T0188860

CHALLENGES IN AD HOC NETWORKING

IFIP – The International Federation for Information Processing

IFIP was founded in 1960 under the auspices of UNESCO, following the First World Computer Congress held in Paris the previous year. An umbrella organization for societies working in information processing, IFIP's aim is two-fold: to support information processing within its member countries and to encourage technology transfer to developing nations. As its mission statement clearly states,

> *IFIP's mission is to be the leading, truly international, apolitical organization which encourages and assists in the development, exploitation and application of information technology for the benefit of all people.*

IFIP is a non-profitmaking organization, run almost solely by 2500 volunteers. It operates through a number of technical committees, which organize events and publications. IFIP's events range from an international congress to local seminars, but the most important are:

• The IFIP World Computer Congress, held every second year;
• Open conferences;
• Working conferences.

The flagship event is the IFIP World Computer Congress, at which both invited and contributed papers are presented. Contributed papers are rigorously refereed and the rejection rate is high.

As with the Congress, participation in the open conferences is open to all and papers may be invited or submitted. Again, submitted papers are stringently refereed.

The working conferences are structured differently. They are usually run by a working group and attendance is small and by invitation only. Their purpose is to create an atmosphere conducive to innovation and development. Refereeing is less rigorous and papers are subjected to extensive group discussion.

Publications arising from IFIP events vary. The papers presented at the IFIP World Computer Congress and at open conferences are published as conference proceedings, while the results of the working conferences are often published as collections of selected and edited papers.

Any national society whose primary activity is in information may apply to become a full member of IFIP, although full membership is restricted to one society per country. Full members are entitled to vote at the annual General Assembly. National societies preferring a less committed involvement may apply for associate or corresponding membership. Associate members enjoy the same benefits as full members, but without voting rights. Corresponding members are not represented in IFIP bodies. Affiliated membership is open to non-national societies, and individual and honorary membership schemes are also offered.

CHALLENGES IN AD HOC NETWORKING

Fourth Annual Mediterranean Ad Hoc Networking Workshop, June 21-24, 2005, Île de Porquerolles, France

Edited by

K. Al Agha
LRI (Université Paris-Sud), France

I. Guérin Lassous
INRIA, France

G. Pujolle
LIP6 (Université Paris 6), France

 Springer

Challenges in Ad Hoc Networking
Edited by K. Al Agha, I. Guérin Lassous, and G. Pujolle

p. cm. (IFIP International Federation for Information Processing, a Springer Series in Computer Science)

ISSN: 1571-5736 / 1861-2288 (Internet)

Printed on acid-free paper

ISBN 978-1-4419-4058-2   e-ISBN 978-0-387-31173-9

Copyright © 2006 by International Federation for Information Processing.
Softcover reprint of the hardcover 1st edition 2006
All rights reserved. This work may not be translated or copied in whole or in part without the written permission of the publisher (Springer Science+Business Media, Inc., 233 Spring Street, New York, NY 10013, USA), except for brief excerpts in connection with reviews or scholarly analysis. Use in connection with any form of information storage and retrieval, electronic adaptation, computer software, or by similar or dissimilar methodology now known or hereafter developed is forbidden.
The use in this publication of trade names, trademarks, service marks and similar terms, even if they are not identified as such, is not to be taken as an expression of opinion as to whether or not they are subject to proprietary rights.

9 8 7 6 5 4 3 2 1
springeronline.com

Contents

Preface

This book contains the refereed proceedings of the Fourth Annual Mediterranean Ad Hoc Networking Workshop, Med-Hoc-Net 2005. After Sardinia (Italy), Mahdia (Tunisia), Bodrum (Turkey), the workshop took place this year on the beautiful island, Île de Porquerolles (France).

The Med-Hoc-Net 2005 event consolidates the success of the previous editions of the workshop series. It aims to serve as a platform for researchers from academia, research, laboratories and industry from all over the world to share their ideas, views, results and experiences in the field of ad hoc networking.

This year, 73 papers were submitted. We accepted 39 papers as full papers and 10 papers as short papers. Each full paper consists in 10 pages in these proceedings and was presented orally at the workshop whereas each short paper consists in 5 pages in these proceedings and was presented as a poster at the workshop. The selected papers were grouped according to the following topics: Physical and MAC layers, Power Consumption, Quality of Service, Routing, Connectivity, Optimization and Testbeds, Multicast and Broadcast, Clustering, Sensor networks, Auto-organization and Adaptation, Security and Evolution and finally Analysis. The accepted papers came from all over the world, mainly from diverse countries in Europe, but also from USA, Brazil, Tunisia, China and Taïwan. We thank all authors for submitting their papers to Med-Hoc-Net 2005.

For each paper, we provided two reviews (sometimes three reviews). This could only be realized by the hard work of the Technical Program Committee composed of 35 members. We thank all the members of the

Technical Program Committee for their invaluable help with the paper reviews.

We have also two tutorials on Security in Wireless Ad Hoc Networking (Bülent Yener) and on Wireless and Ad Hoc Networks: Routing, Quality of Service and Scalability (Khaldoun Al Agha). We thank these speakers for their contribution. We also express our deep gratitude to Jean-François Diouris, Roger Wattenhofer and Mario Gerla for accepting our invitations to become keynote speakers for the workshop. The diversity of the keynote talks were in accordance to the diversity of the technical program.

Finally, the success of the workshop would not have been possible without the hard work of many colleagues. We wish to thank Joëlle Hnautra and Davor Males for the organization part and Ignacy Gawedzki for the nice web site of the workshop.

Khaldoun Al Agha and Guy Pujolle, General Chairs
Isabelle Guérin Lassous, Conference Program Chair

WIRELESS TRANSMISSIONS WITH COMBINED GAIN RELAYS OVER FADING CHANNELS

Theodoros A. Tsiftsis
Dept. of Electrical & Computer Engineering, University of Patras,
Rion, 26500 Patras, Greece
tsiftsis@ee.upatras.gr

George K. Karagiannidis
Dept. of Electrical & Computer Engineering,
Aristotle University of Thessaloniki, 54124 Thessaloniki, Greece
geokarag@auth.gr

Stavros A. Kotsopoulos
Dept. of Electrical & Computer Engineering, University of Patras,
Rion, 26500 Patras, Greece
kotsop@ee.upatras.gr

Abstract   We present a dual-hop relayed wireless communication system where the gain of the relay, called combined gain relay (CGR), is produced after combining the channel state information from both hops, depending on the mean hop's signal-to-noise ratio (SNR). The proposed scheme can be efficiently applied in dual-hop transmissions with unbalanced mean SNRs due to the long-term fading effects produced by the movement of the user in the area served by the wireless network. The overall system performance is studied in Rayleigh fading channels. Closed-form expressions are derived for important system performance metrics, such as average end-to-end SNR, average error probability and outage probability. Furthermore, we investigate the CGR's average power consumption which in certain cases is lower compared to existed relays. Numerical results and simulations show an improvement in the end-to-end system performance.

Keywords: Average bit error probability (ABEP), combined gain relay (CGR), dual-hop transmissions, outage probability, Rayleigh fading.

1.   Introduction

Multihop relaying technology is a promising solution for the throughput and high data rates coverage requirements, in future cellular and ad-hoc wireless communication systems without the need to use large power at the transmitter, and to combat fading and shadowing in wireless channel through spatial/multiuser diversity [1], [2], [3]. Nowadays, there is a great interest in the research community on the potential of multihop and especially on dual-hop transmissions [4], [5], [6], [7].

Looking through the recent up-to-date open technical literature, the performance of dual-hop wireless communication systems are studied in [1], [4], [5], [6], [7]. Hasna and Alouini have presented a useful and semi-analytical framework for the evaluation of the end-to-end outage probability of multihop wireless systems with non-regenerative channel state information (CSI)-assisted relays over Nakagami-m fading channels [1]. Moreover, the same authors have studied the outage and the error performance of dual-hop systems with regenerative and non-regenerative CSI-assisted relays over Rayleigh [4] and Nakagami-m [5] fading channels. The analysis in [1], [4], and [5] is based on an upper bound for the end-to-end signal-to-noise ratio (SNR) which leads to lower bounds for the system's outage and average error probability. This bound corresponds to an ideal relay capable of inverting the channel in the previous hop (regardless of the fading state of that hop) without limiting the output power. Furthermore, in [6], the end-to-end performance of dual-hop systems equipped with non-regenerative fixed gain relays is investigated and a specific relay is proposed, called semi-blind, that benefits from the knowledge of the first hop's average fading power. Recently, Tsiftsis et al. presented a new upper bound for the end-to-end SNR and efficiently evaluated the average error probability in dual-hop collaborative diversity systems, especially at low SNRs [7]. Finally, Anghel and Kaveh in [3] have studied the error performance of a cooperative network of dual-hop transmissions with parallel CSI-assisted relays in Rayleigh fading, where multi-user spatial diversity is used to combat the signal's impairments.

In this paper, we present a dual-hop transmission system, where the gain of the relay, called combined gain relay (CGR), is produced using CSI from both hops, depending on the mean hop's SNR. The proposed scheme can be efficiently used in dual-hop wireless transmissions with unbalanced mean SNRs between the hops due to the long-term fading effects produced by the movement of the user in the area served by the wireless network. The overall system performance is studied in Rayleigh fading channels as follows: Closed-form expressions for the moments, the average bit error probability (ABEP) and the outage probability of the end-to-end SNR are derived. Furthermore, we study the average power consumed by the CGR and it is shown that in certain cases it is less compared to existed relays. Moreover, numerical examples and Monte Carlo simulations show that CGR results in a significant improvement in the end-to-end system performance, compared to existed gain relay schemes.

2. The Combined Gain Relay (CGR) Scheme

2.1 System and Channel Model

A dual-hop wireless communication system with a non-regenerative relay operating over independent, but not necessarily identically distributed Rayleigh fading channels, is considered. The source terminal S communicates with the destination terminal D through the terminal R which acts as relay. Assuming that terminal S transmits a signal with an average power normalized to unity, the received signal at terminal R can be written as

$$r_R = \alpha_1 s + n_1 \tag{1}$$

where α_1 is the fading amplitude of the channel between terminals S and R (first hop), modelled as a Rayleigh random variable and following the probability density function (PDF)

$$f_{\alpha_i}(\alpha_i) = \frac{2\alpha_i}{\Omega_i} \exp\left(-\frac{\alpha_i^2}{\Omega_i}\right), \quad i = 1, 2 \tag{2}$$

where $\Omega_i = \overline{\alpha_i^2}$ is the averaging fading power of the ith hop and n_1 is the additive white Gaussian noise (AWGN) with single-sided power spectral density (PSD) N_0. The signal r_R is then multiplied by the gain g of terminal R and re-transmitted to terminal D. The received signal at terminal D can be written as

$$r_D = g\,\alpha_2\,(\alpha_1 s + n_1) + n_2 \tag{3}$$

where α_2 is the fading amplitude of the channel between R and D (second hop), following the PDF in (2) and n_2 is the AWGN with single-sided PSD N_0. We have omitted the time index in (1) and (3) for brevity. Using (3), the overall instantaneous SNR at the receiving end can be written as

$$\gamma_{end} = \frac{[\alpha_2 g \alpha_1]^2}{\left[(\alpha_2 g)^2 + 1\right] N_0} = \frac{\frac{\alpha_1^2}{N_0}\frac{\alpha_2^2}{N_0}}{\frac{\alpha_2^2}{N_0} + \frac{1}{g^2 N_0}}. \tag{4}$$

2.2 Mode of Operation

When terminal R has available CSI from the first hop, one kind of gain relay proposed and studied in previously published works [8, 9], is given by

$$g_1^2 = \frac{1}{\alpha_1^2 + N_0}. \tag{5}$$

The choice of this gain aims to limit the output power of the relay, if the fading amplitude of the first channel, α_1, is low.

Next, we propose an alternative mode of operation for the relay-node R, called combined gain relay (CGR), as follows:

Step 1: Periodically, and in synchronization with terminal D, terminal R estimates the average SNR of the first hop, $\overline{\gamma}_1$, and terminal D estimates the average SNR of the second hop, $\overline{\gamma}_2$, and sends it to terminal R.

Step 2: Terminal R generates the new gain relay, according to the following rule:

$$g^2 = \begin{cases} g_1^2 : 1\,/\,(\alpha_1^2 + N_0)\,, & \text{if } \xi < \xi_{th} \qquad (7) \\ g_2^2 : 1\,/\,(\alpha_2^2 + N_0)\,, & \text{if } \xi > \xi_{th} \qquad (8) \end{cases}$$

where $\xi = \overline{\gamma}_1/\overline{\gamma}_2$ denotes the degree of the average SNR unbalance. The parameter ξ_{th} is the threshold which signals the transition between the two available gains and depends on the performance criterion under consideration (i.e., either the average end-to-end SNR or the error probability or the outage probability). The way to choose values for ξ_{th} will be discussed in Section 5. Note, that the choice of g_2 does not limit the instantaneous output power of the relay.

The ability of relay R to generate the appropriate gain, depending on the fading conditions in both hops, leads to an end-to-end SNR, which using (4) with (6) and (7) is formulated as

$$\gamma_{end} = \begin{cases} \gamma_1\,\gamma_2/\,(\gamma_1 + \gamma_2 + 1)\,, & \text{if } \xi < \xi_{th} \qquad (9) \\ \gamma_1\,\gamma_2/\,(2\gamma_2 + 1)\,, & \text{if } \xi > \xi_{th} \qquad (10) \end{cases}$$

where γ_i is the instantaneous SNR of the ith hop, following the exponential PDF defined as

$$f_{\gamma_i}\,(\gamma_i) = \frac{1}{\overline{\gamma}_i}\,\exp\left(-\frac{\gamma_i}{\overline{\gamma}_i}\right), \qquad i = 1, 2. \qquad (10)$$

Note that, as mentioned in Section 1, the performance analysis of dual-hop systems with relay given by (6) has been extensively studied in the literature [1], [3], [4], [5], [7]. Thus, in the following, only the case of $g = g_2$ will be further studied.

3.   Performance Analysis

3.1   Moments of the End-to-End SNR

The first and the second order moments of the end-to-end SNR are statistical parameters which can be efficiently used to evaluate important performance system measures, such as average output SNR and variance. By definition, the nth moment of γ_{end}, for $g = g_2$, is given by

$$E \langle \gamma_{end}^n \rangle = \int_0^\infty \int_0^\infty \left(\frac{\gamma_1 \gamma_2}{2\gamma_2 + 1} \right)^n f_{\gamma_1} (\gamma_1) f_{\gamma_2} (\gamma_2) \, d\gamma_1 d\gamma_2 \qquad (11)$$

where $E \langle \cdot \rangle$ denotes expectation and substituting (10) into (11), $E \langle \gamma_{end}^n \rangle$ can be evaluated as (see [10])

$$E \langle \gamma_{end}^n \rangle = \frac{(n!)^2}{2^n} \overline{\gamma}_1^n U \left(n, 0, \frac{1}{2\overline{\gamma}_2} \right) \qquad (12)$$

where $U (\cdot, \cdot, \cdot)$ is the Kummer's function defined in [11, eq. (13.1.3)]

Average End-to-End SNR.   Using (12) for $n = 1$, the average end-to-end SNR can be obtained as

$$\overline{\gamma}_{end} = \frac{\overline{\gamma}_1}{2} \exp \left(\frac{1}{2\overline{\gamma}_2} \right) E_2 \left(\frac{1}{2\overline{\gamma}_2} \right) \qquad (13)$$

where $E_k (\cdot)$ is the exponential integral [12, eq. (5.1.4)] with k being a positive integer.

3.2   Average Symbol Error Probability (ASEP)

The error performance, for several digital modulation schemes, can be efficiently studied using the well-known moment generating function (MGF)-based approach [13]. The MGF, defined here as

$$\mathcal{M}_{\gamma_{end}} (s) \overset{\triangle}{=} E \langle \exp (-s\gamma_{end}) \rangle \qquad (14)$$

can be evaluated in closed-form solving the following double integral

$$\mathcal{M}_{\gamma_{end}} (s) = \int_0^\infty \int_0^\infty \exp \left(-s \frac{\gamma_1 \gamma_2}{2\gamma_2 + 1} \right) f_{\gamma_1} (\gamma_1) f_{\gamma_2} (\gamma_2) \, d\gamma_1 d\gamma_2 . \qquad (15)$$

Substituting $f_{\gamma_i}(\gamma_i)$ into (15), the first integral in (15) (i.e., the one on γ_1) is of the form

$$\mathcal{I}_1 = \frac{1}{\overline{\gamma}_1 \overline{\gamma}_2} \int_0^\infty \exp \left(-s \frac{\gamma_1 \gamma_2}{2\gamma_2 + 1} \right) \exp \left(-\frac{\gamma_1}{\overline{\gamma}_1} \right) d\gamma_1 \qquad (16)$$

which can be solved using [12, eq. (3.310)] as

$$\mathcal{I}_1 = \frac{1}{\overline{\gamma}_2} \frac{2\gamma_2 + 1}{(s\gamma_2 \overline{\gamma}_1 + 2\gamma_2 + 1)} \qquad (17)$$

The second integral in (15) (i.e., the one on γ_2) can now be written using (17) as

$$\mathcal{I}_2 = \frac{1}{\overline{\gamma}_2} \int_0^\infty \frac{2\gamma_2 + 1}{s\gamma_2\overline{\gamma}_1 + 2\gamma_2 + 1} \exp\left(-\frac{\gamma_2}{\overline{\gamma}_2}\right) d\gamma_2. \tag{18}$$

Using [12, eq. (3.352.4)], [12, eq. (3.353.5)] and [11, eq. (5.1.45)], (18) yields to

$$\mathcal{M}_{\gamma_{end}}(s) = \frac{2}{2 + s\overline{\gamma}_1} + \frac{s\overline{\gamma}_1 \exp\left(\frac{1}{2\overline{\gamma}_2 + s\overline{\gamma}_1\overline{\gamma}_2}\right)}{\overline{\gamma}_2 \left(2 + s\overline{\gamma}_1\right)^2} \Gamma\left(0, \frac{1}{2\overline{\gamma}_2 + s\overline{\gamma}_1\overline{\gamma}_2}\right) \tag{19}$$

where $\Gamma(x, y)$ is the incomplete Gamma function, defined in [12, eq. (8.350.2)].

With the aid of $\mathcal{M}_{\gamma_{end}}(s)$, and using the MGF-based approach for the performance evaluation of digital modulations over fading channels, presented in [13], the error rates can be calculated directly for non-coherent binary signalling, such as BFSK and DPSK, while for other cases including M-QAM and M-PSK, single integrals with finite limits and integrands composed of elementary functions have to be readily evaluated via numerical integration.

3.3   Outage Probability

If γ_{th} is a certain specified threshold ratio, then for non-regenerative multihop transmissions the outage probability is defined as the probability that the instantaneous SNR at the final destination falls below γ_{th} and is expressed as

$$P_{out} = \Pr\left[\gamma_{end} \le \gamma_{th}\right] = \int_0^\infty \Pr\left[\frac{\gamma_1\gamma_2}{2\gamma_2 + 1} \le \gamma_{th}|\gamma_2\right] f_{\gamma_2}(\gamma_2)\, d\gamma_2. \tag{20}$$

Following the same method as in [9], the above integral yields to

$$P_{out} = 1 - 2\sqrt{\frac{\gamma_{th}}{\overline{\gamma}_1\overline{\gamma}_2}} \exp\left(-\frac{2\gamma_{th}}{\overline{\gamma}_1}\right) K_1\left(2\sqrt{\frac{\gamma_{th}}{\overline{\gamma}_1\overline{\gamma}_2}}\right) \tag{21}$$

where $K_1(\cdot)$ is the first order modified Bessel function of the second kind defined in [11, eq. (9.6.22)].

4.   Average Power Consumption

In this section, we quantify the average gain of the relay (i.e., average power consumption) when CGR is considered. If τ is the percentage of the time when g_2 is used ($1 - \tau$ corresponds to g_1) then the average power consumed by the relay, $\overline{P}_{CGR}$, can be expressed by

$$\overline{P}_{CGR} = \tau\overline{P}_2 + (1 - \tau)\overline{P}_1 \tag{22}$$

where $\overline{P}_1$ and $\overline{P}_2$ are the average power consumed by the relay, when g_1 or g_2 are used, respectively. For Rayleigh fading channels, $\overline{P}_1$ and $\overline{P}_2$ can be written

Table 1.   Evaluation of ξ_{th} for several values of $\overline{\gamma}_1$

$\overline{\gamma}_1$ (dB)	ξ_{th}
-5	0.6
0	0.54
5	0.58
10	0.68
15	0.84

as [6, eq. (15)]

$$\overline{P}_i = E\left\langle g_i^2 \right\rangle = \frac{e^{1/\overline{\gamma}_i}\Gamma\left(0, 1/\overline{\gamma}_i\right)}{\overline{\gamma}_i N_0}. \tag{23}$$

5.   Numerical Results

In this section, we provide several representative numerical and simulation examples illustrating the performance of the dual-hop system with CGR over Rayleigh fading channels. These results are compared with a system which uses only the gain relay given by (6).   The threshold, ξ_{th}, for the transition

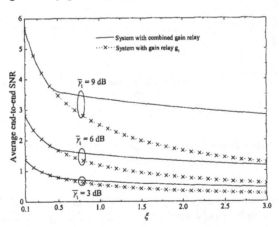

Figure 1.   Comparison of the average end-to-end SNR of a dual-hop system with the relay gain g_1 and CGR versus ξ for several values of $\overline{\gamma}_1$.

from g_1 to g_2, depends on the selected performance criterion and it can be determined after equating the formulae related to this criterion of the gains g_1 and g_2 and solving numerically with respect to ξ. When the criterion considered is the outage probability, then ξ_{th} can be determined by equating (21) to [9, eq.

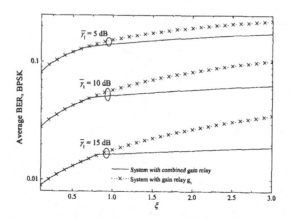

Figure 2.   Comparison of the BPSK average error performance of a dual-hop system with the relay gain g_1 and CGR versus ξ for several values of $\overline{\gamma}_1$.

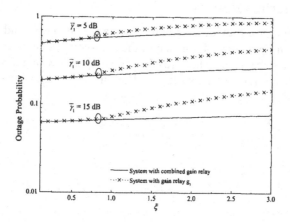

Figure 3.   Comparison of the end-to-end outage probability of a dual-hop system with the relay gain g_1 and CGR versus ξ for several values of $\overline{\gamma}_1$.

(14)] and solving numerically for ξ_{th}. In Table 1, ξ_{th} is evaluated for several values of $\overline{\gamma}_1$. It can be easily verified that almost the same values for ξ_{th} are observed when other performance criteria as the average end-to-end SNR or the ABEP are used.

In Fig. 1 the average end-to-end SNR for a dual-hop system with CGR is plotted versus ξ, for several values of mean SNR $\overline{\gamma}_1$. Monte Carlo simulations are also performed for a system using a relay with the gain g_1 and their results are depicted in the same figure. We observe that depending on the value of ξ, the CGR improves the overall average end-to-end SNR performance. Similar conclusions are also extracted from Figs. 2 and 3, where the BPSK average er-

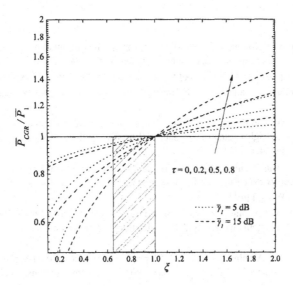

Figure 4. Ratio of the average power consumption versus ξ for several values of τ.

ror rate performance and the outage probability are plotted versus ξ for several values of $\overline{\gamma}_1$, respectively.

Finally, in Fig. 4, the excess average power consumption, expressed by the ratio, $\overline{P}_{CGR}/\overline{P}_1$, is evaluated for several values of ξ. It is very interesting to observe that when $0.65 \leq \xi \leq 1$ (grey region), although the average power consumption of CGR is less than $\overline{P}_1$ (i.e., $\overline{P}_{CGR}/\overline{P}_1 < 1$), the system's performance is improved. Moreover, as expected, the average power consumption of the CGR is increased when $\xi > 1$. However, by substituting (23) in (22) and using [11, eq. (6.5.31)], it can be easily verified that $\lim\limits_{\xi \to \infty} \overline{P}_{CGR} = 1/N_0$.

6.   Conclusion

A dual-hop wireless communication system with a novel combined gain relay, was presented. The new type of relay produced a gain using CSI from both hops, depending on the mean hop's SNR. This approach results to an improved end-to-end system performance compared to existed gain relays, but with an increase in average power consumption. However, it was shown that in certain cases, the average power consumed by the CGR was less compared to existed relays. Furthermore, closed-form expressions for the moments, the average error probability and the outage probability of the end-to-end SNR were derived.

References

[1] Hasna, M.O., and Alouini, M.S. (2003). "Outage probability of multihop transmission over Nakagami fading channels," IEEE Communications Letters, vol. 7, pp. 216-218.

[2] Boyer, John., Falconer, David D., and Yanikomeroglu, Halim. (2004). "Multihop diversity in wireless relaying channels," IEEE Transactions on Communications, vol. 52, pp. 1820-1830.

[3] Anghel, Paul A., and Kaveh, M. (2004). "Exact symbol error probability of a cooperative network in a Rayleigh-Fading Environment," IEEE Transactions on Wireless Communications, vol. 3, pp. 1416-1421.

[4] Hasna, M.O., and Alouini, M.-S. (2003). "End-to-end performance of transmission systems with relays over Rayleigh fading channels," IEEE Transactions on Wireless Communications, vol. 2, pp. 1126-1131.

[5] Hasna, M.O., and Alouini, M.-S. (2004). "Harmonic mean and end-to-end performance of transmission systems with relays," IEEE Transactions on Communications, vol. 52, pp. 130-135.

[6] Hasna, M.O., and Alouini, M.-S. (2004). "A performance study of dual-hop transmissions with fixed gain relays," IEEE Transactions on Wireless Communications, vol. 3, pp. 1963-1968.

[7] Tsiftsis, T.A., Karagiannidis, G.K., Kotsopoulos S.A., and Pavlidou, F.-N. (2004). "BER analysis of collaborative dual-hop wireless transmissions," IEE Electronics Letters, vol. 11, pp. 1732-1745.

[8] Laneman, J.N., and Wornell, G.W. (2000). "Energy-efficient antenna sharing and relaying for wireless networks," in Proc. IEEE Wireless Communications and Networking Conf. (WCNC'00), Chicago, IL, pp. 7-12.

[9] Emamian, V., Anghel, P., and Kaveh, M. (2000). "Multi-user spatial diversity system in a shadow-fading environment," in Proc. IEEE Vehicular Technology Conference (Fall VTC'02), Vancouver, BC, Canada, pp. 573-576.

[10] Tsiftsis, T.A., Karagiannidis G.K., and Kotsopoulos, S.A. (2005). "Dual-hop wireless communications with combined gain relays (CGR)," accepted for publication in IEE Proc. Communications.

[11] Abramovitz M.A., and Stegun, I.A. (1972). Handbook of Mathematical Functions with Formulas, Graphs, and Mathematical Tables, 9th ed. New York: Dover.

[12] Gradshteyn, I.S., and Ryzhik, I.M. (2000). Table of Integrals, Series, and Products, 6th ed. New York: Academic.

[13] Simon, M.K., and Alouini, M.-S. (2005). Digital Communication over Fading Channels, 2th ed. New York: Willey.

ADAPTIVE PROBABILISTIC NAV TO INCREASE FAIRNESS IN AD HOC 802.11 MAC LAYER

Claude Chaudet[1], Guillaume Chelius[2], Hervé Meunier[3], David Simplot-Ryl[3]

[1]*GET-ENST ; LTCI-UMR 5141 CNRS, 46, rue Barrault, 75634 Paris, FRANCE –*
Claude.Chaudet@enst.fr

[2]*CITI/INRIA ARES – INSA de Lyon – Bât L. de Vinci – 21, avenue J. Capelle – 69621 Villeur-banne, FRANCE –* guillaume.chelius@inria.fr

[3]*IRCICA/LIFL, Univ. Lille 1, CNRS UMR 8022 – INRIA Futurs, POPS research group – Bât. M3, Cité Scientifique – 59655 Villeneuve d'Ascq Cedex, FRANCE –*
{meunier,simplot}@lifl.fr

Abstract   The IEEE 802.11 MAC layer is known for its low performances in wireless ad hoc networks. For instance, it has been shown in the literature that two independent emitters nodes can easily monopolize the medium, preventing other nodes to send packets. The protocol we introduce in this article is a simple variation of the original IEEE 802.11 MAC layer which significantly increases the fairness while maintaining a high effective bandwidth. Its principle consists in avoiding systematic successive transmissions by the same emitter through the probabilistic introduction of a waiting time, a virtual NAV, after each emission. The probability to set a NAV is adaptively computed depending on the perceived utility of the previous virtual NAV. This protocol, called PNAV (*Probabilistic NAV*), is shown to be efficient by simulation and is compared to another IEEE 802.11 adaptation.

1.   Introduction

Medium-access control (MAC) protocols for wireless networks have received a considerable attention over the past few years with the aim to reduce the number of collisions while maximizing the bandwidth use. Collisions occur when a node is in the neighborhood of two simultaneous transmitters. If the transmitting stations are neighboring nodes, the collision probability can be reduced through the use of a simple random backoff algorithm and a carrier sense mechanism. These principles are the basics of the widely used CSMA protocol family. If the transmitting stations cannot communicate directly, the collision risk is increased due to the absence of carrier sense. This problem was first described by [Kleinrock and Tobagi, 1975], and is known as the "hidden terminal problem". Several solutions have been proposed to resolve this problem. For instance, communicating nodes can exchange short control messages to inform their neighborhood of the forthcoming data frame. In the IEEE 802.11 *Distributed Coordination Function* (DCF), a node initiating a communication first sends a request-to-send (RTS) frame to the receiver. If the intended receiver correctly receives the RTS frame and if the medium is free in its vicinity, this receiver answers with a clear-to-send (CTS). Upon reception of the CTS frame, the sender transmits its data frame. The RTS and CTS control frames contain the duration of the subsequent data exchange, which gives the opportunity to all neighboring nodes to be aware of the medium occupation induced by the communication. More precisely, nodes that receive RTS and/or CTS frames set a "Network Allocation Vector" (NAV) for the duration of the exchange and will restrain from transmitting during this period.

In addition to collisions, the hidden terminal situation is responsible for several issues. [Ng and Liew, 2004] have shown that along a node string in a multi-hop network, all nodes do not have the same medium access. The unfairness of the MAC protocol is also clearly exhibited by [Chaudet et al., 2005b]. They propose a simple scenario with three pairs of emitters and receivers where two pairs capture the totality of the medium while the third one has no opportunity to compete for the medium access. Such typical scenarios appear when the medium is saturated. There have been some proposals to solve these issues and they usually lead to a traffic limitation. In this paper, we address the fairness problem while ensuring an efficient use of the channel bandwidth. We propose a simple modification of the MAC layer where nodes can probabilistically set a virtual NAV after each sent frame. The probability to introduce such a NAV is adaptively computed according to its observed utility. We show that our approach is efficient compared to already existing solutions. This MAC protocol is called PNAV for Probabilistic NAV and is fully compatible with the IEEE 802.11 standard.

A literature study and a full description of IEEE 802.11 can be found in the extended version of this article, [Chaudet et al., 2005a]. The remainder of the paper is organized as follows: We describe our proposal in Section 2. In Section 3, we describe the simulation environment and results are given in Section 4. Section 5 concludes the paper and presents the future works.

2.   Probabilistic NAV

Under certain circumstances, the IEEE 802.11 DCF function leads to an unbalanced bandwidth repartition or different medium access probabilities between different radio links. For example, let us consider the three pairs topology intensively studied in [Chaudet et al., 2005c, Chaudet et al., 2005b] and showed on Figure 1. In this scenario, three emitters contend for medium access. The topology is unbalanced and one emitter competes with the two others while the other ones only have to deal with the central emitter. Neighbor emitters are in mutual carrier-sense range but cannot directly communicate.

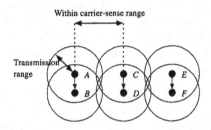

Figure 1. 3-pair topology.

The pair in the middle almost never gains access to the medium that is monopolized by the exterior pairs. In this configuration, the exterior pairs do not even get knowledge of the middle one trying to access the medium. In consequence, IEEE 802.11 DCF adaptations such as AOB ([Bononi et al., 2004]) that estimates the medium occupation using emitters' perception of the state of the medium, only slightly increase the fairness of IEEE 802.11 in this situation. As the middle pair is dumb, exterior pairs do not hear any other communications, do not delay transmission through the classical backoff or NAV mechanisms and thus consider the medium unoccupied which in turn reduce the efficiency of other enhancement proposals.

In the presence of dumb radio links, the only way to increase the fairness is to give these links an opportunity to express themselves. This may be done through the introduction of a NAV in the IEEE 802.11 layer of nodes that frequently access the medium. These silence periods may give the opportunity to dumb radio links to transmit packets and to notify their presence to all surrounding nodes that could in turn activate mechanisms to increase fairness.

Our proposal follows this strategy. According to a varying probability, a node sets a NAV of duration δ after each transmission in order to give other nodes the possibility to gain access to the medium. The NAV probability, p_{nav}, is a function of both the node and other nodes' use of the medium. Qualitatively, it helps emitters answer questions such as "am I monopolizing the medium?" or "did my last NAV give an opportunity to another node's communication?".

In order to estimate the medium occupancy induced by a particular node, we identify three different events. These events will be used by the PNAV automaton to adapt the node probability to introduce a NAV after each of its emissions. Initially, the NAV probability, p_{nav} is set to 0, meaning that no NAV is introduced before the first emission.

- ***t* event**: the *t* event occurs when the considered emitter acquires the medium for two successive transmissions with an inter-emission period inferior to the NAV duration, δ. If a node u only keeps on experiencing *t* events, it means that it is monopolizing the medium, and it should therefore increase its probability to release the medium. Upon observation such an event, the p_{nav} probability is increased by a value p_{step}, parameter of the protocol.

- ***r* event**: the *r* event occurs under two conditions. First, the considered mobile has set a probabilistic NAV after its last emission; second, the medium has been acquired by another node before the NAV expiration. Occurrence of an *r* event means that the introduction of the NAV has been successful in term of medium fairness, as this silence period has been used by another node to access the medium. Therefore, after an *r* event, p_{nav} is set to 1 meaning that a NAV is systematically set as long as it is useful to encourage nodes to delay their transmissions to help starved nodes to access the medium.

- ***s* event**: the *s* event occurs under two conditions. First, the considered node has introduced a probabilistic NAV after its last emission; second, it has reacquired the medium after expiration of the NAV. Occurrence of the *s* event signifies that the introduced NAV was not necessary, as the associated silence period has not been successfully used by another node to access the medium. Therefore, p_{nav} is reinitialized to 0 when an *s* event occurs in order to ensure a low bandwidth waste if the considered node is the only one competing to access the medium.

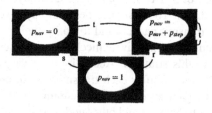

Figure 2.   PNAV automaton

The automaton determining p_{nav} in function of the different events is depicted on Figure 2. The main concerns behind the automaton are to introduce

NAV as soon as a node is monopolizing the medium (*t* event), to keep on introducing NAV if they are useful (*r* event) and finally not to introduce a NAV if it is useless (*s* event). The PNAV mechanism depends on two parameters p_{step} and δ.

3.   Evaluations

This section focuses on introducing the simulation environment and the scenarios we used in order to study some equity issues observed in IEEE 802.11 DCF.

Simulations in this study involve several parallel pairs of nodes, each pair having an emitter node trying to transmit its traffic to a receiver node. For example, Figure 1 illustrates this topology considering 3 parallel pairs. We will first consider that parameters are set in such a way that an emitter node only senses and can communicate with its two closest neighbors (inter-pair distance: 150 m, radio range: 160 m, carrier sense: 160 m). Then we will increase the carrier sense distance and finally fall to the scenarios depicted earlier. Beside the basic parallel pairs, we evaluate the impact of our proposition on chained nodes and random network topologies. These experiments are conducted as follows: given a topology of nodes (couples of emitter/receiver nodes), we basically generate a saturated traffic from the emitters to their respective receivers and we log the amount of data successfully received during the simulation process.

Simulations were performed using the network simulator NS-2[1] in version 2.27 with MAC and physical parameters tuned to reflect the HR-DSSS 11 Mb/s physical layer of IEEE 802.11b. This results in a transmission range of about 160 m and a carrier sense range of 160 m or 400 m, depending on the simulated scenario. The MAC protocol presented above has been implemented into the simulator as well as the AOB flavor presented in [Bononi et al., 2004] with an ACL parameter value corresponding to the high-rate physical layer.

For the first analysis, three types of scenarios have been considered. Pairs of nodes, similar to the situation depicted on Figure 1 that will be described later, chains of flows and random scenarios. In all these scenarios, we used CBR flows saturating the medium. Due to space limitations, only the pairs scenarios results will be presented in the next sections, the other results being included in [Chaudet et al., 2005a].

The simplest scenario consists in a single emitter and a single receiver with a saturated traffic. It provides the opportunity to evaluate the maximum bandwidth provided in no-competition conditions.

The 2-pair saturated traffic scenario has also been evaluated in order to rate the maximum bandwidth over a shared channel, and thus, to rate the synchronization ability of the MAC protocol.

The 3-pair scenario enlightens the typical issue about the fairness of most ad hoc MAC protocols. The middle emitter node has to compete for medium access, with emitters from both sides, which do not have to compete with each other. IEEE 802.11 DCF equity issues typically arise in this topology.

Further increasing the number of pairs then leads to similar fairness issues, whose characteristics depend on the number of pairs.

4.   Performance evaluation

In this section, we present an analytical evaluation of the loss of bandwidth that can be expected on a single link and simulation results for the larger scenarios described above. Simulation results presented in this section are the average of the throughput mean and standard deviation of each flow, computed over 20 simulations, each simulation lasting 30 seconds. To evaluate the performance of the sole MAC protocol, we used a static routing agent for NS-2 developed by T. Razafindralambo, computing offline shortest-paths between any pairs of nodes. Other sources of traffic such as ARP also have been disabled. Results presented here only concern transmissions without RTS-CTS exchange. Simulations also have been performed with RTS-CTS activated and the conclusions are similar in each of these situations, even though the overall performance is different.

Single pair

To begin with the performance analysis of the PNAV mechanism, we consider a single communicating pair. The aim of this first study is to evaluate the waste of bandwidth introduced by the probabilistic NAV when there is no contention on the medium. Indeed, PNAV decreases the maximum bandwidth that can be achieved by a single communication. Consider node u communicating with node v at a packet rate such that the inter-emission period is inferior to δ. Node u will observe consecutive t transitions until it sets a NAV. This NAV will not be used by any other communication as u is the only transmitting node and a s transition will occur, reinitializing p_{nav} to zero. The phenomenon will be repeated periodically, introducing useless NAVs, thus decreasing the effective bandwidth of the communication between u and v. We will now try to evaluate this bandwidth waste as a function of the parameters δ and p_{step}.

Let N_{nav} be the random variable associated to the number of emissions between two probabilistic NAV. As there is only one pair communicating, the only possible transitions are t and r depending on whether or not a NAV has been introduced after the preceding emission. The automaton behavior can be modeled with a simple Markov chain described by Figure 3. In consequence, it is quite simple to compute the expected number of emissions $E(N_{nav})$ between two NAV by solving the Chapman-Kolmogorov equations system associated to the Markov chain.

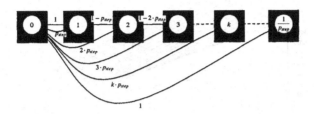

Figure 3. A markov chain describing the automaton behavior in the single pair case

$$p(N_{nav} = k) = p_{step} \cdot \prod_{i=0}^{k-1} (1 - i \cdot p_{step})$$

$$E(N_{nav}) = \sum_{k=1}^{\frac{1}{p_{step}}} \left(k \cdot p_{step} \cdot \prod_{i=0}^{k-1} (1 - i \cdot p_{step}) \right)$$

Given $E(N_{nav})$ and depending on δ, we can also deduce the decrease of effective bandwidth in the case of a single communicating pair. It is illustrated by figure 4. As we can see on the picture, the effective bandwidth of PNAV is close to the maximum available bandwidth (3600 kb/s) even with large values for δ if we consider small values for p_{step}. Further experimentations using different node topologies will be carried out with $\delta = 2000\ \mu s$ and $p_{step} = 0.1$.

Multiple pairs

We simulated two to seven parallel pairs separated by a distance close to the transmission range with a carrier sense area equal to the transmission area. Emitters only compete with their direct neighbors and no collision occurs because the receivers are near enough of their associate emitters to prevent signal jamming. This kind of scenario can happen in an indoor context, for instance. Its purpose is to give basic evaluation of the performance of the different solutions, without signal-level concerns.

Figure 5(a) presents the achieved throughput means and standard deviations as function of the number of parallel pairs. A first observation is that using PNAV leads to an almost null standard deviation, improving fairness, but at the cost of overall performance. AOB also presents a mean throughput decrease and leads to a fairness only a little better than the one achieved by IEEE 802.11.

Increasing the carrier sense range so that emitters compete for medium access with two-hops neighbors leads to the results presented on Figure 5(b).

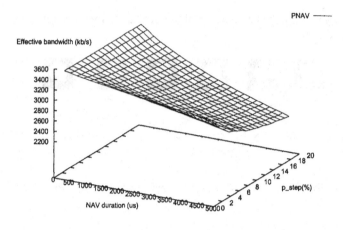

Figure 4.   Effective bandwidth of a single pair using PNAV

On this figure, AOB and PNAV result in similar mean throughput but PNAV improves fairness. The standard deviation peaks for 4-pairs and 7-pairs configurations are due to the particularities of the topology. Let's consider, for instance the 4-pairs scenario. In this situation the central emitters have to compete with all three other emitters for medium access while the exterior ones only compete with two others. This unbalance tends to prevent central nodes from transmitting, leaving a greater share of the medium to the exterior nodes. The 7-pairs situation is indeed the aggregation of two times the 4-pairs situations. Exterior pairs and the very central pair are favored.

5.   Conclusion

In this paper, we have presented PNAV, an adaptation of the IEEE 802.11 DCF protocol in order to increase its fairness in an ad hoc environment. Contrarily to other proposals using the medium occupation – the slot utilization metric for AOB – as an input to the system, our protocol is event-driven. It consists in introducing probabilistic NAV depending on events observed on the radio medium. These events can be qualitatively described as "*I am monopolizing the medium*" or "*my PNAV has been useful for someone's else communication*". The probability to introduce a NAV evolves depending on these

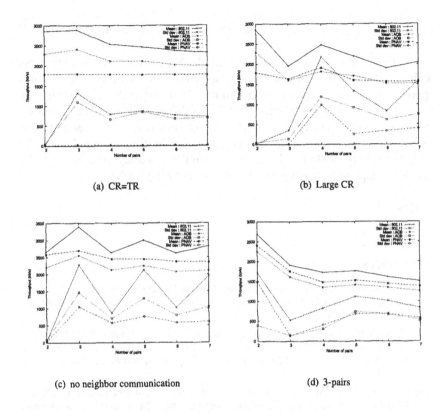

(a) CR=TR   (b) Large CR

(c) no neighbor communication   (d) 3-pairs

events. PNAV has been simulated in several topologies known for their 802.11 DCF fairness issues, the pairs and the chain topologies, as well as pseudo-realistic topologies. It has shown very satisfying performances, inducing more fairness between the different flows than a classical IEEE 802.11 DCF and AOB as well depending on the considered topology, while maintaining a high overall throughput, lower than a classical IEEE 802.11 DCF but higher than AOB.

If the results observed by simulations are promising, several issues remain to be addressed. A theoretical analysis of the PNAV automaton and the NAV probability function is an interesting perspective as it may enlighten the existence of an optimal NAV probability as a function of the network topology, similar to the work done in [Bononi et al., 2004] in the AOB context. Other radio medium events can also be considered in order to refine the PNAV automaton with the aim to continue on increasing the MAC protocol fairness while maintaining a high achieved throughput. We also plan on studying the behavior of the proposed protocol when used in networks called *heterogeneous* by [Bruno et al., 2005], i.e. network composed of emitters using different MAC strategies.

Finally, an interesting point is that the PNAV protocol is not incompatible with other 802.11 DCF adaptations such as AOB. They present two orthogonal approaches that could be combined. While AOB monitors the radio occupation to adapt its deferring probability, PNAV uses different events such as successive transmissions to decide to relinquish the medium. The consequence is that both protocols show their best performances in different topologies. An interesting study would be to combine both of them in order to see whether the resulting adaptation would inherit the best of both approaches.

Notes

1. http://www.isi.edu/nsnam/ns/index.html

References

[Bononi et al., 2004] Bononi, L., Conti, M., and Gregori, E. (2004). Runtime optimization of IEEE 802.11 wireless LANs performance. *IEEE Transactions on Parallel and Distributed Systems*, 15(1):66–80.

[Bruno et al., 2005] Bruno, R., Conti, M., and Gregori, E. (2005). Distributed contention control in heterogeneous 802.11b WLANs. In *Proc. 2nd Annual Conference on Wireless On demand Network Systems and Service (WONS 2005)*, pages 190–199, St Moritz, Switzerland.

[Chaudet et al., 2005a] Chaudet, C., Chelius, G., Meunier, H., and Simplot-Ryl, D. (2005a). Adaptive probability nav to increase fairness in ad hoc 802.11 mac layer. Technical report, INRIA.

[Chaudet et al., 2005b] Chaudet, C., Dhoutaut, D., and Guérin Lassous, I. (2005b). Experiments of some performance issues with IEEE 802.11b in ad hoc networks. In *Proc. 2nd Annual Conference on Wireless On demand Network Systems and Service (WONS 2005)*, pages 158–163, St Moritz, Switzerland.

[Chaudet et al., 2005c] Chaudet, C., Dhoutaut, D., and Guérin Lassous, I. (2005c). Performance issues with IEEE 802.11 in ad hoc networking. *IEEE Communication Magazine*. to appear.

[Kleinrock and Tobagi, 1975] Kleinrock, L. and Tobagi, F. (1975). Packet switching in radio channels: Part i – carrier sense multiple-access modes and their throughput-delay characteristics. *IEEE Transactions on Communications*, 23(12):1400–1416.

[Ng and Liew, 2004] Ng, P. and Liew, S. (2004). Offered load control in IEEE 802.11 multi-hop ad-hoc networks. In *Proc. IEEE International Conference on Mobile Ad hoc and Sensor Systems (MASS 2004)*, Fort Lauderdale, Florida, USA.

A LINK LAYER PROTOCOL FOR SELF-ORGANIZING ULTRA WIDE BAND IMPULSE RADIO NETWORKS

Nan Shi, Liang Xia and Ignas G. Niemegeers
Center for Wireless and Personal Communications, EWI, Delft University of Technology, Mekelweg 4, 2628 CD, Delft, The Netherlands {n.shi;l.xia;i.niemegeers@ewi.tudelft.nl}

Abstract: Ultra Wide Band (UWB) impulse radio, promises to be suitable for short-range, low-power, low cost and high data rate applications. While most UWB research is concentrating on the physical layer, little research has been published on the link layer. A novel self-organizing link layer protocol (SDD) based on time hopping impulse radio was proposed by the authors. In this paper, the SDD protocol is further developed and specified in detail. The simulations are carried out using the GloMoSim simulation environment.

1. INTRODUCTION

Future Personal Area Networks (PANs) should be able to support a large variety of personal applications. Some of the more demanding ones will be, for instance, video conferencing or interactive games. Ultra Wide Band impulse radio (UWB-IR) promises to be suitable for such short-range, low-cost and high data rate applications while having a very low energy consumption. IEEE 802.15 is the standardization body which covers the link layer and physical layer technologies for PANs. UWB-IR is one of the technologies considered within IEEE 802.15.3a.

PANs that meet these expectations will have a hybrid character, consisting mainly of ad hoc networks, using IEEE 802.15 air-interfaces, with occasional access to infrastructures. Because of the mobility of a person and the devices that constitute a PAN, and the dynamics of the applications [1], nodes will join or leave the network, and radio links will be broken or established. Therefore the network should be able to quickly configure and reconfigure itself. These operations should be done without the intervention of a user or a system administrator, and therefore will have to be self-organizing. Self-organization in this context implies the discovery of neighbors, the creation of connections, the scheduling of transmissions and the formation and re-configuration of the network topology.

In [2] we introduced a novel link layer protocol, for PANs based on UWB-IR, i.e., Self-organizing Device discovery and Data transmission (SDD) protocol. The SDD protocol makes use of time hopping multiple access, which is an intrinsic feature of UWB-IR. This protocol is able to automatically discover nodes within radio range, form a distributed link layer topology and assign channel resources for collision-free transmissions.

In this paper we highlight the key aspects in the design of the SDD protocol, present a further developed and optimized version of the protocol and analyze its behavior by means of simulation. In Section 2, we discuss issues related to the design of UWB-IR based networks. In Section 3, we describe the sub-processes of the SDD protocol. In Section 4, the performance parameters which characterize the quality of self-organization in the SDD protocol are specified and analyzed by means of simulation in Section 5.

2.   DESIGN ISSUES OF UWB-IR BASED NETWORKS

In order to design a high data rate and fast medium access in UWB ad hoc networks, a number of facts and design issues related to the UWB-IR technique need to be kept in mind.

- TH impulse radio: Low duty cycle and low power density are crucial properties of TH impulse radio. Multiple access can be achieved by TH spread spectrum, which uses a pseudorandom time hopping sequence, called the TH code. TH impulse radio also has in principle the capability to determine its location with great accuracy, i.e., of the order of sub-centimeter [3].
- Collisions: As a result of the low duty cycle of TH impulse radio, the probability that packets overlapping in time collide is decreased. When multiple packets transmitted on different codes arrive at a node simultaneously, the node is able to decode the information on its own code while the information on other codes is perceived as noise [5]. This enables simultaneous in-range transmissions and receptions on different codes. This improves the aggregate capacity of the network. We base our design on the assumption that no more than 10 nodes communicate simultaneously. This allows us to neglect the multiple access interference

(MAI) in this instance and ensure that the achievable data rate of a node is not affected [4].Furthermore, when overlapping packets sent on the same code arrive (Fig.1), multiple pulses are received in one frame and the pulses may not exactly overlap. The result is an increase in MAI but not a collision since packets are still successfully received. By using a novel blind synchronization method [6], the receiver is able to decode the overlapping packets of the same code. A packet collision happens only when two or more packets with the same code exactly coincide in time at a node; the physical layer will detect this collision.

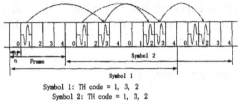

Symbol 1: TH code = 1, 3, 2
Symbol 2: TH code = 1, 3, 2

Figure 1. Packets overlapping on the same TH code.

- Carrier-sensing: The low power density and low duty cycle of TH impulse radio however implies that it is difficult to distinguish idle periods from packet transmission periods in an UWB receiver [7] and then a long channel detection delay can not be avoided. As a result, MAC protocols based on carrier-sensing would result in poor performance.

- Acquisition time: The signal acquisition time of impulse radio receivers is longer than conventional receivers (of the order of ms). The transmission of one data packet between two devices normally requires one or more signal acquisitions. The long signal acquisition time may degrade the achievable throughput [8]. To mitigate this effect we have a physical layer design which targets a relatively short acquisition time, of the order of 0.1ms [6]. Moreover, the link layer protocol design should as much as possible avoid frequent synchronizations.

- Spreading code: TH impulse radio has a large and adjustable code family; it enables each node to be assigned different codes, e.g., a TH sequence [5]. We define three basic types of codes: *common, transmitter-based* and *receiver-based* codes, denoted respectively by C, $C_{i,T}$ and $C_{i,R}$. The receiver-based and transmitter-based codes can be derived from a node's unique 48-bit IEEE MAC address by using a pseudo random process, e.g., using the method proposed in [9]. The common code is defined as a signaling channel for exchanging specific control messages.

- Neighbor discovery: Using TH spread spectrum as the multiple access method implies that data transmission is not possible before the communication codes are known by the sending and receiving nodes.

Neighbor discovery is the process during which nodes get to know the presence and identity of their neighbors.

3.   OPERATIONS OF THE SDD PROTOCOL

In this section we discuss performance related aspects and optimizations of the SDD protocol. For more details on the operation of the protocol we refer to [1]. We consider a scenario where a number of nodes within radio range of each other are expected to form and maintain a single-hop ad hoc network. The protocol consists of two sub-processes: *Device Discovery* (DD) and *Data Transmission* (DT).

3.1   Device Discovery Process

The DD process can discover multiple nodes per synchronization. This is unlike Bluetooth and it clearly speeds up the network formation. For example, Bluetooth needs up to 10.24s to finish one discovery cycle; on average, it spends 5~6s finding only one device (see Bluetooth specifications). We will show that (see Section 5) our protocol uses around 50ms to find 10 nodes and 70ms to find 50 nodes.

We illustrate how the DD process works. To simplify the explanation, the propagation delay is not shown in the following figures. As shown in Fig. 2, if node i is switched on, it first stays in *Idle* state for a random period with uniform distribution. Then, node i broadcasts an Inquiry (IS) packet on the common code C. The acquisition header of the IS packet allows the nodes in range and listening, e.g. node j, to synchronize with node i. After sending the IS packet, node i starts a response scan operation which is able to receive multiple responses from the inquired nodes. During this operation, node i periodically sends Low Rate Synchronization (LRS) packets on code $C_{i,T}$ of node i to keep all inquired nodes synchronized.

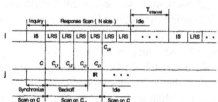

Figure 2. Device Discovery process.

If the link i-j already exists, j doesn't have to reply and returns to *Idle* state monitoring code C. Otherwise, after a random number of time slots, denoted by $T_{j,backoff}$, node j responds with an Inquiry Response (IR) packet on the code $C_{i,R}$ of node i. $T_{j,backoff}$ is determined by node i's scanning window size $w_{i,scan}$. It is uniformly distributed in the range $[0, w_{i,scan}]$. Afterwards, node j returns to *Idle* state. If node j is successful in sending the IR packet containing node j's code $C_{j,T}$, node i and j have discovered each other and are ready for data transmission.

The number of slots during the response scan is called the *response scan window size* $w_{i,scan}$. The larger $w_{i,scan}$, the lower the probability of response packet collisions but on the other hand the longer the response scan duration. Two parameters are related to $w_{i,scan}$, of which one is the initial value of the scan window size W after a node is powered on and the other is the adaptation factor β. β is to scale the changes of $w_{i,scan}$ each time. The information of the discovered node is stored in the neighbor list. The maximum size of the neighbor list is denoted as l_{max}. The discovery interval T_{int_short} and T_{int_long} determines the frequency with which the DD process is executed.

3.2   Data Transmission Process

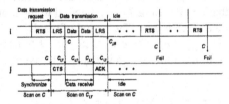

Figure 3. Data Transmission process.

The DT process is initiated by an RTS-CTS handshake using code C. Fig.3 illustrates the unicast data transmission process for two nodes. Node i needs to send data to node j. If node i is *Idle*, it first broadcasts an RTS packet on code C. Without waiting for the response, node i continues to send an LRS packet on code $C_{i,T}$ to keep node j synchronized. Right after node j receives the RTS packet, it replies to node i by sending a CTS packet on code C. In the meantime, node j begins to monitor code $C_{i,T}$. Subsequently, the data packet is transmitted on code $C_{i,T}$ from node i to node j. If it succeeds, node j replies to node i with an ACK packet on code $C_{j,T}$. Finally both nodes i and j return to *Idle* state.

When node i does not receive a CTS packet from node j, node i will periodically attempt to resend an RTS packet in T_s interval for at most m times. This is illustrated in Fig.3. If there is still no response after m number of RTS packets, it means that either node j has left the radio range of node i, node j has been powered off, or the connection between node i and j has been disturbed for a long time.

4.   PERFORMANCE EVALUATION

1) Discovery time:

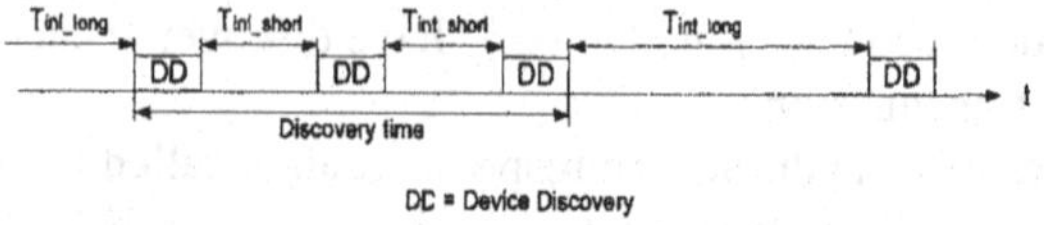

Figure 4. SDD discovery time.

We define *discovery time* $\overline{T}_{disc}$ as the average time spent by a self-organization protocol to enable any newly entering node or group of nodes to discover and incorporate with all or most neighboring nodes. It should be short enough to allow timely configuration and re-configuration of the link topology relative to the dynamics of the network. A relevant measure is the time for a particular node i to detect a neighboring node j has joined or left, denoted by $T_{i,join}^{j}$ and $T_{i,depart}^{j}$.

The discovery time $T_{i,disc}$ of the SDD protocol is defined as the duration of a set of successive DD processes with short average interval. It is counted from the moment that a node using T_{int_short} interval to the moment it changes to T_{int_long} interval mean (see Fig.4). The period of one DD attempt is denoted as $T_{i,dd}$, $T_{i,dd} = \upsilon_{IS} + w_{i,scan} \times \sigma$ where υ_{IS} is IS packet transmission time and σ is the time slot used in response scan window. The average discovery time $\overline{T}_{disc}$ is as follows:

$$\overline{T}_{disc} = \frac{1}{N_{total}} \sum_{i=1}^{N_{total}} (\sum_{k=1}^{r} T_{i,dd}(k) + \sum_{k=1}^{r-1} T_{int\_short}) \qquad (1)$$

There are k ($1 \leq k \leq r$) times DD attempts within the discovery time for a single node. r is obtained from the simulation.

2) Discovery ratio:

We define the *discovery ratio* $\overline{\rho}$ as the average percent of the number of neighbors on the list in the total number of nodes within the radio range. Note that this measure relates to the network as a whole and not to an individual node. Discovery ratio is calculated as the average percentage of discovered neighbors after one discovery time. d_i is the degree of any node i.

$$\overline{\rho} = \frac{1}{N_{total}} \sum_{i=1}^{N_{total}} \frac{d_i}{N_{total} - 1} \qquad (2)$$

3) Effect on throughput:

When network nodes frequently join and leave, the self-organization processes, i.e., device discovery and connection setup, need to be performed more often. We define the *effect on throughput* as the achievable throughput measured when discovery processes are performed to the throughput measured when discovery processes are not performed. We measure the achievable throughput when DD process is performed as well as when DD process is not performed. The comparison of the two measurement results can show the effect of DD process on throughput. Throughput is defined as the average successful transmission rate.

5. SIMULATION RESULTS

We did an initial performance evaluation of the SDD protocol using GloMoSim. Based on an interactive game scenario described in [1], we consider a number of nodes forming a single-hop network within an area of 10m×10m, i.e., corresponding to an in-room environment. The nodes are less than 50 and are uniformly distributed over the simulation area. Node mobility is neglected in this scenario. We assume an error-free channel, hence all packet losses are due to collisions or buffer overflow.

Table 1. Parameter specifications

Parameter	Value	Parameter	Value
Achievable data rate	110 Mbps	Initial time T_{int}	[1ms, 20ms]
Traffic model	CBR	Slot duration for DD σ	20 µs
Packet size	2000 bytes	T_{int_short}	10ms
Buffer size	10000 packets	T_{int_long}	1s
Channel acquisition time	0.1 ms	Retransmission interval mean $E[T_r]$	0.2 ms
IS packet size	36 bytes	Retransmission times m	3
IR packet size	20 bytes	Response scan window initial value W	15 or 32 slots
RTS packet size	36 bytes	Neighbor list size l_{max}	10 to 100 entries
CTS packet size	36 bytes	Neighbor list time out T_{lmax}	100 s

The system parameters used to evaluate the SDD protocol are listed in Table 1. We set the achievable data rate to 110Mbps corresponding to the IEEE 802.15.3a standard. The signal acquisition time is set to 0.1ms, which can be further improved [6]. In order to avoid frequent synchronizations, we use a large packet length of 2000 bytes. The choice of protocol parameters is mostly based on preliminary experiments.

5.1 Discovery time

We first investigate the influence of the response scan window size on *discovery time*. We assume l_{max} is larger than the number of nodes and hence does not impact the discovery time.

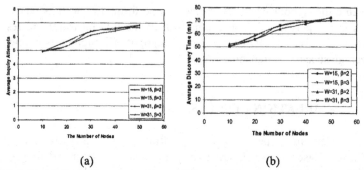

(a)   (b)

Figure5. (a) The average number of DD processes in one discovery; (b) The average discovery time.

In Fig.5, we observed a certain degree of linearity in terms of the number of nodes. Moreover, the maximum discovery time for a 50-node setting is less than 75ms which is much lower than the magnitude of the discovery time in Bluetooth. We also observe that as we use different initial scan window size W and the adaptation factor β (see Fig.5), $\overline{T}_{disc}$ is slightly different within a certain range. The difference is caused by the different adaptation parameters W and β. The difference is not so dramatic because in the initial setting, T_{int_short} is one or two orders of magnitude larger than the response scan window period which is from 0.2 ms to 0.7ms. We now investigate the influence of the neighbor list size l_{max} on average discovery time $\overline{T}_{disc}$ for different numbers of in-range nodes. In this experiment, the initial scan window size W is chosen as 31, and the adaptation factor β is 2.

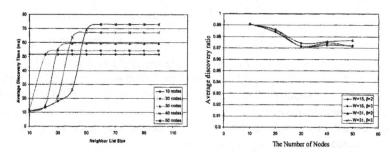

Figure 6. The average discovery time   *Figure 7.* Average discovery ratio.
for different neighbor list sizes.

As shown in Fig.6, we can see that when the neighbor list size l_{max} is smaller than the number of nodes, the discovery time increases as l_{max} increases. The reason is that the DD processes with T_{int_short} interval terminate only according to one condition that the neighbor list is full. More time is needed by each node to fill in its neighbor list when l_{max} increases. In this case, the degree d_i of each node is equal to l_{max}. If l_{max} is equal to or larger than the number of adjacent nodes, when the network is fully connected, the discovery time reaches a steady maximum value. This is because the DD processes with T_{int_short} interval terminate due to the fact that no new neighbor has been found in the last three contiguous discovery processes.

5.2 Discovery ratio

With the same parameter settings as in the initial experiments, the average discovery ratio was measured. We set the neighbor list size l_{max} much larger than the total number of node. From Fig.7, we observe that the average discovery ratio $\bar{\rho}$ is always higher than 0.97 for different number of nodes. It shows that most nodes can find most of their neighbors in one discovery time. Thus, the degree of any node is very close to the number of in-range nodes. Therefore, the node similarity can be satisfied in the network topology formed by SDD protocol. In Fig.7, when the number of nodes increases, $\bar{\rho}$ slightly decreases. This is because when more nodes come up in the network, the probability that more DD processes overlap with each other increases, as well as the probability of collisions of packets.

5.3 Throughput behavior

This experiment evaluates the influence of the DD processes on the system throughput. We only consider 4 nodes in this experiment and thus the effect of MAI and routing protocol can be neglected. In both the situations of without and with DD processes, the initial DD process has to be executed.

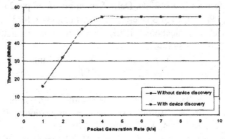

Figure 8. Throughput behavior with/without device discovery.

When the packet generation rate is smaller than 4000 pkts/sec and the network is lightly loaded, the throughput increases with the packet generation rate (see Fig.8). For higher packet arrival rates, the network is saturated and the throughput stays above 54 Mbit/s. When the network is either lightly loaded or saturated, we observe that the device discovery has very little influence on the system throughput. It benefits from the high data rate and capability of multiple transmissions offered by TH impulse radio.

The fast transmission of control packets on the common code reduces the probability of collision occurrence between the DD and the DT processes. The multiple transmissions on different codes enable the two simultaneous processes to be successfully executed.

6.   CONCLUSION

In this paper, the key characteristics in the design of the self-organizing link layer protocol SDD for impulse radio UWB were described. The SDD protocol was implemented in a GloMoSim simulator. Results show that the SDD protocol has good performance in the operations of neighbor discovery and medium access. In the current experiment conditions and assumptions, the average discovery time is much lower than the discovery time in Bluetooth. The node similarity can be satisfied in the single-hop network topology. The device discovery process has very little influence on the system throughput. Presently, we are working on the multi-hop case and on performance analysis using different traffic models.

REFERENCES
1. W. Lu, A. Lo and I. Niemegeers, "On the Dynamics and Self-organization of Personal Networks", MAGNET Workshop in Shanghai, November, 2004.
2. N. Shi and I. Niemegeers, "A Self-organizing Link Layer Protocol in UWB Ad Hoc Networks", Proceedings of Personal Wireless Communications: IFIP TC6 9th International Conference, PWC 2004, Delft, September 2004, pp. 248-261.
3. M.G.M. Hussain, "Principles of Space-time Array Processing for Ultrawide-band Impulse Radar and Radio Communications", IEEE Transactions on Vehicular Technology, vol. 51, issue 3, May 2002, pp 393-403.
4. L. Zhao, A.M. Haimovich, "The Capacity of an UWB Multiple Access communication System", Communications, 2002. ICC 2002. IEEE, vol.3, 28 April-2 May 2002, pp.1964 – 1968.
5. M.Z. Win, R.A. Scholtz, "Ultra-Wide Bandwidth Time-Hopping Spread-Spectrum Impulse Radio for Wireless Multiple-Access Communications", IEEE Transactions on Communications, vol. 48, no. 4, April 2000, pp. 679-689.
6. R. Djapic, G. Leus and A-J. van der Veen, "Blind Synchronization in Asynchronous Multiuser UWB Networks Based on the Transmit-reference Scheme", The Asilomar Conference on Signals, Systems, and Computers, Pacific Grove CA, November 7-10, 2004.
7. I. Oppermann, "The Role of UWB in 4G", Special Issue on Adaptive Global Net: Vision Towards a Modern Communication Infrastructure, Wireless Personal Communications, April 2004, vol. 29, no. 1-2, pp. 121-133(13).
8. S.S.Kolenchery, J.K.Townsend, J.A. Freebersyser, "A Novel Impulse Radio Network for Tactical Military Wireless Communications", Proceedings of IEEE Milcom '98, Boston, October 1998.
9. J.J. Garcia-Luna-Aceves, J. Raju, "Distributed assignment of codes for multihop packet-radio networks", MILCOM 97 Proceedings, vol.1, November, 1997, pp. 450-454.

POWER CONTROL AND CLUSTERING IN WIRELESS SENSOR NETWORKS

Lahcène Dehni[1], Francine Krief[2], Younès Bennani[1]

[1] *Laboratoire d'Informatique de l'Université Paris Nord, Institut Galilée, 99, Avenue J.B. Clément, 93430 VilletaneuseFrance ;* [2] *LAboratoire Bordelais de Recherche en Informatique Domaine Universitaire,351, cours de la Libération, 33405 Talence Cedex, France*

Abstract: The use of the wireless sensor networks (WSNs) should be increasing in different fields. However, the sensor's size is an important limitation in term of energetic autonomy, and thus of lifetime because battery must be very small. This is the reason why, today, research mainly carries on the energy management in the WSNs, taking into account communications, essentially. In this context, we compare different clustering methods used in the WSNs, particularly EECS, with an adaptive routing algorithm that we named LEA2C. This algorithm is based on topological self-organizing maps. We obtain important gains in term of energy and thus of network lifetime.

Key words: Wireless sensor networks, clustering, power control, adaptive routing algorithm, and topological self-organizing maps.

1. INTRODUCTION

WSNs present a vast application field, for example, in the scientific, logistic, military and health field. According to MIT'S Technology Review[1], *"this technology is one of the ten new technologies which will change the world and our manner of live and work"*.

The battery is an important component of a sensor. Generally, it is neither replaceable nor rechargeable. With its small size, it provides an energy quantity very limited on a scale of 2J by a sensor[2]. So, it limits the lifetime of the sensor and influences the total operation of the network. This is the reason why, today, protocols ensuring low energy consumption occupy an important research orientation in this field.

A sensor ensures acquisition, data processing and communications. The communications are the most energy consuming. Thus, a good diagram of energy management must, in priority, take into account communications.

The two principal classes of protocols used in the wireless networks are based on the multi-hops routing or clustering techniques. Several approaches are proposed to calculate the optimal path in the multi-hops routing protocols. Some[3] propose to take into account the shortest path, in term of distance, to the base station. Others[4] still, choose an optimal path by privileging some sensors whose presence in the path reduces the energy consumption.

However, the main disadvantage of the multi-hops routing is the periodicity of the messages sent to maintain the valid paths. These messages overload the network and consume additional energy.

Today, clustering gives the best results[5]; this is the reason why we adopted this approach. It is a problem of classification which interests the numerical learning for a long time, in particular, the connectionist models and, more particularly, the topological Self-Organizing Maps (SOMs). This last approach has proved its efficiency in this type of problem.

We proposed to adapt an unsupervised connectionist learning method by introducing the evolutionary and dynamic clustering aspect. This new approach of clustering allows us improving the efficiency of the routing in WSNs. In this paper, we compare the proposed routing algorithm with different clustering methods used in the WSNs, particularly EECS[6] (Energy Efficient Clustering Scheme in Wireless Sensor Networks). We obtain better results with our method.

Our paper is organized as follows: first, we present an energy consumption model in the WSNs. Then, we study different clustering protocols. We also present the unsupervised numerical learning technique for the clustering, called the self-organizing maps. The adaptation of this classification technique to the problem of routing allowed us to propose a routing algorithm adapted to the WSNs. Finally, we show, through an experiments series, some validation results of our new algorithm and we present the future prospects.

2.   ENERGY CONSUMPTION MODEL IN WSNS

A sensor uses its energy to carry out three main actions: acquisition, communication and data processing. The power consumption to perform the data acquisition is not very important. Nevertheless, it varies according to the phenomenon observed and monitoring type. The communications consume much more energy than the other tasks, in emission as well as in reception. Fig. 1 presents an antenna model and the energy consumption rules associated[9]. To transmit a k bits message over a distance of d meters, the transmitter consumes:

$$E_{Tx}(k,d) = E_{Tx}(l) + E_{Tx\_amp}(k,d) \tag{01}$$

$$E_{Tx}(k,d) = \begin{cases} k.E_{elec}(k,d) + k.\varepsilon_{friss}.d^2 & \text{if} \quad d < d_{crossover} \\ k.E_{elec}(k,d) + k.\varepsilon_{two\_ray\_amp}.d^4 & \text{else} \end{cases} \tag{02}$$

To receive a k bits message, the receiver consumes:

$$E_{Rx}(k) = E_{Rx\_elec}(k) = k.E_{elec} \tag{03}$$

Where : E_{elec} : energy of electronic transmission/reception; k : size of a message; d : distance between the transmitter and the receiver; E_{Tx_amp} : amplification energy; ε : amplification factor; $d_{crossover}$: limit distance over which the transmission factors change of value.

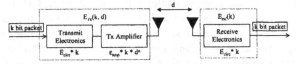

Figure 1. Communication power consumption model in WSNs

Power consumption in aggregation is calculated by: $E_{DA} = 5$ nJ/bit/msg   (04)

3.   CLUSTERING PROTOCOLS USED IN WSNS

Heinzelman and al.[8-9] have proposed the LEACH protocol and a centralized version of this protocol, called LEACH-C. These protocols are based on clustering.

Clustering consists in the segmentation of the network into groups (clusters). Sensors transmit their data towards group representatives called clusterheads (CHs), which send these data to the base station (BS). In some applications, CHs make a simple data processing (aggregations...) on the received data before retransmitting them to the BS. Clustering permits the bandwidth re-utilization. It also offers a better resource allocation and helps to improve the energy control in the network[10-11]. With the clustering sensors establish small communication distances with their CHs. The data aggregations and compressions minimize energy consumption by reducing the data flow and thus the total communications.

LEACH protocol is based on a probabilistic demand model and fixes the optimal clusters number according to some parameters such as the network topology, the communications and the computational cost. (Generally, CHs represent 5% of the sensors number in the network). CHs create TDMA tables according to the number of sensors in a cluster. Each sensor transmits data to CH using the time slots specified in the TDMA tables. Sensors turn off their antennas and wait for their speaking time. It permits to minimize the energy dissipation. CHs leave their receivers on to receive the sensors data.

Each CH chooses randomly a code in a list of CDMA propagation codes; it transmits this list to its sensors in the cluster. The sensors use this list for their transmissions. It permits to minimize the communication interferences between closed CHs. The use of TDMA/CDMA techniques allows a hierarchy built on a multilevel clustering, it can increase the amount of saved energy.

An extension of this algorithm, called LEACH-C[9], has been proposed to avoid these drawbacks. In this centralized iterative algorithm, the clusters structure is computed by the BS using the "Simulated annealing" optimization method[12]. At each step, the sensors are given their role, either CH or simple sensor, by the BS. Then, operations continue like in the LEACH protocol.

Authors[6] present EECS (Energy Efficient Clustering Scheme in WSNs). It is a LEACH-like clustering scheme. CHs are elected depending on there communication residual energy while achieving a well CH distribution; furthermore, a new method is introduced in order to balance the load among the CHs. The simple sensors choose their CH by considering not only saving its own energy but also balancing the workload of CHs. To do that, two distance factors are introduced: $d(P_j, CH_i)$ (distance between a node P_j and a CH_i) and $d(CH_i, BS)$ (distance between a CH_i and the BS) and two proposed normalized functions to get a *cost* function. P_j chooses CH_i with min $\{cost\}$. Simulation results show that EECS outperforms LEACH significantly and prolongs the network lifetime over 35% [6].

4.   THE UNSUPERVISED CONNECTIONIST LEARNING AND THE SOM

Unsupervised numerical learning, or automatic classification, consists in determining a partition of an instance space from a given observations set, called training set. It aims to identify potential trend of data to be gathered into classes. This learning approach, namely *clustering*, seeks for regularities from a sample set without being driven by the use of the discovered knowledge. Euclidian distance is usually used by clustering algorithms to measure similarities between observations. Self-Organizing Maps (SOM) implement a particular form of competitive artificial neural networks; when an observation is recognized, activation of an output cell – competition layer – leads to inhibit activation of other neurons and reinforce itself. It is said that it follows the so called "Winner Takes All" rule. Actually, neurons are specialized in the recognition of one kind of observations.

The learning is unsupervised because neither the classes nor their number is fixed a priori.

A SOM consists in a two dimensional layer of neurons (Fig. 2) which are connected to n inputs according n exciting connections of respective weights w and to their neighbors with inhibiting links.

The training set is used to organize these maps under topological constraints of the input space. Thus, a mapping between the input space and the network space is constructed; closed observations in the input space would activate two closed units of the SOM.

An optimal spatial organization is determined by the ANN from the received information, and when the dimension of the input space is lower than three, both position of weights vectors and direct neighborhood relations between cells can be represented visually. Thus, a visual inspection of the map provides qualitative information of the map and the choice of its architecture. The connectionist learning is often presented as a minimization of a risk function. In our case, it will be carried out by the minimization of the distance between the input samples and the map prototypes (referents), weighted by a neighborhood function h_{ij}. To do that, we use a gradient algorithm. The criterion to be minimized is defined by:

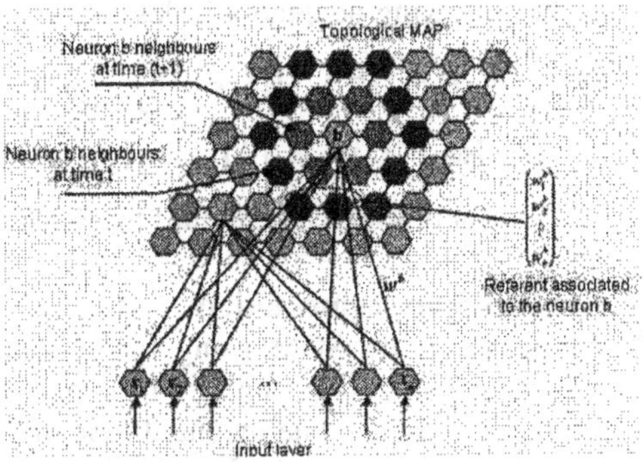

Figure 2. MAP structure (2D network)

$$E_{SOM} = \frac{1}{N} \sum_{k=1}^{N} \sum_{j=1}^{M} h_{j\,NN\,(x^{(k)})} \left\| w_{.j} - x^{(k)} \right\|^2 \tag{06}$$

N represents the learning samples number, M the neurons number, $NN(x^k)$ is the neuron having the closest referent to the input form $x^{(k)}$, and h the neighborhood function. The neighborhood function h can be defined as:

$$h_{rs} = \frac{1}{\lambda(t)} \exp\left(-\frac{d_1^2(r,s)}{\lambda^2(t)} \right) \tag{07}$$

$\lambda(t)$ is the temperature function modeling the neighborhood extent, defined as:

$$\lambda(t) = \lambda_i \left(\frac{\lambda_f}{\lambda_i} \right)^{\frac{t}{t_{max}}} \tag{08}$$

λ_i and λ_f are respectively initial and the final temperature. t_{max} is the maximum number allotted to the time (number of iterations for the x learning sample). $d_1(r,s)$ is the Manhattan distance defined between two neurons r and s on the map grid, with the coordinates (k,m) and (i,j) respectively:

$$d_1(r,s) = |i-k| + |j-m| \tag{09}$$

The learning algorithm of this model proceeds essentially in three phases:
- Initialization phase where random values are assigned to the connections weights of each neuron of the map grid. - Competition phase during which, for any input form $x^{(k)}$, a neuron $NN(x^k)$, with neighborhood $V_{NN(x^{(k)})}$, is selected like a winner. This neuron has the nearest weight vector by using Euclidean distance:

$$NN(x^{(k)}) = \operatorname*{argmin}_{1 \leq i \leq M} \left\| w_i - x^{(k)} \right\|^2 \tag{10}$$

- Adaptation phase where the weights of all the neurons are updated according to the following adaptation rules: If $w_{.j} \in V_{NN(x^{(k)})}$ then adjust the weights

using: $w_{.j}(t+1) = w_{.j}(t) - \varepsilon(t) h_{j\,NN(x^{(k)})} \left(w_{.j}(t) - x^{(k)} \right)$ (11)

else $\quad w_{.j}(t+1) = w_{.j}(t)$ (12)

Repeat this adjustment until the SOM stabilization.

• **SOM map segmentation**:

We segment the SOM using the K-means method (Fig. 3). It is another clustering method. It consists in choosing arbitrarily a partition. Then, the samples are treated one by one. If one of them becomes closer to the center of another class, it is moved into this new class. We calculate the centers of new classes and we reallocate the samples to the partitions. We repeat this procedure until having a stable partition.

The criterion to be minimized in this case is defined by:

$$E_{K-means} = \frac{1}{C} \sum_{k=1}^{C} \sum_{x \in Q_k} \|x - c_k\|^2$$ (13)

Where C represents the number of clusters, Q_k is the cluster k, c_k is the center of the cluster Q_k or the referent.

The basic algorithm requires fixing K, the number of clusters wished. However, there is an algorithm to calculate the best value for K assuring an optimal clustering. It is based principally on the minimization of Davies-Bouldin index, defined as follows:

$$I_{DB} = \frac{1}{C} \sum_{k=1}^{C} \max_{l \neq k} \left\{ \frac{S_c(Q_k) + S_c(Q_l)}{d_{ce}(Q_k, Q_l)} \right\}$$ (14)

With $\quad S_c(Q_k) = \dfrac{\sum_i \|x_i - c_k\|^2}{|Q_k|}$ (15)

$$d_{cl}(Q_k, Q_l) = \|c_k - c_l\|^2$$ (16)

C is the number of clusters, S_c is the intra-cluster dispersion, and d_{ce} is the distance (centroid linkage) between the clusters centers k and l.

This clustering procedure aims to find internally compact spherical clusters which are widely separated. There are several methods to segment the SOMs[13]. Usually, they are based on the visual observations and the manual assignment of the map cells to the clusters. Several methods use the K-means algorithm with given ranges for K value. Our work is based on the approach of Davies-Bouldin index minimization[14].

We note that the K-means approach can be applied directly to the data instead of SOMs. In our work, we applied it to the SOMs results. The idea is to use SOMs as a preliminary phase in order to set a sort of data pretreatment (dimension reduction, regrouping, visualization...). This last has the advantage to reduce the clusters calculation complexity and also ensure a better visualization of the automatic classification results. Moreover, the use of SOMs for visualization is crucial, especially in the case of data multivariate: dimension > 2 or 3. In this last case, the SOMs permit to reduce the data space dimension and to visualize the clusters in the plan.

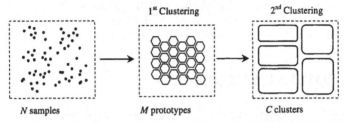

1st Clustering 2nd Clustering

N samples M prototypes C clusters

*Figure 3.*Two successive clusterings: SOM followed by K-means

5.   LEA2C: A NEW ROUTING APPROACH IN WSNS

We use clustering methods based on the unsupervised connectionist learning techniques and different properties of LEACH-C in order to propose a new routing approach in WSNs, so called LEA2C (Low Energy Adaptive Connectionist Clustering). In our approach the sensors have a GPS system (Global Positioning System). It allows the BS to localize the sensors. As in LEACH-C protocols[8-9], we use the power consumption model of the Fig. 1.

Our algorithm is iterative: In each iteration the BS calculates the clustering according to sensors alive coordinates. It affects roles to the sensors by assigning transmission codes and frequencies. Sensors clustering is done with the SOMs and the number of clusters is optimized using the *k*-means algorithm. In each cluster, the CH choice can be made using one of the three following criteria: - The sensor having the maximum power level in the cluster. - The nearest sensor to the gravity center of the cluster or to the BS.

LEA2C algorithm:

To compare our approach with other methods such as EECS method, we use the same communication and data model; also we run our simulation in two different scenes[6].

1) Initialization: Random deployment of the N homogeneous sensors in a given space and with the same energy level.

2) Clustering

2.1) Clustering of the WSN by using the SOM and *K*-means algorithms by using the sensors coordinates.

2.2) CHs selection according to one of the selection criteria cited above.

2.4) Roles affecting to each the sensors (CH or simple sensor).

3) Data transmission

3.1) Data transmission from the simple sensors to the CHs: consumed energy is calculated using the Eqs. (01) and (02).
3.2) We calculate, for each CH:
- The data reception and aggregation energy using the Eq.(03, 04)
- The results transmission energy to the BS by using the Eq.(01).
3.3) When the CH is chosen according to the first criterion (maximum energy), the same CHs are reelected after each transmission.
3.4) Repeat the steps 3.1) to 3.4) until the death of one sensor.
4) Repeat the steps 2) and 3) until the death of all the sensors in the network.

6.   SIMULATIONS RESULTS

Figure 4.a. SOM clustering 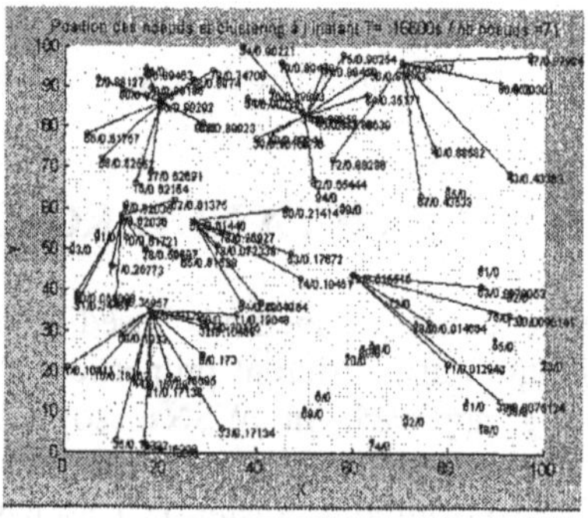   *Figure 4.b.* LEA2C communications

To simulate our algorithms, we have used SOMs core (SomToolbox) proposed by HUT researchers[15] (Helsinki University of Technology). We have applied our algorithm on the same data used in EECS[6]. The figures below present the results obtained.

Fig. 4.a. represents the neurons segmentation of the SOM map.

Fig. 4.b. represents the sensors network, and shows the sensors clustering.

Figs. 5.a and 5.b represent respectively the variation of the number of sensors alive according to the number of received messages by the BS in the normal scene (400) and the large scene (1000) motes. In each figure, we consider the corresponding variations according to the four scenarios:
- Direct transmission from the sensors to the BS.
- The clustering according to our approach with the three CH selection criteria already mentioned.

Figs. 6.a and 6.b represent the same variations with the EECS protocol.

In general, Figs. 5.a and 5.b show, for our algorithm, that the choice of the CH according to the criterion of maximum energy is better than the choices according to the other criteria. Choices according to the criteria of proximity to the GC and to the BS have nearly the same performances. They are enough far from the criterion of maximum energy but better than the performances of the direct transmission protocol and EECS ones.

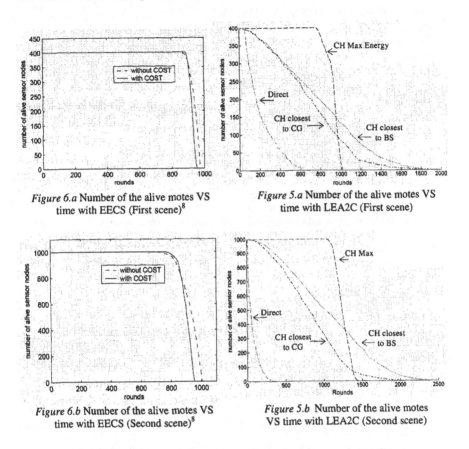

Figure 6.a Number of the alive motes VS time with EECS (First scene)[8]

Figure 5.a Number of the alive motes VS time with LEA2C (First scene)

Figure 6.b Number of the alive motes VS time with EECS (Second scene)[8]

Figure 5.b Number of the alive motes VS time with LEA2C (Second scene)

Figs. 6.a and 6.b show the effectiveness of the EECS. Moreover, EECS with *cost* gives better results than the without-*cost* scenario.

By comparing the Figs. (5.a, 5.b) and Figs. (6.a, 6.b), we notice that the graphs have the same paces with very apparent profits brought by our algorithm compared with the EECS protocol.

On the graphs 6.a and 6.b, we notice that LEA2C, with the better selection criterion of CHs (Max energy level), makes it possible to ensure a totality survival of sensors during 90% of the network lifetime. Compared to EECS, our algorithm offers a profit of 50% more important in term of total network lifetime when the CH retained is with the max energy level, and 100% times more when the CH retained is the nearest sensor to the BS.

7.   CONCLUSION AND PROSPECTS

LEA2C ensures an important profit compared with the EECS protocol. The results obtained are very promising with a lifetime up to 50% longer. The network coverage is insured during 90% the total time of treatment.

To improve our results, we plan the following adaptations: - Application of a super-clustering on the CHs, and the spreading of the clustering over several levels. - Use of other SOMs versions and the coupling with other communication protocols. - Optimization of the parameters of the learning algorithms (SOMs, *K*-means) - Integration of other parameters in the clustering process, such as the moving speed of the sensors in the case mobiles sensors.

8.   REFERENCES

1. Technology Review: 10 Emerging technologies that till change the world (February 2003); http://www.technologyreview.com.
2. G.J. Pottie and al. Wireless integrated network sensors; *Communications of the ACM* 43 (5), pp. 551– 558. (2000)
3. C. Perkins and E. Royer, Ad-Hoc on-demand distance vector (AODV) routing; *The Second IEEE Workshop on Mobile Computing Systems and Applications (WMCSA'99).* (1999)
4. K. Scott and N. Bambos, Routing and channel assignment for low power transmission in PCS; *5th IEEE Int. Conf. on Universal Personal Communications*, volume 2. (1996)
5. S. Ghiasi et al. Optimal energy aware clustering in sensor networks; *SENSORS Journal*, Vol. 2, Issue 7, pp. 258-269, July 2002.
6. M. Ye, C. Li, G. Chen and J. Wu, EECS: An energy efficient clustering scheme in wireless sensor networks; *IEEE IWSEEASN'05.* (2005)
7. I. F. Akyildiz, W. Su, Y. Sankarasubramaniam, and E. Cayirci, A survey on sensor networks"; *IEEE Communications Magazine*, Vol. 40, No. 8, pp. 102-114, (2002).
8. W. Heinzelman, A.P. Chandrakasan and H. Balakrishnan; Energy-efficient communication protocol for wireless microsensor networks; *Sensor 2002*, 2, pp. 258 –269. (2002)
9. W. Heinzelman, A.P. Chandrakasan and H. Balakrishnan, An application-specific protocol architecture for wireless microsensor networks; *IEEE Transactions on Wireless Communications*, Vol. 1, No. 4, pp. 660-670. (2002)
10. E.-S. Jung and N. H. Vaidya, A power control MAC protocol for ad-hoc networks; *ACM MOBICOM.* (2002)
11. V. Kawadia and P. R. Kumar, Power control and clustering in Ad Hoc networks; *IEEE INFOCOM.* (2003)
12. T. Murata and H. Ishibuchi, Performance evaluation of genetic algorithms for flowshop scheduling problems; *1st IEEE Conference Evolutionary Computation*, volume 2. (1994)
13. A. Juha and A. Esa, Clustering of the self-organizing map; *IEEE Tractions On Neural Networks*, volume 11, n° 3, (2000)
14. David L. Davies and Donald W. Bouldin, A cluster separation measure; *IEEE Trans. on Pattern Analysis and Machine Intelligence*, PAMI-1(2): pp. 224-227. (1979)
15. E. Alhoniemi and al. SOM Toolbox, (2000). http://www.cis.hut.fi/projects/somtoolbox/

PROTECTING TRANSMISSIONS WHEN USING POWER CONTROL ON 802.11 AD HOC NETWORKS

Alexandre Andrade Pires and José Ferreira de Rezende
GTA - COPPE
Universidade Federal do Rio de Janeiro, Brazil
Email: {andrade, rezende}@gta.ufrj.br

Carlos Cordeiro
Philips Research USA
Briarcliff Manor, NY 10510
Email: Carlos.Cordeiro@philips.com

Abstract   This paper presents the ALCA (Asymmetric Link Collision Avoidance) protocol. ALCA was designed to deal with a known deficiency of the Basic Scheme
Gomez et al., 2001 for power control in 802.11 ad hoc networks, which occurs
when links become asymmetrical as a result of power control. The proposed
ALCA mechanism conveys transmission duration information to these terminals
through a simple modification of the 802.11 MAC protocol. Through extensive
simulation, the performance of ALCA is investigated and compared to PCM
(a solution that requires major hardware updates). Results indicate that ALCA
outperforms PCM while being a considerably less complex solution.

Keywords: ad hoc, power control, IEEE 802.11

Introduction

A number of proposals have been made in order to reduce power consumption in ad hoc networks so as to provide longer autonomy to mobile nodes, and
hence increase the network lifetime. Among the areas of vigorous research,
power-aware routing has attracted considerable attention, and is based on the
idea of appropriately selecting routes in order to minimize power consumption
Narayanaswamy et al., 2002; Gomez et al., 2001; Agarwal et al., 2001; Monks
et al., 2001. A complementary research area focuses on designing protocols
that save energy through the use of transmit power control. The basic idea is
to avoid exceeding the transmission power level needed for link establishment.

Power control techniques are often based on a feedback mechanism, which is responsible for information exchange between receiver and transmitter so as to adjust transmission power to the minimum necessary level required for link maintenance Agarwal et al., 2001; Monks et al., 2001. Besides saving transmission energy, power control has the advantage of contributing to a potential spatial reuse of the channel. In other words, transmissions at a lower power level are kept in a reduced range, which decreases medium contention and results in a higher aggregated throughput by allowing other transmissions to take place simultaneously in the network. Also, power control reduces co-channel interference, which leads to better signal-to-noise ratio at the receivers.

We can identify three broad approaches to establish a power control loop between transmitters and receivers in IEEE 802.11 ad hoc networks: those employing a separate control channel Lin et al., 2003; those making use of busy tones Monks et al., 2001; and those adding extra information fields in all control and data frames Agarwal et al., 2001. The first two schemes usually give good performance as power control feedback is provided while the transmission is ongoing. On the other hand, these schemes require that two transceivers be available, which make them expensive and complicated solutions. In what concerns the third approach, its main drawback is the introduction of asymmetric links among medium contenders. Asymmetric links increase the likelihood of collisions, putting at risk the benefits obtained from power control.

In this paper, we propose a solution to avoid collisions in the presence of asymmetric links. This scheme, named ALCA (Asymmetric Link Collision Avoidance), has the advantage of being simple, efficient and easily implementable. Through extensive simulations, we have compared ALCA with existing solutions that are based on the same approach, and the results are very promising. The remainder of this paper is organized as follows. Section 1 presents the existing work on power control for IEEE 802.11 ad hoc networks. Next, in Section 2 the ALCA mechanism is described in detail. Section 3 presents the simulation environment and results. Finally, this paper is concluded in Section 4 with some future directions.

1.   Power Control on IEEE 802.11 Networks

This section describes the major existing schemes that add extra information fields in the IEEE 802.11 frames to perform power control in ad hoc networks.

BS: Basic Scheme

A simple mechanism for power control on IEEE 802.11 networks is based on power information exchange during the RTS, CTS, DATA and ACK frame exchange Gomez et al., 2001; Agarwal et al., 2001, and constitutes the starting point for several possible enhancements. In short, this technique is based on the idea of transmitting the RTS and CTS frames at the maximum transmit power level. This frame exchange is then used to determine the minimum power level needed for a successful communication between the two nodes, thus allowing them to transmit the DATA and the ACK frames with the minimum required power. Clearly, this method does not take any advantage of the potential spatial channel reuse, as the reservation of the channel is always done at the maximum power level. On the other hand, it conserves significant energy as DATA and ACK frames are transmitted at lower power levels.

On the downside, the reduction on the transmit power of the DATA and ACK frames may cause collisions in the receiver (with the DATA frame) as well as in the transmitter (wit the ACK frame). This is due to the introduction of asymmetric links between the communicating nodes and other potential transmitters that cannot sense the medium busy during the ongoing low power transmission. Such collisions result in frame retransmission and hence increased energy consumption, eliminating any possible gain obtained from power control. In the next section we elaborate on this problem and present the PCM protocol Jung and Vaidya, 2002 as a possible solution.

PCM: Power Control MAC

The virtual carrier sensing mechanism of IEEE 802.11 works well for terminals inside the transmitter's transmission range, where they are able to successfully decode the frame received. However, a problem occurs with the terminals located within the carrier-sensing zone (CS-Zone) of the transmitter, which is characterized by the fact that nodes in this zone can only sense the carrier in the channel, but cannot decode the frames received. As a result, these nodes do not have access to the duration information contained in the frame headers. Considering that propagation effects are the same in both directions, the transmitter is also in these nodes' CS-Zone. In this situation, a collision will take place if any of these terminals decide to initiate a transmission during the ongoing low power transmission. In an attempt to minimize the occurrence of this scenario, the standard specifies that if a node receives a signal with sufficient power to trigger a carrier detection, but not high enough to result in a correct frame reception, it shall set its NAV to an inter-frame space called EIFS (Extended Inter Frame Space) once the carrier detection is over. Nodes within the transmission range and CS-Zone adjust their NAVs during RTS-CTS-DATA-ACK transmission. Nodes in transmission range correctly set their NAVs when receiving RTS or CTS. However, since nodes in the C-Zone cannot decode the packet, they do not know the duration of the packet transmission. To prevent a collision with the ACK reception at the source node, nodes within the C-Zone set their NAVs for the EIFS duration. The main purpose of the EIFS is to provide enough time for a node to receive the ACK.

However, when power control is employed the above sequence may fail. For example, consider the Basic Scheme. After a CTS transmission, a terminal located in the CS-Zone of the CTS transmitter will set its NAV with the EIFS value. Next, as the DATA transmission will be carried out at a lower power level there will be a consequent reduction of the CS-Zone. Once the EIFS expires, it may so happen that the terminal senses the medium as idle if it is no longer inside the CS-Zone of the original transmission. In this case, the node concludes that the channel is free and, after the backoff process is over, initiates an RTS transmission.

This problem was studied in Jung and Vaidya, 2002 which shows that this failure may result in a significant increase in the number of collisions and retransmissions. As a result, instead of the desired energy conservation effect, the power consumption in the network would actually increase. To overcome this problem, the authors propose a power control MAC (PCM) scheme that avoids these collisions through a periodic in-frame variation of transmit power level for DATA frames. During the low power DATA frame transmission, the transmitter must advertise nodes within the original CS-Zone (i.e., the zone defined by the power level used for transmission of the RTS/CTS) that the transmission is still going on. To this end, PCM mandates that during the transmission of DATA frames the terminal should raise its transmit power to the maximum power level, triggering carrier detection and further NAV setting to EIFS duration for those terminals in the CS-Zone. After a period of time transmitting at the maximum power level, the power is again reduced to the minimum level. This periodic increase/decrease of the transmit power level continues indefinitely until the DATA transmission is completed, triggering carrier detection at the terminals within the original carrier sensing range and preventing them from accessing the medium and causing collisions. PCM achieves a better energy conservation, as it minimizes collision probability and guarantees that the power saving gain obtained from power control is not eliminated by excessive retransmissions. However, a major drawback with this solution is that it requires transmitters to vary their transmission power very quickly and with high precision.

BSM: Basic Scheme with Memory

In the Basic Scheme, RTS and CTS frames are always sent at the maximum transmit power. In other words, the power control loop is used for the sole purpose of reducing the DATA and ACK frames transmission power. As an enhancement, the Basic Scheme with Memory (BSM) employs a table at each terminal that maintains the previous transmission power level used by the terminal to communicate with each one of its neighbors. For each MAC address of a neighbor terminal, there is an entry in the table that keeps the exact power necessary for communication with that node, which is obtained from the last RTS-CTS-DATA-ACK exchange between the nodes. As opposed to the Basic Scheme, a node uses the reduced power level for all its transmissions, i.e., RTS-CTS-DATA-ACK.

Among the advantages of BSM scheme, we can observe a higher power saving and a higher potential to channel spatial reuse. The channel reuse is enhanced as the union of the CS-Zone for the RTS frame and the CS-Zone for the CTS frame represents the reserved area for a transmission. If these frames are sent at reduced power level, such zones will be reduced, allowing for the occurrence of simultaneous transmissions. On the other hand, this mechanism provides a lower protection for DATA transmissions, possibly increasing the collision probability. Also, the BSM scheme should be enhanced with mechanisms for scenarios with mobility since it does not calculate the needed transmit power in a per-packet basis.

2. ALCA: Asymmetric Link Collision Avoidance

As discussed in 1, asymmetric links due to power reduction on DATA and ACK frames may result in frame collisions and further retransmissions, leading to poor performance. This problem is inherent to any mechanism of power control based on the Basic Scheme Gomez et al., 2001; Agarwal et al., 2001. As a result, a solution to the asymmetric link problem is critical and essential to any power control protocol employing high power control frames (i.e., RTS and CTS) for medium reservation and collision avoidance, and reduced power DATA and ACK frames.

The solution proposed in this work, the ALCA (Asymmetric Link Collision Avoidance) protocol, overcomes this problem by allowing terminals in the carrier sensing zone of a transmission to have access to transmission duration information despite the fact that terminals within this zone are not able to correctly receive and decode a frame, and so cannot read the duration field present in RTS and CTS frames. As we have showed in 1, the asymmetric link problem is a consequence of this inability.

Although terminals located in the carrier sensing zone cannot decode the correct type of a packet, but they can detect a data carrier on the channel. Moreover, they can sense with some level of accuracy the instants of time when carrier sense turns on and off. The proposed scheme is based on conveying the Current Transmission Duration Information (CTDI) through the physical duration of the carriers that transport RTS and CTS frames. This way, terminals within the CS-Zone will be able to determine the CTDI, preventing them from accessing the channel until the current transmission successfully terminates.

The physical duration of the RTS/CTS frames can be increased by simply adding a few bits to them. However, it is important to keep in mind that these additional bits do not carry any information by themselves, but are just a way to enlarge the frames according to the CTDI. Thus, the ALCA protocol provides a discrete set of N different Carrier Durations (CD) for RTS and CTS frames. For terminals inside the reception zone the CD is simply ignored, as these terminals are able to access the CTDI included in RTS and CTS duration field. However, terminals located in the CS-Zone use the CD information to extract the CTDI and hence avoid collisions.

Broadly, the ALCA protocol operation is comprised of two major parts. In the first one, a node that is going to initiate a transmission calculates the respective CTDI and stores it in an RTS frame. In addition, it determines which CD it will have to use in order to allow terminals in the carrier sensing zone to recover the intended CTDI. This selection is made by comparing the CTDI to predefined thresholds. Thus, the transmitter chooses a CD_i among those N possible CDs. Finally, the transmitter includes the necessary word of bits in the RTS frame, so that the transmission has the intended duration on the channel (those bits are ignored by nodes inside reception zone). Obviously, to ensure protocol consistency, ALCA requires that all terminals in the network know beforehand both the thresholds as well as the set of possible CDs.

In the second part of ALCA operation, a terminal in the CS-Zone of the considered transmitter senses a data carrier on the channel. As the frame cannot be successfully decoded, the information of signal duration (i.e., the CD) is extracted. In this case, instead of setting the NAV to the standard EIFS value as in IEEE 802.11, the node selects an appropriate value for the EIFS based on the extracted signal duration. Clearly, this value has to be larger than the CTDI calculated using the signal duration in order to avoid a collision. The same protocol operation applies in case of CTS frames so as to convey transmission duration to nodes in the carrier sensing zone of the receiver. Last, but not the last, it is important to note that the ALCA protocol may work in combination with any power control scheme based on the BS methodology.

3.   Simulation Results

We have used ns-2.26 to perform our simulations. For the evaluation of the power control schemes, we have used random scenarios generated by arbitrary location of 40 nodes inside a specified physical area. A total of 20 terminals are transmitters, while the other 20 are receivers. Although all flows are single hop, but they do not always occur with the closest node to the transmitter. Any node inside of transmitter reception zone can be chosen to be a receiver. Reception zone is a circle of 250 m of radius, while CS-Zone has a radius of 500 m. We run simulations varying the aggregated rate of the CBR sources. Two metrics are considered: aggregated throughput (in Mbps) and the amount of data transmitted by unit of energy (in Megabytes per Joule). Each point is an average of 50 runs, each of them with nodes in different locations. The error bars in the curves correspond to 99% confidence intervals. Packet size is fixed in 1024 Bytes.

The simulations were run varying the physical area where nodes are placed and the noise power. The noise power, or noise floor, corresponds to the power at the receivers when all transmitters are turned off. We use two values for physical area, 1 km^2 and 4 km^2. For noise power, we also consider two values, namely, -100 dBm (the typical noise of office environments) and -83 dBm (which corresponds to a noisy environment). Our goal is to study the behavior of the schemes with respect to network densities and noise variations. Finally, we have focused on three configurations: large area with low noise, large area with high noise, and small area with low noise.

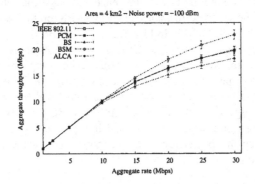

Figure 1. Sparse network with low noise - Aggregate throughput.

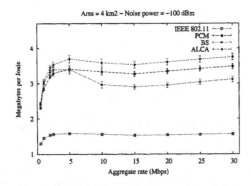

Figure 2. Sparse network with low noise - Energy efficiency.

Figures 1 and 2 present aggregated throughput and Megabytes per Joule when using an 4 km^2 area and noise power of -100 dBm. We can see that there is minimal difference in aggregated throughput achieved by the five schemes and that they are equivalent with respect to data delivery, under these conditions. Aggregated throughput was evaluated for each configuration, always resulting in similar curves: small differences in averages, always smaller than error bars. While the maximum aggregated offered load was 30 Mbps (on a 11 Mbps channel), which corresponds to a 1.5 Mbps CBR source on each transmitter, we conclude that full network capacity is never reached. This explains why aggregated throughput curves for the schemes are similar, even if collisions and retransmissions occur more or less frequently in each one of them. As aggregated throughput curves are always similar, we now discuss only energy related curves for the other two configurations.

From Figure 2, we note important differences amongst the schemes. Pure IEEE 802.11 has the worst performance. PCM and BS, on the other hand, are seen to outperform IEEE 802.11. In low offered loads, BS is more efficient in terms of energy savings. However, as CBR load increases so does the asymmetrical link problem, hence causing collisions and consequent performance degradation. With its periodic variation of transmit power, PCM triggers EIFS in the CS-Zone and is thus able to avoid the asymmetrical link problem and achieve higher energy conservation as compared to BS. Clearly, the ALCA protocol works well in solving asymmetrical link problem without the need to increase the transmit power level of data frames, thus achieving superior energy conservation.

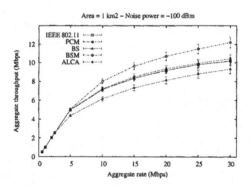

Figure 3.   Dense network with low noise - Aggregate throughput.

Figures 3 and 4 present results of reduced physical area, with low noise. As area is reduced and network density increases, channel contention is higher and we can see that the point where BS and PCM schemes have similar performance occurs in reduced rates in contrast to the large area, low noise config-

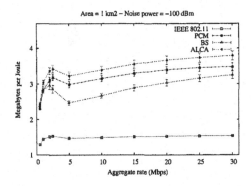

Figure 4.   Dense network with low noise - Energy efficiency.

uration. As the total number of collisions increases, relative gain of ALCA is reduced when compared to PCM, but it still achieves superior performance.

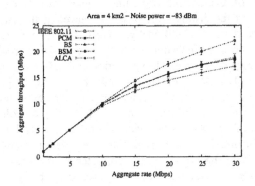

Figure 5.   Sparse network in a noisy environment - Aggregate throughput.

Figures 5 and 6 investigates the scenario when the area is large (4 km^2) and noise raises to -83 dBm, and reflects numerous situations such as industry plants. Once more, ALCA exhibits best performance while we can see that PCM follows ALCA more closely, as noise increases the occurrence of collisions.

4. Conclusions

This work has presented the ALCA (Asymmetrical Link Collision Avoidance) protocol, which is intended to solve asymmetrical link problem, a known deficiency of Basic Scheme (BS) based power control mechanisms. ALCA was evaluated together with BS which supplies power control while ALCA

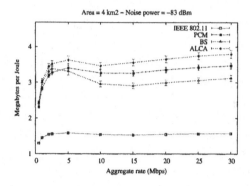

Figure 6.   Sparse network in a noisy environment - Energy efficiency.

works on solving asymmetrical link problem. Therefore, ALCA can be used in conjunction to any other power control protocol based on the BS method.

The results confirm that asymmetrical link problem can increase the number of collisions and retransmissions, possibly canceling the energy saving obtained by power control. Additionally, results show that ALCA protocol presents a good performance in dealing with asymmetrical link problem. ALCA has experienced energy savings slightly superior to PCM, and much superior than other schemes. Therefore, we can conclude that the ALCA protocol provides higher energy conservation than other existing schemes without the need for drastic changes in hardware or in the 802.11 MAC protocol. As future work, we plan to evaluate ALCA behavior in a mobile network environment and analyze its performance when used with other power control schemes. Also, we will evaluate the impact of the coexistence of devices supporting ALCA with legacy 802.11 devices without any power control.

References

Agarwal, S., Krishnamurthy, S., Katz, R. H., and Dao, S. K. (2001). Distributed power control in ad-hoc wireless networks. In *IEEE PIMRC'01*.

Gomez, J., Campbell, A. T., Naghshineh, M., and Bisdikian, C. (2001). Conserving transmission power in wireless ad hoc networks. In *ICNP'01*.

Jung, E. and Vaidya, N. H. (2002). A power control MAC protocol for ad hoc networks. In *ACM MOBICOM'02*.

Lin, X.-H., Kwok, Y.-K., and Lau, V. K. N. (2003). A new power control approach for ieee 802.11 ad hoc networks. In *IEEE PIMRC'03*.

Monks, J. P., Bharghavan, V., and mei W. Hwu, W. (2001). A power controlled multiple access protocol for wireless packet networks. In *IEEE INFOCOM'01*.

Narayanaswamy, S., Kawadia, V., Sreenivas, R. S., and Kumar, P. R. (2002). Power control in ad-hoc networks: Theory, architecture, algorithm and implementation of the COMPOW protocol. In *European Wireless 2002*.

A POWER-SAVING ALGORITHM AND A POWER-AWARE ROUTING SCHEME FOR IEEE 802.11 AD HOC NETWORKS

Nikos Pogkas[1] and George Papadopoulos[2]

[1]*Department of Electrical and Computer Engineering University of Patras, Campus of Rio, Greece E-mail: npogas@ee.upatras.gr;* [2]*Industrial Systems Institute, Rion Patras Greece*

Abstract: This paper proposes a local power saving algorithm combined with a power-aware routing scheme to provide energy-efficient operation of the network. The power saving algorithm reduces communication energy consumption whereas the power aware routing scheme increases node lifetime. Another objective of the proposed routing strategy is the selection of stable paths in order to achieve robust network operation; to accomplish this scope a new routing metric is presented combining the residual energy level of nodes with an estimation of the stability of links. Simulation studies indicate a reduction in energy consumption and a significant increase in node lifetime whereas the network performance (delivery ratio and routing overhead) is not affected significantly.

Key words: Power aware routing, power saving mode, low power mode,

1. INTRODUCTION

In recent years there has been increased research interest in the area of ad-hoc networks, which can operate without the presence of any preinstalled network infrastructure, have distributed robust operation and can adapt well in network dynamics such as mobility of hosts or topological changes. These network properties are desirable in many situations such as military, law enforcement or disaster relief operations.

This work is based on the design and implementation of a low cost ad-hoc network for disaster relief operations[1]. Our application objective was a search and rescue operation[2] after an earthquake in a collapsed apartment, building or house. In each apartment or building there should be a number of small preinstalled, low-cost, battery operated autonomous devices (sensor nodes) equipped with a camera CMOS sensor, an audio microphone and a wireless interface. The rescue teams using mobile central units, roaming over the collapsed building should collect captured images and recorded audio from the remote sensor nodes inside the collapsed building in order to find trapped people and rescue them.

This work focuses on routing and network energy consumption issues. A combined efficient way for dealing with idle time (low power mode) and communication (power aware routing) is proposed for a powerful network energy management solution. Although this work is based on DSR[3] and IEEE 802.11b, the principles apply to other routing and MAC protocols.

2.   LOW POWER MODE ALGORITHM

Since the mobile nodes of an ad hoc network operate using batteries, it is important to minimize the power consumption of the network. Existing network solutions that improve energy efficiency focus on: transmit power control, low power mode algorithms and power aware routing algorithms.

While transmit power control increases the network capacity and reduces interference, its use in reducing energy consumption is based heavily in the hardware specifications of the wireless interface[4]. The use of multi-hop paths saves energy only when the path attenuation dominates the static energy consumption of the hardware, a case that occurs less frequently than is typically believed. As a result our energy efficient solution is based on the combination of a low power mode algorithm and a power aware routing strategy, presented in the next sections.

The basic idea of the proposed Low Power Mode algorithm (LPM) is to reduce the idle power consumption by turning off the radios of nodes that are idle. The algorithm's operation is driven entirely by the communication in the network. The main design considerations of our LPM implementation are the following: distributed robust operation in ad hoc networks, the use of the algorithm should not affect significantly network performance, no need for synchronization between the nodes (the synchronization of nodes proposed in various Chen[5] is difficult to implement in dynamic topologies and induces a significant network overhead), no periodic exchange of packets or beacons (periodic transmission of packets or beacons proposed by Zheng[6] increases the energy consumption unnecessarily when the network is idle, also channel bandwidth and network capacity is decreased while the beacons or control packets contend for channel access with normal data packets), low implementation complexity and no need for modifications at the MAC layer (in order to be easily deployed with current commercial and future wireless products).

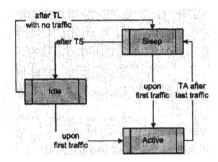

Figure 1. State diagram of the LPM algorithm

The algorithm has been implemented as an intermediate network driver at the LLC OSI layer for commercial IEEE 802.11 wireless cards. In Fig. 1 we present the state diagram of the algorithm. When a node is idle it periodically turns off its radio for duration T_S entering the *Sleep* state. After T_S it enters the *Idle* state for a period of T_L where it listens for incoming packets. When it receives a broadcast or unicast packet addressed to that node it enters the *Active* state where it remains for duration of T_A. The same state transition occurs when there is a packet available at the egress queue ready for transmission. When a node is in the *Sleep* state it cannot receive any packets from any other node. As a result, a mechanism must be implemented in order to guarantee the successful reception of packets for a node that periodically enters the *Sleep* sate. This mechanism is presented in Fig. 2. Every node that transmits a packet remains in the *Active* state for T_A. If the destination is a node that is possibly in the power saving state (namely transits periodically between the *Idle* and the *Sleep* state), the source node must retransmit the packet R times with an interval T_O in order to overlap the packet transmission with the destination's *Idle* state.

In order to reduce possible local congestion or overhead in the network the following mechanism has been implemented. Each node maintains a table (*Next-hop Nodes Table*) with the possible states of its next-hop neighbours in order to decide if it has to make the R re-transmissions or not. If the node transmits or receives a packet from a neighbour node, it marks this node as active in its table. After T_A seconds it marks the same node as possible-inactive (power-saving state) until it transmits successfully or receives another packet from that node. If the wireless interface is working in promiscuous mode, the nodes can trace any packet transmission in the network in order to update the status of next-hop nodes, improving the algorithm's performance.

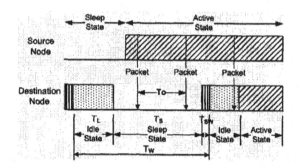

Figure 2. Packet retransmission mechanism

The information regarding the active state of a destination node in the next-hop table is accurate enough to coordinate transmissions since the source node has detected a successful transmission or reception of a packet from that node based on a MAC layer acknowledgement. If the destination node is in the power saving state then the source node will initiate the retransmission mechanism. If the destination node enters the active state the source node will receive an acknowledgement and will stall any pending retransmissions of the packet.

However, during a broadcast transmission there is no MAC-ACK, so the source node has to transmit a broadcast packet every T_O seconds for R times. In order to reduce this overhead, a variable is maintained (*T_last_broadcast*) which contains the last time that a broadcast packet has been transmitted. Broadcast packets will cause every next-hop node to enter the active state for at least a period of T_A. Thus, when a sending node transmits a broadcast packet at time $t < T_A + T\_last\_broadcast$ it assumes that all its next-hop nodes are still in the active state and the packet is transmitted normally without any retransmissions. This mechanism reduces significantly the number of retransmissions in the network which are caused by the use of the algorithm.

In the presence of unstable links or high mobility, the above mechanism performs sufficiently well and in some cases improves network performance as a result of the additional retransmissions imposed in unicast and broadcast packets. The major disadvantages of the proposed LPM algorithm are the increased latency during a route discovery (a basic problem found in most of the asynchronous low power mode algorithms) and the additional overhead induced by broadcast packets that are transmitted in the network (and especially for packets that are flooded in the entire network).

In the next paragraphs we present a systematic approach to address the LPM algorithm's design parameters and we calculate the maximum achieved energy efficiency of such an algorithm. An idle node not implementing the LPM algorithm in a time period $T_W = T_L + T_S + T_{SW}$ will consume energy

$$E_1 = P_L * T_L + P_L * T_S + P_L * T_{SW} \tag{1}$$

During the same period an idle node that implements the algorithm will consume energy

$$E_2 = P_L * T_L + P_S * T_S + P_{SW} * T_{SW} \tag{2}$$

where P_L is the power consumed at the idle state, P_S is the power consumed when the radio is off, Ts is the time a node spends in the sleeping state and T_L in the listening state. Tsw is the time needed to switch the radio from off to on plus the time needed to switch from on to off and, during this period, the power consumption is approximately equal to P_L ($P_{SW} \approx P_L$), as measured in many experimental scenarios[4, 8].

Using Eqs. (1) and (2) we define the power efficiency factor P_{EFF} of the algorithm for idle nodes by

$$P_{EFF} = \frac{E_1 - E_2}{E_1} = \frac{(P_L - P_S) * T_S}{P_L * T_W} \tag{3}$$

$$K_{DEV} = \frac{(P_L - P_S)}{P_L} \tag{4}$$

The constant value K_{DEV} depends on the hardware specifications of the wireless card and bounds the maximum value of the power efficiency factor. The maximum number of retransmissions required for a sleeping node to receive a packet is defined by

$$R = T_w / T_O \text{ , where } T_L > T_O \tag{5}$$

Also we define the ratio $D = T_S / T_O$ \hfill (6)

Using Eqs. (3), (4), (5) and (6) the power efficiency is found to be,

$$P_{EFF} = K_{DEV} * \frac{D}{R} \text{ , where } R \in N^+ \text{ and } R > 1 \tag{7}$$

A guideline to select adequate parameters for the algorithm is the following; T_S must have a small value to reduce latency. A positive integer is selected for the number of retransmissions R in order to achieve the desirable energy efficiency. The minimum value of T_L depends on the MAC layer specifications. Also T_O must be lower than T_L by an amount that reflects possible transmission delays caused by the driver, operating system, packet transmission delay or the MAC congestion avoidance mechanism. A set of values that has been used in the implementation and in the simulations of Section 5 is the following: T_L=69ms, T_{SW}=1ms, T_S=290ms, T_O=60ms and R=6. This set in case of the Orinoco wireless card (P_{TX}=1408mW, P_{RX}=914mW P_{IDLE}=785mW P_{SLEEP}=65mW) can achieve $PEFF$=0.73.

3.   POWER AWARE ROUTING

There have been several research efforts regarding power aware routing algorithms. These algorithms must select the best path to minimize the total power needed to route packets on the network and maximize the lifetime of all nodes. Minimum cost battery routing MCBR[9] proposes the remaining battery capacity of the nodes as a metric. Min-max battery routing MMBR[10] defines as a cost metric of a route the maximum battery cost value of the nodes that constitute the path. Although the previous algorithms reduce network consumption and increase node lifetime, or both, in networks where the wireless channel is characterized by multi-path propagation it is observed that some links may experience an increased packet error rate. These unstable links can decrease the network performance significantly[7] due to packet losses and the initiation of the route discovery mechanism.

Efforts towards this direction have been also made to add criteria based on a combination of shortest-path, link quality, or least congested paths, that is, network load. Link quality estimations can be based on either the signal-to-noise ratio or the expected transmission count (ETX) metric[12]. The results Couto[12] and Draves[13] show that with stationary nodes the ETX metric significantly outperforms shortest path routing; also network-load and packet delay metrics perform poorly because they are load-sensitive and hence suffer from self-interference. However, Draves[13] concludes that in a mobile scenario shortest-path routing performs better, compared to ETX, because it reacts more quickly to fast topology change. Therefore the path length is also considered in the metric for our route selection.

In this work we present a route selection algorithm that combines link stability metric with the battery level of the nodes and the route length. When the nodes have battery levels above some threshold and the links are stable, shortest path routing is performed. In case of link failures stable links are preferred and as the battery level of nodes is decreased a combination of the above metrics is encountered in route selection. Following the methodology proposed by Singh[9] we define the path cost $C(n_0, n_k)$ of a path from a source node n_0 to a destination node n_k by:

$$C(n_0,n_k) = \sum_{i=1}^{k} z(n_{i-1},n_i)$$

(8)

where $z(n_{i-1}, n_i)$ is the cost of the link from node n_{i-1} to node n_i. The path cost C depends on the path length of the route and the cost of the links that compose the route. The link cost is defined as a function of the energy cost Zen and the stability cost Zst of the link from node n_{i-1} to node n_i by:

$$z(n_{i-1}, n_i) = f(Zen(n_i), Zst(n_i)) = Zen(n_i) * Zst(n_i) \qquad (9)$$

The multiplication of the above metrics increases the cost of nodes that have unstable links and low energy levels. As a result longer hop paths are preferred and packets are routed over these nodes. The energy cost metric of a node is defined as:

$$Zen(n_i) = 1 + EF * g(n_i) \qquad (10)$$

where $g(n_i)$ is the normalized energy consumed by the node, $g(n_i) = (E_{INITIAL} - E(n_i))/E_{INITIAL}$, EF is the energy cost factor which bounds the maximum value of the energy cost, $E_{INITIAL}$ is the initial and $E(n_i)$ the current residual energy level of the node. The stability cost metric is defined as:

$$Zst(n_i) = 1 + \frac{1 + SF}{stability(n_i)} \qquad (11)$$

where $stability(n_i)$ is the stability metric of that node and SF a stability cost factor which bounds the maximum value of the stability cost. An optimal assignment of the EF and SF factors is required for meeting the network communication constraints. Increasing EF a priority is given to power aware routing, whereas increasing SF more stable links are preferred.

The stability metric was first proposed by Hu[11] in order to estimate a dynamic link timeout cache policy, the Link-Max-Life (LMF) link cache. When a node is added in the cache it has an initial link stability value $(SINITIAL)$. When a link from the route cache is used in routing a packet originated by that node, the stability metric of the two end point nodes is additively increased by a stability increase factor $SINCF$, $stability(n_i) = stability(n_i) + SEDCF$.

Upon a link error, the source node will receive a route error packet containing the broken-link. In this case the stability metric of the two end point nodes is multiplicatively decreased by a stability decrease factor $1/SDECF$ (where $SDECF \geq 2$), $stability(n_i) = stability(n_i)/SEDCF$.

In any case the stability metric is bounded in a set [2, MAX_STAB]. Using Eqs. (10), (11) and (12) the path cost is equal to:

$$C(n_0, n_k) = \sum_{i=1}^{k} (1 + EF * g(n_i)) * \left(1 + \frac{1 + SF}{stability(n_i)}\right) \tag{12}$$

In the presence of unstable links in the network, nodes that route packets capture the received route error messages and update the stability metric of the nodes in the network. Each node maintains in the route cache a local view of the stability metric of links in the network. As a result, nodes that experience a high link loss ratio have decreased values of stability. Using Eq. (12) source nodes in the network route packets avoiding the use of unstable links and nodes with low energy, increasing the network lifetime and communication robustness. In Table 1, a comparison is presented between different wireless cards: the Agere Orinoco Gold and the Cisco Aironet PC4800B. In the case of the Orinoco wireless card, the increased value of K_{DEV} implies that the LPM algorithm is more effective, as the P_{EFF} can attain higher maximum values. A set of values that has been experimentally evaluated in the deployed wireless ad hoc network is the following: $EF=1$, $SF=2$, $SDECF=2$, $SINCF=2$, $SINITIAL=25$, $MAX\_STAB=300$.

Table 1. Measured power consumption of IEEE 802.11 wireless cards

WLAN card	P_{TX} (mW)	P_{RX} (mW)	P_{IMAX} (mW)	P_{MMAX} (mW)	K_{DEV}
Aironet	1729	1380	1300	320	0.7538
Orinoco	1408	914	785	65	0.9171

4.   SIMULATION STUDY

In this section we evaluate the performance of the proposed LPM and PAR algorithms and their effect in communication efficiency with simulations using the ns-2 network simulator. The network topology consists of 50 nodes randomly distributed in a 1000mx1000m square area. The results are average values for a number of simulations in which the nodes are either static or have a random way point movement with relatively low mean speeds varying from 0 to 5m/sec.

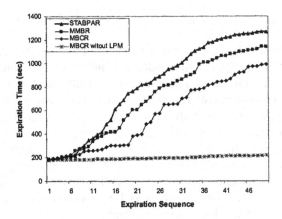

Figure 3. Expiration time vs. expiration sequence

In Fig. 3 we present the expiration time of each node in the network (i.e., the time when a node exhausts its battery) for four different cases: when the LPM is not used and the routing strategy is MMBR, when LPM is used with MBCR and MMBR routing and when LPM is used with the proposed power aware routing (STABPAR). The presented simulation results are in a network topology with 50 nodes and 5 simultaneous CBR traffic flows of 80Kbps. As we can observe, the combination of the proposed power aware routing and the LPM algorithm can achieve a significant increase in the lifetime of nodes. In this case energy efficient routes that experience a lower link-loss ratio are preferred for routing packets, as a result there is a significant decrease in route errors and route discovery operations that waste energy.

5. CONCLUSIONS

In this paper we have presented a Low Power Mode (LPM) algorithm and a Power Aware Routing (PAR) strategy to reduce network consumption and increase node lifetime in an efficient way. Although this work is focused on 802.11 and DSR it can be applied to other MAC and routing protocols, as well. The LPM algorithm can reduce the energy consumption of the wireless card up to 70%, while the network performance is not affected significantly. The PAR strategy proposes a new metric for route selection which combines the link stability and the node battery levels. As a result, energy efficient stable links are preferred for routing packets and, thus, node lifetime and network robustness is increased. The combination of the proposed LPM and PAR algorithms can lead to powerful energy efficient solutions for ad-hoc wireless networks.

During some preliminary experiments in real wireless networks, deployed with embedded sensor nodes and mobile PCs as central units, the network lifetime was increased significantly and the network performance was improved. The experimental evaluation of the stability metric in the presence of high attenuation and interference show that more stable routes were selected increasing the throughput in multi-hop TCP connections between the sensor nodes and the central stations, compared to shortest-path routing. As part of our on-going work we experimentally evaluate the PAR and LPM algorithms and several aspects of the protocol stack, such as TCP performance and tuning, in a wireless network with a large number of nodes.

REFERENCES

1. "LOCCATEC: Low Cost Catastrophic Event Capturing," European Research Project IST-2000-29401, www.loccatec.org
2. N. Pogkas et al. "System for acquiring and surveying data following catastrophic events, with scope of facilitating eventual aid or intervention," European Patent No. 03425667.7.
3. D. B. Johnson, D. A. Maltz, and J. Broch. "The Dynamic Source Routing Protocol for Mobile Ad Hoc Networks," Internet Draft, MANET Working Group, draft-ietf-manet-dsr-09.txt, April 2003.
4. R. Min and A. Chandrakasan, "Top 5 Myths about the Energy Consumption of Wireless Communication," IEEE Mobihoc 2002.
5. B. Chen, K. Jamieson, H. Balakrishnan, and R.Morris, "Span: An Energy- Efficient Coordination Algorithm for Topology Maintenance in Ad Hoc Wireless Networks," Proc. of the International Conference on Mobile Computing and Networking, pp. 85–96, 2001
6. R. Zheng, J. C. Hou and L. Sha, "Asynchronous Wakeup for Ad Hoc Networks," MobiHoc 2003.
7. K. Benekos, N. Pogkas, G. Kalivas, G. Papadopoulos, "TCP Performance Measurements in IEEE 802.11-based Wireless LANs," IEEE MELECON, May 2004.
8. J. C Cano., P. Manzoni, "A Performance Comparison of Energy Consumption for Mobile Ad Hoc Networks Routing Protocols," IEEE ACM MASCOTS, 2000.
9. S. Singh, M. Woo, C. S. Raghavendra, "Power-Aware Routing in Mobile Ad Hoc Networks," Proc. Mobicom, Oct. 1998.
10. C. K. Toh "Maximum Battery Life Routing to Support Ubiquitous Mobile Computing in Wireless Ad Hoc Networks," IEEE Communications Magazine, June 2001, pp 138-147.
11. Y. C. Hu and D. B. Johnson., "Caching Strategies in On-Demand Routing Protocols for Wireless Ad Hoc Networks," Proc. ACM International Conference on Mobile Computing and Networking, August 2000.
12. D. Couto, D. Aguayo, J. Bicket, and R. Morris, "A High-Throughput Path Metric for Multi-Hop Wireless Routing," MobiCom 2003, September 2003.
13. R. Draves, J. Padhye, and B. Zill, "Comparison of Routing Metrics for Static Multi-Hop Wireless Networks," ACM SIGCOMM, August 2004.

OPTIMIZED FLOODING AND INTERFERENCE-AWARE QOS ROUTING IN OLSR*

Dang Quan Nguyen[1] and Pascale Minet[1]

[1]*INRIA Rocquencourt, Domaine de Voluceau*
Rocquencourt - B.P. 105
78153 Le Chesnay Cedex, France
dang-quan.nguyen@inria.fr, pascale.minet@inria.fr

Abstract   Radio interferences and low capacity resources in ad-hoc wireless networks make more complex the quality of service (QoS) support. We propose a solution taking into account radio interferences in mobile ad-hoc networks routing and providing an optimized flooding based on multipoint relays. This solution is based on a modified version of the OLSR routing protocol that considers bandwidth requests and interferences in route selection while providing a very efficient flooding. A comparative performance evaluation based on NS simulations shows that despite the overhead due to QoS support, this solution outperforms classical OLSR in terms of maximum number of acceptable flows, bandwidth amount granted to a flow and route stability. Moreover, the efficiency of the optimized flooding is equal to that provided by the native version of OLSR.

Keywords: Interference, quality of service, optimized flooding, QoS routing, OLSR, multipoint relay (MPR).

1.   Introduction

In a MANET, QoS support is harder than in a wired network because of interferences. The transmission of a node is said to interfere with the transmission of other nodes if at the receivers, the carrier to interference ratio is lower than a threshold value.

Another diffi culty of QoS support in MANETs is that they are characterized by low capacity time-varying resources. The bandwidth of already accepted fbws may signifi cantly decrease as a new fbw is introduced. That is why an admission control is needed. Both the admission control and QoS routing must

*This study has been funded by DGA/CELAR (French Ministry of Defence), in MANET project. Technical point of contact: thierry.plesse@dga.defense.gouv.fr

be interference aware. Furthermore, disseminating information (e.g.; network topology in a proactive routing protocol) or information request (e.g.; route request in a reactive routing protocol) is frequently needed. In order to avoid resources wastage, optimized flooding is required. A solution based on multipoint relays (MPR) is more adaptive than a solution based on a predefined connected dominating set and leads to less retransmissions. As a consequence, a solution based on OLSR routing providing QoS support and optimized flooding is needed. This is the purpose of this paper.

2. Interference aware QoS OLSR

In [3], it is shown that finding a path from a source to a destination that satisfies a bandwidth constraint is made NP-complete by the interferences. That is why we propose a heuristic.

2.1 General presentation

We choose a QoS routing algorithm based on OLSR where the hop count is the primary criterion and the local available bandwidth is the secondary one, for the following reasons:

- The shortest routes, having the minimum hop count, tend to minimize the network resources used for the transmission of a packet from its source to its destination. That is why the hop count must be taken into account in order to reduce the bandwidth loss due to interferences.

- Some flows have bandwidth requirements. Hence the local available bandwidth must be taken into account in the route selection.

- Being called upon any topology change, the chosen routing algorithm must have a complexity similar to Dijkstra algorithm.

- Resources in a MANET having low capacity, the chosen algorithm is based on a partial topology knowledge, like OLSR.

QoS parameters values are disseminated in the network by means of MPRs. The selection of MPRs is modified to consider the bandwidth locally available at each node. The main drawback of this solution lies in the overhead generated: each flooded message leads to a number of retransmissions higher than that obtained with the native OLSR. In this paper, we show how to conciliate the optimized performances of MPR flooding with QoS support. For that purpose, we distinguish two types of MPRs:

- Those, called MPRF, are selected according to the native version of OLSR and are used to optimize flooding.

- The other ones, called MPRB, are selected considering the local available bandwidth and are used to build the routes.

We now detail each component of our solution.

2.2   QoS signaling

Measure of the local available bandwidth.   The Local Available Bandwidth (LAB) of a node is measured locally at the MAC level: the percentage of time the channel is sensed idle and the node is not in back-off state, multiplied by the channel capacity.

Dissemination of the bandwidth available.   Any node broadcasts its LAB as well as the LAB of its one-hop neighbors in its *Hello* message. Consequently any node knows the LAB of each node in its one-hop neighborhood and two-hop neighborhood.

Any MPRB node broadcasts in its *TC* message the LAB of its MPRB selectors and the minimum LAB in its interference area. Notice that according to OLSR rule, only MPRF nodes of the sender retransmit the received message and only if they receive it for the first time.

2.3   MPR selection

Each node performs two MPR selections. The first one is to determine the MPRFs. It is done as specified in the OLSR RFC. The second one is to determine the MPRBs. Knowing the LAB of its neighbors and two-hop neighbors, any node N_i selects its MPRBs in order to reach each two-hop neighbor by a path of maximum bandwidth. If for a two-hop neighbor, there are several one-hop neighbors reaching it, the one with the highest LAB is selected.

The Hello message sent by a node contains both its MPRFs and its MPRBs. A node selected as MPRB broadcasts a TC.

2.4   QoS routing

Two QoS routing algorithms are used. Algorithm 1, unconstrained, aims at providing the widest shortest path between any two nodes (i.e.; the path with the minimum hop number and in case of equality, the path with the largest available bandwidth). It is the default algorithm used to compute the routing table. On the other hand, Algorithm 2, constrained by a bandwidth request, is used to compute a route offering the requested bandwidth to reach a destination. It is called by the admission control for a new fbw f requesting B_f bandwidth units.

2.5   Admission control

The purpose of an admission control is to accept a new fbw f if and only if the QoS of already accepted fbws is not compromised by the acceptance of f and the QoS requested by f can be met. It checks that all nodes on the path of

f provide the requested bandwidth and any node in the interference area of a
node on the path of f has enough bandwidth.

3.   Performance evaluation

We evaluate the performance of our solution by simulation with NS. According to the default value of NS-2, the reception range of a node is $250m$
and the carrier-sense range is $550m$. We use the IEEE 802.11b MAC protocol
without RTS/CTS. The nominal bandwidth is $11Mbps$. OLSR parameters are
set as recommended in [1].

3.1   Flooding optimization

We consider a network with 200 nodes, randomly located on a $2000x2000m^2$
area. Figure 2 shows that our solution with MPRB-optimized generates as
many TCs as MPRB that is used by QOLSR [4]. Notice that this is necessary
for computing paths with maximum bandwidth. The interesting point is that
our solution maintains the number of retransmissions per TC generated as low
as MPRF. Therefore, MPRB-optimized performs effi cient fboding.

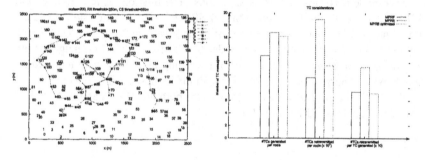

Figure 1.   Ad hoc network with 200 nodes.   *Figure 2.*   TC considerations, 200 nodes.

3.2   QoS support

Configuration studied.   We now simulate 7 CBR fbws with this confi gu-
ration (see Figure 1). The fbws are CBR. Each fbw requires $175Kbps$ at the
application layer. The packet size is $1500bytes$.

Bandwidth granted to flows.   Figures 3 and 4 respectively show the bandwidth received at the application layer of each fbw in the two following scenarios: 7 fbws with Interference-Aware routing and 7 fbws with the native
OLSR protocol. The simulations show that Interference-Aware routing can
provide bandwidth guarantee to QoS fbws when the bandwidth resource is
still available. The native OLSR cannot offer this guarantee because it does
not take into account the availability of bandwidth resource.

With our solution, we can notice that in Figure 1, fbws 6 and 7 are routed around the center of the network because there is not enough bandwidth available in the center to support them. Routing fbws 6 and 7 across the center of the network would degrade the bandwidth already granted to the other fbws as shown in Figure 4.

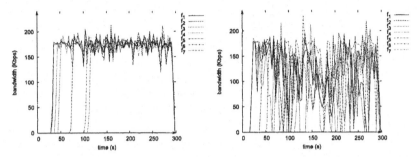

Figure 3.   Interference-Aware routing.   *Figure 4.*   Native OLSR protocol.

Moreover, our solution achieves much less packet loss. Indeed, the loss rates averaged on all fbws and measured at the application level of each fbw destination is equal to 53.08% with native OLSR whereas it is only 1.85% with our solution.

4.   Conclusion

In this paper, we have shown how to conciliate an interference-aware QoS support with an effi cient fboding. Our solution distinguishes two types of multipoint relays: those in charge of MPR fboding that are selected as specifi ed in the classical OLSR version and the other ones that are used to select routes considering bandwidth demand and interferences. Simulation results have shown that the proposed solution allows to accept more fbws, routes are more stable and accepted fbws receive the bandwidth they have requested. Moreover, the overhead due to this QoS support, is kept low and fboding achieves the very good performances of native OLSR.

References

[1] C. Adjih, T. Clausen, P. Jacquet, A. Laouiti, P. Minet, P. Muhlethaler, A. Qayyum, L. Viennot: *Optimized Link State Routing Protocol*, RFC 3626, IETF, 2003.

[2] Y. Ge, T. Kunz, L. Lamont: *Quality of Service Routing in Ad-Hoc Networks Using OLSR*, HICSS'03, Big Island, Hawai, January 2003.

[3] G. Allard, L. Georgiadis, P.Jacquet, B. Mans: *Bandwidth Reservation in Multihop Wireless Networks: complexity, heuristics and mechanisms*, International Journal of Wireless and Mobile Computing (inderscience), accepted for publication in May 2004, To appear (ISSN-1741-1084).

[4] H. Badis and K. Al Agha: *QOLSR, QoS routing for Ad Hoc Wireless Networks Using OLSR*, in European Transactions on Telecommunications, vol. 15, n ° 4, 2005.

OLSR AND MPR: MUTUAL DEPENDENCES AND PERFORMANCES*

Jérôme Härri, Christian Bonnet and Fethi Filali

Institut Eurécom †
Department of Mobile Communications
B.P. 193
06904, Sophia Antipolis, France
{ Jerome.Haerri,Christian.Bonnet,Fethi.Filali } @eurecom.fr

Abstract   Since the initial draft, the Optimized Link State Routing (OLSR) protocol has been associated with the Multipoint Relay (MPR) protocol to reduce the flooding of OLSR topological messages. Many papers have been written on solutions to improve OLSR by replacing MPR by another topology control protocol, or by modifying MPR heuristic. But few of them have dealt with the particular interactions between MPR and OLSR. In this chapter, we argue that OLSR optimality is bound to the deep cooperation between MPR and OLSR. We also illustrate how OLSR suffers from convergence problems, and finally suggest that solving these convergence issues will open new paths to improve OLSR.

Keywords: Convergence, dependence, MPR, OLSR, MANETs.

1.   Introduction

Optimized Link State Routing (OLSR) is one promising algorithm selected by the IETF for routing in Mobile Ad Hoc Networks (MANETs). It has recently reached the experimental request for comments status under the label OLSR3626. In order to compute and maintain routes from and to any nodes in a mobile ad hoc network, OLSR performs for each node a loop discovery on each path to any nodes in the network. Therefore, at convergence, each node fills a routing table that indicates the next hop node to reach any destination node. This path is unique and loop-free. In order to perform this task, each node periodically broadcasts Topology Control (TC) messages contain-

---

*An extended version of this chapter is available as a technical report under the reference RR_05_138 at http://www.eurecom.fr/people/haerri.en.htm

†Institut Eurécom's research is partially supported by its industrial members: Bouygues Télécom, Fondation d'entreprise Groupe Cegetel, Fondation Hasler, France Télécom, Hitachi, Sharp, ST Microelectronics, Swisscom, Texas Instruments, Thales.

ing link state information. Since these TC messages are broadcast to the entire
network, a serious flooding control mechanism needs to be implemented.

Multipoint relays (MPR, A. Laouiti *et al.*) provide a localized and optimized
way of flooding reduction in a mobile ad hoc network. Using 2-hops neighborhood information, each node determines a small set of forward neighbors for
message relaying, which avoids multiple retransmissions. MPR has been designed to be part of OLSR to specifically reduce the flooding of TC messages
sent by OLSR to create optimal routes. Depicted like this, one might think
that both protocols are completely separated and could even be independently
tested, improved, or even changed. However, OLSR has a much different relationship with MPR.

In this chapter, we support that OLSR optimality is closely related to the
particular relationship between OLSR and MPR. We also illustrate some critical convergence issues of OLSR and MPR, which allows us to think that OLSR
and MPR effectively never converge. We argue that this issue is mainly due to
the loss of critical packets and to the correct reception but discarding of inconsistent packets. Finally we suggest that solving these convergence issues might
open new paths to improve OLSR.

The rest of the chapter is organized as follows. Section 2 illustrates OLSR
and MPR mutual dependences, while Section 3 exhibits the convergence issues
in OLSR and MPR. Finally, in Section 4, we draw some concluding remarks.

2.   Mutual Dependences of MPR and OLSR

The most important property OLSR needs from a topology management
protocol for broadcast reduction is its low fraction of nodes implied in flooding. MPR has been particularly designed for flooding reduction but does not
optimize the number of MPR nodes. When designing a topology management protocol, we also want to obtain a minimal number of relays. Therefore
we could think of CDS flooding instead of MPR flooding. There are a large
number of teams that proposed heuristics that solve this task: V. Bharghavan
et al., J. Wu *et al.*, I. Stojmenovic *et al.*, to name only a few. In order to
keep the MPR assets while improving its drawbacks, the first CDS Jaquet *et
al.* (RR.4597) imagined was the set of all MPR nodes. Unfortunately, their
results on this particular CDS showed that it contained too many nodes, and
was therefore suboptimal. They later proposed two MPR reduction protocols
called CDS-MPR (RR.4597) and NCDS (RR.5098). The authors then compared their protocols with MPR flooding applied to OLSR and the results they
obtained were somehow surprising. As expected, the number of dominators
was much smaller than with MPR. But the most astonishing results were that,
although the set of relays in a CDS is much smaller than MPR's, the average

fraction of nodes implied in MPR flooding and CDS flooding are identical. Moreover, they also showed that CDS flooding does not improve OLSR.

Two conclusions may be drawn based on these results. First, a key property for OLSR for being optimal is to have a good flooding reduction protocol at a low communication overhead. Since MPR communication overhead is small ($O(n)$) and is optimal in term of flooding reduction, a CDS would be of no use in order to improve OLSR.

Second, OLSR's advertised link state information need to be kept to a minimal level. OLSR does not only build its optimal routes based on advertised relaying nodes, but on advertised candidates for relaying. In other words, OLSR does not need to have a list of *MPR* nodes, but a list of *MPR Selector* node, or nodes that request other particular nodes to relay their traffic. Therefore, since CDS-based topology management is not configured to this task, such approach will not be appropriate for OLSR. The only way to keep route optimality, and avoid cycles, is to advertise MPR selector links and not dominators.

3. Convergence Issues in MPR

We consider convergence as the number of steps needed to make the protocol end. Still, we must distinguish logical from physical steps. In order to elect a MPR node, it usually takes 2 logical steps, recursively performed until all two hops neighbors are covered. The physical steps are MPR's ability to notify the elected MPR nodes of their election. Indeed, in a perfect environment, MPR converges after successfully having notified all its MPR nodes of their respective elections. Yet, we noticed that packet losses and the order of packet receptions were altering the whole process.

Let us first consider the order of packet decoding. In OLSR, upon reception of a packet, a node first considers in that order, Asymmetric links, Symmetric links, MPR links and Lost links, and in the order of the increasing node ID. A typical example of such decoding problem is depicted in Figure 1. Yet, we can find several other message discarding problems that are connected to the message decoding order, either within similar or different statuses. Unfortunately, several implementations of OLSR ignore this problem and rely on multiple retransmissions to correct this issue. Consequently, several physical iterations are needed for each node to elect the correct MPRs and reach optimality.

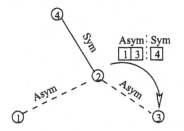

Node 3 first decodes the Asymmetric link between node 2 and node 1. Yet, since node 2 is also an Asymmetric neighbor to node 3 and cannot have 2-hop neighbors, this logical status is discarded. The Symmetric logical status of the link between node 2 and node 4 is also ignored if decoded before node 3 decode the Asymmetric link between node 2 and node 3.

Figure 1. Illustration of OLSR convergence issues

Then, another serious issue that cannot be improved by a particular implementation is the network inconsistency due to message losses. We consider here two kinds of message losses in MPR. In order of their increasing importance: *messages containing links physical status*, and *messages containing links logical status*. While the former naturally represents the channel status, the latter is what we call critical packets. Actually, the **weakest link** in OLSR comes from the **strongest link** of MPR. MPR flooding optimality comes from its selective retransmission. However, this is a very critical issue since perfect flooding for MPR and efficient routes for OLSR highly depend on this particular feature.

Therefore, incorrect decoding and the losses of critical packets bring serious convergence issues that we depicted in Figures 2(a) and 2(b). The following results were obtained using the Naval Research Laboratory ns-2 implementation of the OLSR protocol (NRLOLSR). The following results were obtained by measuring the metrics after the population of 60 nodes were uniformly distributed in a $A \times B$ grid, were A and B depend on the required density of nodes. Each node has a transmission range of $250m$. The density is obtained by the following formula $\#nodes \cdot \frac{\pi \cdot range^2}{A \cdot B}$. We normalized the density with respect to the density of nodes obtained with 60 nodes distributed in a $900m \times 700m$ grid. As we want to show convergence issues, we simulated OLSR on a static network without traffic. We are convinced that nodes mobility and traffic will even worsen our results. Finally, the convergence time is defined as the time before all nodes obtain symmetric links to all of their neighbors, while the MPR convergence time is defined as the time before all selected MPR nodes have been correctly notified of their status by all MPR Selector nodes. The number of iterations is similar to the MPR convergence time, but measured in terms of physical iterations.

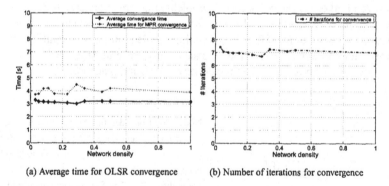

(a) Average time for OLSR convergence   (b) Number of iterations for convergence

Figure 2.   Illustration of OLSR convergence issues

On Figure 2(a), we see that MPR needs on average 3 seconds to converge, before which non-stable MPRs are elected. We also see on the same figure that no stable and optimal MPRs are obtained before 4 seconds on average. Therefore, OLSR cannot expect to create stable routes during this time interval. We also show in Figure 2(b) the average number of iterations before MPR converges. We see that MPR needs on average 7 iterations before being able to provide OLSR with accurate topological data. These observations are important since they are obtained based on a static network. If we consider mobility, each time the topology is changed, OLSR looses between 3 to 4 seconds before being able to reorganize its routes.

4. Conclusion and Clues for Improving OLSR

In this chapter, we presented OLSR requirements and MPR properties and illustrated the convergence issues of OLSR. We observed that MPR needs on average 3 seconds to obtain symmetric links to all its neighbors, and cannot compute stable MPRs before 4 seconds on average. In number of iterations, this mean that MPR needs at least 7 iterations before being able to provide OLSR with MPR selectors. We argued that this problem comes from the losses of critical packets, and also from inconsistent decoding of correctly received packet, which is more alarming and which has never been reported before. Yet, this has long been occulted by relying on multiple retransmissions, without any guarantee that OLSR built its routes on accurate MPR nodes. Therefore, solving MPR's ties to the notification of MPR status might open a new path to OLSR global improvement by reducing the network inconsistency and by increasing its convergence time.

References

A. Laouiti *et al.*, "Multipoint Relaying: An Efficient Technique for Flooding in Mobile Wireless Networks", *35th Annual Hawaii International Conference on System Sciences (HICSS'2001)*, Hawaii, USA, 2001.

T. Clausen and P. Jacquet, "Optimized Link State Routing Protocol (OLSR)", www.ietf. org/rfc/rfc3626.txt, Project Hipercom, INRIA, France, October 2003.

C. Adjih, Ph. Jacquet, and Laurent Viennot, "Computing connected dominated sets with multipoint relays", in *INRIA Rapport de Recherche No. 4597*, INRIA Rocquencourt, France, 2002.

Philippe Jacquet, "Performance of Connected Dominating Set in OLSR protocol", in *INRIA Rapport de Recherche No. 5098*, INRIA Rocquencourt, France, 2004.

NRLOLSR, http://pf.itd.nrl.navy.mil/projects.php?name=olsr

OLSR IMPROVEMENT FOR DISTRIBUTED TRAFFIC APPLICATIONS

Laurent Bouraoui, Arnaud de La Fortelle, Anis Laouiti
INRIA, Rocquencourt
BP 105, 78153 Le Chesnay Cedex, France
{laurent.bouraoui, arnaud.de_la_fortelle, anis.laouiti}@inria.fr

Abstract

This paper presents the experimental framework currently being developed at INRIA on mobile traffic applications using ad hoc communication. In this paper we propose a set of modifications to the OLSR protocol in order to adapt it to vehicle ad hoc networks. This work is the fruit of a collaboration between two INRIA research teams: HIPERCOM and IMARA. HIPERCOM is working on ad hoc routing protocols and IMARA is working on intelligent vehicles.

Keywords: ad hoc, network, OLSR, communication, traffic

1. Wireless communication in transportation

Mobile wireless communication has become a very popular topic to most actors in the transportation area. Car manufacturers associated with service providers want to offer new services to their customers, in order to increase comfort and safety (e.g. real time traffic state or routing recommendations or advanced drivers assistance systems). Road authorities see the opportunity to have all embedded systems using the communication and computation power of modern vehicles to monitor and regulate the traffic avoiding investments in static equipments. Public authorities would like to increase safety and security: automatic emergency calls reduces the fatalities, vehicle transporting dangerous goods can be tracked, etc. There is a strong support for research in this area, as numerous project attest: Car2Car Communication consortium [8] or Network on Wheel [9] in Europe, the Vehicle Infrastructure Integration initiative [6] in USA or SMARTWAY [3] in Japan.

Among these applications, many of them use a centralized architecture with GPRS or UMTS data transmission. However, there are several limitations to such an architecture.

The fi rst limitation is the time scale: typically in the minute range. This is suffi cient for traffi c monitoring and control applications does not pertain to urban environments for small journeys with many different paths possibilities or local traffi c regulation (e.g. at an intersection).

The second limitation is that a Big Brother type server can not scale to the service demanded by the hundreds of thousands of cars driving in the region it covers. If all cars are communicating in real time to the server and want to adapt quickly their journey to the traffi c conditions, there will be, fi rst, a problem of bandwidth and, second, processing diffi culties, notwithstanding privacy issues.

2.   Ad hoc communication in transportation

The possibilities and limitations of a centralized architecture draw the suit-able place for distributed architecture and car ad hoc networks: for local appli-cations that need less than a minute reaction time. There will always remain a central server who is in charge of monitoring the roads network at a regional level. But there will be local applications that run autonomously most of the time, except if there is a special need at the global level to monitor directly a given place.

In the sequel, we shortly present the OLSR protocol and the specifi c changes that are going to be implemented to fi t the vehicles ad hoc networks require-ments.

3.   The OLSR protocol

OLSR is an optimization of a pure link state routing protocol. It is based on the concept of *multipoint relays (MPRs)* [4]. First, using *multipoint re-lays* reduces the size of the control messages: rather than declaring all links, a node declares only the set of links with its neighbors that are its *"multipoint relay selectors"*. This means that we declare only a partial set of links to the network, which is suffi cient to routing table calculation. The use of *MPRs* also minimizes flooding of control traffi c. Only *multipoint relays* forward non duplicated control messages. In fact, each node maintains a duplicate set to prevent transmitting the same *OLSR* control message twice. This technique of *MPR* signifi cantly reduces the number of retransmissions of broadcast control messages [2, 4]. The two main *OLSR* functionalities are, Neighbor Discov-ery and Topology Discovery and Dissemination. Each node in the network maintains a neighbor information database (as a result of a neighbor discov-ery mechanism), and a topology information database (as a result of topology discovery). These databases are refreshed periodically, and they enable each node to compute the routes to all known destinations. These routes are com-puted with Dijkstra's shortest path algorithm [5]. Hence, they are optimal as concerns the number of hops. The routing table is computed whenever there is a change in neighborhood or topology information. Further details of *OLSR* can be found in [2].

3.1 Using OLSR in car communication

This article aims at adapting *OLSR* parameters, in order to take into account the context of car ad hoc networks. In this section, we fi rst defi ne the properties that a routing protocol should satisfy in a transportation applications. Then we introduce a set of suggested changes to the *OLSR* protocol to meet these requirements.

3.1.1 Properties. We enumerate three properties that an ad hoc routing routing protocol should respect to be adapted to the transportation applications:

1 Enabling communication and information exchange between cars: the routing protocol should ensure and maintain a correct knowledge of the existing links and routes. Communicating car networks should be created quickly, and car appearance (i.e radio link appearance), or disappearance, should not affect, the global functioning of the network.

2 High reactivity is required: in general car traffi c is very dynamic. Moreover, each car can change its direction (turning left or right street for example) at any moment. The car ad hoc network should be able to react rapidly to these changes.

3 Small car networks are preferred: everyday, several thousand of cars are driving in cities at the same moment. Building an ad hoc network which include all of them is at the same time useless and infeasible. Global or distant information broadcasting is the role of a central server.

3.1.2 OLSR changes and parameters tuning. As defi ned, *OLSR* protocol is not well suited for wireless car communication. We now, present the modifi cations we recommend to adapt *OLSR* to communicating transportation applications.

- The proactive behavior of *OLSR* protocol satisfi es the fi rst property. In fact, it continuously exchanges control traffi c, by the mean of *Hellos* and *TCs* messages. As a result, all nodes can calculate routes and communicate with each other in a dynamic mobile ad hoc network. Upper layers transportation applications can simply rely on the routing information collected by *OLSR* to have a correct view of the network topology and exchange data.

- In order to satisfy the second property, we simply need to tune the re-freshing period of topological information broacasted by *OLSR*. The default parameters values in OLSR protocol are as follow:

  - Refreshing Hello period is equal to 2 sec (i.e*HELLO_INTERVAL*).

  - Refreshing TC period is equal to 5 sec (*TC_INTERVAL*).

  Moreover, the holding time period is usually three times the refreshing period. Therefore, a symmetric link breakage is detected after 6 seconds in worst case. This may be too long for car ad hoc networks which are moving quickly. It would be better to react on link breakage in term of one second. Hence, we suggest to reduce the *HELLO_INTERVAL* to some value lesser than one second. The refreshing TC period could be set to one second. In this manner, we increase the reactivity of the nodes to recover possible link breakage.

- To fulfi ll the third requirement, we should restrict the propagation of the *OLSR* control traffi c in a predefi ned area. This area should at least include the 2-hop neighbors, then nodes can select their *MPRs* and take profi t from the optimized flooding technique of *OLSR*. The idea here is to use the geographical position which can be obtained by using Global Navigation Satellite System (GNSS, i.e. GPS or Galileo) devices embedded into the cars. This geographical information is used to drop unwanted control traffi c coming from far cars. Since the *OLSR* topological information are relayed by the mean of *TC* messages, we need to include the geographical position of the originator inside these packets. For more precision, we can also add the geographical position of each address node declared in the *TC* message. Before relaying such a message, a node have to check the distance separating it from the originator. If the distance is greater than a certain threshold, the packet will be dropped.

Each car will have a limited topology view of the global network (see fi gure 1 left). The routing table offers routes to all the nodes belonging to the predefi ned area, and the car can communicate with them directly.

Notice that the upper layer application data could be broadcasted outside these limited ad hoc networks. In fact, we can defi ne a wider area, where application data could be relayed. Of course we need to include the geographical position inside the data packet to send. In fi gure 1 right, the inner area defi nes the range for topological information relaying, and the wider area defi nes the range for application data diffusion.

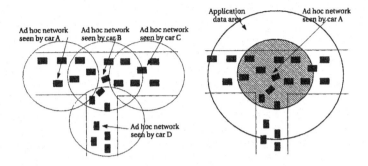

Figure 1.   Ad hoc network view and data range

4.   Conclusion

The proposed modifi cations to the *OLSR* for vehicles ad hoc networks are currently being tested using four wheeled electric vehicles that have robotic abilities, i.e. that can be run fully autonomously: the CyCabs. We are at the beginning of the experimental phase. We are conducting range and bandwidth measurements, and testing the routing information stability in a fully mobile environment. These tests aims at tuning the different parameters of *OLSR* to adapt it to vhicle ad hoc networks.

References

[1] C. Adjih, T. Clausen, P. Jacquet, A. Laouiti, P. Minet, and L. Viennot. Multicast optimized link state routing. Technical Report 4721, INRIA, 2003.

[2] P. Jacquet, P. Muhletaler, P.Minet, A. Qayyum, A. Laouiti, T. Clausen, L. Viennot, and C. Adjih. Optimized link state routing protocol. In *IETF RFC3626*, October 2003.

[3] Japanes Ministry of Land, Infrastructure and Transport, Intelligent Transport Systems, www.its.go.jp/ITS/index/indexSmartWay.html. *Smartway Project Advisory Committee.*

[4] A. Qayyum, A. Laouiti, and L. Viennot. Multipoint relaying technique for flooding broadcast messages in mobile wireless networks. In *HICSS: Hawai Int. Conference on System Sciences*, 2002.

[5] A. S. Tanenbaum. *Computer Networks.* Prentice Hall, 1996.

[6] US Department of Transportation, Intelligent Transportation Systems, www.its.dot.gov/initiatives/initiative9.htm. *Vehicle Infrastructure Integration (VII).*

[7] David Ward. Developments in vehicle to vehicle communications. In *Proceedings of the 9th International Forum on Advanced Microsystems for Automotive Applications*, March 2005.

[8] *Car2Car Communication Consortium.* www.car-to-car.org.

[9] *Network-on-Wheels.* www.informatik.uni-mannheim.de/pi4/lib/projects/NoW.

MULTILEVEL NETWORK MODELING TO ACHIEVE CROSS LAYER MECHANISMS

M. Issoufou Tiado, R. Dhaou and A.-L. Beylot
mahamadou.issoufou.tiado@enseeiht.fr, Riadh.Dhaou@enseeiht.fr, beylot@enseeiht.fr
ENSEEIHT – IRIT, 2 rue Camichel BP 7122, 31071 Toulouse Cedex France +33 56158 8306

Abstract: A new way to improve the performance of ad hoc networks consists in using cross layer mechanisms. Currently, several protocols have demonstrated some reachable performance gain. Global integration on each level of the protocol stack has to be ensured. We present some efficient methods that may either produce or update cross–layer models. Those models, developed on different levels, allow an efficient organisation of the wireless systems and could take several forms. A cross–layer conceptual model is composed of: cross–layer interaction models and interactions description arrays. In this paper, we propose a method which has been applied to a chosen protocol stack.

Key words: Ad hoc Network, Cross–layer Method.

1. INTRODUCTION

Ad hoc Networks are wireless networks characterised by a dynamic topology, limited bandwidth, and energy consumption constraints. The link quality quickly changes and causes bursts of errors. Moreover, it has a large–scale variation: the average state of the channel depends on user position and on interferences [1]. Wireless networks are generally less efficient than wired ones and classical protocols were not optimized in such a context. Some innovating techniques have to be developed to improve their performance. Protocols are generally designed independently. In an opposite operating mode, the cross–layer concept adapts them by sharing information between layers and by an overall optimisation instead of multiple optimisations at different levels. Several significant experiments were performed [2,5,6,19]. The Cross–layer technique can be used by all the protocols if there are interactions whose execution improves the performance of the global system. Specific protocols such as those improving TCP throughput have been proposed in [2]. Other large models implementing cross–layer interactions have been designed [3,4]. Nevertheless, because of the diversity of protocols, of their behaviour (even at the same layer), and of the possible interactions, it is important to design a generic method, ensuring a continuous evolution of cross–layer models and allowing the integration of new protocols and interactions. An interaction may be defined as an information exchange between protocols, not necessarily adjacent, that may be located in one or several nodes. Their architecture may be complex and may lead to a partial model design or produce apparent antagonist models when taken separately. A conceptual method allows integrating different aspects of the cross–layer Interaction Model (CLIM). For example, in [3], the MobileMan system based on "full cross–layer design" has been proposed in opposite to "layer triggering signals". We will show that triggering signals such as ECN or L2 triggers are a kind of cross–layer interactions gathered in cross–layer Atomic Action of Notification. In fact, the two concepts are different aspects of a global cross–layer model. A part of this model consists of cross–layer information collection and their exposition to other layers, the other part of messages or signals exchanged between layers when particular events occur. In [4], different cross–layer methods such as "Packet Header" or "ICMP Messages" are presented. The designed method has the advantage to highlight the impact of each cross–layer interaction on each protocol in order to update its source code and adapt it to this context. These modifications will not affect the behaviour of the protocol if the interaction is disabled. The method may be applied to a given protocol stack or to integrate interactions in an existent cross–layer model. By considering CLIM as a conception and protocols and interactions as an implementation, we propose a reverse method, "reverse" materialises the evolution from concrete models to conceptual models. This method aims at an efficient organisation and uses potentialities that may improve the performance of the designed system.

2.   CROSS–LAYER DESIGN METHOD

2.1   Cross–Layer Atomic Action (CLAA) Concept

A Cross–Layer Atomic Action (CLAA) may be the setting or the utilisation of a layer parameter, the utilisation of other layers services, and layer events that have to be exposed to other layers. "Atomic" means that the action can not be divided into actions that do not impact the same protocols.

Actions such as "the coordination of the point-to-point link layer communication with the end-to-end transport layer communication" [4] or "the utilisation of channel state" are not atomic. The first one is imprecise and the second one refers to the use of parameters such as BER, SNR, carrier power, existence of carrier signal, retransmission/acknowledgement , ...

Three kinds of CLAA may be distinguished:

Exported States CLAA (ES-CLAA) correspond to CLAA that export parameters to other layers. They may be used for admission control, QoS ... MobileMan system, distributed WCI servers [4] are Exported States models.

Notified Events CLAA (NE-CLAA): they report events to other layers. Examples of those interactions are error control coordination, delay jitter notification when transmitting a packet during a temporally "bad" channel state (avoiding sending new data), retransmission avoidance notification. CLASS system is consequently a model of "Notified events".

Available Services CLAA (AS-CLAA): when specific mechanisms are developed to give interesting parameters or services to other layers.

2.2 Modeling of Interactions

ES-CLAA and AS-CLAA are local interactions within a node. They can be characterised by variables/environment parameters. For example, the activation of a service such as VMAC[14,19] depends on a Boolean variable. Using this service, environment variables such as estimation of local delay, jitter and collisions, will be regularly updated. NE-CLAA includes both local interactions (significant energy drop notification) [5] and distant interactions (ECN) [6]. Thus the cross–layer interaction model is divided into an environment subsystem including environment variables/parameters, an interface subsystem allowing communication between non adjacent layers and a distant subsystem allowing communication between layers of separate nodes. To fit the necessary standardisation of communication mechanisms, we suggest for the environment system input/output functions (read or write values). For the interface system, we can choose input/output functions or a standard protocol. The choice will be refined when simulation will be produced. Information conveyed by each interaction will allow defining a protocol or input/output functions. For the distant subsystem, standardised protocols will be used according to each CLAA.

2.3 Method steps

We propose the following seven steps method:
1. Select a protocol stack to produce the cross–layer Interaction Model;

2. Cross–layer Atomic Action census : it could be either a set of CLAA for which a performance evaluation has to be performed;

3. Production of Protocols interaction array that represents the interactions between CLAA (array lines) and protocols (array column). Each array cell can take those values: S (local to a node - by default, or distant) if the protocol is source of the interaction, D if the protocol is the destination of the CLAA, U if the protocol uses the CLAA data, X if the protocol exchanges signals for the setting of the CLAA. The number following "S/D" shows the chronology of conveying CLAA informations;

4. Production of the Protocol functions interaction array: protocols are divided into functions. The previous array is modified: each column corresponds now to a protocol function. This new array shows the functions to be modified for this CLAA implementation;

5. Deduction of an interaction model for each kind of CLAA: the array produced in step 3 shows the cross–layer interaction model for each kind of CLAA. This model shows the layered protocol stack chosen in step 1 with an additional subsystem and interactions arrows;

6. Production of an interaction description array for each protocol. For each CLAA and each protocol, it indicates the origin of the CLAA, the source or the destination function, the kind of communication to use (direct, via subsystem) and its possible exploitation by the protocol's function;

7. Deduction of the implementation mode of each interaction model: every CLAA belongs to an upper predefined subsystem. Each subsystem has a standardised communication method.

3.   APPLICATION OF THE METHOD

3.1   Protocols stack choice

To experiment our method for the design of cross–layer models, we choose some specific protocols: TCP, DSR (Dynamic Source Routing) [7-10], IP, IEEE 802.11 (link and physical layer) [11]. Each protocol contributes to the definition of the functions of the protocol in the layered protocol stack. These functions are influenced by the listed CLAA. This step aims to fix one or more wired protocol that may be adjusted to wireless environment within Cross – Layer mechanisms and concepts.

3.2 CLAA census

At this CLAA census step, all potentially wireless environment interesting events and variables are considered.

3.2.1 Available services: AS-CLAA

VMAC (Virtual MAC) [14, 19] introduced at link layer is an example of AS-CLAA. It monitors the radio channel to establish delay, jitter, collisions and packets loss estimations using DIFS free time measure, virtual packets, simulation of transmissions and virtual packets stamps. A virtual source adjusts its application parameters and determines the accepted service level. Additional services can be considered as AS-CLAA such as IntServ [4, 15], RSVP [15], DiffServ [4, 15] at network layer, FEC [4, 16], ARQ [4, 16, 17, 18] at link layer.

3.2.2 Exported states CLAA (ES-CLAA)

Let us examine some exported states CLAA. The Energy level [5, 17] is an ES-CLAA of the system energy manager, it implements the interaction that updates the battery level so that protocols adapt their behaviour. Gallager pioneer works [17] define a reliable communication through energy constraints. Nodes have a finite energy and thus a finite number of bits before energy exhausts. Bit allocations become an interesting optimisation problem that requires co-operation between all the layers. Physical layer Received Signal Strength ES-CLAA [4, 18] materialises the update of environment subsystem variable that gives a signal intensity received from a node. Its value allows to evaluate the distance between two nodes or to establish their direct access, for the needs of routing protocols. The link layer PLR [4], Physical layer SNR [4], The Physical layer BER [4] are other examples of ES-CLAA.

3.2.3 Notified events CLAA – NE-CLAA

ECN [1,6] and ELN [4,19] are NE-CLAA. When routers detect congestions, they set the ECN bit in the header. The receiver node reports the congestion to the sender by turning "on" the ECN bit in TCP header. The sender invokes then the congestion avoidance mechanism. In the case of wireless networks with infrastructure, a "snoop agent" can be introduced at the base station. It keeps the trace of non acknowledged segments lost on the wireless link. It sets the ELN bit in the duplicate ACK if it corresponds to a segment of the list. Then the sender will retransmit the next segment and do not take any congestion control action. The use of snoop agent on a mobile node is not appropriate because the sender can not know if the loss occurs on the wireless link or elsewhere in the network because of congestion. That is why in our ad hoc network, this CLAA will not be used. There are many other examples of NE-CLAA such as jitter of sent packets [4], retransmission avoidance [4, 19] (for instance in IP layer handoff [18], retransmission are needed and new traffic admission freezed), link layer acknowledgements (used for example by DSR and based on link layer grouping of acknowledged frames containing complete IP datagram [7-8] by using SIFS intervals of 802.11 [11]), significant energy lowering event [5], DSR packet salvaging [7-8], ...

3.3   Protocols Interactions Array

The CLAA will now be classified in a protocol interaction array which includes the protocols using them, the source and the destination of the interactions. To read this array, for example, by the physical layer SNR ES-CLAA, the 802.11 updates environment subsystem parameters that give SNR value. This parameter is used by 802.11 link layer, TCP and application layer. The source of received signal power NE-CLAA is physical 802.11. It informs 802.11 link layer which at sends a notification to DSR protocol.

Table 1. Cross-Layer Atomic Action Array

Cross – Layer Atomic Actions	Protocols					
	Appli.	TCP	DSR	IP	Link 802.11	Phys. 802.11
Jitter of sent packets NE		D			S	
Retransmission avoidance NE		D	D		S	
Acknowledgement NE		D3	D2, S3		D1, S2	S1
Explicit congestion NE		D		S distant		
Significant energy decrease NE	D	D	D	D	D	S
Salvaging packet NE			D		S	
Sending jitter due to Route error NE		D	S			
Sending jitter due to Route modification NE		D	S			
Packet loss ratio ES	U	U			S	
SNR, RSS, BER ES	U	U			U	S
Energy level ES	U	U	U	U	U	S
Delay constraint RSVP AS	X			X	X	
VMAC AS	U				U	S
IntServ, DiffServ AS	U			S		
FEC, ARQ AS		U			S	

3.4   Functions Interaction array

DSR protocol ensures functions such as routing, route discovery, transmission control, ... Let us now produce a DSR function interaction array which presents the CLAA used by DSR, DSR functions and the others protocols. For example, the transmission control function is the effective network layer destination of the Retransmission avoidance NE-CLAA originated by 802.11 link layer. This function may be modified at the 6th step (Interaction description array). For an efficient presentation of the method, we will limit protocol function interaction array to one example.

Table 2: Cross-Layer Atomic Action Notified Events (NE-CLAA) of DSR

NE – CLAA	DSR Functions						Other Protocols			
	Rout ing	Route Discov	Trans. Ctrl	Route error	Salvag ing	Seg ment	App.	TCP	Link 802.11	Phys. 802.11
Retransmission avoidance			D					D	S	
Acknowledgements			D2, S3					D3	D1, S2	S1
Significant energy decrease	D	D		D	D	D	D	D	D	S
Salvaging packet				D					S	
RSS	D2								D1, S2	S1
Sending jitter due to R. error			S					D		
Sending jitter due to R. modification					S			D		
Energy level	U	U		U	U	U	U	U	U	S

3.5   Deducing of CLAA interaction models

A model of each kind of interaction can now be deduced. The model aims to show additional subsystems due to interactions and to explicit internal cross–layer mechanisms. For model readability, interface subsystem and distant subsystem are not represented in lower models, they are implicit.

3.5.1 Notified events CLAA case

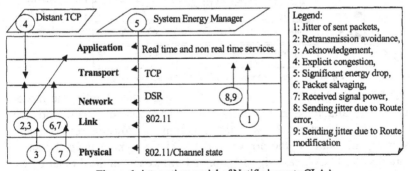

Figure 1: interaction model of Notified events CLAA

The system energy manager and a distant TCP can then be represented as follows. Note that the number represents the CLAA given in legend, the circle symbol the CLAA source layer and the arrow the CLAA destination layer. Here, the number 5 shows that if the energy level reaches a crucial threshold, the system energy manager sends this information to all the layers.

3.5.2 Exported states CLAA case

The model given by Exported States CLAA on the protocol stack, the environment subsystem and the system energy manager is as follows. In this model, according to our CLAA census step, the DSR protocol uses only the battery level variable regularly updates by the system energy manager. Here, the number represents the CLAA given in legend, the circle symbol contains CLAA list concerned by the arrow, the arrow indicates the use or the update of variables from or towards environment subsystem. For example, in number 1, the 802.11 link layer updates the packet loss ratio variable that is use by TCP and application independently of other CLAA in the list.

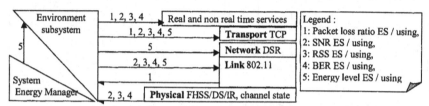

Figure 2: interaction model of Exported state CLAA

3.5.3 Available services CLAA case

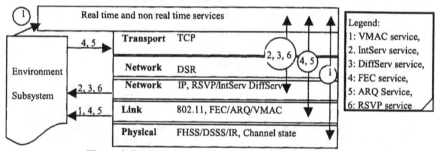

Figure 3: interaction model of Available services CLAA

By the same deducing mechanism of the interaction model, the model given by Available Services CLAA on the protocol stack and the environment subsystem is as follows. From or towards environment subsystem, the number, the arrows and the circle symbol have the same Exported states CLAA case signification. At difference, in the 3 other cases, the double arrows show information exchange between layers (through Interface Subsystem that do not appear for readability reasons). Theses exchanges aim at activating services in appropriate layer. For example, Applications ask the concerned layer for services activation. When services are activated, environment subsystem is setup. The other layers use activation indicators or active services parameters to adapt their behaviour.

3.6 Interactions description arrays

Table 3 : Cross-Layer Atomic Actions of TCP

CLAA	TCP Function	TCP using of CLAA
Sending jitter due to Route error NE	Transferred data control	If a possible expiration of the ACK waiting timeout, then cancel and reset packet ACK waiting timeout. Do not retransmit the packet during the new timeout. Do not invoke congestion control mechanism.
Sending jitter due to R. modification NE		
Retransmis. avoidance NE		Freeze the transmissions and retransmissions for the time specified in the message ⇒ reset all timeouts.
ECN NE	Congestion ctrl	Invoke the congestion control mechanism.
Significant energy decrease NE	Transferred data control	Modify the retransmission frequency and/or transmission output.
Packet loss ratio ES		Adjust the retransmission frequency and transmission output according to the high value of this parameter that is established by threshold (indicate channel state).
SNR, BER ES		
RSS ES		Use the link layer ACK if the threshold of this parameter indicates that the destination node is directly accessible.
Energy level ES		Modify the retransmission frequency and the transmission throughputs according to high value of this parameter that is established by threshold.
FEC AS	error correction	Cancel the data checksum control mechanism.
ARQ AS		Cancel the data error correction function if the DSR protocol ensures that the destination is directly accessible.

At this step, we are able to deduce the interaction description array of each protocol. Each array aims to explicit the possible exploitation of the CLAA by the influenced protocol's function. For document readability, we limit the interaction description presentation to: the CLAA, the protocol function and the use of the CLAA by the function. Only the TCP case is described in the present paper. Its interaction description array indicates the use of each CLAA by TCP functions and the modification of TCP source code proposed.

4. CONCLUSION

Cross–layer design is required for mobile ad hoc network to improve their performance. It is important to do that design in a standard framework to promote the evolution of protocols interaction models by taking into account new interactions or building new models for other protocols. This work aims at creating useful formal steps that produces conceptual interaction models and efficient interaction description arrays, as it has been shown in a significant example.

On-going work consists of implementing that cross–layer interaction models in NS (Network Simulator). The three subsystems (environment, interface, distant), have to be implemented first as additional objects in NS.

Then every CLAA of each subsystem have to be placed into the ns source code. It is necessary to identify the existing or the additional fields or instructions or methods of the source protocol, the destination protocol and the subsystem of the CLAA. A simulation will be run to quantify the obtained gain of each CLAA.

5.   REFERENCES

1.   S. Shakkottai, T. S. Rappaport, P. C. Karlsson, "Cross-Layer Design for Wireless Network", IEEE Comm. Mag., Oct. 2003.
2.   V. T. Raisinghani, et al., "Improving TCP performance over Mobile Wireless Environments using Cross – Layer Feedback", IEEE ICPWC , 15-17 Dec. 2002, p81–85.
3.   M. Conti, G. Maselli, G. Turi, S. Giordano, "Cross – Layering in Mobile Ad hoc Network Design", IEEE Computer society Magazine, February 2004.
4.   Q. Wang, M. A. Abu-Rgheff,, M. A., "Cross – Layer Signalling for Next – Generation Wireless Systems", IEEE WCNC 2003, Volume: 2 , 16-20 Mar 2003 p1084-1089 vol.2.
5.   W. Li, Z. Bao – yu, "Study on Cross – Layer Design and Power Conservation in Ad hoc Network", IEEE PDCAT'2003, 27-29 Aug. 2003 Pages: 324 – 328.
6.   K. Ramakrishnan, S. Floyd, D. Black. « The Addition of Explicit Congestion Notification (ECN) to IP. » RFC3168 September 2001.
7.   J. G. Jetcheva, Y. Hu, D. Johnson, D. Maltz, "The Dynamic Source Routing Protocol for Mobile Ad hoc Networks (DSR)", Internet Draft, IETF MANET WG, Nov 2001
8.   D. B. Johnson, D. A. Maltz, "Dynamic Source Routing in Ad hoc Wireless Networks", Mars 1998 http://www.monarch.cs.cmu..edu/monarch -papers/
9.   T. Demir, "Simulation of Ad hoc Networks with DSR Protocol", May2001. http://netlab.boun.edu.tr/papers/Iscis2001-DSR-TamerDEMIR+.pdf
10. " The Dynamic Source Routing Protocol for Mobile Ad hoc Networks (DSR)", 21 february 2002, www.ietf.org/proceedings/02mar/I-D/draft-ietf-manet-dsr-07.txt
11. P. Almquist « Type of Service in the Internet Protocol Suite. ». RFC 1349, July 1992.
12. Y. Bernet et al., "A framework for Integrated Services Operation over DiffServ Networks", RFC 2998, Nov. 2000.
13. M. Luby et al., "The use of FEC in Reliable Multicast", RFC 3453, December 2002.
14. G. Fairhurst, L. Wood, "Advice to link designers on link ARQ", RFC 3366, August 2002
15. S. Dawkins et al., "E.-to-E. Perf. Implications of Links with Errors", RFC 3155, 08/2001
16. Veres, A.T. et al., "Supporting service differentiation in wireless packet networks using distributed control", IEEE JSAC, Vol. 19, No 10, pp. 2094-2104, October 2001.
17. R. G. Gallager, "Energy limited channels: coding, Multi – access, and Spread Spectrum", 1998 Conf. Info. Sci Sys. Mar 98
18. Y. Min-hua, L. Yu, Z. Hui-min, "The IP Handoff between Hybrid Networks", IEEE PIMRC, Sept. 2002, Vol.1, pp265-269
19. H. Balakrishna, R. Katz, "Explicit Loss Notification and Wireless Web Performance", IEEE Globecom, Sydney, Nov 98.

BANDWIDTH MEASUREMENT IN WIRELESS NETWORKS

Andreas Johnsson, Bob Melander, and Mats Björkman
The Department of Computer Science and Electronics
Mälardalen University
Sweden

Abstract   For active, probing-based bandwidth measurements performed on top of the unifying IP layer, it may seem reasonable to expect the measurement problem in wireless networks, such as ad-hoc networks, to be no different than the one in wired networks. However, in networks with 802.11 wireless links we show that this is not the case.

Our experiments show that the measured available bandwidth is dependent on the probe packet size (contrary to what is observed in wired networks). Another equally important finding is that the measured link capacity is dependent on the probe packet size *and* on the cross-traffic intensity.

The study we present has been performed using a bandwidth measurement tool, DietTopp, that is based on the previously not implemented TOPP method. DietTopp measures the end-to-end available bandwidth of a network path along with the capacity of the congested link.

Keywords: Available bandwidth, link capacity, measurement, testbed, TOPP, wireless

1.   Introduction

Wireless networks, used when connecting to the Internet or when several nodes want to communicate in an ad-hoc manner, are becoming more and more popular. Because of the increased dependence on wireless network technology, it is important to ensure that methods and tools for network performance measurement also perform well in wireless environments. In this paper, we focus on performance measurements in terms of network bandwidth, both link bandwidth and the unused portion thereof; the available bandwidth.

Measurement of network properties such as available bandwidth in for example ad-hoc networks are important for network error diagnosis and performance tuning but also as a part of the adaptive machinery of network applications such as streaming audio and video. Since the exact route between two nodes in an ad-hoc network usually is unknown and may change without notification to the application layer the end-to-end measurement of the available bandwidth should not require any infrastructure or pre-installed components at each node. To achieve that, common end-to-end bandwidth measurement methods can be applied.

State-of-the-art bandwidth measurement methods are for example Pathchirp [Ribeiro et al., 2003], Pathload [Jain and Dovrolis, 2002], Spruce [Strauss et al., 2003] and TOPP [Melander et al., 2002]. The basic principle is to inject a set of measurement packets, so called *probe packets*, into the network. The probe packets traverse the network path to a receiver node, which time stamps each incoming probe packets. By analyzing these time stamps estimates of the link capacity and/or the available bandwidth can be made. For many end-to-end available bandwidth measurement methods no previous knowledge of the underlying network topology is needed. That is, bandwidth estimation methods are well suited for end-to-end performance measurements in ad-hoc networks. The existing methods differ in how probe packet are sent (the flight patterns) and in the estimation algorithms used (see [Prasad et al., 2003] for an overview).

In the following sections, we describe and measure bandwidth estimation characteristics when probing in 802.11 wireless networks. We show that both the measured available bandwidth and the measured link capacity are dependent on the probe packet size. Furthermore, our measurements indicate that the measured link capacity is also dependent on the cross-traffic rate.

The measurements have been performed in a testbed containing both wireless and wired hops. Our testbed topology only consist of one wireless hop, but we believe that our results illustrate the measurement problem for larger ad-hoc networks, consisting of several wireless hops, as well. To produce measurement results we have used DietTopp, a tool that measures the available bandwidth and link capacity of an end-to-end path. For comparisons and to illustrate that our observations are not tied to a certain measurement tool, we have also used the tool Pathload, that measure the available bandwidth of an end-to-end path, in our experiments.

Earlier work has touched upon the problem of active measurements of bandwidth in wireless networks. In [Johnsson et al., 2004] we discuss the main problem areas when deploying existing bandwidth measurement methods in ad-hoc networks. For example, we observed using ns-2 simulations, that the measured link capacity show dependence on the cross-traffic rate.

Measurement results presented in [Lakshminarayanan et al., 2004] indicate that the available bandwidth is dependent of the probe packet size. Our study extends that study by showing that *both* the available bandwidth and the measured link capacity depends on both the probe packet size and the cross-traffic rate. Further, we use a more complex measurement topology to verify their findings.

2. Experimental setup

This section describes our experimental setup. That is, the measurement tool (DietTopp), our testbed and what kind of measurements we have performed and their relevance to ad-hoc networks.

2.1 DietTopp

DietTopp has its origins in the previously not implemented TOPP method [Melander et al., 2002]. It uses the measured dispersion of probe packet trains to calculate bandwidth estimates.

In short summary DietTopp works as follows. Starting at some offered probe rate o_{min}, DietTopp injects m probe packet trains, where each train contains k equally sized probe packets, into the network path. When all probe trains corresponding to a probe rate o_{min} have been transmitted, DietTopp increases the offered rate o by Δo. Another set of probe packet trains are sent into the network with the new probe rate. This is repeated i times until the offered probe rate reaches some specified probe rate o_{max}.

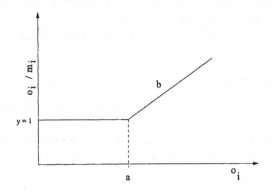

Figure 1. Plot of the ratio o_i/m_i as a function of o_i.

The probe packet dispersion may change as the probe packets traverse the network path between the probe sender and the probe receiver. This is due to the *bottleneck spacing effect* [Jacobson, 1988] and/or interactions with competing traffic.

The receiver time stamps each probe packet arrival. Hence, any change in probe packet separation can be measured. The time stamps are used to calculate the measured probe rate m_i.

When all measurements are collected, DietTopp computes the ratio o_i/m_i for all i. If plotting the ratio o_i/m_i on the y-axis and o_i on the x-axis for all i, we get a plot like the theoretical one in Figure 1. If the dispersion of the probe packets would remain unchanged after traversal of the network path, the measured rates, m_i, on the receiver side would be the same as the offered rates o_i. Expressed differently, the ratio o_i/m_i would equal 1. The link that limits the available bandwidth of the path will eventually get congested when increasing the offered probe rate. This causes the curve to rise since the rate m does not increase as much as the rate o. If the link capacity is l and the available bandwidth is a the relation between o_i and m_i is given by $o/m = (1 - a/l) + o/l$ (when one link is congested) [Melander et al., 2002].

Segment b in the figure is linear and the slope corresponds to the link capacity of the congested link. The available bandwidth of the end-to-end path is defined as the intersection of $y = 1$ and b (i.e. a in the figure) [Melander et al., 2002].

To speed up the probing phase of DietTopp we want to avoid measurements below a. That is, we want to ensure that $o_{min} > a$. This is done by estimating m_{max} which is done by injecting a set of probe packets at rate o_{max} and then measure their separation at the receiver. According to [Melander et al., 2002] m_{max} is greater than the available bandwidth (m_{max} is referred to as the asymptotic dispersion rate in [Dovrolis et al., 2001]).

Having a value of $o_{min} > a$ the procedure described above is executed to find the link capacity and available bandwidth.

DietTopp is implemented in C++ on Unix platforms and can be downloaded from [Johnsson, 2005].

2.2   The testbed

The testbed used consists of 9 computers running Linux, shown in Figure 2. The link speed for each link is shown in the figure. The links between $Xw1$, $Xw2$ and $R1$ are 802.11b wireless links (sharing the same channel) while the link between S and $R1$ either can be a 802.11b wireless link or a 100 Mbps wired link.

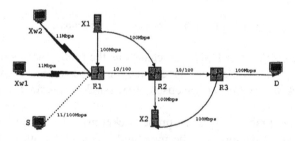

Figure 2.   The testbed is constructed by one wireless link, three routers and several cross-traffic generators (on both the wireless and the wired links)

The cross traffic is generated by a modified version of *tg* [McKenney et al., 2002]. The cross traffic is either constant bit rate (CBR), exponential or pareto distributed (shape = 1.5). Further, the cross traffic consists of 60 (46% of the packets), 148 (11%), 500 (11%) and 1500 (32%) byte packets. This distribution of packet sizes originates from findings in [Choi et al., 2000].

2.3   Experiments

In this paper we want to identify possible problems associated with bandwidth measurements in wireless networks, such as ad-hoc networks.

The measurements have been performed using DietTopp. We elaborate on the impact of probe packet size, the cross-traffic distribution and on the number of cross-traffic generators in the wireless network. We compare our results to results obtained from Pathload.

This work is related to the work presented in [Lakshminarayanan et al., 2004]. We extend and complement that work in the following way: We use our newly developed tool DietTopp, that measured both the link capacity and the available bandwidth of the bottleneck link. Previous work has only focused on the available bandwidth on wireless links. Further, we use a more complex testbed scenario.

3.   Experimental results

This section presents the results obtained from running DietTopp in different experiment scenarios. We have used Pathload [Jain and Dovrolis, 2002] to compare the obtained measurement results. In the diagrams all measurement results are shown with a 95% confidence interval.

3.1   Measurement results in wireless networks

This subsection presents our results from measurements using DietTopp where the bottleneck is a wireless link (the link between S and R1 in the testbed as described in subsection 2.2) which is the case in ad-hoc wireless networks. Cross traffic is present on both of the wired links R1 - R2 and R2 - R3, but the rate is limited to approximately 9% of the corresponding link capacity (100 Mbps in this case). That is, the wireless link is the link that limits both the link capacity and the available bandwidth. The cross traffic at the 100 Mbps links between R1, R2 and R3 is pareto distributed (with respect to cross-traffic packet arrival times) and consists of 4 different packet sizes. The cross-traffic configuration on the wired links is the same for each experiment presented in this section.

The probe-packet size affects both the measured link capacity and the available bandwidth estimate when the bottleneck on an end-to-end path is a wireless link. We illustrate and describe this phenomenon in a set of diagrams below.

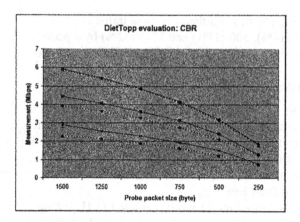

Figure 3. Available bandwidth (dashed lines) and measured link capacity (solid lines) measured under 0, 250 Kbps and 500 Kbps cross-traffic rates.

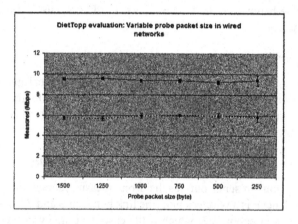

Figure 4. Available bandwidth (dashed line) and link capacity (solid line) measured by DietTopp in a wired network using different probe packet sizes. The cross traffic is a 3.26 Mbps pareto distributed stream on a 10 Mbps link.

The two upper curves in Figure 3 show the measured link capacity (solid line) and the measured available bandwidth (dashed line) when no cross traffic is present on the wireless link. Varying the probe packet size from 1500 bytes down to 250 bytes gives decreasing values of both the measured link capacity and the measured available bandwidth. It should be observed that the total number of bits remains constant independent of the probe packet size. The total amount of probe data sent by DietTopp in these measurements is 1.2 Mbit. Each probe train consists of 16 probe packets and we send 5 probe trains on each probe rate level. The number of probe rate levels depends on the probe packet size; decreasing the probe packet size increases the number of probe rate levels.

The two middle curves show measurement estimates when there is a 250 Kbps CBR cross-traffic stream on the wireless link. The two bottom curves correspond to the case when a 500 Kbps CBR stream is present. Both the measured link capacity and the measured available bandwidth decrease with decreasing probe-packet size. Another equally important behavior is that the measured link capacity decreases when increasing the cross-traffic rate. Yet another interesting phenomenon is that the difference between the measured link capacity and the measured available bandwidth tends to be smaller for small probe packet sizes. Why this is the case is a subject of further research.

For comparison we have varied the probe packet size in an all wired network. The measurement results can be seen in Figure 4. Both the measured link capacity and the available bandwidth are quite stabile, that is independent of the probe packet size.

We have also done measurements using Pathload, a tool that estimates the available bandwidth using 300 byte packets. The results obtained from using Pathload in our testbed with different cross-traffic distributions and intensities can be seen in Table 1. When comparing results obtained by Pathload (in Figure 3) to those of DietTopp we can see that Pathload reports available bandwidth measurement estimations that are in line with estimations made by DietTopp (using interpolation between packet sizes 250 and 500 bytes).

Cross traffic	Measurement (Mbps)
0	2.32 - 2.39
250k cbr	1.67 - 1.67
250k exp	1.73 - 1.73
250k par	1.40 - 1.63
500k cbr	0.96 - 0.99
500k exp	0.87 - 0.95
500k par	1.27 - 1.29

Table 1. Measurement results obtained from Pathload under the influence of different cross-traffic distributions.

Figures 5 and 6 report results from the same type of measurements as in Figure 3. The available bandwidth and the measured link capacity decrease with decreasing probe-packet size and increasing cross-traffic rate. However, in these two scenarios we have used more complex cross-traffic distributions. In Figure 5 we have used exponentially distributed arrival times for the cross-traffic packets while in Figure 6 we have used pareto distributed arrival times. As can be seen in both figures the confidence intervals are larger when the cross traffic is burstier. It is also obvious that the curves are less smooth compared

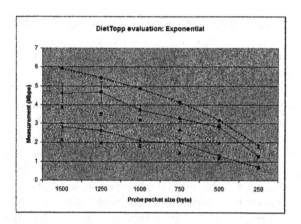

Figure 5. Available bandwidth (dashed lines) and measured link capacity (solid lines) measured under 0, 250 Kbps and 500 Kbps exponentially distributed cross-traffic.

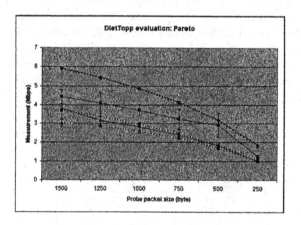

Figure 6. Available bandwidth (dashed lines) and measured link capacity (solid lines) measured under 0, 250 Kbps and 500 Kbps pareto distributed cross-traffic.

to the CBR case in Figure 3. In the pareto case (Figure 6) it is hard to distinguish between the 250 Kbps and 500 Kbps measurements of link capacity and available bandwidth. However, we can still see that the measured link capacity and available bandwidth is dependent on both the probe packet size and the cross-traffic rate. Again, comparing the measurement results (at the 300 byte probe packet size level) with results obtained by Pathload (in Table 1) we can conclude that the available bandwidth estimate characteristics are compatible.

In Figure 7 two cross-traffic generators are generating 250 Kbps of CBR cross traffic each. Comparing Figure 7 to the measurement results in Figure

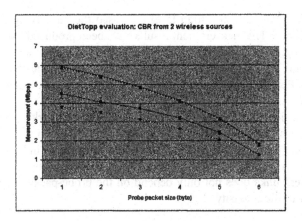

Figure 7. Available bandwidth (dashed lines) and measured link capacity (solid lines) measured under 0 and 500 Kbps CBR cross-traffic. The cross traffic is generated by two different sources (250 Kbps each).

3 we see that the confidence intervals are larger when having multiple cross-traffic generators. Otherwise the curves in Figure 3 and in Figure 7 are similar.

3.2 Wireless measurement results discussed

The reason for the varying measurement estimates of the link capacity and the available bandwidth in our experiments (as seen in the previous section) can be derived from the link-level acknowledgments and the contention phase used in 802.11 networks. That is, if a probe packet is small, the relative overhead induced by the link-level acknowledgment and the contention phase is larger than if the probe packet were large. This will affect the probe-packet separation. In the DietTopp model the probe-packet separation is used to form estimates of both the link capacity and the available bandwidth. Hence, a smaller probe packet size will result in a lower bandwidth estimate. Due to the lack of space a more in-depth mathematical description is left out.

The results concerning the available bandwidth are in line with results discussed in [Lakshminarayanan et al., 2004]. We validate and extend the findings in [Lakshminarayanan et al., 2004] by using more complex testbed scenarios and by showing the impact of the probe-packet size and cross-traffic intensity on the measured link capacity. We also use our own tool DietTopp, that measures both the end-to-end available bandwidth and the link capacity.

4. Conclusion

In this paper we have shown measurements that illustrate the difference between bandwidth measurements in wired and wireless networks, such as ad-hoc networks. We have at a high level discussed the underlying reasons for these differences. The measurement results have been produced using our own tool, DietTopp, throughout the paper. For comparison and validity we have used Pathload. The measurements have been performed in a testbed where we have used different kinds of cross traffic, from simple CBR to bursty pareto distributed cross traffic.

Our conclusions are that measurements in wireless networks are associated with difficulties that can result in misleading bandwidth estimations. We have shown that the probe-packet size is critical to the measured link capacity and the available bandwidth. Further, we have shown that the measured link capacity on wireless links does not only depend on the probe-packet size, but also on the cross-traffic intensity.

References

Choi, Yongmin, Lee, Heung-No, and Garg, Anurag (2000). Measurement and analysis of wide area network (wan) traffic. In *SCS Symposium on Performance Evaluation of Computer and Telecommunication Systems*.

Dovrolis, Constantinos, Ramanathan, Parameswaran, and Moore, David (2001). What do packet dispersion techniques measure? In *Proceedings of IEEE INFOCOM*, pages 905–914, Anchorage, AK, USA.

Jacobson, Van (1988). Congestion avoidance and control. In *Proceedings of ACM SIGCOMM*, pages 314–329, Stanford, CA, USA.

Jain, Manish and Dovrolis, Constantinos (2002). End-to-end available bandwidth: Measurement methodology, dynamics, and relation with TCP throughput. In *Proceedings of ACM SIGCOMM*, Pittsburg, PA, USA.

Johnsson, Andreas (2005). Diettopp implementation, beta version. http://www.idt.mdh.se/äjn12/.

Johnsson, Andreas, Björkman, Mats, and Melander, Bob (2004). A study of dispersion-based measurement methods in ieee 802.11 ad-hoc networks. In *Proceedings of the International Conference on Communication in Computing*, Las Vegas.

Lakshminarayanan, Karthik, Padmanabhan, Venkata N., and padhye, Jitendra (2004). Bandwidth estimation in broadband access networks. In *In Proceedings to the Internet Measurement Conference*.

McKenney, Paul E., Lee, Dan Y., and Denny, Barbara A. (2002). Traffic generator software release notes. SRI International and USC/ISI Postel Center for Experimental Networking.

Melander, Bob, Björkman, Mats, and Gunningberg, Per (2002). Regression-based available bandwidth measurements. In *Proceedings of the 2002 International Symposium on Performance Evaluation of Computer and Telecommunications Systems*, San Diego, CA, USA.

Prasad, R.S., Murray, M., Dovrolis, C., and Claffy, K. (2003). Bandwidth estimation: metrics, measurement techniques, and tools. IEEE Network Magazine.

Ribeiro, Riedi, Baraniuk, Navratil, and Cottrel (2003). pathchirp: Efficient available bandwidth estimation for network paths. In *Passive and Active Measurement Workshop*.

Strauss, Katabi, and Kaashoek (2003). A measurement study of available bandwidth estimation tools. In *ACM SIGCOMM Internet Measurement Workshop*.

PERFORMANCE EVALUATION STUDY OF AN AVAILABLE BANDWIDTH MEASUREMENT TECHNIQUE IN MULTI-HOP WIRELESS AD HOC NETWORKS

Soumer Brahim, Kamoun Farouk, Tounsi Hajer
CRISTAL Laboratory ENSI, Manouba University
brahim.soumer@cristal.rnu.tn, frk.kamoun@planet.tn, Hajer.Tounsi@cristal.rnu.tn

Abstract   In an ad hoc network, mobile nodes communicate with each other using multi-hop wireless links. There is no stationary infrastructure; for instance, there are no base stations. Each node in the network also acts as a router, forwarding data packets for other nodes. A central challenge in the design and evaluation of ad hoc networks is the estimation and the monitoring of network resources such as available bandwidth. Considering the dynamic routing protocols that can efficiently find routes between two communicating nodes, the high level of loss and the interference between node transmissions, the available bandwidth measurement techniques already provided by the literature may be inaccurate.Our goal is to carry out a systematic performance study of SloPS's [1] behavior when acting with three dynamic routing protocols for ad hoc networks: the Dynamic Source Routing protocol (DSR) [2, 3], the Ad Hoc On-Demand Distance Vector protocol (AODV) [4, 5] and the Destination-Sequenced Distance Vector (DSDV) [6].

Keywords: measurement techniques, available bandwidth, ad hoc networks

1.   Introduction

The research community is developing a set of metrics and techniques for bandwidth measurement. Many of them [7] are well understood and can provide accurate estimates under certain conditions. Network measurement techniques can be classified into two categories: passive measurement [8] and active probing [9] [10]. Passive measurement tools use the trace history of existing data transmission. While potentially very efficient and accurate, their scope is limited to network paths that have recently carried user traffic. Active probing, on the other hand, can explore the entire network. The packet pair technique [10] is one of the most popular active probing techniques. The basic idea of packet pairs is that the sender sends a pair of packets, which are echoed back by the destination. By measuring the changes in the packet spacing, the sender can estimate the bandwidth properties of the network path. While the packet pair mechanism is a reliable method for measuring the bottleneck link capacity of a network path [10], its use to measure the available bandwidth has had more mixed results. The capacity C of an end-to-end path is the maximum IP layer rate that the path can transfer from source to sink. In other words, the capacity of a path establishes an upper bound on the IP layer throughput that a user can expect to get from that path. The minimum link capacity in the path determines the end-to-end capacity C. The hop with the minimum capacity is the narrow link on the path. We note that some layer-2 technologies do not operate with a constant transmission rate. For instance, IEEE 802.11b wireless LANs transmit their frames at 11, 5.5, 2, or 1 Mbps, depending on the bit error rate of the wireless medium. We can define this rate as the link capacity during time intervals in which the capacity remains constant. Another important metric is the available bandwidth of a link or end-to-end path. The available bandwidth of a link relates to the unused, or "spare", capacity of the link during a certain time period. So even though the capacity of a link depends on the underlying transmission technology and propagation medium, the available bandwidth of a link additionally depends on the traffic load at that link, and is typically a time-varying metric.At any specific instant in time, a link is either transmitting a packet at the full link capacity or it is idle, so the instantaneous utilization of a link can only be either 0 or 1.Previous measurement techniques performance comparisons [9][17] had demonstrated that Pathload [1] is the most accurate technique to estimate available bandwidth. In this study, we cover Pathload measurement technique as well as its behaviour in ad hoc network environment using simulation. We carry out a systematic performance study of SloPS's [1] behaviour when acting with three dynamic routing protocols for ad hoc networks: DSR [2,3], AODV [4,5] and DSDV [6].The paper is organized as follows. Section 2 gives a taxonomy of the related work in bandwidth estimation. The simulation parameters and scenarios are presented in section 3.1 while the various measurement techniques and methodology are illustrated in section 3.2. The simulation results are examined in section 4 and we conclude in section 5.

2.   Related work

2.1   Available Bandwidth measurement techniques

The Available bandwidth must be averaged over a reasonable time interval, so packet pair techniques often use packet trains. A typical example of an active measurement tool for available bandwidth is PBM (Packet Bunch Mode) [11]. If routers in the network implement fair queueing, the bandwidth indicated by the back-to-back packet probes is an accurate estimate of the "fair share" of the bottleneck link's bandwidth [12]. Another tool, cprobe [13], sends a short sequence of echo packets between two hosts. By assuming that "almost-fair" queueing occurs during the short packet sequence, cprobe provides an estimate for the available bandwidth along the path between the hosts. Treno [14] uses flow control and congestion control algorithms similar to those used by TCP to estimate available bandwidth. The work in [10] mentions a technique for estimating the available bandwidth based on the Asymptotic Dispersion Rate (ADR). Pathload [1] tool proposes to characterize the relationship between probing speed and available bandwidth by measuring the one way delay of probing packets.

2.2 SloPS (Self Loading Periodic Streams) : The Pathload technique

SLoPS is a recent measurement methodology for measuring end-to-end available bandwidth[1]. The source sends a number K= 100 of equal-sized packets (a "periodic packet stream") to the receiver at a certain rate R. The methodology involves monitoring variations of the one way delays of the probing packets. If the stream rate R is greater than the path's available bandwidth A, the stream will cause a short term overload in the queue of the tight link. One way delays of the probing packets will keep increasing as each packet of the stream queues up at the tight link. On the other hand, if the stream rate R is lower than the available bandwidth A, the probing packets will go through the path without causing an increasing backlog at the tight link and their one way delays will not increase. One way delays increase only when the stream rate R is larger than the available bandwidth A. In SLoPS the sender attempts to bring the stream rate R close to the available bandwidth A, following an iterative algorithm. The sender probes the path with successive packet trains of different rates, while the receiver notifies the sender about the one-way delay trend of each stream. The available bandwidth estimate A may vary during the measurements. SLoPS detects such variations when it notices that the one-way delays of a stream do not show a clear increasing or non-increasing trend;(a grey region) which is related to the variation range during the measurements.

3. Simulation study

3.1 Simulation scenarios and parameters

The overall goal of our simulation experiments is to measure the ability of SloPS to resist to network topology change while continuing to successfully measure available bandwidth based on estimating the One Way Delay along the path. In this sense, our basic methodology is to apply to the network a variety of workloads in order to define the measurement techniques performance under some conditions.The measurement techniques evaluation is based on the simulation of 50 wireless nodes forming an ad hoc network, moving over a square flat space (500m-500m) during 900 seconds of simulated time. In order to enable fair comparisons of the routing protocols effect, it was critical to challenge SLoPS with identical loads and environmental conditions. Each run of the simulator accepts in input a scenario file that describes the exact motion of each node and the exact sequence of packets originated by each node, with the exact time at which each change in motion or packet origination is to occur. We choose our cross traffic sources to be constant bit rate (CBR) sources. Nodes in the simulation move according to the "random waypoint" model [3]. The movement scenario files that we used for each simulation are characterized by a pause time. Each node begins the simulation by remaining stationary for pause time seconds. It then selects a random destination in the 500m-500m space and moves to that destination at a speed, distributed uniformly between 0 and some maximum speeds. We have fixed two maximum speeds: 1m/s for low speed motion and 20m/s for high speed motion. Each simulation ran for 900 seconds of simulated time. We ran our simulations with movement patterns generated for 8 different pause times: 0, 30, 60, 120, 300, 600, 800 and

900 seconds. Because the performance of the measurement technique is very sensitive to movement pattern, we generated scenario files with 80 different movement patterns, 10 for each value of pause time. All three routing protocols were run on the same 80 movement patterns.We implemented SLoPS as an application object in NS (Network Simulator). Thus Pathload consists of two processes. The sender (SND) running at the server and the receiver process (RCV). The control channel transfers messages regarding the characteristics of each stream (the abortion or end of the measurement process etc). We fixed the receive timeout as two seconds because we noticed that less than this value, the reactive routing protocols may not have already routes in their cache for our scenarios. In the other hand, this timer must not be very large because the execution time of all the process may increase and consequently Pathload can't converge before the route definition changes. Another important parameter is the acceptable loss. In fact when considering the analysis of the stream, Pathload ignore all the streams that present a loss more than a certain limit. We fixed the value of the acceptable loss as 0.25 because of the delivery ratio in low mobility conditions is higher than 75% for all the routing protocols [15].

3.2   Error measurement methodology

3.2.1   Metric.   We define the relative measurement error of Pathload as where AB-pathload is the available bandwidth estimated by Pathload, AB-simu is the available bandwidth along the path given by NS traces, and Capacity is the bottleneck link capacity. This metric is measured for the three routing protocols to compare Pathload reliability for each one of them.

3.2.2   Collecting methodology.   To measure the relative-error, we must know every variable in the formula. But we know that available bandwidth is a dynamic variable and it changes along the simulation, so we decided to execute Pathload algorithm every 100 seconds, this is a sufficient time for Pathload to terminate the measurement. We added also the number of hops aspect, that's why we choose randomly a path for each length. For example, before starting the simulation, we have by an internal mechanism all the one hop length paths between all nodes every 100 seconds interval and then we choose just one of them to experiment pathload along it. We repeat this process for two, three and four hops paths long and of course for the nine hundred seconds intervals of the total simulation time. We noticed that for almost all the routing protocols, there are no paths with more than four hops that still with stable length within the 100 seconds interval especially when the pause time is very little and the movement speed is 20 m/s. Once the path definition is fixed, we know all the intermediate nodes. We can trace all the packets that these nodes are forwarding even with other nodes of the map. So we can, for every 100 seconds intervals, measure the amount of data forwarded by each node and consequently in each link of the path. With this method we can have at each time interval the minimum available bandwidth along the path and also because we fix the capacity as the bottleneck link rate which is 1, 2, 5 or 11 Mb. Thus we have for each scenario hop length an output file with nine relativ-error values and this for each routing protocol. As pathload gives us an interval for the AB, we take its center as AB-pathload variable. Finally, the relative-error for each pause time scenario is $\sum_{i=1}^{9} \frac{relative-error_i}{9}$

4.   Simulation results

4.1   Available bandwidth measurement

The first set of experiments uses differing numbers of pause time with a low mobility speed of 1 m/s and 10 traffic sources. Fixing for example the pause time at 500s, the available bandwidth for DSR, DSDV and AODV measured by NS traces and Pathload technique are illustrated in Figure 1 for the 900s measurement period.

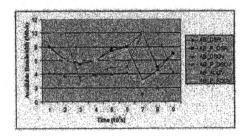

Figure 1.   Available bandwidth for 1 Hop Pause=500s Speed=1m/s sources=10

We call AB-P-x the available bandwidth measured by Pathload and AB-x the available bandwidth measured by NS traces and this when x is the routing protocol.First, we must notice that DSR and AODV outperforms DSDV in the real available bandwidth value performance during almost all measurement period. This is due to the low delivery percentage of DSDV comparing to the two other routing protocols especially for this pause time mobility (500s) [15].Figures 2 and 3 highlight the relative-error performance of Pathload when acting with the three routing protocols on our traffic loads of 10 sources. We consider in figure 2 the case of one hop routes and in figure 3 the case of two hops routes.The figure 1 presents the details of our measurements for the first case, using always the same method to compute relative-error for each 100 seconds interval. We notice in this figure that we measure first for each one hop route the available bandwidth using Pathload then we apply the technique described above to measure manually using NS traces the utilization of each link and then obtain the real value of the available bandwidth. Using a pause time equal to 500 s, we can notice that we can have three main cases.

The first case is when Pathload can converge with a good performance and the relative-error is less than 10% for the three routing protocols (between 300 sec and 600 sec when the relative-error is 3%, 10% and 8% for respectively DSR, DSDV and AODV).The second case is when all the routing protocols give a bad performance (between 600 sec and 700 sec). This is because Pathload can't converge due to cross traffic that increases the delivery time of Pathload Packet trains and consequently obliges the algorithm to ignore many times the same stream. In fact, Pathload uses a TCP connection to control

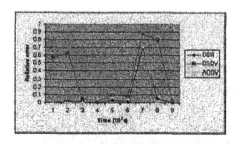

Figure 2.   Relative-error for 1 Hop Pause=500s Speed=1m/s sources=10

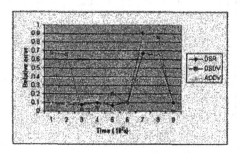

Figure 3.   Relative-error for 2 Hops Pause=500s Speed=1m/s sources=10

and validate each stream before calculating the heuristics metrics and decide the increasing trend of the One Way delay (OWD)[1]. This case can exist when the routing protocol packet delivery percentage is very low due to mobility or when the link utilisation is very high due to cross traffic. The last case is when Pathload gives good performance with one or more routing protocols and fail to converge with one other. This is for example the case of DSDV between 0 and 200 sec and also between 700 and 800 sec. This case is due to the routing protocol proactive nature. In fact, in these time intervals DSDV could not find any route between the chosen pair of nodes or take a long time to complete the exhaustive list of routes between all nodes and this especially in the simulation starting. To evaluate the impact of hop length over Pathload performance, we fix the same sources for our one hop and two hops chosen paths (we must choose of course paths that have to still stable during the measurement 100s period and this at least for two hops). This hypothesis is only for this experiment need and we keep the random paths selection for all the other experiments. We remark that more the path length grows more the Pathload accuracy decreases. In fact for the same time period we have for example between 0 and 100 seconds the relative error is 1%, 57% and 1% for one hop path and 9%, 67% and 9% for two hopspath and this respectively for DSR, DSDV and AODV routing protocols. This increase is more important when the path utilizationis greater.

---

[1]When Pathload can't converge we fix AB-Pathload as 10 Mb which is the initial rate value.

We can take the [700-800] seconds interval when the relative error is 5%, 80% and 2% for one hop path and 65%, 85% and 64% for two hops path and this respectively for DSR, DSDV and AODV routing protocols.

4.2 The mobility effects

The next set of experiments (Figure 4) demonstrate the effect of mobility. We choose the average relative-error value calculated for different pause times and for all the four path length cases of one, two, three and four hops. As expected, the relative-error metric is converging to 1 when there is a very high node motion. For example, figure 4-a shows this metric as a function of both node mobility rate (pause time) and the routing protocols. For DSR and AODV, packet delivery ratio is between 95% and 100% of the packets in all cases that's why all Pathload packet trains are validated and a very little number of streams are ignored. DSDV fails to converge below pause time 300, where it delivers about 92% of its packets. At higher rates of mobility (lower pause times), DSDV does poorly, dropping to a 70% packet delivery alternate routes. Nearly all of the dropped packets are lost because a stale routing table entry directed them to be forwarded over a broken link. In fact, DSDV maintains only one route per destination and consequently, each packet that the MAC layer is unable to deliveris dropped since there are no alternate route. Figures 4-b, 4-c and 4-d show that more the path length increases more the relative-error is greater. This is due to the cross traffic which is more important when the path contains larger number of hops. Also, the probability to have a path definition changes during Pathload execution time is more important when the number of hops in the path grows. In fact, we abort the measurement operation when we detect that a routing changes have occurred even when we have another route between the same source and destination. In summary, for low mobility and

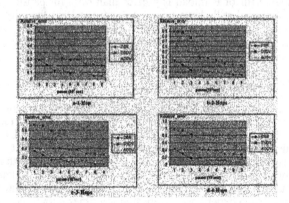

Figure 4.   Relative error =f(pause-time) when Speed=1m/s sources=10

with 10 sources of cross traffic, pathload can have an accuracy of 90% for DSR and AODV and of 70% for DSDV. For higher mobility (pause time <300 s), pathload is not the accurate tool. In fact, its relative error is greater than 40% for DSR and AODV and 90% for DSDV.

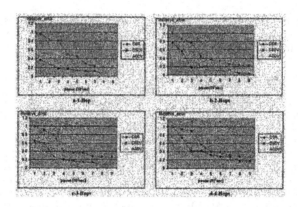

Figure 5.   Relative error =f(pause-time) when Speed=1m/s sources=30

4.3   Cross traffic effects

In figure 5, we have 30 sources of cross traffic. In this experiment, we have noticed that DSR expresses more overhead to find routes. This is because DSR put all the route definition in the packet header of its route request messages and consequently the links bandwidth utilization is very important. Comparing between figure 4-a and 5-a results, we find that when there is no pause time, the relative-error has increased from 30% to 40% for DSR and AODV and from 70% to 95% for DSDV. For longer paths (figures 5-b,5-c and 5-d), the pathload performance degrades with DSR and high mobility conditions. In fact, the relative error of Pathload is greater than 60% for pause time <200s. With AODV, Pathload stills have good performance (less than 40% for high mobility and one, two and three hops). This is not the case of four hops when the relative-error of Pathload is 70% and 57% respectively when the pause time=0s and 100s.

4.4   The mobility speed effects

In order to explore how the Pathload measurement technique scales with the change of the topology, we changed the maximum node speed from 1 m/s to 20 m/s and re-evaluated it with all three protocols over scenario files using this lower movement speed In this experience, a general remark is that many measurement tentatives fail because the routing changes occur during the measurement operation. In fact, we started the Pathload process each 100 sec and we have noticed that among the 360 measurement tentative that we have done for each experience (each experience is repeated ten times with 9 values for each hop count) 161, 152 and 201 routing changes during the measurement operation and this respectively for DSDV, DSR and AODV have been occurred. So these routing changes increase when the mobility speed increases and they are the principal source of error of the Pathload measurement technique. In fact, when the speed is 1 m/s we have only 71, 64 and 82 routing changes during the measurement execution for respectively DSDV, DSR and AODV. In figure

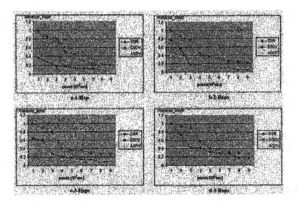

Figure 6. Relative error =f(pause-time) when Speed=20m/s sources=10

6, we fix the mobility speed to 20 m/s and we keep all the other conditions as paragraph 3.2. We notice that the performance of Pathload degrades with almost all the routing protocols, especially for DSR and AODV in comparison with their results when the mobility speed is 1m/s. The difference between DSR and AODV, however, has grown from a factor of 1.2 to nearly a factor of 1.6 for four hops paths because DSR's caching is even more effective at lower speeds where the cached information goes stale more slowly. Although, due to its largely periodic nature, pathload with DSDV continues to have a constant relative-error as the case of the mobility speed equals to 1m/s.

5. Conclusions

The area of ad hoc networking has been receiving increasing attention among researchers in recent years. Over the past few years, a variety of new available bandwidth measurement techniques targeted specifically at the ad hoc networking environment have been proposed, but little performance information on each technique and no detailed performance study of these techniques has previously been available in ad hoc network environment. In this work, we describe first SloPS technique and its integration into the ns network simulator. This new simulation environment provides a powerful tool for re-evaluating this technique and its behavior when operating in an ad hoc network. Then, we present the results of simulation comparing three multi-hop wireless ad hoc network routing protocols DSDV, DSR, and AODV. We present the results for a range of node mobility rates and movement speeds.This technique performs well in some cases yet has certain drawbacks in others. With DSDV, SloPS performs quite well, with an acceptable error-rate when node mobility rate and movement speed are low, and doesn't converge when node mobility increases. The performance of SloPS in presence of DSR was good at all mobility rates, however the use of source routing increases the number of routing overhead bytes required by the protocol so the measurement relative-error increases when movement speeds increases or the cross traffic is very large. Finally, Slops in presence of AODV performs almost as well as with DSR at almost all mobility rates and movement speeds and accomplishes its goal of eliminating source routing overhead. However, topology changes can occur during the measurement process which can lead Pathload packets train to switch to another path and consequently available bandwidth estimation will not be accurate especially when movement speed is 20m/s.Many extensions can be applied to this study. It is obvious that this is not a complete study of all the major measurement techniques. In fact, other available bandwidth measurement techniques implementation in NS like IGI [16] or cprobe [13] can be added to the performance comparison. In addition, we believe that we must have a real integrated wireless ad hoc testbed that supports the different routing protocols and also ad hoc networks adapted monitoring techniques to collect real actives available bandwidth measurement techniques information's. This testbed is useful to validate our future measurement techniques performance studies and also the mobility impact over their behavior.

References

[1] Manish Jain and Constantinos Dovrolis. Pathload: A measurement tool for end-to-end available bandwidth. In Passive and Active Measurements, *Fort Collins CO, March 2002.*
[2] J.Broch, D. Johnson, and D. Maltz. *The Dynamic Source Routing Protocol for Mobile Ad Hoc Networks.* http://www.ietf.org/internet-drafts/draft-ietfmanet- dsr-03.txt, IETF Internet draft, Oct. 1999, work in progress.
[3] D. Johnson and D. Maltz. *Dynamic Source Routing in Ad Hoc Wireless Networks.* T. Imielinski and H. Korth, Eds. Mobile Computing, Ch. 5, Kluwer, 1996.
[4] C. E. Perkins and E. M. Royer, *Ad Hoc On-demand Distance Vector Routing.* Proc. 2nd IEEE Wksp. Mobile Comp. Sys. and Apps., Feb. 1999, pp. 90-100.
[5] C. E. Perkins, E. M. Royer, and S. R. Das, *Ad Hoc on Demand Distance Vector (AODV) Routing* http://www.ietf.org/internet-drafts/draft-ietfmanet- aodv-06.txt, IETF Internet Draft, July 2000, work in progress.
[6] Charles E. Perkins and Pravin Bhagwat. *Highly dynamic Destination- Sequenced Distance-Vector routing (DSDV) for mobile computers..* In Proceedings of the SIGCOMM '94 Conference on Communications Architectures, Protocols and Applications,
[7] Prasad, R.S., Murray, M., Dovrolis, C., Clay, K *Bandwidth estimation: metrics, measurement techniques, and tools..* IEEE Network Magazine (2003)
[8] S. Seshan, M. Stemm, and R. H. Katz *SPAND: shared passive network performance discovery.* in In Proc 1st Usenix Symposium on Internet Technologies and Systems
[9] Federico Montesino-Pouzols Instituto de Microelectrnica de Sevilla (IMSE-CNM) Seville, Spain Federico.Montesino@imse.cnm.es *Comparative Analysis of Active Bandwidth Estimation Tools .*
[10] C. Dovrolis, P. Ramanathan, and D. Moore, *What do packet dispersion techniques measure?.* in Proc. the Conference on Computer Communication (IEEE Infocom), Anchorage, Alaska, USA, Apr. 2001, pp. 905-914.
[11] Vern Paxson. *Measurements and Analysis of End-to-End Internet Dynamics..* PhD thesis, U.C. Berkeley, May 1996.
[12] Srinivasan Keshav. *Packet pair flow control.* IEEE/ACM Transactions on Networking, February 1995.
[13] Robert L. Carter and Mark E. Crovella. *Measuring bottleneck link speed in packet-switched networks.* Technical report, Boston University Computer Science Department,
[14] Matthew Mathis and Jamshid Mahdavi. *Diagnosing internet congestion with a transport layer performance tool. .* In Proc. INET'96, Montreal, Canada, June 1996.
[15] Josh Broch David A. Maltz David B. Johnson Yih-Chun Hu Jorjeta Jetcheva *A Performance Comparison of Multi-Hop Wireless Ad Hoc Network Routing Protocols.*
[16] Ningning Hu, Student Member, IEEE, Peter Steenkiste, Senior Member, IEEE *Evaluation and Characterization of Available Bandwidth Probing Techniques.*
[17] Soumer B. *Measurement techniques in wired and wireless heterogeneous environments.* Cristal Laboratory ENSI Tunisia Master report Juin 2004.

UNIFIED SUPPORT FOR QUALITY OF SERVICE METRICS MANAGEMENT IN MOBILE AD HOC NETWORKS USING OLSR

Djamal-Eddine MEDDOUR, Laurent REYNAUD, Yvon GOURHANT, Bertrand MATHIEU
France Telecom R&D Division 2, Avenue Pierre Marzin 22307 Lannion CEDEX, France

Abstract: This article focuses on technical issues related to quality of service provisioning at routing layer in ad hoc networks. It describes the design and implementation of a unified support for quality of service (QoS) metrics within the routing protocol OLSR. This is achieved by the extension of both signalling messages and route calculation process. Major benefits of the proposed approach are to allow dynamic enforcing and adaptation of QoS metrics according to policies defined into the network. QoS metrics information are inserted in a generic way within OLSR signalling messages taking advantage of Linux kernel plug-ins. These messages are used by the routing process in order to compute routes with respect to the chosen QoS metrics.

Key words: Routing protocol, OLSR, QoS metrics, kernel Plug-ins.

1. INTRODUCTION

Ad hoc networks [1] [2] emerged as an outcome of several projects on mobile computing and packet radio networks financed by the DARPA (Defense Advanced Research Project Agency) during late 60s [3]. One of the key concepts of this paradigm is that the terminals communicate directly between themselves in a multi-hop fashion in an infrastructure-less environment. Each terminal will thus behave both as a router as well as an end-terminal. Consequently, new routing protocols are designed and applied in order to handle terminal mobility and enable multi-hop communication for the network.

In conjunction with the maturity observed on the routing protocol design [4][5], implementation and test, the growing need for multimedia application highlights the need to set up an accurate quality of service support for ad hoc networks. The quality of service provisioning in ad hoc networks is a difficult goal to achieve and the inherent properties of ad hoc network (shared links, limited resources, malign users ...) exemplify the complexity to enforce an effective solution. Nevertheless, several solutions treating QoS provisioning in ad hoc networks have been proposed at various levels of the network stack, more particularly at the routing level. At the routing level, the quality of service provisioning is addressed through the optimization of one or several metrics in the route calculation process. Many metrics may be considered like energy [6], node load [7], bandwidth or delay [8][9], node capacity [10], link stability [11]....

To recapitulate, what commonly follows is a set of two distinct QoS solutions:

• Firstly, most commonly admitted solutions narrow the scope of the problem to a very specific issue. (E.g. security, Energy, link stability ...). This brings good overall performance with respect to the chosen metric, but it targets only a very specific issue of QoS in ad hoc networks, and cannot be considered as a global QoS solution. There is a multiplication of the different QoS models that target different environments.

• Secondly, there are some solutions which try to define statically an extensive set of metrics combinations [12]. However, the definition of an optimal QoS metrics combination is still an NP-hard problem [13] which means that the greater the amount of metrics in a combination is, the more complex the combination maximization will become. At most, what can be expected with these approaches is a comprehensive and complex QoS model that, unfortunately, when applied to a given ad hoc routing protocol, will often dramatically decrease the overall performance. This performance loss is of concern if one or many of the QoS criteria are inappropriate within the ad hoc network were the model is deployed.

However, the diversification of application requirements and the dynamic context of ad hoc networks highlight the insufficiency of such approaches which may consider only one metric or metrics heuristic with a given routing protocol. In order to deal with these limitations, a unified framework for quality of service metrics support is desirable as an alternative to meet the need of a dynamic strategy to set up and adapt QoS metrics at routing level following policies defined in the network. To achieve this goal, we propose a QoS metric management architecture that operates distinctly from the routing module. QoS metrics information are inserted on the routing signaling messages in a generic way taking advantage of Linux kernel plugins, and these enhanced messages are therefore used by the routing algorithm itself or transferred to an external module in order to compute routes with respect to the chosen QoS metrics.

2. MOTIVATIONS

Existing QoS approaches for ad hoc networks advocate the use of a specific metric or a combination of several metrics applicable to explicit use-cases (bandwidth, delay, reliability, energy etc). These solutions utilize static QoS management. When the corresponding QoS metric chosen by the routing protocol does not meet the application requirements, the global QoS efficiency achieved will not be optimal. For instance, the use of delay metric is not judicious if we want to satisfy bandwidth-sensitive applications and vice versa. Moreover, ad hoc network heterogeneity (in term of type of terminal, attached or not to a reliable infrastructure, communication sensibility...) must be taken into account for the design of an effective QoS solution.

To deal with this shortcoming, we propose and implement a new approach that aims at providing an open and generic framework for the management of QoS metrics at routing level. Our approach allows dynamic adaptation of QoS metrics with respect to predefined ad hoc network QoS policies. The use of such a solution allows more effective QoS management. Routing based application requirements is also enabled.

3. OUR APPROACH

In this section, we present our approach allowing a dynamic adaptation of the QoS metric at the routing protocol level. Even if the solution principals could be applied for any routing protocol, we advocate in our case the use of the proactive routing protocol OLSR.

3.1 Solution requirements

In order to enable a dynamic QoS metrics adaptation in ad hoc networks, the following modules are needed:
- **Extended routing protocol:** signalling message should be extended to carry QoS metrics information. The route calculation process is also modified to be able to compute routes with respect to the chosen metrics.

- **Network level QoS metrics manager:** to ensure an effective QoS metrics choice, a network level manger is required. Its decision must be made based on the available network resources and the applications needs; this decision is then transferred to all the nodes involved into the routing process. This mechanism could be centralized or fully distributed (ad hoc network relayed to a fixed infrastructure/pure ad hoc network).

In this work, we address mainly the routing protocol part. For the choice of the QoS metrics, we set up a centralized mechanism that uses a simple algorithm to take its decision (an example of such algorithm is given in section 4.1). Nevertheless, for more reliability, a distributed solution is needed and we intend to investigate such a problem in our future works.

3.2   OLSR description

Type	Description
HELLO.	Neighbors detection
TC.	MPR declaration
MID.	interfaces declaration
HNA.	Gateways detection s

Table 1. List of messages used in OLSR

The standard routing protocol OLSR [4] is a link-state protocol which provides optimal routes in term of number of hops. It is particularly suitable for dense networks where the use of its broadcast technique via Multi-Point Relays (MPR) seems more effective in such a context. MPR are a sub set of 1 hop neighbours which allow a node to reach its 2 hops neighborhood. OLSR ensures the construction of routing table following a periodic exchange of signalling messages (see Table 1). These letters are then used to build a graph of the topology which will be used for route calculation.

Furthermore, we can distinguish two main components for route calculation within OLSR

- Topology maintenance: in order to handle topology changes due to node motion (mobility, entrance and exit), a periodic exchange of signalling messages is used and then network topology information is gathered, thus, a graph of the topology is built. Moreover, this mechanism encompasses a system that allows minimizing global network overhead by the selection of special nodes on the networks called MPR (Multi Point Relay). In OLSR, only nodes selected as MPR will act as routers and therefore will retransmit networks traffics.

- Path selection: the Dijkstra algorithm is applied on the graph of topology in order to compute best paths between the network nodes.

We note here that the standard OLSR is a non QoS-aware routing protocol since the route selection criterion is the number of hops only.

3.3 Architecture of the proposed solution

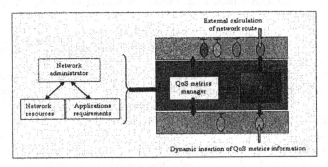

Figure 1. Proposed architecture

The complete architecture is presented in figure 1. A central entity playing the role of a network administrator monitors the available network resource and the application requirements. It takes its decision based on this information and the pre defined QoS policies. This decision is then transmitted to and enforced by the network nodes.

The main idea of our approach is to re-use the existing signalling messages of OLSR without redefining new messages. To be able to manage any type of metric, the following extensions are introduced:

- Extending existing signalling message TC in manner that can transport QoS metrics related information. The core OLSR is therefore modified in order to enable the treatment of the new TC message.
- Dynamic insertion and calculation of QoS metrics information via external modules. Moreover, we introduce the possibility to manage several metric through an external route calculation module. Indeed, the routing protocol transmits to this module the graph of topology enriched by QoS metrics information. Therefore, this module can directly update the kernel routing table.
- The routing protocol connected to a component so-called "QoS metrics manager" which transmits to the routing protocol the QoS metrics to apply in the network. Furthermore, it is responsible for the set up of the needed modules for both dynamic QoS insertion and route calculation.

3.3.1   Extended TC messages

The integration of QoS support within OLSR consists on building a topology graph enriched by QoS metrics information. As the construction of such a graph is based on TC messages, the latter will thus be used to transport QoS information. A "normal" TC message includes these fields:

- ANSN: presents a number of sequences in order to identify the most recent TC;

- Reserved: Field not used, fixed by defect at 0;

- Advertised Neighbour Main Address 1..N: The addresses of MPR nodes of the TC message transmitter.

We propose to introduce a QoS metrics support within the TC message. The Field RESERVED is used to indicate the number of neighbours transported in the message TC and to delimit the part of the original TC message and the extension. The extension part contains the following fields (see figure 2):

- For each address, we associate the value of metric defined below in the message (Example: bandwidth or delay towards this neighbour).

- Nb_Metrics: an integer of 1 byte, it indicates the number of metrics transported by the message TC, It is followed by a field on 1 byte not used;

- A pair (metric type, metrics id) of integers of 1 byte each one. It represents respectively the type of metric, and its identifier.

3.3.2   Dynamic insertion of QoS metrics information

In order to achieve dynamic insertion of QoS metrics information, we advocate the usage of PromethOS [14]. PromethOS is an extension of the standard Linux mechanism Netfilter which offers a support to set up on the fly software components called "plug-ins", which has the capacity to apply treatments to the received packages. Plug-ins are kernel modules that are used to reprogram the behaviour of the IP stack and are installed and controlled by PromethOS framework.

Therefore the insertion of QoS metrics values will be done via the use of a PromethOS plug-in. This is useful to intercept the TC messages during transmission, and to modify them in order to include various data related to QoS metrics.

Once the decision concerning the QoS metrics to apply is transmitted to the "*QoS metrics manager*", it deploys the component "*metrics calculation*" which calculates the QoS metric value and is carried out in user space. Thereafter, these values will be transferred to the kernel module "*metrics_add*" which inserts them in the TC message. The frequency of calculation of these parameters depends on the sensitivity of the metric. Metrics like the bandwidth, the time or link stability should be calculated more frequently than metric like energy.

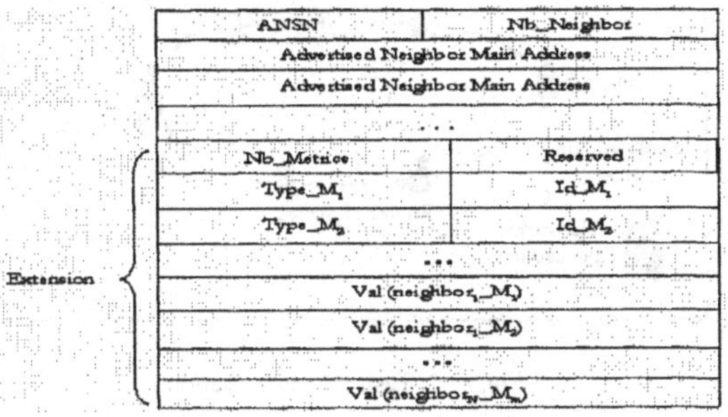

ANSN	Nb_Neighbor
Advertised Neighbor Main Address	
Advertised Neighbor Main Address	
. . .	
Nb_Metrics	Reserved
Type_M₁	Id_M₁
Type_M₂	Id_M₂
. . .	
Val (neighbor₁_M₁)	
Val (neighbor₁_M₂)	
. . .	
Val (neighbor_n_M_m)	

Extension {

Figure 2. Measured delay for all approaches (performed on the time before metrics changing)

3.3.3 Route calculation

The new TC messages once collected on the level of OLSR will be used to build a graph of the topology, each element of the graph being represented in the following way < @source, @destination, metric1, metric2...... >. The route calculation will be done based on the chosen metric.

In order to be able to compute routes based on multiple metrics and overcome limitation present in the current algorithm, we provide an API that allows an external route calculation. An external module that implements a heuristic of route calculation methods based on needed metrics should be used. Information concerning the graph of topology is transferred to this module. Therefore, routes are calculated and injected into the Linux kernel.

4. EXPERIMENTATION

The experimentation presented here shows how a dynamic adaptation of QoS metrics can respond efficiently to the observed changes of network conditions. We integrated the proposed scheme within the OLSR implementation provided by [15].

Figure 3 depicts the ad hoc network topology used for our experimentation. The network is composed of 7 nodes running the routing protocol OLSR including our modification, implemented under Linux. All nodes are equipped by 802.11b wireless cards with a maximum of 11Mbits/s data rates. Within this topology, a source node transmits several traffics with different QoS requirements towards the destination.

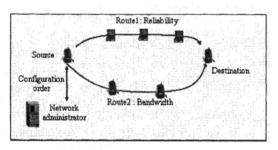

Figure 3. Testbed configuration

4.1   Scenario

Figures 4 and 5 show how the use of bandwidth metric allows us to obtain good bandwidth level. This will be advantageous for the applications requiring important bandwidth. Nevertheless it penalizes applications which are delay sensitive. We could observe the same phenomenon when using the metric delay. Our solution based on the use of a dynamic QoS metric will enable us to meet application needs, by respecting the constraints of the applications (in term of metric) and to obtain the best compromise.

Two paths between the source node and the destination node with different capacities are set up, the first one (Route 1) composed of 3 PC with high capacities proposing more reliability but less bandwidth, the second one (Route 2) composed of 2 PDA with low capacities but it contains less hops, it hence offers more bandwidth but a less reliable path. The reliability in our case is related to terminals capacities.

In this topology, we consider two kinds of traffic conveyed in the network between the source node and the destination node. The first one uses TCP and requires bandwidth (example: HTTP, FTP), the second using UDP requires real time and more reliability (Example: multimedia...).

In order to enforce the choice of QoS metrics, a module emulating the network administrator is integrated in the source node. It sets up a system called **Event_collector** that gathers the application related QoS requirements. The following algorithm is then run to decide on the QoS metrics that are to apply to the network (note that such an algorithm must be modified to fit the requirements of each ad hoc network. For instance, secure routes should be privileged in the case of a military based communication).

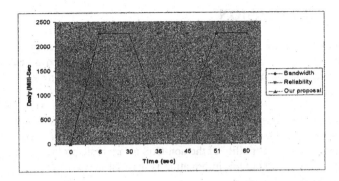

Figure 4. Measured delay (performed on the time before metrics changing)

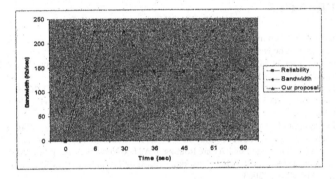

Figure 5. Measured bandwidth (measures performed on the time before metrics changing)

This algorithm tests whether all the applications have chosen the correct metric i.e. to identify if there is no conflict between the expressed QoS needs. Otherwise, the reliability metric will be chosen by the network administrator. Therefore, following the QoS metrics chosen by the network administrator, traffic will be routed through route 1 (reliability) or route 2 (bandwidth).

We can thus notice the effectiveness of our approach from the obtained results. Moreover, they show clearly the need for a dynamic management of QoS metric in ad hoc networks. Compared to a standard approach with a static QoS metric, our proposal offers needed flexibility with respect to the QoS policy defined in the network.

5.   CONCLUSION

In this article, we have described a novel approach for the design and the implementation of QoS support at routing level. Our proposal enables dynamic adaptation of QoS metrics to meet predefined ad hoc network QoS policies.

The evaluations carried out show clearly the generated QoS profit generated by the use of a dynamic metric compared to a classic approach. This profit is achieved with a negligible network overhead. Also, our approach keeps compatibility of the non-QoS aware basic protocol, which is relating to the fact that QoS information is inserted in a separate way from neighborhood information.

REFERENCES

[1] IETF MANET Working Group. MANET Charter, 2000.
[2] IRTF RRG Ad hoc Network Systems Research Subgroup.
[3] J. Freebersyser et al, "A DoD Perspective on Mobile Ad Hoc Networks", Ad Hoc Networking, ed. C. E. Perkins, Addison-Wesley, 2001, pp. 29–51
[4] T.Clausen, P.Jacquet "Optimized Link State Routing Protocol (OLSR)". RFC3626.
[5] D. B. Johnson et al "The Dynamic Source Routing Protocol for Mobile Ad Hoc Networks" IETF Draft, April 2004.
[6] J. Gomez et al "PARO: Supporting Dynamic Power Controlled Routing in Wireless Ad Hoc Networks", ACM/Kluwer Journal on Wireless Networks (WINET), September 2003.
[7] S.-J. Lee et al "Dynamic Load-Aware Routing in Ad hoc Networks", IEEE ICC 2001.
[8] H. Badis et al "QoS for Ad Hoc Networking Based on Multiple Metrics: Bandwidth and Delay", IFIP MWCN 2003
[9] C. Perkins, E. Belding-Royer, and S.R. Das "Quality of Service in Ad hoc On-Demand Distance Vector Routing", IETF Internet Draft, draft-ietf-manet-qos-00.txt, July 2000.
[10] R. Meraihi et al "Cross-layer QoS and terminal differentiation in ad hoc networks for realtime service support", IFIP MedHocNet 2003,
[11] R. Sivakumar, P. Sinha, and V. Bharghavan, "CEDAR: A Core-Extraction Distributed Ad Hoc Routing Algorithm", IEEE Journal on Selected Areas in Communications,
[12] X. Yuan, "Heuristic Algorithms for Multi-Constrained Quality of Service Routing", IEEE/ACM Transactions on Networking, April 2002
[13] Z. Wang et al "Quality-of-service routing for supporting multimedia applications", IEEE JSAC, September, 1996.
[14] R. Keller et al "PromethOS: A Dynamically Extensible Router Architecture Supporting Explicit Routing", Proceedings of IWAN 2002
[15] http://qolsr.lri.fr : OLSR implementation from the LRI.

A FRAMEWORK FOR ROUTING IN LARGE AD-HOC NETWORKS WITH IRREGULAR TOPOLOGIES

Marc Heissenbüttel, Torsten Braun, David Jörg, Thomas Huber*
Institute of Computer Science and Applied Mathematics
University of Bern, Switzerland
{heissen, braun, joerg, thuber}@iam.unibe.ch

Abstract   In this paper, we consider routing in large wireless multihop networks with possibly irregular topologies. Existing position-based routing protocols have deficiencies in such scenarios as they always forward packets directly towards the destination. Greedy routing frequently fails and costly recovery mechanisms have to be applied. We propose the Ants-based Mobile Routing Architecture (AMRA) for optimized routing, which combines position-based routing, topology abstraction, and swarm intelligence. AMRA routes packets along paths with high connectivity and short delays by memorizing past traffic and by using ant-like packets to discover shorter paths. The geographic topology abstraction allows AMRA to cope with high mobility and large networks. Simulative evaluation indicate that compared to other position-based routing AMRA finds significantly shorter paths with only marginal overhead protocols.

Keywords: Ad-hoc networks, routing, swarm intelligence

Introduction

Routing in wireless multihop networks has generated a lot of interest and a large number of routing protocols have been proposed. In position-based routing protocols like GFG [1] and GPSR [2], nodes are aware of their positions e.g. through GPS. Each node forwards packets greedily to one of its neighbors closer to the destination. A recovery mechanism has to be applied if no neighbor is closer and this greedy routing fails.

*The work presented in this paper was supported (in part) by the National Competence Center in Research on Mobile Information and Communication Systems (NCCR-MICS), a center supported by the Swiss National Science Foundation under grant number 5005-67322.

Position-based protocols require only little control traffic and do not need to maintain paths. Thus, they are scalable and robust to changes in the network, which make them the preferred choice for large and highly dynamic networks. However, position-based routing protocols show also some shortcomings.

- Routing a packet along the line-of-sight between the source and destination may often not be possible in realistic networks due unpopulated areas, mountains, or lakes. Thus, greedy routing of position-based protocols will fail and the recovery mechanism must be applied. The path chosen may be very suboptimal.

- Each packet is sent completely independently of all others. If greedy routing fails and the recovery mechanism forwards the packet along a very long path even though a much shorter exists, all subsequent packets will follow the longer path. The protocols have no way to adapt and to learn from experiences.

To summarize, the stateless approach of position-based protocols is not only the reason for their advantages, but is also the source of new drawbacks such as the lack of knowledge about network topology on a large scale. Thus, if we assume that the overall node distribution in the network remains quite static and only varies slowly over time, it is beneficial to accumulate such information at the nodes to facilitate communication with distant nodes.

We propose the Ants-based Mobile Routing Architecture (AMRA) whose objective is to overcome these aforementioned drawbacks of conventional position-based protocols. It is designed for routing in large wireless multihop networks with possibly tens of thousands of nodes with irregular topologies. In such scenarios, AMRA is able to find more optimal paths than other position-based protocols by memorizing past traffic such that packets are not routed necessarily directly towards the destination anymore. The required memory to keep track of the traffic can be kept small, in the order of some hundred bytes, by applying an aggregated and fisheye-like view on the network. Furthermore, if only few data traffic is in the network and existing paths are not known, additional ant-like control packets can be emitted to actively discover shorter paths. Both types of packets, data and ants, increase the probability for their traveled path depending on the encountered quality. Thus, packets are attracted to travel along the good path already traveled by other packets, which in turn increase the probability for these paths even more.

This principle of self-reinforcing of traveled paths through packets is basically the principle of ant-colony optimization where ants find shortest paths between the nest and a food source. The ant colony optimization principle has been applied lately to routing in ad-hoc networks in several papers [3, 5, 4]. All these ant-based routing algorithms are similar to other topology-based protocols and have a route discovery, a route maintenance, and a route error phase. They mainly make use of the ant colony optimization to improve the resilience and reliability of paths or to improve existing paths compared to other topology-based protocols. Therefore, they still have the same characteristics of other topology-based protocols such as large control traffic overhead and, thus, are not suited for large networks with highly dynamic topologies as considered in this paper.

The remainder of this paper is organized as follows. In Section 1, we describe AMRA and the used protocols in detail. AMRA is evaluated in Section 2 by simulations and finally Section 3 concludes the paper.

1. The Ants-based Mobile Routing Architecture

AMRA is a two-layered framework with three independent protocols rather than an actual routing protocol. Three specific protocols are presented exemplarily within the AMRA framework. The two protocols used on the upper layer are called Topology Abstracting Protocol (TAP) and Mobile Ants-Based Routing (MABR). Straight Packet Forwarding (StPF) is situated on the lower layer and functions as an interface to the physical network for MABR. Due to lack of space only the general concepts are given in this section, for more details cf. [6].

Topology Abstraction Protocol (TAP)

TAP is the key to make routing scalable and provides in a transparent manner an aggregated and static topology with fixed "logical routers" (LR) and fixed "logical links" (LL) to MABR. Logical routers are fixed geographical areas of equal size arranged in a grid to cover the whole global area. Depending on its current position, each node is part of one specific logical router. A node can easily detect, based on its position, when it crosses the border of the current logical router and then it automatically becomes a member of the new logical router. In order to scale to large networks, each logical router groups other logical routers into zones $Z_{i,j}$ as shown in Fig. 1. The zone size increases exponentially with the distance i to the center router and allows covering large areas with few zones. This is justified by the circumstance that from the view of a fixed node, close-by nodes that move some distance may be located in an entirely different direction, whereas the same movement of a node far away only marginally affects the direction. It is important to notice that the view of zones is relative. Each logical router resides in the center of its own zone model.

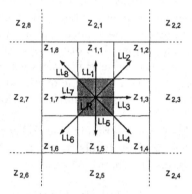

Figure 1. Logical router LR in the center, the zones in its view $Z_{i,j}$, and its logical links LL_k indicated as arrows

A logical link LL_k represents a path along a straight line to an adjacent logical router over possibly multiple physical hops. In this way, we introduce a static logical topology on the network independent of the actual node distribution.

The Mobile Ants-Based Routing Protocol (MABR)

The routing protocol MABR operates on top of abstract topology provided by TAP and thus does not have to cope with changing topologies. Basically, all what MABR has to do now is that whenever a node receives or overhears a packet, it determines where the packet originates from and from which direction it arrived. More precisely, it determines the source zone $Z_{i,j}$ of the packet by the coordinates of the source node as given in the packet header. Note that this zone is relative to the view of the current node. Furthermore, the node determines the last logical router in which the packet was forwarded before having entered the current logical router, i.e., it determines the logical link LL_k which approximates most closely the followed path over the last few physical hops. Nodes maintain a probabilistic routing table where all the zones and the logical links are organized in rows and columns, respectively. The value of the field in the routing table corresponding to the determined zone $Z_{i,j}$ and logical link LL_k is increased. The other seven entries in the row of $Z_{i,j}$ are decreased proportionally such that the sum over all logical links in a row for a certain zone remains 1. A high value indicates that there exists a path in the direction of that logical link to the respective zone.

Eventually, the best paths will emerge and MABR is able to circumvent areas with bad or no connectivity. Then, data packets will always be routed over logical links with high connectivity such that greedy routing is possible. MABR routes data packets by determining to which zone a packet should be routed from the destination coordinates as given in the packet header. The node then selects the logical link with the highest probability to this zone. Consequently, data packets are routed logical-hop by logical-hop over the logical links, i.e. from one logical router to one of its adjacent logical routers and so on. Furthermore, ants can be transmitted periodically to explore new paths if there is only little data traffic. Unlike data packets, ants are routed purely position-based, i.e., they are not influenced by the probabilistic routing of MABR but forwarded directly towards the destination by StPF. If a node does not have a logical link with a high probability, the data packets are also routed purely position-based and adapt therefore the role of ants.

In irregular topology, the logical link pointing directly towards the destination zone may often not have a high value as no packets arrive out of this direction. Consider again the same exemplarily topology as before in Fig. 2. A node S that wants to route to a destination node D does not forward the packet towards node C, because LL_3 pointing in this direction has a very low probability as no packets from zone $Z_{3,3}$ traveled over this link. S forwards the packet either over LL_1 or LL_6 because the received data packets originating from zone $Z_{3,3}$ arrived from the direction of LL_1 and LL_3. The possible paths for packets from a node D in zone $Z_{3,3}$ to S are depicted exemplarily. Thus, for any destination node located in zone $Z_{3,3}$, the packets are also routed over these two links with high probability.

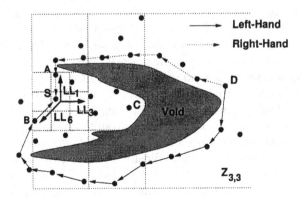

Figure 2.　Routing packets to $Z_{3,3}$ over LL_1 and LL_6

If a node moves to another logical router, its view on the network changes, and it adapts its routing table accordingly by having the probability of all logical links approaching a uniform distribution. The reason is that previously collected information about good paths looses its relevance because zones and links are relative to a node's view and do no longer correspond to previous geographical areas.

Straight Packet Forwarding (StPF)

StPF is a position-based routing protocol and responsible to physically forward packets over the logical link determined by MABR to the next logical router. StPF can be basically any standard position-based routing protocol such as GFG/GPSR [1, 2]. In GFG/GPSR, packets are forwarded to the neighbor closest to the final destination. If no such neighbor exists and greedy routing fails, GFG/GPSR applies a perimeter routing mode to recover. Therefore, each node extracts locally a planar subgraph of the actual network graph, which is necessary to avoid loops, and forwards packets on the faces of this subgraph according to the right-hand rule. Packets are again routed in greedy mode as soon as they are received at a node that is closer to the final destination than where the packet entered the perimeter mode.

2. Evaluation

As AMRA is designed for large networks, we also conducted simulations with several thousand nodes. Unfortunately, realistic network simulators like ns-2 are not able to run such large simulations. Therefore, we implemented and simulated AMRA in a Java network simulator and compared it to GFG/GPSR and a shortest path algorithm. The Java simulator does not account for any physical propagation medium properties or MAC layer functionality and thus is able to run simulations with thousands of nodes. Therefore, packets cannot be dropped due to collisions or congestion and packets do not experience delay. We use the hop count metric in order to asses the performance. The hop count metric is typically considered a good indication for the delay because CSMA based MAC protocols such as IEEE 802.11 have high cost for acquiring the medium. The nominal transmission range and the logical router side length were both set to $250\,m$. The results are averaged over 10 simulation runs and given with a double-sided 90% confidence interval. Data packets are transmitted periodically between two randomly chosen communication peers at a rate of 1 packet/s. The simulation time was set to $1800\,s$, but no data is transmitted in the initial first $900\,s$ to reach a stable state of the mobility model. AMRA was always simulated with unidirectional and bidirectional traffic between the source and the destination. The reason is that AMRA can use traffic flowing in the opposite direction to update the routing tables towards the destination. On the other hand, GFG/GPSR and the shortest path algorithm are not affected by bidirectional traffic and thus they were only simulated with unidirectional traffic.

To simulate large networks with irregular topologies, we use the restricted random waypoint mobility model [7]. The model defines rectangular city areas and highways connecting selected cities, but otherwise is similar to the standard random waypoint mobility model. Nodes choose a next waypoint within their current city or in one of the adjacent cities connected by highways. Consequently, there may be void areas with no nodes such that direct routing between some cities is not possible. A typical scenario is depicted in Fig. 3 with four cities and three highways.

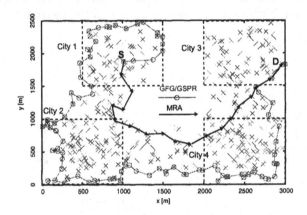

Figure 3.   Path of MRA and GFG/GPSR in irregular topology

We defined four cities of $1000\,m$ x $1000\,m$ interconnected by three highways with 500 nodes on an area of $3000\,m$ x $2500\,m$. Nodes in the city move at a speed in the interval $[1, 15]\,m/s$ and at a higher speed on the highway $[10, 30]\,m/s$. A typical path chosen by AMRA and GFG/GPSR is also shown in the figure. Although it is definitely a worst-case scenario for GFG/GPSR, it again clearly highlights the problem of position-based protocols, namely the inability to know which are good paths to a distant node on a large scale. We first conducted simulations where the number of transmitted ants was varied and we had a fixed number of traffic sources set to 10.

In Fig. 4, we can see that GFG/GPSR has on average an about 2.5 times higher hop count than the shortest possible path. Considering the fact that often the traffic flow is between nodes in the same city or one of the adjacent cities, we may conclude that the hop count for traffic flows between non-adjacent cities is much more than 2.5 times the shortest path. If nodes are in adjacent cities, routing along a straight line between them is possible and the performance of GFG/GPSR is almost identical to the shortest path.

AMRA with only unidirectional traffic and no ants performs even worse than GFG/GPSR. However, as soon as few ants are transmitted the hop count drops sharply. With only 50 ants transmitted per second in the whole network, i.e. with 500 nodes, each node transmits an ant each 10 seconds, the hop count is about 15 compared to 10 of the shortest path and 25 for GFG/GPSR. The further increase of ants does not further reduce the hop count however. On the other hand, if we have bidirectional traffic, the hop count is completely independent of the number of ants. The data packets in the opposite direction are sufficient to establish high probability entries in the routing tables.

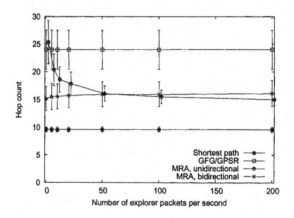

Figure 4.   Irregular network with varying number of ants

In a next step, we simulated a scenario where no ants are transmitted at all and only the number of traffic flows was varied Fig. 5. Again, the performance of GFG/GPSR shows an about 2.5 times higher hop count than the shortest path. Unlike before, the graphs for GFG/GPSR and the shortest path are no longer exactly constant, but only statistically constant within the confidence intervals. The reason is that, unlike the number of ants, a varying number of sources may yield slightly different results among the different simulation runs. AMRA with bidirectional traffic remains almost unaffected by the number of traffic flows, i.e. traffic flowing in different directions does not distort the entries in the routing tables for traffic flows to other destinations. As before where we had 10 traffic flows, AMRA with unidirectional traffic suffers if we have no ants and only few traffic flows. The chance that a node has overheard a lot of traffic to a given destination zone is low and, thus, when it has to forward a packet to that zone the risk is high that it forwards the packet in a wrong direction. However, as more traffic flows there are in the network, the performance of AMRA with unidirectional traffic approaches the performance of AMRA with bidirectional traffic. If we have sufficient traffic, the entries in the routing tables are updated accurately by the data packet themselves. The reason is that if there are no useful entries in the routing tables, data packets are routed purely position-based and thus adopt the role of ants.

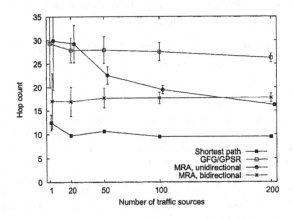

Figure 5.   Irregular network with varying data traffic and no ants

3.   Conclusion

In this paper, we presented the Ants-based Mobile Routing Architecture (AMRA), which makes use of topology abstraction, a principle from swarm intelligence, and position-based routing. AMRA is used to optimize routing in large network with irregular topologies where routing along a a straight line towards the destination is not possible. Results showed that AMRA is able to cope efficiently with irregular network topologies, i.e. realistic topologies for large networks. In a scenario with a horseshoe-like topology, AMRA was able to find paths that are up to 40% shorter than of GFG/GPSR. Consequently, AMRA would also yield much shorter delays and reduce congestion in the network. In simple and flat network topologies, AMRA performed comparable to GFG/GPRS. Unlike GFG/GPSR, AMRA uses ants to discover new paths and, thus, introduces additional control traffic however. Simulation showed that the number of ants can be kept small. For scenarios with bidirectional traffic or a lot of unidirectional traffic, even no ants are required. Therefore, the overhead compared to GFG/GPSR reduces to little additional memory to store the routing table. Realistic network traffic is typically bidirectional, e.g. simply because TCP is used on the transport layer. We can summarize the main features of AMRA as follows.

- AMRA allows nodes to learn by memorizing past traffic such that disadvantageous paths are avoided and packets are routed along paths with high connectivity.

- Due to the abstract topology, AMRA can easily cope with high mobility and is scalable in terms of number of nodes and the covered geographical area of the network.

- The overhead due to ants can be minimized as only few or even none are required to find good paths.

References

[1] P. Bose, P. Morin, I. Stojmenovic, and J. Urrutia, "Routing with guaranteed delivery in ad hoc wireless networks," in *Proceedings of ACM Workshop on Discrete Algorithms and Methods for Mobile Computing and Communications (DIALM '99)*, Seattle, USA, Aug. 1999.

[2] B. Karp and H. T. Kung, "GPSR: Greedy perimeter stateless routing for wireless networks," in *Proceedings of the 6th Annual ACM/IEEE International Conference on Mobile Computing and Networking (MOBICOM '00)*, Boston, USA, Aug. 2000, pp. 243–254.

[3] M. Güneş, M. Kähmer, and I. Bouazizi, "Ant-routing-algorithm (ARA) for mobile multi-hop ad-hoc networks - new features and results," in *Proceedings of the 2nd Mediterranean Workshop on Ad-Hoc Networks (Med-Hoc-Net'2003)*, Mahdia, Tunesia, June 2003.

[4] M. Roth and S. Wicker, "Termite: Ad-hoc networking with stigmergy," in *Proceedings of IEEE Global Telecommunications Conference (GLOBECOM'03)*, San Francisco, USA, Dec. 2003.

[5] G. Di Caro, F. Ducatelle, and L. Gambardella, "AntHocNet: An adaptive nature-inspired algorithm for routing in mobile ad hoc networks," *European Transactions on Telecommunications*, vol. 16, no. 2, 2005.

[6] M. Heissenbüttel, "Routing and Broadcasting in Ad-Hoc Networks", Ph.D. dissertation, University of Bern, Switzerland, June 2005.

[7] L. Blazevic, S. Giordano, and J. Y. L. Boudec, "Self organized terminode routing simulation," in *Proceedings of MSWiM 2001*, Rome, Italy, July 2001.

ROUTING IN EXTREMELY MOBILE NETWORKS

Géraud Allard
INRIA - Domaine de Voluceau
Rocquencourt, France
geraud.allard@inria.fr

Philippe Jacquet
INRIA - Domaine de Voluceau
Rocquencourt, France
philippe.jacquet@inria.fr

Bernard Mans
Dpt. of computing - Macquarie University
Sydney, NSW 2109, Australia
bmans@ics.mq.edu.au

Abstract   To become realistically untethered, wireless communication networks need to be self-organised, rapidly deployable, infrastructureless and mobile. Existing protocols are efficient in routing data dynamically between mobile nodes that belong to the same connected component. Concrete applications such as Defence and Disaster-Relief cannot always assume that the network is connected (*i.e.*, not partitionned). However, even if the network is continuously partitioned, a "communication path" may be available through time and mobility using intermediate mobile nodes (temporally within reach of each other) - we have coined these "Extremely Mobile Networks". We consider the problem of routing in a highly mobile network which, possibly, may never be fully connected. We introduce new algorithms that always allow to route a packet toward a remote destination. The packet bounces from connected components to connected components, thanks to node mobility.

Keywords: Network partition, Routing, MANET, Mobile Network, Wireless Network.

1.   Introduction

Existing MANET protocols are highly efficient in routing data between mobile nodes that belong to the same connected component. What about a disconnected network where source and destination may be located in two different connected components? In this case usual routing protocols drop packet due to host unreachable. A simple idea is to allow the router that has no available route to the destination to keep the packet in buffer until the conditions become more appropriate for forwarding. The forwarding conditions will change because of mobility: the router can move closer to the destination so that they belong to the same connected component and the packet can be delivered. Realistically, the network may be continuously partitionned due to high mobility, and the traditional approach to allow a mobile node to wait for the network to be fully connected (*i.e.,* form a unique component) or to wait to be in range of the destination may lead to unacceptable delays. Furthermore, concrete applications, such as Defence and Disaster-Relief, cannot always rely on such assumptions. Nevertheless, even if the communicating nodes may *never* be within the same connected component, it is important to observe that a "communication path" may be available through time using intermediate nodes that are temporarily within reach of each other while moving, hence making such networks viable for critical applications - we have coined these *Extremely Mobile Networks*. Initial works have highlighted the importance of the problem by demonstrating the difficulty at hand. For torus-like networks, the authors in [9] propose algorithms using counting timers combining a simple random policy with the sophistication of utility-based policies and evaluate their performance. In [5], Li and Rus proposed to actively modify the trajectories of the mobile nodes to guarantee transmissions in minimal time while minimising the trajectory modifications, but this requires that the movement and the positions of the nodes are known (*e.g.,* using GPS). In [8], Shah proposed to deliver messages in disconnected MANET by broadcasting multiple copies of the message in the connected component (while limiting the number of multiple copies among neighbours and providing time-out for holding messages). However, for small networks, the replication of the messages increases the traffic substantially as well as reducing the capacity. Earlier studies [3, 10] have developed protocols for networks that exhibit correlated movement patterns. The rest of previous studies on mobility have assumed the continuous connectedness of the networks (in order to find adequate routing paths). This assumption has deflected the effort of researchers towards designing consensual mobility models for simulations in order to provide consistent and comparable conclusions [1]. The problem of bandwidth optimization by using space and mobility in a fully connected network is a different problem and is addressed in [2][4].

In this paper, we make the important assumption that the node motions are unpredictable. We introduce a novel routing algorithm based on information aging. We compare its efficiency with the basic routing strategies by providing comprehensive simulations and characterising the desired properties.

2. Simple Routing Strategies

We first review three simple strategies: Source Only (SO); Random Jumps (RJ); Flood Routers (FR). For each strategy we briefly highlight the pros and cons in particular with regard to the mobility models.

Source only. With this algorithm the packet stays on the source router until a route to destination is available, *i.e.*, when the router and the destination are in the same connected component. *Advantages:* The number of transmission is limited to the number of hops in the same connected component. This hopefully makes better use of the capacity. *Drawbacks:* The delivery delay may be extremely large when routers move randomly like in random walk model. It can be infinite when the source and destination are far apart and do not move.

Random jumps. With this algorithm the current router transmits the packet to a random router of the connected component of the current router. The new router becomes the current router which will retransmit the packet (and so forth), until the current router is in the same connected component of the destination (thanks to mobility). *Advantages:* The process is not limited by the relative mobility of the source and the destination. *Drawback:* The frequency at which the packet is retransmitted may lead to a bandwidth waste. The frequency must be frequent enough so that the node can jump to another connected component when there is a temporary merge. In random mobility models the move of the packet is equivalent to a random walk which may take a huge amount of time to reach the connected component of the destination. *Remark:* The frequency of retransmissions could be limited by only allowing transmissions toward new nodes in the connected component. This is still a random walk anyhow.

Flood routers. The packet is flooded to all members of the connected component. Every time a new node comes into the connected component it receives directly the packet from a border node, then the node floods the packet to its neighbors, *i.e.*, only node which receives the packet for the first time retransmits it. The packet will eventually reach its destination (possibly, through multiple routes). *Advantages:* The packet will arrive to destination much faster than with a random walk. In fact, without considering physical constraints (*e.g.*, interference and collisions), this is clearly the fastest strategy as any route used by another strategy is one of the branch of the flooding. There is no need to manage the connected component membership (flooded packets do that by themselves). *Drawback:* The cost of maintaining and flooding a huge number of packet copies in the network may be prohibitive and may impede the network capacity. Flooding may be optimized using MultiPoint Relays (MPR) as in the OLSR protocol [6]. However, there is no way, except using timeout or sophisticated acknowledgment flooding, to kill redundant copies when the destination received its own.

3.   Forward to Best Gateway

We now introduce a strategy, that we call Forward to Best Gateway (FBG), based on information aging. This algorithm aims to get similar fast convergence of the flood router algorithm without the cost of multiple packet flooding. Like in FO and RJ, the packet is stored in only one router at a time. The router forwards to the best gateway to the destination when there is a new one. The current router is always the best gateway. The best gateway is the relay which has the most recent and shortest route to the destination. To compute the most recent and shortest route the algorithm relies on a link aging protocol.

Link aging protocol. Every node maintains a topology database of the links with the age. Age(L) is the age of link L in the database. The age of the link is obtained from the information obtained from other nodes. When two nodes are just connected by a rising link they compare they database. Then they flood (via MPR) their connected component with the most recent link age. In other words each of the two nodes retransmits a tuple (link, age) when the age is smaller than the age(link) which was previously in its database.

Most recent and shortest route calculation. We define age(route) as the minimum value of age(link) for all links in the route. A route is an increasing age route when the value age(link) increases on the route. There are two options: (1) shortest path of the less aged route, (2) shortest of the less aged increasing (link) age route. In the first case one computes the shortest route with the metric age-length, where age-length(route1)$<$ age-length(route2) iff (i) age(route1)$<$ age(route2), or (ii) length(route1)$<$ length(route2) when age(route1) = age(route2). This is not a basic Dijskstra algorithm since the optimal route is not necessarily the concatenation of optimal routes. For example age(AC)=10, age(AB)=0, age(BC)=0, age(CD)=20, age(AD)=30. In this case the optimal route from A to C is (A,B,C), from C to D is (C,D), but from A to D it is (A,C,D). However this can be computed via a vector Dijkstra. In the second case one computes the shortest less aged increasing age route by a simple Dijkstra algorithm since any optimal increasing age route is the concatenation of optimal increasing age routes.

THEOREM 1 *For any route route1 there exists an increasing age route route2 such that age(route1)=age(route2).*

Proof. The proof comes from the fact that the information from the status of a link necessarily came to the node via a link less aged (a link which was active when the link age update went through). ■

Aged distance vector variant. The shortest less aged increasing route can be computed as follow: for any destination d, each node keeps a distance vector (next hop, age, length). If its next hop is aged (not active) then the node is said to be gateway to d. Gateways to d continuously advertized their tuple (age, length) in their connected component. The nodes in the connected component compute their next hop to their best gateway according to the metric age-length by adding to the length the distance to the gateway. In the process the node may lose its status of best gateway. *Rational:* The gateway nodes are likely to be on the border the closest to the destination. The closer a connected component is to the destination, the smaller should be the age to this destination (a node in the same connected component shares the same age for a given destination). When two connected components merge, the one with the smaller age should be closer and enforces its gateway nodes and the gateway nodes in the other connected component lose their status. Therefore the packet directly jumps towards a gateway node of the connected component with the smallest age. By following this strategy, the packet is expected to get closer to the destination.

4. Models and parameters of interests

First of all, we assume that the speed of packet propagation inside a connected component is infinite (very large compared to the node speed). We need to take into account the three following parameters v_m, v_a and v_p. Quantity v_m is the average speed of the destination node, v_a is the speed at which a flooding via FR protocol propagates. Quantity v_p is the speed at which the packet heads towards its destination in the best gateway FBG. We expect the following inequality: $v_p \leq v_a$. The flooding should propagate faster than the best gateway (which can be seen as one branch of the flooding tree). Quantity v_a should also be the speed at which the age toward a given destination propagates. In other words if a node was at position z at time t then the nodes which have route of age θ at time $t + \theta$ should be at average distance $\theta \times v_a$. Therefore it is expected that the condition for the aging protocol to give a good indication of node position (without assuming the use of devices such as GPS) be: $v_m < v_a$. Looking carefully it looks also as a condition for the FR algorithm to work properly (*i.e.,* better than Random Jump). If v_a is about the speed of sound then the destination should move at subsonic speed. Furthermore, for the FBG algorithm to work properly, we need that the packet moves at speed faster than v_m in order to eventually reach the destination and to let the algorithm work better than a basic random walk: $v_m < v_p$. Notice that we must consider the asymptotic speed of the mobile, *i.e.,* the average distance between initial position and final position when the time tends to infinity. In the case of a random walk this speed tends to zero. Therefore the algorithm will work with any random walk model even if the domain of the network is unbounded.

Therefore the performance of the FBG algorithm compared to FR algorithm can be described with the ratio $\frac{v_p}{v_a}$. The quantity v_a is a function of the node mobility model and the node density (*e.g.,* [4]). The faster the nodes move the larger is v_a. It should be interesting to consider the random walk model under the three alternative conditions: (i) the free space distance is smaller or of same order than the radio ranges; (ii) the free space distance is smaller or of same order than the connected component average radius (shapes may be intricate); (iii) the free space distance is much larger than the connected component average radius. In the later case the performance should be similar to the random way point model. *Conjecture:* if the average speed v_m for traveling across a connected component is the same in every component then the (v_a, v_p) tuple should be similar accross any model.

5.   Simplification and improvement

Jump to best age. When a connected component with lesser age merges with the current connected component, the packet could simply jump to any node in the less aged connected component (instead of traveling to the new best gateway). In this case there is no need to maintain the complicated gateway system. Only the age to the destination (and not the path) in the connected component would suffice (in addition to the membership monitoring inside the connected component).

Jump to the oldest of the same age. Instead of randomly jumping on a mobile router that have the least age before the merge, one can make the packet jumping to the router whose actual age has changed the less recently, *i.e.,* to the oldest in the age in the connected component (since all nodes in the connected component got the same age).

Use of the Doppler effect. We introduce a new improvement using the well known phenomenon of frequency shift named after Doppler (1803-1853). We define the Doppler effect of a node A as the average rate at which the age to the destination varies. A large Doppler effect indicates that the node is traveling toward the destination. The Doppler effect could be used for the protocol: the packet likely moves to the nodes which have the largest Doppler effect. For example, when the connected component merges with a connected component with a younger age then the packet moves to the node with highest Doppler effect in the new connected component.

Use of the average age of the nodes. Let A and B be two nodes and let $age(AB)$ be the age of the link AB stored in A's database. The *average age* of AB, denoted as $\overline{age}(AB)$, is recomputed as follows each time $age(AB)$ changes: the new value of $\overline{age}(AB)$ is $\rho \times \overline{age}(AB) + (1 - \rho) \times age(AB)$ with $0 < \rho < 1$ as a fixed parameter. Thereby a node can keep track of its past ages and use this parameter for routing by sending packets to the node that has the smallest average age. The number of retransmissions is limited since a packet is only forwarded when an age modification is detected.

6.   The road model

In this model we assume an unbounded highway with a stream of cars moving to the left and another stream of cars moving to the reverse direction, all with uniform speed v_m. We assume that on both lanes the car distribution follows the law of Poisson with density D. We use the unit disk graph model (the radio range is exactly one unit). Using basic algebra, we can prove the following theorem.

THEOREM 2 *When D is the density on a single lane, $v_a = \frac{e^{2D}+1}{2} v_m$.*

If we properly use the Doppler effect then we can get $v_p = v_a$.

Proof. We consider a packet that is routed toward the right. The average length L of the connected component containing the car that holds the packet and made of cars of both lanes satisfies the identity: $L = \ell + (1 - e^{-2D})L$ with $\ell = \int_0^1 2Dxe^{-2Dx}dx = \frac{1-(2D+1)e^{-2D}}{2D}$. The age information instantaneously travels in the connected component. When the packet arrives at the end of the connected component it has to wait $\frac{1}{Dv_m}$ before jumping of one unit distance and then entering a new connected component. Therefore the average age propagation speed on this lane in the referential of the car is $(L + 1)v_m D = \frac{e^{2D}-1}{2}v_m$. Adding the car speed v_m yields the desired result. ∎

Remark: the speed tends to v_m when $D \to 0$ since the connected components tend to vanish. The speed is proportional to v_m which is expected but also proportional to the exponential of car density.

7.   Simulations

We first present some simulations that show the impact of our algorithm on the behaviour of the routers and packets. We then compare the performances of our algorithm, and its variants, with the basic strategies.

Routing and packet paths. We consider the random walk model where at each step nodes move in average of unit distance (the radio range). We display for different maps size and router number: (1) the router map and the packet path: *i.e.,* the actual location where the packet has jumped until it reaches its destination The router map corresponds to the positions of the routers when the packet reached his destination. (2)The router age histogram and the packet history: the router age histogram gives the distribution of age versus distance to destination, the packet history gives the time at which the packet has jumped to a new router versus the distance of this router to the destination. The simulations show that the FBG algorithm works very well in dense networks but show great variations in the behavior of the packet routing in sparse networks. For instance the packet may travel quickly to its destination or may stay a very long time far from the destination even if it jumps frequently from routers to routers.

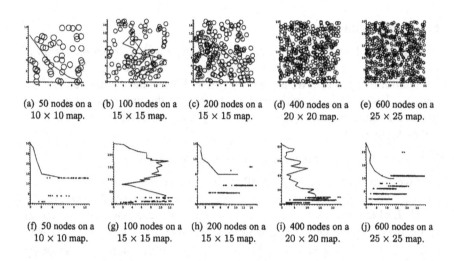

(a) 50 nodes on a   (b) 100 nodes on a   (c) 200 nodes on a   (d) 400 nodes on a   (e) 600 nodes on a
    10×10 map. 15×15 map. 15×15 map. 20×20 map. 25×25 map.

(f) 50 nodes on a   (g) 100 nodes on a   (h) 200 nodes on a   (i) 400 nodes on a   (j) 600 nodes on a
    10×10 map. 15×15 map. 15×15 map. 20×20 map. 25×25 map.

FBG-based routing algorithms performance. We conducted 400 simulations using five different algorithms: SO, RJ, FBG and two algorithms based on FBG denoted as *FBG with Oldest Same Age* (FBG-OSA) and *FBG with Average Age* (FBG-AA). We considered 600 mobile routers located on a $250m \times 250m$ area. Transmission ranges are supposed to be equal to $10m$ for all the routers. We used the Random Waypoint mobility model with speeds randomly chosen between $5m.s^{-1}$ and $10m.s^{-1}$. For each scenario, we randomly choose a source node and a destination node respectively denoted as *orig_node* and *dest_node*. Let us consider a packet issued by *orig_node* that must be delivered to *dest_node*. Let t_a be the time elapsed between the packet's first transmission by *orig_node* and its reception at *dest_node* using algorithm a. For a given scenario, let us define $T_{a,b}$ as $T_{a,b} = t_a - t_b$, with a and b two different routing algorithms. If $T_{a,b} > 0$ (*resp.* $T_{a,b} < 0$) then the algorithm b (*resp.* a) has delivered the packet to *dest_node* faster than the algorithm a (*resp.* b). In the sequel, we will use $T_{a,b}$ to compare the packet delivery time of two algorithms.

We show pairwise comparison between algorithms. Each *Algo1 vs. Algo2* comparison depicted shows the probability that either *Algo1* or *Algo2* leads to the fastest packet delivery. It also shows the probability that delivery time is the same for both algorithms (denoted as "=" on the figure). First, *RJ vs. SO* indicates that RJ and SO have almost the same probability of fastest packet delivery ($\approx 40\%$). Then, analysing *FBG-based* algorithms performance shows that FBG-OSA and FBG-AA allow a faster packet delivery than SO and RJ with a significant probability ($\approx 60\%$ for FBG-AA). Furthermore, although *FBG-OSA vs. FBG-AA* have 40% of identical delivery time, FBG-AA's per-

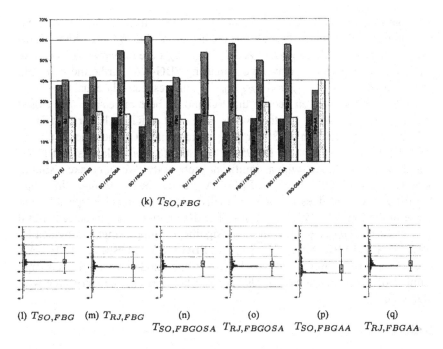

(k) $T_{SO,FBG}$

(l) $T_{SO,FBG}$ (m) $T_{RJ,FBG}$ (n)   (o)   (p)   (q)

$T_{SO,FBGOSA}$ $T_{RJ,FBGOSA}$ $T_{SO,FBGAA}$ $T_{RJ,FBGAA}$

Figure 1.   Probability of Packet delivery time and Pairwise Comparison of Algorithms.

formance seems to be slightly better than FBG-OSA. On the other hand, FBG does not really improve the probability of fastest time delivery compared to SO and RJ since the performance is quite similar for these algorithms. In addition, FBG-OSA and FBG-AA are better than FBG for almost 50% and 55% of the simulations while they lead to same results for 30% and 25%. We depict the distributions of $T_{Algo_1,Algo_2}$ with $Algo_1 = \{SO, RJ\}$ and $Algo_2 = \{FBG, FBG - OSA, FBG - AA\}$. We leave aside the FR algorithm since we do not want the network to carry several copies of the same packet, which could lead to heavy network load. The left part of each figure describes the distribution of $T_{Algo_1,Algo_2}$ in seconds for the 400 simulations. The boxplot on the left indicates some noteworthy values of the distribution. The lower and the upper tails represent respectively the 5th and the 95th percentile (*i.e.*, respectively 5% and 95% of the results are lower than this value). The lower and the upper bound of the rectangle represents respectively the 25th and the 75th percentile of the data set. The line and the point inside the rectangle indicates respectively the median (*i.e.*, the 50th percentile) and the mean value of the distribution. First, it is important to note that the 25th percentile and the median are close to zero for all the distributions: 25% of the values are quite similar for the compared algorithms. Next, let us focus on the FBG-AA algorithm. Since the mean values of $T_{SO,FBG-AA}$ and $T_{RJ,FBG-AA}$ are respectively 7.59s and 5.63s we can expect a good average gain using FBG-AA. Furthermore, the 5th percentile of $T_{SO,FBG-AA}$ and $T_{RJ,FBG-AA}$ are respectively equal to $-11.7s$ and $-8.4s$, hence we can deduce that SO and RJ best values are very closed to FBG-AA worst ones. In other words, when SO or RJ are better than FBG-AA, the gain brought on by SO or RJ is rather small. On the other hand, the 75th percentile (13.75s) and the 95th percentile (36.1s) indicates that FBG-AA leads to a high gain with a significant probability. We can make a similar analysis for FBG-OSA however FBG-AA presents better results. Note that, the FBG algorithm does not achieve really good performance especially because of the low 5th, 25th percentiles. The distribution tends to be center at 0 especially for $T_{RJ,FBG}$. It shows how significant improvements provided by FBG-OSA and FBG-AA are. To sum up, FBG-OSA and especially FBG-AA not only avoid SO and RJ drawbacks (*i.e.,* source node immobility and large number of retransmissions) but also achieve better packet delivery time with high gain.

References

[1] T. Camp, J. Boleng, and V. Davies, 'A Survey of Mobility Models for Ad Hoc Network Research', *Wireless Communication & Mobile Computing (WCMC): Special issue on Mobile Ad Hoc Networking: Research, Trends and Applications*, **2(5)**, (2002), pp. 483-502, 2002

[2] M. Grossglauser and D. Tse, "Mobility increases the capacity of ad hoc wireless networks", IEEE infocom 2001.

[3] X. Hong, M. Gerla, G. Pei and C. Chiang, 'A Group Mobility Model for Ad Hoc Wireless Networks', *ACM Workshop on Modeling and Simulation of Wireless and Mobile Systems*, 1999.

[4] P. Jacquet, "Space-time information propagation in Mobile ad hoc Networks", IEEE Information Theory Workshop, Texas, October 2004.

[5] Q. Li and D. Rus, *Communication in disconnected ad hoc networks using message relay*, Journal of Parallel and Distributed Computing, vol. 63, pp. 75-86, 2003.

[6] T. Clausen, P. Jacquet, et al., *Optimized Link State Routing Protocol*, IETF-RFC-3626, http://www.ietf.org/

[7] R. Rajaraman, 'Topology Control and Routing in Ad hoc Networks: A Survey', *SIGACT News*, **33**, (2002),pp. 60-73.

[8] R. Shah and N.C. Hutchinson, 'Delivering Messages in Disconnected Mobile Ad-Hoc Networks', *ADHOC-NOW*, LNCS 2865, Springer-Verlag, pp. 72-83, 2003.

[9] T. Spyropoulos, K. Psounis, C. Raghavendra, "Single-Copy Routing in Intermittently Connected Mobile Networks," IEEE SECON, October 2004.

[10] K. Wang and B. Li, 'Efficient and guaranteed service coverage in partitionable mobile Ad Hoc Networks', *IEEE-Infocom*, vol. 2, 2002, pp. 1089-1098.

MORHE: A TRANSPARENT MULTI-LEVEL ROUTING SCHEME FOR AD HOC NETWORKS

Michael Voorhaen
PATS Research Group, University of Antwerp
Dept. Mathematics and Computer Science
Middelheimlaan 1, B-2020 Antwerpen, Belgium
michael.voorhaen@ua.ac.be

Erwin Van de Velde
PATS Research Group, University of Antwerp
Dept. Mathematics and Computer Science
Middelheimlaan 1, B-2020 Antwerpen, Belgium
erwin.vandevelde@ua.ac.be

Chris Blondia
PATS Research Group, University of Antwerp
Dept. Mathematics and Computer Science
Middelheimlaan 1, B-2020 Antwerpen, Belgium
chris.blondia@ua.ac.be

Abstract   This paper presents a transparent multi-level routing scheme, named MORHE, that improves the scalability of the OLSR protocol by exploiting the heterogeneous nature of nodes in the network. In our work we try to take an approach that focuses on scenarios where ad hoc technology can be applied, but where we also find nodes in the network with varying capacity. The MORHE protocol makes use of nodes which have a large capacity (e.g. more energy, larger transmission range) to build something that could best be described as an ad hoc infrastructure. Nodes are grouped in clusters that need to be interconnected by specific nodes. This implies that a node no longer needs to know the entire network topology as is the case of the OLSR protocol, but only needs to maintain routes to the nodes inside its own cluster and to the other clusters. Using this approach the signalling overhead - which is one of the main reasons why OLSR is not scalable - is greatly reduced. We also introduce a simple mobility management scheme to allow nodes to roam the different ad hoc clusters.

Keywords: Routing, Scalability, OLSR, Hierarchical, Click, IP Address Compacting

Introduction

Mobile Ad-hoc NETworks (MANETs) can be used for a wide variety of applications, from small scale day-by-day extensions of infrastructured networks that allow users to communicate and have access to multimedia information, up to large scale disasters where fixed infrastructure has failed and an ad hoc network can be used as a temporary, much needed, replacement. The latter case is especially interesting for public safety users who need a system that can be deployed quickly without end user intervention and that allows access to all types of information.

Much of the current research on ad hoc has focused on flat network topologies where the nodes are assumed to have more or less the same capacities and similar needs to have access to the network. Ad hoc routing protocols like OLSR, AODV and DSR ([6], [7], [8]) are meant to allow best effort multihop communication in wireless networks while being resilient to mobility. However research has shown that flat routing protocols do not scale to large networks, since they need to maintain a seperate route for every host in the network.

In this paper we present a transparent multi-level routing scheme called MORHE (*M*ulti-level *O*LSR *R*outing using the *H*NA *E*xtension) that allows any OLSR compliant node to participate in the network without modifications. Our approach takes advantage of the heterogeneousity of the nodes that are present in the network. E.g. units that are less power constrained can be equipped with multiple interfaces, have a larger transmission range, more available bandwith or a combination of the previous. The MORHE protocol will use these nodes to form what can be best described as an ad hoc infrastructure. The ad hoc network is divided into several seperate clusters that are interconnected using the less constrained units, present in the network. During the remainder of this paper these nodes are addressed as *backbone enabled nodes* or simply backbone nodes. Using concepts that were previously defined in the OLSR standard [6] such as the HNA extension and the concept of hierarchical addressing we were able to implement a transparant scheme that allows an overlay network to be built and that minimizes overhead in the network, while still allowing nodes to roam between the different clusters. This transparancy is important since the protocol only affects the backbone enabled nodes but it does not require any fundamental changes to the OLSR protocol. Every OLSR compliant node can thus join a MORHE network.

We assume that the backbone enabled nodes are chosen before network deployment. In a public services scenario this is feasible since there the backbone enabled nodes could be police cars or fire trucks and the public service units normally only move in the vicinity of these vehicles. However the resilience to mobility that is inherent to ad hoc protocols is needed since the public service units should not be limited to staying near these vehicles for communication.

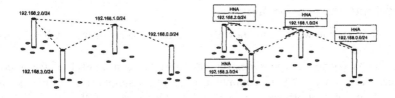

Figure 1.   Example topology of a MORHE network

Figure 2.   Building the overlay network using HNA messages. step 1.

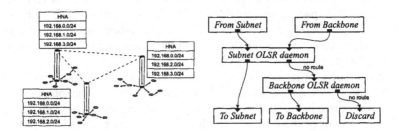

Figure 3.   Building the overlay network using HNA messages. step 2.

Figure 4.   Operation of the backbone nodes

The *Hierarchical OLSR* protocol [11] improves the scalability of the OLSR protocol by adding HTC messages that are used to build a hierarchy in the network. MORHE behaves similarly to HOLSR, however it builds a hierarchical network using the HNA extension allowing it to be backwards compatible with existing OLSR implementations.

1.   A Transparent Multi-level Routing Scheme

Figure 1 shows an example of the topology of a MORHE network with 2 levels. All the nodes in the network are grouped into smaller ad hoc clusters and each cluster is provided with a node that is backbone enabled, i.e. it has two interfaces: one for communicating in the cluster and another for communicating on the backbone. This scenario could be extended by having several levels in the backbone, or allowing all the nodes in the clusters to act as relays for their Personal Area Network (PAN) equipment. As explained in the following sections, the MORHE protocol allows for any number of levels in the network given that the address space is large enough.

Building the overlay network

In this section we describe how the main components of the MORHE protocol work.

The backbone enabled nodes run an OLSR deamon on each of the interfaces. These two deamons communicate in a very simple setup displayed in Fig. 4: if a packet arrives at a backbone enabled node it will first attempt to look for a route to the destination on the subnet. If this failed the packet is passed to the backbone where another route lookup is performed. If a route is found the packet is forwarded, else the packet is discarded and the source node is notified that there is no route to the host.

The routes to the different clusters are advertised using Host and Network Association (HNA) packets that are described in the OLSR RFC [6]. Each backbone node periodically sends out a HNA message informing the other backbone nodes that it can reach all the nodes in the subnet that it is connected to. This is shown in Fig. 2.

The same process is repeated for the clusters: when a backbone node receives a HNA message it updates its association database. This association database is then advertised in the cluster, again using a HNA message, informing all the nodes in the cluster about what other clusters can be reached. This procedure is shown in Fig. 3.

Mobility Management

We now propose a transparant mobility management scheme that only affects the modules that generate the HNA messages at the backbone nodes. This minimizes the impact on the nodes that are deployed in the network, i.e. each OLSR compliant node can operate without problems in this network.

The scheme is based on the proactive nature of OLSR, being that each of the MPR (Multi Point Relay) nodes advertises its neighbors at a regular basis. This way each node in the network learns of the routes to the different destinations in the network. This means that all the backbone enabled nodes also learn of the visitors that are in their subnet by looking at the IP address prefix. Each time a HNA message is generated by a backbone node it will not only advertise reachability of its own subnet, but also reachability of the visiting nodes, which it learns of by scanning its routing tables. A node that receives one of these HNA messages will then add a host specific entry to its routing table as specified by the OLSR standard.

Minimizing the size of HNA messages

The use of HNA messages reduces the network overhead already significantly. However it is possible to use the subnet notation and the fact that all traffic has to pass through the backbone for even further reduction of the overhead. We will propose a solution in two parts: Redundancy Check and IP Address Compacting.

Redundancy Check. If a backbone node has an own subnet and e.g. it has 192.168.1.0/24, it will communicate this to all other backbone nodes using HNA messages. If e.g. node 192.168.1.5 is visiting another subnet, the backbone node of that subnet will communicate the reachability of this node to all other backbone nodes. If this is the case, all other backbone nodes receiving both the HNA messages would tell their subnets that they can reach 192.168.1.0/24 and 192.168.1.5/32. It is easy to see that the information about 192.168.1.5 is redundant as 192.168.1.0/24 contains this address allready. The redundancy check finds this redundant information and deletes it, before sending information into the subnet. Of course, this information is not redundant in the routing tables of the backbone node, where it is possible that there is another gateway for 192.168.1.0/24 than for 192.168.1.5/32.

This is an easy algorithm when the information of the HNA messages of other backbone nodes is kept sorted in a table:

1 If a new element has to be inserted, search through the list to find its place (sort).

2 When the location for the element has been found, check with the previous element if that element contains the new element. If so, do not insert the new element, otherwise insert it.

3 When a element has been inserted, check if the new element contains the next element. If so, delete the next element and repeat this step. Otherwise, stop.

The second step is correct when the entries have the form ⟨ Network IP address, subnet mask ⟩ where the network IP address is the network prefix followed by all zeroes (in binary notation). All IP addresses in this subnet will have a host postfix that is not equal to zero and will come after the subnet element in the sorted list.

IP Address Compacting. This algorithm is applicable in any backbone node whose subnet has visiting mobile nodes. When two visiting nodes have IP addresses that differ only in the last bit, e.g.: 192.168.1.2/32 and 192.168.1.3/32, these addresses can be brought together using the subnet mask as 192.168.1.2/31. In this section, we will explain the algorithm. The same compression can be executed on the redundancy check table after the successful execution of the redundancy check and before broadcasting this information into the cluster. We will explain the case of the visitor table first.

Every time the backbone node has to update its routing and visitor tables, OLSR drops the entire routing table and all visitor information. So the algorithm must be able to reconstruct the entire visitor table, compressed, with a low cost. The algorithm works iterative and will keep a sorted visitor table.

1 Insert the first visiting node in the visitor table with subnet mask 255.255.255.255 (/32)

2 Insert another visiting node in the visitor table with subnet mask 255.255.255.255 (/32), so that the IP addresses with their subnet masks in the visitor table are ordered from the lowest to the highest address.

3 If the previous or next pair of ⟨ IP address, subnet mask ⟩ has the same subnet mask and they differ only in the last bit of the network prefix, these elements will be taken together as a pair ⟨ A, B ⟩ where A is formed by taking the IP address of one of the elements and making the last bit of the network prefix (in binary notation) 0. B is the subnet mask of one of the elements with the last 1-bit (in binary notation) made 0.

   ■ e.g. ⟨ 192.168.8.0, 255.255.255.0 ⟩ and ⟨ 192.168.9.0, 255.255.255.0 ⟩ will be replaced with ⟨ 192.168.8.0, 255.255.254.0 ⟩

4 Repeat the previous step untill the current element cannot be taken together with the previous or the next one.

5 If there are more elements to be inserted, go to step 2, otherwise stop.

The identical algorithm is possible on the redundancy check table.

2.   Simulation Study

Simulation Parameters.   For our simulations we will use the nsclick [3] simulation platform. Nsclick embeds the Click Modular Router Platform [4] into the ns-2 [1] simulator allowing us to run actual routing protocols developed for the click platform inside a simulation. We based our work on a click based implementation of the OLSR protocol. The parameters used for OLSR are the default parameters described in [6].

Simulated Scenario.   The scenario consists of an ad hoc network that is split into 4 clusters with 16 nodes each, one of which is a backbone node. The only way that a node can communicate with a node that is in another cluster is through the overlay network. Except for the backbone nodes, the nodes are placed randomly inside the area of the cluster they belong to. The backbone nodes are placed in the center of the area. An example is given in Fig. 5: the backbone nodes are shown in grey. The backbone nodes are configured with two 802.11 interfaces, that operate on different channels. The interface that is

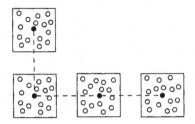

Figure 5. Simulated Scenario

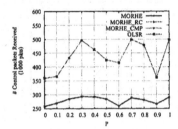 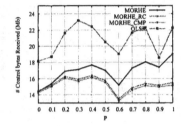

Figure 6. Routing signalling overhead (# packets received)

Figure 7. Routing signalling overhead (# bytes received)

connected to the overlay network has a range of 300m, while the interface on the subnet has a much smaller coverage (100m). The nodes in a cluster are randomly distributed on a 200m by 200m surface.

Each cluster is assigned 256 consecutive addresses: 192.168.0.0/24, 192.168.1.0/24, 192.168.2.0/24, 192.168.3.0/24 respectively. The backbone nodes are given the 192.168.x.253 address for the interface on the subnet and the 192.168.x.254 address for the interface on the backbone. The nodes are addressed upwards from 192.168.x.1.

For this scenario we define a parameter P as the probablity that a node is visiting another cluster during the simulation run. P is varied from 0.0 to 1.0 in steps of 0.1. The nodes that are visiting another cluster are uniformly distributed among the remaing clusters. Using this scenario we can investigate the behaviour of the MORHE protocol in scenarios with a varying amount of visiting nodes in the clusters.

10 pairs of nodes initiate a unidirectional call, with each call staggered by 30s. The calls are CBR connections sending packets of size 500 bytes at a rate of 16 kbps.

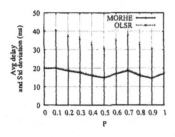
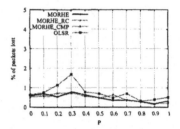

Figure 8.   Average end-to-end delay   Figure 9.   % packets lost

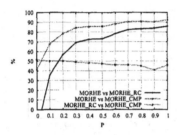
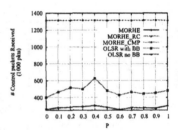

Figure 10.   Reducing the overhead   Figure 11.   Reducing the overhead
with redundancy check and compacting   with redundancy check and compacting

3.   Simulation Results

We will now compare the results of:

- OLSR using Multiple Interface Description (MID) support: MID should be supported by any OLSR implementation that wishes to comply with RFC3626 (In the graphs we refer to this as OLSR). This approach will actually make sure that one big ad hoc network is created.

- MORHE without redundancy check and IP address compating

- MORHE with redundancy check (In the graphs we refer to this as MORHE_RC).

- MORHE with redundancy check and IP address compacting (In the graphs we refer to this as MORHE_CMP).

We will start by looking at the total amount of overhead measured as the amount of routing signalling packets and bytes received during the simulation run. The results are shown in Figs. 6 and 7. As you can see in Fig. 6 MORHE offers a reduction in the amount of signalling packets received of about 40%

independently of the amount of nodes visiting a foreign cluster. Neither the redundancy check, nor the compacting have an effect on this result, since they only reduce the size of the HNA packets.

We can observe the same behaviour for the amount of bytes sent when there are less than 60% of the nodes visiting another cluster.(Fig. 7). However in scenarios where 60% or more nodes are visiting another cluster the overhead in bytes received increases and comes close to that of OLSR. This can be explained by the increase in the size of the HNA packets when there are more visiting nodes inside a cluster. Fig. 10 shows exactly how much using the redundancy check and the IP address compacting improves the MORHE protocol in terms of HNA overhead. It is clear that the redundancy check removes much of the overhead when many nodes are visiting another subnet. If both redundancy check and IP address compacting are active the overhead in bytes caused by the HNA packets is reduced by almost 90% if P is large. In fact by choosing the address ranges for the subnets in such a way that they can be compacted when advertised on the subnet - 192.168.0.0/24, 192.168.1.0/24, 192.168.2.0/24 and 192.168.3.0/24 compact to 192.168.0.0/22 - the HNA overhead, compared to using only redundancy checks, is reduced by almost 40% to 50% depending on the value of P. If one of the subnets were to become unreachable at some point, the overhead would increase since MORHE would not be able to compact the addresses into one subnet anymore, however connectivity among the remaining subnets is still guaranteed.

Fig. 9 shows that MORHE and OLSR have similar results when it comes to packet loss. Almost no packets are lost. One can observe a slight improvement which is caused by the medium being less congested by broadcast packets, which is a direct consequence of the fact that MORHE reduces the overhead in the network. The average end-to-end delay in the network is shown in Fig. 8. For clarity only MORHE without extensions and OLSR are displayed and in terms of end-to-end delay there is no significant performance difference between MORHE and OLSR.

4. Conclusion

In this paper we have presented a transparent multi-level routing protocol based on OLSR. Our approach takes into account the heterogenous nature of the nodes in an ad hoc network and builds an ad hoc infrastructure that improves the scalability of the OLSR protocol. MORHE was developed in such a way that any OLSR compliant node can join a MORHE network and roam the different ad hoc clusters without any problems.

We have described how this protocol can be easily integrated into a working OLSR implementation and have implemented the protocol using an OLSR implementation for the Click Modular Router Project. Using the ns-2 simulator and the nsclick extension we simulated several scenarios allowing us to compare OLSR with the MORHE protocol. The following conclusions can be made: Proactive ad hoc routing protocols need a large amount of signalling overhead to work and do not scale to large networks. MORHE avoids much of this overhead by dividing the network into smaller clusters and building an ad hoc infrastructure. Although the MORHE protocol was not primarily designed for scenarios where many nodes are visiting a foreign subnet the protocol behaves well even in these scenarios. By managing the address space of the ad hoc network, schemes such as the redundancy check and IP address compacting can be used to decrease the size of the signalling packets, while leaving the protocol behaviour unchanged.

5.   Future Work

The focus in this paper was on scenarios with a static overlay network and non-overlapping clusters. We intend to further investigate the consequences of nodes which roam between overlapping ad hoc clusters, as well as the effects of mobile clusters. Scenarios based on group mobility models will be investigated to measure the performance of the MORHE protocol when the backbone network is more dynamic. Support for fast handovers between clusters should be a further research topic.

References

[1] The Network Simulator ns-2

[2] OOLSR: Projet Hipercom, INRIA.

[3] Michael Neufeld, Ashish Jain, Dirk Grunwald, Nsclick: bridging network simulation and deployment, In *Proceedings of the 5th ACM international workshop on Modeling analysis and simulation of wireless and mobile systems, Atlanta, Georgia, USA*, 2002

[4] Eddie Kohler, The Click modular router, November 2000

[5] Andreas Tønnesen, Implementing and extending the Optimized Link State Routing protocol, Master thesis, UniK, November 2004

[6] P. Jacquet, T. Clausen, RFC 3626: Optimized Link State Routing Protocol (OLSR), Oct 2003.

[7] C. Perkins, E. Belding-Royer, S. Das, RFC 3561: Ad hoc On-Demand Distance Vector (AODV) Routing, July 2003.

[8] David B., Johnson David A., Yih-Chun Hu, The Dynamic Source Routing Protocol for Mobile Ad Hoc Networks (DSR), July 2004.

[9] G. Pei, M. Gerla, Mobility Management in Hierarchical Multi-hop Mobile Wireless Networks, In *Proceedings of IEEE ICCCN'99, Boston, MA, pp. 324-329*, 1999

[10] C. Perkins, RFC 3344: IP Mobility Support for IPv4, August 2002

[11] Y. Ge, L. Lamont, L. Villasenor, Improving Scalability of Heterogeneous Wireless Networks with Hierarchical OLSR, August 2004

VIRTUAL TRELLIS ROUTING

How Regular Structures can ease Network Operations

Julien Ridoux, Anne Fladenmuller, Yannis Viniotis
LIP6 - UPMC   ECE Department - NCSU
8, rue du C. Scott - Paris, France   Box 7911 - Raleigh, NC 27695, USA
{julien.ridoux, anne.fladenmuller}@lip6.fr, candice@eos.ncsu.edu

Abstract   The mobility characteristic of Ad Hoc and Sensor networks implies that
the topological information contained in the traditional IP address can
no longer reflect the position of a node in the network. In this paper we
propose a new approach to resolve the location-identification coupling
contained in the IP address. The approach uses a Virtual Regular Structure (VRS) to describe the addressing space of the entire network; such
a structure provides additional desired properties such as robustness
and multi-paths. Our approach explores a distributed implementation
of the VRS based on a trellis graph description of routing tables instead
of the traditional trees. We show that the construction of the optimal structure is an NP-Complete problem; in this paper, we propose a
heuristic and evaluate its performance via simulations.

Keywords: Self-Organized Networks, Regular Structures

1.   Introduction

Unlike traditional (wired) networks, the Ad Hoc and Sensor networks
we target in this study face unique challenges: they do not rely on any
routing infrastructure, their topology is flat and not known in advance,
their links are not reliable and they have to be tolerant to transient
node presence. The main functions of a network layer, namely, building a
routing table, performing lookups in this table, taking a routing decision,
and efficiently processing packets, have to be performed in the presence
of these challenges.

IP addressing, as it is commonly used, does not suit the nature of such
Ad Hoc and Sensor networks. Because of the transient presence of nodes,
the node identity and location can not be maintained in the same piece
of information. The implicit association between identity and location
used in wired IP networks eases the process of building, maintaining

and using routing tables. As soon as the nature of the network forces separation of identity and location, a lookup on the identity has to be realized in order to retrieve the location. Indirect routing approaches [6] or geographic approaches [4] are examples of this explicit association retrieval. From a high-level point of view, putting all the information needed by the network layer in a *single* data element would improve the functions of the network layer. Such a perfect situation is, of course, not realistic, and, depending on the nature of the networks studied, several association combinations are possible.

In this paper, we want to introduce a new topological space (i.e., an addressing scheme different from the traditional IP address space and tree-like routing tables) that is suitable for and facilitates network layer operations in the presence of mobility, node faults, network mergers and splits. The precise definition and distributed construction of the addressing scheme used by the network layer is the fundamental and first step to realize. In this paper, we focus our attention to this point only. For a more detailed description of how one can use our new addressing scheme to perform data forwarding, see [3].

The study done by Castro *and al.* in [7] shows that imposing *a structure* in this scheme eases the functions of the network layer and thus improves its overall performance. Since Sensor or Ad Hoc networks cannot rely on a physical structure by themselves, we propose to introduce structure in a *virtual* manner.

The Virtual Regular Structure (VRS) we propose maintains an organized, logical topology, in spite of mobility effects. The basic idea is to define and build the VRS in a *recursive* manner, using the same building block (a trellis graph), in order to ease the network management operations when nodes move or network splits/mergers occur. The construction of the VRS is based on physical neighborhood information only, to reflect the physical topology of the nodes that form the network. The set up of the VRS is "constructive" and realized locally, in order to avoid the need of a global view of the network, difficult to obtain in our context. This mechanism avoids widespread flooding on the network for any management operation and owns, by nature, good properties in terms of scalability.

In section 2, we detail how the topological location space is constructed. We show that the trellis construction problem is NP-Complete and provide a heuristic solution. In section 3, we present simulations showing the feasibility of constructing a VRS based on topological information.

2.   VRS based on Trellis Graphs

Our proposal to create the Virtual Regular Structure (VRS) is based on the following hypotheses, reflecting the nature of Ad Hoc and Sensor networks. The network is built from scratch and the physical topology created by the nodes arrival process can not be predicted. We make no assumption on the properties of the topology and suppose that no infrastructure is present to help supporting the addressing or routing mechanisms. We make the hypothesis that each node joining the network possesses a unique Universal Identifier (UI), which could be an IP address. The definition of this identifier is not handled by the system, but reference [2] provides information for such a definition.

Trellis graphs are used here to implement the VRS for Ad Hoc and Sensor networks. To the best of our knowledge, trellis graphs have been used only in [8] at the networking level but with a different purpose from ours. A trellis graph can be generated by a Convolutional Encoder [9].

A trellis is a connected graph, repeating a set of vertices, all of which have the same degree. The number of vertices of a trellis is 2^L, L defining the trellis size. Another representation of such a trellis graph is a Finite State Machine (FSM). An example of trellis graphs is shown in the right part of figure 1. The vertices of a trellis, labeled by binary values (in the example from 00 to 11), represent the different FSM states. The trellis edges represent the FSM transitions. A number of trellis graphs can be generated, with different node degrees, introducing more or less redundancy and so, more or less possible paths between two distinct vertices. In the rest of this section we consider trellis graphs of size 4 for explanation purposes.

2.1   Description of a Single Cluster

In order to set up the VRS in a distributed manner, the FSM defining the trellis is known *a priori* by all the nodes composing the network. The trellis pattern defines the routing table layout that is used by nodes in a cluster. The clusters are formed by associating nodes (labeled with their UI) to vertices of a trellis (entries of the routing table). This association creates a mapping of the physical topology into the virtual one (the trellis graph). The label of the vertex of the trellis associated to a node is called its Local Relative Address (LRA). This mapping introduces the correlation between the identity of the nodes (their UI) and their address (their LRA). Depending on the node arrival sequence (even if resulting in the same physical topology), the construction heuristic we propose possibly produces different mappings.

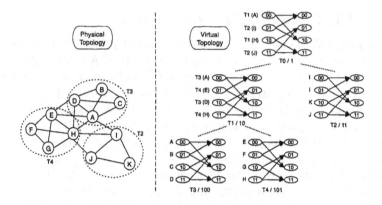

Figure 1.   Spanning the Network.

Figure 1 gives an example of such a clustering. The topology in figure 1 contains the four nodes A, B, C and D, which are associated to the vertices of a the trellis labeled T_3. In this case, each node of the physical topology is associated to a unique vertex of the trellis. In trellis T_3, node A is associated to the vertex labeled 00 and nodes B, C and D are respectively associated to vertices 01, 10 and 11. This mapping operation results in the creation of a cluster of nodes. This cluster represents a subset of the nodes' physical connectivity. Figure 1 shows that a node can be associated to different vertices of a trellis. As an example, node I in trellis T_2 is associated to two vertices, *i.e.*, I is being given two LRA in the virtual structure: 00 and 01. This shows that one or several LRA can be allocated to a physical node.

2.2   Spanning the entire Network

As we presented, a trellis graph defines a cluster of a maximum number of nodes. In order to be able to span the entire network and include each node in the VRS, our mechanism adds clusters (*i.e.*, trellis graphs) in a recursive manner. This recursive construction introduces trellises of trellises, repeating the same regular structure.

Figure 1 shows trellis graphs T_3, T_4 and T_2 mapping respectively the nodes $\{A, B, C, D\}$, $\{E, F, G, H\}$ and $\{I, J, K\}$. This mapping of nodes creates a first level of clusters. In order to allow all the nodes in the network to communicate, the trellis graphs T_2, T_3 and T_4 are interconnected recursively. Figure 1 gives an example of a VRS with two levels of recursion. As an example, T_1 associates T_3 to its states 00 and 10, while it associates T_4 to its states 01 and 11. T_0 and T_1 can then be described as "trellis of trellis graphs".

Even if trellis graphs are defined in a virtual space, the actual communication between them has to be ensured by the physical nodes interconnecting them. The two nodes chosen to represent their trellis in higher recursive levels are always those whose labels have the smallest and highest values in the trellis. We name these two nodes the Trellis Heads. In figure 1, T_3 is represented in T_1 by its Trellis Heads $A(00_{T_1})$ and $D(10_{T_1})$. In the same manner, T_4 is represented by nodes $E(01_{T_1})$ and $H(11_{T_1})$ in T_1.

We define a Trellis Prefix (TP) to identify each regular structure. By definition each trellis of size 2^L gathers $2^{(L-1)}$ sub-trellis. Each trellis T attributes a prefix p written as a bit string of size $(L-1)$ to the nodes representing a common sub-trellis. A sub-trellis' TP is the recursive concatenation of the higher level trellis' prefix and p. The highest trellis in the recursive hierarchy possesses the label "1". An example of the resulting TP attribution is illustrated in figure 1, where T_4's TP is 101, the concatenation of T_1's TP (10) and T_4's prefix in T_1 (1).

At each step of the VRS construction, each label of each trellis composing the VRS is associated to a physical node. It is then possible for a source to retrieve the path in the VRS to any destination. This path is represented by the Local Relative Address of the destination in its trellis and the Trellis Prefix of the cluster it belongs to.

In figure 1 example, let suppose that F and J need to reach K. For J, the case is trivial. J and K belong to the same cluster and share the same mapping information. J knows K's LRA as 10_{T_2} and can reach it based solely on its knowledge of the trellis connectivity. From F's point of view, the path to reach K is represented by the Trellis Prefix of the cluster F belongs to (the trellis T_4 with prefix 101) and the LRA of F in T_4 (01_{T_4}). The forwarding of packets is realized on per cluster basis, by processing the Trellis Prefix of the destination contained in the packet header. When the packet reaches the destination's cluster, it is forwarded to the destination thanks to its LRA information. Since we introduce redundancy in the structure, several paths can be defined for each cluster the packets go through, giving the multi-path property.

2.3   Construction Complexity and Heuristic

Finding the optimal construction of the recursive clusters (*i.e.*, one that minimizes the number of clusters) is an NP-Complete problem. In the following we formalize the problem in terms of graph theory and show the equivalence with the well-known H-Matching problem [5].

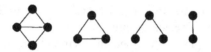

Figure 2.   The 4 Derived Graphs of the trellis of size 4.

The cluster resulting from the mapping of nodes' UI to the trellis vertices corresponds to a connected subgraph of the physical network topology. We name this connected subgraph the trellis Derived Graph. The mapping operation producing this Derived Graph can be represented by the following steps.

(1) Let $\mathcal{M}$ be the FSM representation of a trellis with a number s of states s_i. $\mathcal{M}$ can be represented as an edge-labeled, directed graph M. We first make the adjacency matrix of M be symmetric and put the values on the diagonal to 0 (to remove the self loops), resulting in the connected undirected graph M'.

(2) Let W be a set of vertices such that $|W| \in [2, s]$. W represents the nodes of the physical topology belonging to a common cluster. Then, the mapping operation is represented by an application $\mathcal{A}$ such that $\forall\, i \in [1, |W|], \forall\, j \in [1, s]$, $v_i \mathcal{A} s_j$ produces an instance of M'.

(3) The presence of a physical node in the cluster, mapped to different labels of the trellis, results in duplicate entries in M' adjacency matrix. By removing these entries we obtain one of the trellis Derived Graphs $D = (W, F)$, whose cardinality corresponds to the number of nodes in the cluster. Figure 2 gives all the possible Derived Graphs of the trellis of size 4 where $|W| \in [2, s]$.

Let $G = (V, E)$ be the undirected, connected graph representing a given network topology. Let $D = (W, F)$ be one of the possible Derived Graphs of a trellis of a given size. Creating the clusters on G that will map the nodes to the trellis is equivalent to an H-Matching of G, where H is the Derived Graph D. Then,

(i) if $|W| = 2$, the H-Matching of G by D is realized in a polynomial time.

(ii) if $|W| \geq 3$, the H-Matching of G by D is NP-Complete (the proof of this result can be found in [5]).

The smallest trellis of interest to us produces Derived Graphs of more than two vertices, leading to the definition of clusters along an H-matching where $|W| \geq 3$. An optimal H-Matching in our context consists in placing as many nodes as possible in a trellis, *i.e.*, using the Derived Graphs for which $|W|$ is maximal, and is then NP-Complete.

As said, the complete construction of the VRS is a recursive process. This implies to realize the H-matching described, at each level of recursion, on the Trellis Heads obtained from the previous clustering step. Each step of the construction corresponds to the solution of an NP-Complete problem.

Since the construction of the VRS is an NP-Complete problem, we propose a heuristic to set it up, based on the fact that nodes join the network in an incremental manner. Our heuristic builds the top trellis of the VRS first, and adds lower level trellises as new nodes join. We describe in the following algorithm 1 the key points of the heuristic only. When a node joins a network, it tries to join the existing VRS by being inserted in an existing trellis. If no possible position is available, because of physical connectivity constraint, the arriving node creates a new trellis with its neighbor. This heuristic ensures that any new node joining the network can be configured and adapts the total size of the addressing space to the number of nodes present in the network.

This heuristic shows how our addressing space is built in a distributed but local manner among physical neighbor nodes. The VRS is built without widespread flooding mechanisms, by maintaining locally the common mapping in use in a cluster. Having a regular structure of finite size, and a construction mechanism realized locally gives natural scalability properties to our proposal.

Algorithm 1 Construction Heuristic

---

node N joins the network
if N detects some neighbors **then**
    each neighbor returns the list of trellises it belongs to
    N sorts the trellises by their decreasing level in the VRS and then the decreasing number of
    nodes they contain
    for each trellis **do**
        N lists the available positions in the trellis
        for each position **do**
            N checks recursively the position in lower trellis
            if the position is one of the Trellis Head **then**
                N checks recursively the position in upper trellis
            end if
            if position is valid **then**
                break
            end if
        end for
    end for
    if No available position has been found **then**
        for each trellis **do**
            N selects two neighbors that do not belong to a lower trellis
            N creates a new trellis with these two neighbors
        end for
    end if
else
    N creates a new trellis

end if

---

3.   Evaluation and Simulations

With the definition of our heuristic, it is always possible to build a recursive trellis-based VRS containing all the network nodes. Since the complexity of such construction is NP-Complete for an existing topology, it is important to simplify the construction as much as possible. It is also important to maintain performance in terms of computational load on the nodes for the routing, minimization of the information storage required for our VRS or matching of the physical minimum route and the path in the VRS to the destination. Analyzing the structural properties of the VRS produced gives a first estimate of such costs.

3.1   Definition of performance estimates

The computation required to route packets along the VRS mostly depends on the length of the path between nodes. The longer the path in the VRS, the more processing time is required to compute it, since more nodes are involved in forwarding packets. Statistically, it seems intuitive that the *depth* of the VRS will have an impact on the average length of the path between nodes. The depth of the VRS can give us some insight on the performance in terms of average routing processing load for a given topology.

Each trellis stores information on each association (LRA, UI) of its own trellis and of all the trellises of longer prefixes below it. The number of LRA per trellis is fixed, and several LRAs can be associated to one UI. So, in order to optimize the amount of information stored in the VRS, we need to minimize the number of trellises and to create the shortest structure possible. This is clearly what our heuristic tends to do, by limiting the creation of new trellises.

As a result of this analysis, we can deduce that the depth of the virtual structure and the number of trellises has an impact on the performance of our approach. Although our heuristic tends to minimize both metrics, it can not be guaranteed they will both be optimized. One major characteristic of our proposal is that, although we are sure a VRS can be built, we can not predict its resulting shape. Then, for a given topology, several VRS can be built, depending on the node arrivals: the number of trellises as well as the maximum number of recursive trellises (depth of the VRS) can differ. It is thus important to understand which parameter will impact performance the most.

In order to evaluate these structural performance estimates, we generated topologies where nodes are placed randomly in a square geographic area. Each wireless node has a transmission range of 250 meters. The dimension of the square area is defined by the geographical density of

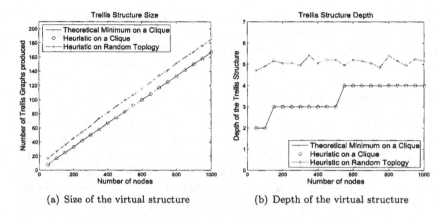

(a) Size of the virtual structure   (b) Depth of the virtual structure

Figure 3. Heuristic Quality Evaluation.

the topology, fixed to 35 nodes per km^2. The value for a topology size corresponds to an average over 25 runs in the same conditions. In these simulations, we studied the construction heuristic we propose by using a trellis of size 8.

3.2   Heuristic Evaluation

In order to evaluate the proposed heuristic, we computed the theoretical minimum number of trellises and the minimum depth of the VRS for a given number of nodes, respectively shown in figure 3(a) and 3(b). These bounds correspond to a physical topology that can be represented as a clique, *i.e.*, whithout any physical connectivity constraint. In both figures 3(a) and 3(b) we observe that the proposed heuristic leads to the theoretical minimum bounds on a clique topology. This clearly shows that the heuristic achieves its goal on a topology where the physical constraints does not have to be taken into account.

On the random topology we produced, figure 3(a) shows that our heuristic remains close to the optimum number of trellis. Even if our heuristic does not clearly lead to the optimum because of the nodes arrival process and the physical connectivity constraint, we observe that the number of trellis graphs produced does not increase exponentially with the size of the topology.

Figure 3(b) shows that the depth of the structure on a random topology can be more than twice the optimal depth computed. For topologies of smaller sizes, the connectivity of the network does not allow new nodes to be inserted in trellises of higher level in the structure. This leads to the construction of new sub-trellises that increase the overall depth of the structure. Having a VRS of higher depth while the total number of trellises stays close to the optimum indicates that the VRS is not well balanced. Nevertheless, we again observe that the depth of the VRS does not increase exponentially with the number of nodes.

4.   Conclusions

In this paper we have proposed the use of virtual Trellis structures to (a) organize the addressing space of a self-organized Ad Hoc and Sensor networks in a structured fashion, and, (b) to perform data routing in such an environment. Thanks to the redundancy and recursion introduced in the trellis-based VRS, we provide a distributed dynamic addressing scheme, with the following advantages: localized operations, no size limit in the addressing space, a built-in multi-path routing structure, computed locally, and robustness to various kinds of mobility. The construction of the optimal trellises was proven to be an NP-Complete problem. A heuristic was provided to build the VRS and evaluated via simulations. Future work will study the impact of group mobility on our scheme and compare the performance of our approach to other schemes.

References

[1] C.E. Perkins (1996). IP Mobility Support. RFC 2002, IETF.

[2] I.Stoica, R.Morris, D.Karger, M.F.Kaashoek, H.Balakrishnan (2001). Chord: A Scalable P2P Lookup Service for Internet Applications. In *Proc. of ACM SIG-COMM*.

[3] J.Ridoux, A.Fladenmuller and Y.Viniotis (2004). Beyond the Tree Structure: a new way to configure nodes in SONs. Technical report. http://www-rp.lip6.fr/~ridoux/Publications/TR_BeyondTrellis.pdf.

[4] J.Li, J.Jannotti, D.De Couto, D.Karger and R.Morris (2000). A Scalable Location Service for Geographic Ad Hoc Routing. In *Proc. of ACM MOBICOM*, pages 120–130.

[5] Kirkpatrick, D. G. and Hell, P. (1978). On the Completeness of a generalized Matching Problem. In *Proceedings of the tenth annual ACM symposium on Theory of computing, San Diego, CA*.

[6] L. Blazevic, L. Buttyan, S. Capkun, S. Giordano, J. P. Hubaux and J. Y. Le Boudec (2001). Self-Organization in Mobile Ad Hoc Networks: the Approach of Terminodes. *IEEE Communications Mag.*, 39(6).

[7] M.Castro, M.Costa and A.Rowstron (2003). Should we build Gnutella on a Structured Overlay? In *HotNets-II. Cambridge, MA, USA*.

[8] S.D.Nikolopoulos, A.Pitsillides, and D.Tipper (1997). Addressing Network Survivability issues by finding the K-best paths through a Trellis Graph. In *Proc. of IEEE INFOCOM*.

[9] S.Lin, D.J.Costello (1983). *Error Control Coding: Fundamental and Applications*. Electrical Engineering Series. Prentice-Hall.

CONNECTIVITY PROPERTIES OF RANDOM WAYPOINT MOBILITY MODEL FOR AD HOC NETWORKS*

Pasi Lassila, Esa Hyytiä, and Henri Koskinen
Helsinki University of Technology (TKK), Networking Laboratory
P.O. Box 3000, FIN-02015 TKK, Finland
{pasi.lassila, esa.hyytia,henri.koskinen}@tkk.fi

Abstract   We study the connectivity properties of an ad hoc network consisting of n nodes each moving according to the Random Waypoint mobility model. In particular, we focus on estimating two quantities, the probability that the network is connected, and the mean durations of the connectivity periods. The accuracy of the approximations is compared against numerical simulations. For the probability of connectivity, an approximation is given that is remarkably accurate. By numerical examples we also show that in sparse network the mobility has a positive effect on connectivity, whereas in dense network the situation becomes the opposite. For the mean length of the connectivity periods results are also accurate in the important region where the probability of connectivity rises rapidly.

Keywords: ad hoc networks, mobility modelling, k-connectivity, RWP.

1.   Introduction

The connectivity problem in wireless networks deals with determining if it is possible to transfer information between any two nodes, typically ignoring all capacity and traffic related phenomena, most notably interference effects. The most popular network model – and the one used in this study – defining when two nodes are directly connected has been the Boolean one, in which two nodes are connected if they are both within each other's transmission ranges. When this model is augmented with an assumption that all nodes have an equal transmission range, the connectivity problem reduces to determining the distribution of the threshold range for connectivity: for a given set of nodes, this is equal to the greatest edge length in the minimum spanning tree of the nodes [6]. It has been shown in [7] that for uniformly distributed nodes in the unit

*We are grateful to Laura Nieminen for the help with the simulations. This work has been supported by the Academy of Finland (grant n:o 74524), the Finnish Defence Forces Technical Research Centre and partly the Nokia Foundation.

square, as the number of nodes tends to infinity, the threshold range for connectivity has asymptotically the same, previously known, distribution as the threshold range for minimum degree 1, i.e., the greatest edge length in the nearest-neighbor graph. The result has been generalized to k-connectivity in [8]. Furthermore, the identity in the case $k = 1$ has been shown to hold for normally distributed points in [9]. Recently, the asymptotic distributions of the threshold range for k-connectivity when $k > 1$, for uniformly distributed points inside a circle and square have been derived in [10]. The distribution of the threshold range for k-connectivity is not known when the number of nodes is finite. The results above motivate approximating k-connectivity of finite networks by minimum degree k, as has been done, e.g., in [11]; this is also the basis of our approach.

In this paper we present approximations for the probability that a network with n nodes is k-connected. The network nodes are assumed to move according to random waypoint (RWP) mobility model [1–4], which concentrates more nodes in the center of the area. In particular, for our purposes an important quantity is the stationary node distribution. For this approximate results for various movement areas (circle, rectangle) have been obtained in [1, 3], and, as a part of our earlier work, in [4] we have also derived an exact expression for an arbitrary convex domain. In the RWP model the nodes move independently and the number of neighbors a given node has is binomially distributed with a certain parameter p. These are needed in our approximation for the probability that all nodes have at least k neighbors, which is used to approximate the probability of k-connectivity. In our first approximation the parameter p is computed exactly using the results of our earlier work [4]. Additionally, two numerically simpler approximation schemes are given, which are based on making some additional poissonian assumptions. Our approach is similar to the one in [11], with the distinction that in [11] the binomial distribution characterizing the number of neighbors a given node has is approximated by a Poisson distribution. Also, we have an exact result for the node distribution, whereas in [11] an approximation has been used (although a rather accurate one). The quality of the approximations for 1-, 2- and 3-connectivity are evaluated by means of numerical simulations in a unit disk, while the approach itself is not limited to any special geometry. In the simulations, the threshold ranges for k-connectivity have been determined using the efficient algorithms given in [12]. The results show that especially our first approximation gives remarkably accurate results. We also give an approximation for the mean time a network remains 1-connected (or disconnected). The approximation utilizes the results on the node arrival rate into a given subset given in [5]. The numerical simulations show that the approximation gives reasonably accurate estimates in the most important region where the probability of connectivity rises rapidly.

2. Preliminaries

In the **RWP model**, a node moves, independently of the others, directly towards the next waypoint at a certain velocity v in a convex domain denoted by $\mathcal{A}$. Upon reaching the waypoint, the next waypoint and velocity are drawn randomly from the uniform distribution over $\mathcal{A}$ and the velocity distribution, respectively. Next we state the necessary results from [4, 5] for our purposes. Let $\bar{\ell}$ denote the mean length of a leg and A the area of the domain $\mathcal{A}$. Define

$$h(\mathbf{r}, \phi) = \frac{1}{2} \cdot a_1 a_2 (a_1 + a_2),$$

where $a_1 = a_1(\mathbf{r}, \phi)$ denotes the distance from $\mathbf{r} \in \mathcal{A}$ to the border of $\mathcal{A}$ in direction ϕ, and a_2 denotes the distance to the border in the opposite direction. The stationary distribution of an RWP node is given by (see [4])

$$f(\mathbf{r}) = \frac{1}{C} \int_0^{2\pi} h(\mathbf{r}, \phi) \, d\phi = \frac{h(\mathbf{r})}{C}, \qquad \text{where } C = \bar{\ell} A^2. \tag{1}$$

The mean arrival rate into a subset $\mathcal{A}_j \subset \mathcal{A}$ is given by [5]

$$\lambda(\mathcal{A}_j) = \int_{\partial \mathcal{A}_j} \lambda(\mathbf{r}, \theta(d\mathbf{r})) \, d\mathbf{r}, \tag{2}$$

where $\theta(d\mathbf{r})$ is the direction of the tangent at point $\mathbf{r}$, and

$$\lambda(\mathbf{r}, \theta) = \frac{1}{C \cdot \mathrm{E}[1/v]} \int_0^\pi \sin \phi \cdot h(\mathbf{r}, \theta + \phi) \, d\phi.$$

For **unit disk** the pdf of node location, denoted by $f(r)$ with $r = |\mathbf{r}|$, is given by

$$f(r) = \frac{2(1 - r^2)}{C} \int_0^\pi \sqrt{1 - r^2 \cos \phi} \, d\phi, \tag{3}$$

where $C = 128\pi/45 \approx 8.936$ [4]. Let $\lambda(r, d)$ denote the mean arrival rate into a disk with a radius of d located r units from the origin. Using (2) gives

$$\lambda(r, d) = \frac{45/64}{\pi \, \mathrm{E}[1/v]} \int_{\alpha_0}^\pi d\alpha \, d(1 - x^2) \int_0^\pi d\phi \, \sin \phi \sqrt{1 - x^2 \cos^2(\phi + \alpha - \beta)}, \tag{4}$$

where $x^2 = r^2 + 2rd \cos \alpha + d^2$, $\beta = \arctan(r + d \cos \alpha, d \sin \alpha)$, and

$$\alpha_0 = \begin{cases} 0, & \text{when } r + d < 1, \\ \arccos \frac{1 - r^2 - d^2}{2rd}, & \text{when } r - d < 1 \leq r + d, \\ \pi & \text{otherwise.} \end{cases}$$

For the special case $r = 0$ we have $x = d$, $\alpha_0 = 0$ and $\alpha = \beta$ yielding

$$\lambda(d) = \frac{45 \cdot d(1 - d^2)}{64 \cdot \mathrm{E}[1/v]} \int_0^\pi \sin \phi \cdot \sqrt{1 - d^2 \cos^2 \phi} \, d\phi. \tag{5}$$

3.   Analytical Approximations for Connectivity

We study k-connectivity and focus on the case where the movement of the nodes is restricted to a unit disk. In particular, we are interested in the probability that a network with n nodes is k-connected at an arbitrary point of time and denote this by $C_{n,k}(d)$, where d is the transmission range. A network is said to be (1-)connected if there exists a path between all node pairs, and k-connected if for each node pair at least k node disjoint paths exist. Due to the assumed circular shape, the node distribution depends only on the distance $r = |\mathbf{r}|$ from the center, as given by (3). The coverage area of each node is also assumed to be circular with a radius of d and is denoted by $B_d(\mathbf{r})$. Note that in principle, the domain of movement can be any convex region, and our general result (1) on the pdf $f(\cdot)$ holds. The approximations presented below depend on the shape of the domain through $f(\cdot)$ and thus hold for any convex region.

Approximation 1: Denote by $Q_{n,k}(d)$ the probability that an arbitrary node has at least k neighbors. Consider an arbitrarily chosen node and condition on its location, denoted by $\mathbf{r}$. Let $p(r, d)$ denote the probability that a given node is within $B_d(\mathbf{r})$, where we emphasize that this probability depends only on the distance $r = |\mathbf{r}|$ from the center. We can express $p(r, d)$ as

$$p(r, d) = \int_{\mathbf{x} \in B_d(\mathbf{r})} f(|\mathbf{x}|)\, dA,$$

where $\mathbf{x}$ denotes the vector for the location of a point inside $B_d(\mathbf{r})$. With a probability of $1 - p(r, d)$ the arbitrary node is outside $B_d(\mathbf{r})$. Since all nodes are independent, the number of other nodes within domain $B_d(\mathbf{r})$ obeys a binomial distribution, $N_{r,d} \sim \mathrm{Bin}(n - 1, p(r, d))$, and the probability that a given node is connected to at least k nodes equals

$$1 - \sum_{i=0}^{k-1} \binom{n-1}{i} \cdot p(r, d)^i \cdot (1 - p(r, d))^{n-1-i}.$$

With the RWP model in unit disk the probability density that a node is at a distance r from the center is $2\pi r f(r)$, and $Q_{n,k}(d)$ is given by

$$Q_{n,k}(d) = 2\pi \int_0^1 r f(r) \left(1 - \sum_{i=0}^{k-1} \binom{n-1}{i} p(r, d)^i (1 - p(r, d))^{n-1-i} \right) dr, \quad (6)$$

which is an exact result. As in [11], we approximate k-connectivity by

$$C_{n,k}(d) = \mathrm{P}\{n \text{ nodes are } k\text{-connected}\} \approx (Q_{n,k}(d))^n. \quad (7)$$

Note that for $n{=}2$ and $k{=}1$ one should use the exact result $C_{2,1}(d){=}Q_{2,1}(d)$ given by (6) instead.

The formal motivation of this approximation is as follows. As remarked in [7], for uniformly distributed random points, the asymptotics of the greatest edge length in the nearest neighbor graph are as if the nearest-neighbor distances were independent, and the longest edge is likely to be the same for the nearest neighbor graph and the minimum spanning tree. Because this holds for normally distributed points [9], the same can be expected to hold for more general spatial distributions. Here, we make the additional assumption that this generalizes to k-connectivity and the k-nearest neighbor graph. Note that $Q_{n,k}(d)$ can, as a function of d, be interpreted as the cumulative distribution function of a single k-nearest-neighbor distance. Hence $(Q_{n,k}(d))^n$ is the cumulative distribution of the maximum of n such i.i.d. k-nearest-neighbor distances, and by the above, this is approximated to be the distribution for the greatest k-nearest-neighbor distance. The final approximation then sets this distribution equal to that of the threshold range for k-connectivity.

Approximation 2: A more simple approximation can be developed by also making an approximation in computing the probability that a certain number of nodes exist within the coverage area of a given node. More specifically, we make a local Poisson assumption and assume that the nodes within the coverage area $B_d(\mathbf{r})$ result from a homogeneous Poisson point process with intensity $\lambda = f(\mathbf{r})$, i.e., the number of nodes within $B_d(\mathbf{r})$ obeys a Poisson distribution with mean equal to λ times the area of $B_d(\mathbf{r})$.

Similarly as in the case of Approximation 1, we condition on the location of a single node, and have a superposition of $n-1$ identical Poisson point processes yielding a total intensity of $(n-1) \cdot f(\mathbf{r})$ per unit area. Consequently, the number of nodes residing in $B_d(\mathbf{r})$ obeys a Poisson distribution with mean

$$a(r) = (n-1)\pi d^2 \cdot f(\mathbf{r}), \qquad (8)$$

and the probability that the number of nodes within $B_d(\mathbf{r})$ is less than k is given by $\sum_{i=0}^{k-1} \frac{a(r)^i}{i!} e^{-a(r)}$. Thus, our approximatation for $Q_{n,k}(d)$ is

$$\hat{Q}_{n,k}(d) = 1 - 2\pi \int_0^1 r\, f(r) \sum_{i=0}^{k-1} \frac{a(r)^i}{i!} \cdot e^{-a(r)}\, dr. \qquad (9)$$

In the above, it is assumed that the coverage area is a full circle even on the border of the RWP domain. The limiting effect of the border can be taken into account by introducing a function $A(r, d)$ which gives the area of the intersection of the unit disk and a disk with radius d at a distance of r from the origin, $A(r, d) = |B_1(0) \cap B_d(\mathbf{r})|$. With this notation the slightly more accurate approximation for $a(r)$ can be expressed as

$$a(r) = (n-1) \cdot A(r, d) \cdot f(\mathbf{r}). \qquad (10)$$

Finally, we use the same approximation for the probability of k-connectivity as in (7), i.e., $C_{n,k}(d) \approx (\hat{Q}_{n,k}(d))^n$.

Length of Connectivity Periods

Another important performance measure is the mean time the network remains connected. Let random variables T_c and T_d denote the lengths of the time periods the network is connected and disconnected, respectively. Clearly,

$$C_{n,1}(d) = P\{n \text{ nodes are 1-connected}\} = \frac{\bar{T}_c}{\bar{T}_c + \bar{T}_d}. \qquad (11)$$

As we are interested in $\bar{T}_c$, knowledge of $C_{n,1}(d)$ and $\bar{T}_d$ is sufficient. For small values of d the network is disconnected with high probability, but as d increases beyond a critical value (depends on n) the probability of connectivity starts to increase rapidly. In practise, this is perhaps the most interesting region, where, when n is large, typically only one node is separated from the network when the network becomes disconnected. We propose estimating $\bar{T}_d$ by the mean interarrival time of nodes into a disk $B_d(\mathbf{r})$ (radius d, center r units away from the origin). Recall that, $\lambda(r, d)$ denotes the arrival rate of a single node into a disk $B_d(\mathbf{r})$, and using either (4) or (5), as the case may be, one can compute $\lambda(r, d)$. Let $\bar{T}_d^{(r)}$ denote the mean disconnectivity time on condition that a single node gets isolated at point r, which we can estimate by

$$\bar{T}_d^{(r)} \approx \hat{T}_d^{(r)} = \frac{1}{(n-1) \cdot \lambda(r, d)}.$$

Next we approximate $\bar{T}_d$ by $\hat{T}_d^{(r)}$ with some r,

$$\bar{T}_d \approx \hat{T}_d^{(r)} \qquad (12)$$

or in general case by the integral

$$\bar{T}_d \approx \int_r T_d^{(r)} \cdot g(r)\, dr, \qquad (13)$$

where $g(r)$ corresponds to the probability that the isolated node is located at the distance of r from the origin. Note that in (12) and (13) we assume that disconnectivity is due to one isolated node. In (12) we are parameterizing the approximation with respect to the distance r from the center, and in the numerical experiments we use $r = 0$ and $r = 1$, which imply that we assume that the network network typically becomes disconnected when a single node gets isolated either at the center ($r = 0$) or on the border ($r = 1$). In (13) we assume some distribution for the location of the isolated node, and in the numerical experiments we use the uniform distribution, $g(r) = 2\pi r(1/\pi) = 2r$. Finally, combining the above with (7) gives us an estimate for $\bar{T}_c$:

$$\bar{T}_c = \frac{C_{n,1}(d)}{1 - C_{n,1}(d)} \bar{T}_d \approx \frac{p^n}{1 - p^n} \cdot \hat{T}_d, \qquad (14)$$

where p denotes the probability that a node has at least one neighbor, $p = Q_{n,1}(d)$.

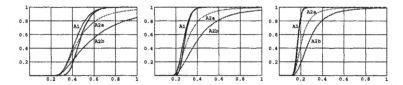

Figure 1. Validation of 1-connectivity for $n = 20, 100, 500$ nodes (from left to right) as a function of d, dashed lines depict simulations and solid lines analytical results.

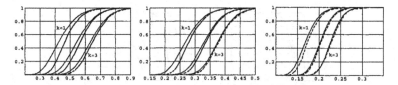

Figure 2. Validation of k-connectivity for $n = 20, 100, 500$ nodes (from left to right) as a function of d, dashed lines depict simulations and solid lines analytical results.

4. Numerical Examples

Probability of Connectivity

First we compare the accuracy of the approximations for 1-connectivity for the different number of nodes n. We refer as A1 to Approximation 1. Approximation 2 contains two approximations and they are referred to as A2a and A2b, where A2a refers to the approximation with $a(r)$ given by (8), i.e., the domain $B_d(\mathbf{r})$ is a full circle even at the border, and A2b refers to the approximation with $a(r)$ given by (10), i.e., the "border effect" is taken into account. The results are shown in Fig. 1, where the dashed lines correspond to simulated results and solid lines to the approximations (as indicated in the figures). As can be seen, A1 is remarkably accurate as n increases. Also, both A2a and A2b are able to predict well the initial rise, but they do not rise as steeply as they should. Somewhat surprisingly, the more detailed approximation A2b which includes the proper handling of the border effect, is less accurate than the simpler A2a.

The results for 2- and 3-connectivity are shown in Fig. 2, where in each graph we show simultaneously 1-, 2- and 3-connectivity as a function of d. In the simulations the k-connectivity has been determined using the algorithms from [12]. The results only compare the accuracy of A1 (solid lines) to simulated results (dashed lines) as the accuracy of A2a and A2b is similar to that already shown before. It can be seen that A1 is very close to the simulated values as n increases, and the higher the value of k the better the fit.

Finally, we compare A1 with the approximation given in [11], where the aim has been to study connectivity in large networks. Fig. 3 shows the results of 1-connectivity for A1 (solid lines), the approximation from [11] (dotted lines)

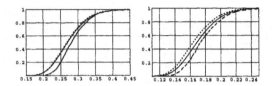

Figure 3.   Comparison of the accuracy of A1 (solid lines) and the approximation in [11] (dotted lines) against simulations (dashed lines) for $n = 100, 500$ (left, right) nodes.

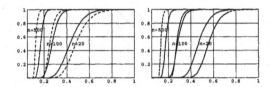

Figure 4.   Comparisons for $C_{n,1}(d)$ with RWP node distribution (solid lines) and uniform node distribution (dashed lines) using our approximations (left) and simulations (right).

and simulations (dashed lines) for $n=100$ nodes (left figure) and $n=500$ nodes (right figure). As can be seen, A1 is more accurate, especially for $n=500$.

Next we compare the impact on 1-connectivity of a **uniform vs. the RWP node location distribution**. The analytical results for the RWP case correspond to approximation A1, and the results for the uniform case are obtained from A1 by using $f(r) = 1/\pi$. The results are shown in Fig. 4, where the figure on the left contains results obtained by using our analytical approximations, and the figure on the right contains the corresponding simulated results. Each figure depicts $C_{n,1}(d)$ as a function of d for $n = 20, 100, 500$. Solid lines correspond to connectivity under RWP node distribution and dashed lines to connectivity under uniform node distribution. It can be seen that the mobility induced by the RWP model can either improve or degrade the connectivity probability depending on the number of nodes. In particular, for small number of nodes, connectivity properties gain from mobility. However, as the number of nodes is increased, the situation becomes the opposite. This phenomenon occurring in the simulations is also captured by our analytical approximations although numerical accuracy is not perfect for small number of nodes.

Mean Length of Connectivity Periods

In Fig. 5 the estimated mean lengths of the connectivity periods are depicted as a function of d and compared against simulations, when the speed is constant, $v = 1$, and the number of nodes $n = 20, 100, 500$. Simulation results are indicated with dashed lines and triangle markers. Lines with square

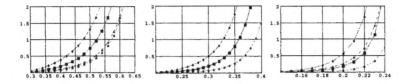

Figure 5. Mean connectivity period length for $n = 20$, 100, 500 nodes (from left to right). Dashed curves corresponds to simulated results and solid curves to estimates.

markers correspond to our approximation where we have assumed a uniform location for isolated node. Lines with star markers correspond to our approximation with $\bar{T}_d \approx \hat{T}_d^{(0)}$, i.e., that a node becomes most likely disconnected in the center. Lines with diamond markers correspond to our approximation with $\bar{T}_d \approx \hat{T}_d^{(1)}$, i.e., that a node becomes most likely disconnected on the border. The results show that in the interesting region, where connectivity probability rises steeply, using $\bar{T}_d \approx \hat{T}_d^{(0)}$ and $\bar{T}_d \approx \hat{T}_d^{(1)}$ act as if they were lower and upper bounds for the mean connectivity durations, while the approximation with uniform assumption for the isolated node gives rather accurate results.

Finally we study how the **velocity distribution** affects the mean length of the connectivity period. Note that as the quantity $\lambda(r, d)$ is inversely proportional to quantity $E[1/v]$, our approximation (14) is directly proportional to quantity $E[1/v]$. In Fig. 6 the simulation results with three different velocity distributions are illustrated for $n = 20, 100, 500$ nodes, i) $v = 1$ (i.e., constant), ii) $v \sim U(0.1, 1.9)$ (i.e., $\bar{v} = 1$), and iii) $v \sim U(0.356, 2.156)$ (i.e., $E[1/v] \approx 1$). Diamond markers correspond to i), star markers to ii), and square markers to iii). It can be seen that with $n = 20, 100, 500$ nodes i) and iii) are almost identical, while ii) generally leads to longer connectivity durations. Also note that the relative difference in the results for ii) and cases i,iii) is close to $E[1/v] \approx 1.64$, in agreement with our approach.

5. Conclusions

In this paper, we have studied the connectivity properties of ad hoc networks where the nodes move according to the RWP mobility model. Analytical approximations have been given for estimating the probability that a network consisting of n nodes is k-connected based on estimating the probability that the network has minimum degree k. The approximations were validated by numerical simulations showing remarkably good agreement.

Additionally, we have also studied the mean lengths of the connectivity periods, for which we have given an (parameterized) approximation, which utilizes the results on the arrival rate of the RWP process into a given subset area. The

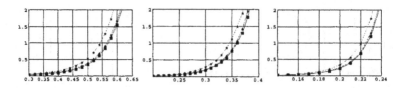

Figure 6.   Mean connectivity period length for $n = 20,\ 100,\ 500$ nodes (from left to right) with different velocity distributions.

numerical results show that in the interesting region where connectivity probability rises steeply, approximation works fairly well. Furthermore, according to our approach the mean length of the connectivity period is directly proportional to quantity $E[1/v]$, which matches well with the numerical experiments.

References

[1] C. Bettstetter, G. Resta, and P. Santi, "The node distribution of the random waypoint mobility model for wireless ad hoc networks," *IEEE Trans. on Mobile Computing*, vol. 2, no. 1, pp. 25–39, 2003.

[2] J. Yoon, M. Liu, and B. Noble, "Random waypoint considered harmful," in *Proceedings of IEEE INFOCOM*, San Fransisco, California, USA, April 2003, pp. 1312–1321.

[3] W. Navidi and T. Camp, "Stationary distributions for the random waypoint mobility model," *IEEE Trans. on Mobile Computing*, vol. 3, no. 1, pp. 99–108, 2004.

[4] Esa Hyytiä, Pasi Lassila, and Jorma Virtamo, "Spatial node distribution in the random waypoint mobility model with applications," submitted for publication, available at http://www.netlab.tkk.fi/julkaisut/bib/, Mar. 2005.

[5] Esa Hyytiä and Jorma Virtamo, "Random waypoint mobility model in cellular networks," *ACM/Kluwer Wireless Networks*, 2005, to appear.

[6] M. Sánchez, P. Manzoni, and Z. J. Haas, "Determination of critical transmission range in Ad-Hoc networks," in *Proceedings of Multiaccess Mobility and Teletraffic for Wireless Communications 1999 Workshop (MMT'99)*, Oct. 1999.

[7] M. D. Penrose, "The longest edge of the random minimal spanning tree," *Annals of Applied Probability*, vol. 7, no. 2, pp. 340–361, 1997.

[8] M. D. Penrose, "On k-connectivity for a geometric random graph," *Random Structures and Algorithms*, vol. 15, no. 2, pp. 145–164, 1999.

[9] M. D. Penrose, "Extremes for the minimal spanning tree on normally distributed points," *Advances in Applied Probability*, vol. 30, no. 3, pp. 628–639, 1998.

[10] Peng-Jun Wan and Chih-Wei Yi, "Asymptotic critical transmission radius and critical neighbor number for k-connectivity in wireless ad hoc networks," in *Proceedings of ACM MobiHoc '04*. 2004, pp. 1–8, ACM Press.

[11] Christian Bettstetter, "On the connectivity of Ad Hoc networks," *Computer Journal*, vol. 47, no. 4, pp. 432–447, July 2004.

[12] H. Koskinen, "A simulation-based method for predicting connectivity in wireless multihop networks," *Telecommunication Systems*, vol. 26, no. 2-4, pp. 321–338, June 2004.

ON IMPROVING CONNECTIVITY OF STATIC AD-HOC NETWORKS BY ADDING NODES*

Henri Koskinen[t], Jouni Karvo[‡], and Olli Apilo[§]
Helsinki University of Technology (TKK), Networking Laboratory
P.O. Box 3000, FIN-02015 TKK, Finland
{Henri.Koskinen, Jouni.Karvo, Olli.Apilo}@tkk.fi

1.   Introduction

Ad hoc networks are by nature constructed "automatically", by the nodes adapting to the neighboring nodes and building up a network. In this context, the network topology is random, and in particular, no connectivity is guaranteed: the nodes may be so sparsely located that they are unable to make up a connected network.

This has motivated a wide range of research, with a primary interest in the connectivity of random networks. In this paper however, we are concerned with what can be done when an ad hoc network needs to be formed but the users are too far apart to form a network with a desired level of connectivity. More precisely, we study the option of improving the connectivity of a static ad-hoc network by carrying extraneous nodes to the scene. The problem is where to put these nodes so as to minimize the number of nodes required for a connected network, or to maximize the utility of the network. We present algorithms that suggest locations for such additional nodes. Networks where adding extraneous nodes is feasible are some sensor networks and such ad-hoc networks that are used in a controlled situation where some central entity can organize the deployment of the nodes. To our knowledge, the connectivity problem in ad hoc networks has not been addressed so far from this practical viewpoint.

This paper is organized as follows: in the next section we describe the problem setting and the underlying assumptions, and define essentially two opti-

*We thank the anonymous reviewers of this paper for their constructive suggestions, and Petteri Kaski (TKK) for pointing out the reference [2].
[t] Financially supported by the Finnish Defence Forces Technical Research Centre and in part by a grant from the Nokia Foundation.
[‡] Funded by the EU FP6-507572 project WIDENS.
[§] Funded by the Academy of Finland (grant n:o 202204).

mization problems for the node addition. Section 3 describes the first heuristic algorithm, the Minimum Spanning Tree algorithm. A more efficient algorithm, the Greedy Tessellation algorithm is presented in Section 4, and the last and most evolved algorithm, the Greedy Triangle algorithm in Section 5. Section 6 contains performance analysis of the algorithms, aided by simulation results. Finally, Section 7 concludes the paper with some final remarks.

2.   Problem Statements

The motivation for our problem stems from an emergency scenario. We consider a group of agents, e.g. fire fighters, deployed in some region, who need to establish communications in the form of an ad hoc network. For this purpose, each agent is equipped with a terminal device; from now on, we will refer to these devices as *terminal nodes*. In support of forming the network, there is a team in possession of additional transceivers that can be used as relays in the network; we will call these transceivers *relay nodes*. We assume that both the terminal nodes and the relay nodes are based on same standard hardware and therefore have equal transmission and reception capabilities. The task of the support team is to place relay nodes in the region so that the terminal nodes and the relay nodes together can form a connected wireless multihop network where each link can provide a desired rate of communication to support the service required by the agents, say, a speech application. The problem we are interested in is to optimize the points where the support team should place relay nodes, given the locations of the terminal nodes.

The key assumptions behind our problem statement are that the locations of the terminal nodes are known and that the location information of these nodes can be collected even though the network is not connected. The motivation behind the latter assumption is that depending on the solutions on the physical layer, it can be possible to be able to sustain low bitrate communications over much further distance than to provide quality of service. In this case, the network is able to convey control information even if efficient communications are not possible. In other words, in this problem we define connectivity using a linkwise throughput requirement.

We use the commonly studied Boolean model for the network. Within this model, any two nodes are assumed to be directly bidirectionally connected if and only if they are within a common transmission range from each other.

Formally, we assume that the network deployment region (where the terminal nodes are located and the relay nodes may be placed) is a bounded convex subset S of the Euclidean space $\mathbb{R}^d$, $d > 1$. In all the problems that we are about to define, the problem instance is completely defined by the set of locations of N terminal nodes, $\mathcal{N} = \{\mathbf{x}_i \in S \,|\, i = 1, 2, \ldots, N\}$, and the transmission range r. Together these imply the pre-existing network topology in the form of an undirected geometric graph $\mathcal{G}(\mathcal{N}, \mathcal{E}(\mathcal{N}, r)) = \mathcal{G}(\mathcal{N}, r)$ with vertex set $\mathcal{N}$ and edge set $\mathcal{E}(\mathcal{N}, r) = \{(\mathbf{x}_i, \mathbf{x}_j) \mid \mathbf{x}_i, \mathbf{x}_j \in \mathcal{N}, i \neq j, \|\mathbf{x}_i - \mathbf{x}_j\| \leq r\}$.

A solution to any of the problems is a set of locations to place relay nodes, $\mathcal{N}_r = \{\mathbf{y}_i \in \mathcal{S} \mid i = 1, 2, \ldots, N_r\}$. Given a configuration of terminal and relay nodes $\mathcal{N} \bigcup \mathcal{N}_r$ and transmission range r, we call a *cluster* the set of all *terminal nodes* in a single maximal connected component in the graph $\mathcal{G}(\mathcal{N} \bigcup \mathcal{N}_r, r)$.

We are hereby ready to define the first optimisation problem:

> **Problem 1** Given $\mathcal{N}$ and r, find $\mathcal{N}_r$ with minimum cardinality that makes the graph $\mathcal{G}(\mathcal{N} \bigcup \mathcal{N}_r, r)$ connected.

We point out that in the limit $r \to 0$, this problem reduces to finding the Euclidean Steiner minimal tree for the set $\mathcal{N}$: the optimal solution is then to place the relay nodes along the edges of this tree. Finding Steiner minimal trees is known to be **NP**-hard [3]. In the general case, our problem poses the additional complications that we are not connecting single points to each other, but clusters where the best points in the clusters for connecting to other clusters must be chosen, and that the objective function has been discretized from the total length of edges in the Steiner tree to the number of added relay nodes. In the following, we suggest heuristic algorithms that are suboptimal but give results without excessive computing requirements.

A greedy approach to solving the problem is to add new relay nodes trying to get as good an improvement as possible in each step, until the connectivity target has been met. A utility metric is required for this approach, and it should reflect how close we are to achieving the target. The utility metric is also needed for cases where it is not possible to make the network connected, due to having too few relay nodes available. This gives rise to the second problem:

> **Problem 2** Find $\mathcal{N}_r$ that maximizes the chosen utility metric U, subject to $N_r \leq N_r^{\max} \in \mathbb{Z}_+$.

Provided that the constraint $N_r \leq N_r^{\max}$ actually prevents us from achieving connectivity, this problem can be viewed as the maximization of the chosen utility metric in $\mathcal{S}^{N_r^{\max}}$. This is a difficult task but allows applying, e.g., simulated annealing. Our algorithms can readily be used for greedy approaches to Problem 2 as well as Problem 1.

The choice of the utility metric depends on the target application. In all examples and simulations where applicable in this paper, we have used the number of nodes in the biggest cluster after each step as the utility metric.

3. Minimum Spanning Tree Algorithm

Our first algorithm arises naturally if we only require that each relay node or contiguous chain of relay nodes connect exactly two clusters of the graph

$\mathcal{G}(\mathcal{N}, r)$. Under this limitation, the optimal solution is to place the relay nodes along the edges of the Euclidean minimum spanning tree (MST) calculated for the clusters, when the distance between two clusters is defined as the shortest distance between two terminal nodes in these distinct clusters.

In fact, it is not difficult to show that this MST consists of exactly those edges that are longer than the transmission range r, in the MST calculated for all the terminal nodes. This can be seen by considering Kruskal's algorithm for finding the MST (see e.g. [4]).

The steps of the algorithm are thus as follows:

1 Calculate the Euclidean minimum spanning tree for $\mathcal{N}$.

2 Place the relay nodes on the edges of the minimum spanning tree that are longer than r. If there are too few relay nodes available to span all such edges, select the edges that result in maximizing the chosen utility metric.

In two dimensions, step 1 can be completed in $O(N \log N)$ time by utilizing the Delaunay triangulation; when $d = 3$, the complexity of finding the minimum spanning tree has at least been brought down to $O(N^{4/3} \log^{4/3} N)$ [1]. In a higher number of dimensions, step 1 is likely to require exhaustively calculating the distance matrix of the terminal nodes, which is a quadratic task. Step 2 is linear in N if all the necessary edges can be spanned, since the whole minimum spanning tree has $N - 1$ edges. If, on the other hand, not all necessary edges can be spanned, the optimal selection of edges generally requires going through all possibilities. In this case, we propose the greedy method of selecting edges in the order of added utility (with respect to the initial clusters) per used relay node. In this method, the initial clusters can be found in linear time by traversing the minimum spanning tree (edges longer than r in the tree separate different clusters), and rating and sorting the $O(N)$ potential edges takes $O(N \log N)$ time. With this approach, the overall complexity of the algorithm is in any case determined by step 1.

The Minimum Spanning Tree algorithm is illustrated in Figure 1.

4.   Greedy Tessellation Algorithm

The stricter requirement that a single relay node should, when possible, connect more than two clusters suggests points that are equally distant from several clusters as potential points of placement. Such points can be found from the Voronoi tessellation (or Voronoi diagram) of the nodes: see [1] for a rather comprehensive survey on Voronoi diagrams.

What makes the Voronoi tessellation interesting for our problem is that it efficiently captures the geometric neighbor relationships of the nodes: points equally distant from three clusters are a subset of the vertices, i.e. the coincid-

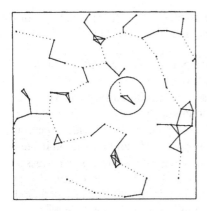

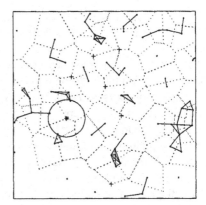

Figure 1. Minimum Spanning Tree algorithm. The initial clusters in this example realization of 70 terminal nodes are connected with solid edges, and the edges to place relay nodes are dotted. The transmission range is 10% of the side of the domain, as illustrated by the circle.

Figure 2. The Greedy Tessellation algorithm, applied to the same realization as in Figure 1. The edges of the Voronoi tessellation are shown with dotted lines, the candidate points for relay node insertion with '+'-signs. The first location to add a relay node is marked with an asterisk.

ing corners of the convex sets also called cells, of the Voronoi tessellation of the nodes. Note that in practise, points equally distant to more than three nodes do not exist. However, placing a relay node at a vertex close to other vertices may well result in connecting more than three clusters.

For this reason, we examine coinciding corners of Voronoi cells that contain nodes all in different clusters, and the corner where inserting a new node yields the maximal increase in the chosen utility metric is selected as the place to insert the next relay node. To sum up:

1. Find the maximal connected components and clusters of the graph $\mathcal{G}(\mathcal{N} \bigcup \mathcal{N}_r, r)$. (Initially, $\mathcal{N}_r = \emptyset$.)

2. Construct the Voronoi tessellation of $\mathcal{N} \bigcup \mathcal{N}_r$.

3. Regard as candidate points the coinciding corners of such Voronoi cells that contain nodes all in different connected components, excluding corners further than r from the nodes and corners not in $\mathcal{S}$.

4. Add to $\mathcal{N}_r$ the candidate point that yields maximal increase in the chosen utility metric.

5. If there were more than one candidate points in step 3 and the problem constraints allow further addition of points, go to step 1.

6 If allowed by the constraints and the graph $\mathcal{G}(\mathcal{N} \bigcup \mathcal{N}_r, r)$ is not yet connected, finish with the Minimum Spanning Tree algorithm.

The last step is required since connected components can be too far apart to be connected with the addition of a single relay node.

Our complexity analysis is mainly based on results gathered in [1]. On the first run through steps 1–5, step 1 amounts to finding and traversing the minimum spanning tree of the nodes, as described in the previous section. The computational complexity of constructing the Voronoi tessellation in step 2 is $O(N \log N)$ in the plane, quadratic in three dimensions, and increases exponentially with the number of dimensions, along with the maximal size of a diagram. The number of vertices in the tessellation to consider potential candidate points in steps 3 and 4 is $O(N)$ in the plane and $O(N^2)$ in $\mathbb{R}^3$.

On subsequent rounds, the addition of new points to $\mathcal{N}_r$ can be updated to the connected components and the tessellation without having to find them from scratch. Updating the tessellation is the more complicated task but takes only $O(n)$ time, where $n = N + N_r$, when $d = 2$ or $d = 3$. Although updating the candidate points should also be a light task, the increase in utility must still be checked for each one in step 4, on every round. The number of rounds made (i.e., the number N_r before proceeding to the last step) with fixed N depends on the density of the network: a very sparse network is unlikely to result in any addition due to too large distances between clusters, as is a very dense network due to a high probability of being connected. With fixed average density of terminal nodes and transmission range, the number of additions is $O(N)$, since it is bounded by the number of initial clusters.

As a conclusion, because of the $O(N)$ repetitions of step 4, the overall running time of this algorithm before the final step is $O(N^2)$ in $\mathbb{R}^2$ and $O(N^3)$ in $\mathbb{R}^3$, which also dominates the final step. Figure 2 illustrates the algorithm.

5.   Greedy Triangle Algorithm

The Greedy Tessellation algorithm uses points that are equally distant from different clusters as potential places for relay nodes. However, with a closer look we see that this is not always optimal: for example, the point marked in Figure 2 as the place for the first relay node falls outside the triangle spanned by the three terminal nodes to be connected, meaning that it cannot be the optimal place for a relay node to connect the three terminal nodes (optimal in the sense that the range required from the relay node to connect the terminal nodes is minimized). Hence, taking only the vertices of the Voronoi tessellation into account, one may not find all the places where connecting three clusters with a single relay node is possible.

Having made this observation, we may simply select triplets of nodes where the nodes are pairwise at most $2r$ apart and all belong to different clusters, as corners of *candidate triangles*. The point equally distant from the corners of a candidate triangle is a candidate point for node insertion only if this point is inside the triangle; if the point is outside the triangle, the midpoint of the longest side of the triangle is the candidate point (see Figure 3(a) and compare with Figure 2). Finally, it needs to be checked whether the distance from the candidate point to each corner of the triangle is less than r. Of these feasible candidate points, the one yielding the maximal increase in the chosen utility metric is chosen as the location of the next added relay node.

It is of course possible for a single relay node to connect more than three distinct clusters. The occurrence of such cases is, however, rare, and thus deliberately seeking these cases is omitted in order to simplify the algorithm. It should be noted however that a proper candidate triangle can still result in connecting more than three clusters.

This method is easily extended to handle triangles whose vertices are too far apart to be connected by a single relay node. The idea is to place two nodes optimally in order to connect the clusters. Consider an addition of two nodes, targeting in connecting three clusters: find a candidate triangle with no side longer than $4r$, and find jointly optimal points for two relay nodes (optimality being defined as above). Where to add these two nodes optimally is divided into different cases, depending on the shape of the triangle; we omit the analysis of these cases in this paper due to space limitations.

Like the Greedy Tessellation algorithm, this algorithm must also be finished with the Minimum Spanning Tree algorithm. The Greedy Triangle algorithm has thus the following phases:

1. Find the maximal connected components and clusters of the graph $\mathcal{G}(\mathcal{N}, r)$, and the candidate triangles.

2. Find the point (if any exist) where adding a single relay node results in connecting the candidate triangle that yields the maximal increase in the chosen utility metric, and add this point to $\mathcal{N}_r$. Maintaining the connected components, the clusters, and the candidate triangles, repeat this as long as new candidate triangles can be connected and the problem constraints permit.

3. Repeat the previous step, now adding to $\mathcal{N}_r$ pairs of points where relay nodes connect candidate triangles.

4. If allowed by the constraints and the graph $\mathcal{G}(\mathcal{N} \bigcup \mathcal{N}_r, r)$ is not yet connected, finish with the Minimum Spanning Tree algorithm.

The Greedy Triangle algorithm can be used as such in a Euclidean space with an arbitrary number of dimensions. However, because among n nodes there are altogether $\Theta(n^3)$ triplets of nodes, it is again a good idea to utilize the geometric neighbor relationships of the nodes in finding sensible candidate triangles,

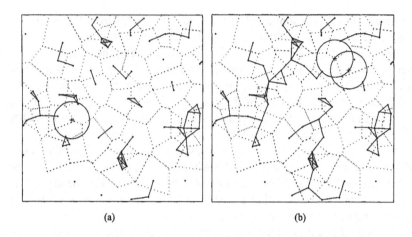

(a)   (b)

Figure 3.   Applying the Greedy Triangle algorithm to the realization of Figure 1. (a): The first point to place a relay node, as determined in step 2 and indicated by the '+'-sign. Note the difference from Figure 2 in the placement. (b): The first pair of points to place relay nodes, as determined in step 3, after several relay nodes have been added in step 2. Note that in this case, four clusters are connected.

at least in the two-dimensional case. In this case, we propose requiring that at most one pair in any considered triplet of nodes not have neighboring cells in the Voronoi tessellation of the nodes, which limits the number of triplets to examine down to $O(N)$. (We found requiring all three nodes to have pairwise neighboring cells, i.e. considering only the triangles in the Delaunay triangulation, too restrictive.) With this choice, the complexity of the algorithm is the same as that of the Greedy Tessellation algorithm, namely, $O(N^2)$ in $\mathbb{R}^2$ and $O(N^3)$ in $\mathbb{R}^3$. The phases of the algorithm are illustrated in Figure 3.

6.   Performance Analysis

In this section, we present and discuss results from applying our three algorithms to simulated realizations of randomly and uniformly distributed terminal nodes in a square-shaped domain in the plane. The purpose is partly to compare the performance of the algorithms relative to each other, and in part to gain some idea on how close to optimal their solutions are.

The latter is a problematic task, as finding the optimal solution for a general realization is very difficult. As mentioned in Section 2, when the transmission range is infinitely shrunk, the optimal solution to Problem 1 is to cover the edges of the Euclidean Steiner minimal tree for the terminal nodes with chains of relay nodes. In this limit, we know the so-called Steiner Ratio: for any set of points in the plane, the total edge length of their Euclidean minimum spanning tree is at most $2/\sqrt{3} \approx 1.15$ times the optimal solution, i.e. the total edge length of their Euclidean Steiner minimal tree [2]. However, with a non-negligible transmission range the case is completely different: as a simple example, consider a regular pentagon whose vertices are on a circle with radius equal to the transmission range, and assume one terminal node at each of these vertices. These initially disconnected terminal nodes can be connected with a single relay node placed at the center of the circle, whereas utilizing the minimum spanning tree results in placing four relay nodes.

Nonetheless, we used as a benchmark for our algorithms the method of placing the relay nodes on those edges of the Euclidean Steiner minimal tree that connect different clusters. This method should be close to optimal with sparse networks, i.e. when the transmission range is small compared to the typical distance between neighboring terminal nodes. Figure 4 shows the average number of relay nodes needed to connect random configurations with varying number of terminal nodes using each of the different algorithms. The transmission range was set to 10% of the side of the square domain, in order to demonstrate a "feasible" scenario where the number of relay nodes needed is still a fraction of the number of terminal nodes, making the addition of relay nodes sensible. As expected, our three algorithms produce gradually better solutions. The two greedy algorithms also outperform utilizing the Steiner tree with these parameters, as the Steiner minimal tree simply optimizes the wrong measure from our problem's viewpoint.

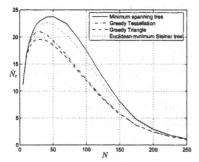

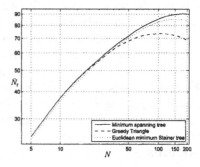

Figure 4. Average number of relay nodes needed to connect the network, as a function of the number of terminal nodes initially in the network, taken over 1000 random realizations. The transmission range is 10% of the side of the square-shaped domain.

Figure 5. Average number of relay nodes needed to connect the network, taken over 1000 random realizations and plotted on log-log -scale. The transmission range is 5% of the side of the domain. The Greedy Tessellation algorithm has been omitted for clarity.

The gain from utilizing the Steiner tree is captured in Figure 5 which shows corresponding results with the transmission range set to 5% of the side of the domain. In a very sparse initial network, the existence of suitable candidate triangles is unlikely, and the Greedy Triangle algorithm practically reduces to the Minimum Spanning Tree algorithm, while the Steiner tree yields the best results. As the density of the initial network increases, the Greedy Triangle algorithm surpasses the Steiner tree method in performance.

The quantity that best describes what we referred to as the density of the network is the average number of other terminal nodes directly connected to a random terminal node in the initial configuration. Not accounting for boundary effects, this quantity is given by $N/A \cdot \pi r^2$ where A is the area of the domain. In essence, this quantity determines which method yields the best results, and for example the two greedy algorithms bring significant advantage to using the MST at proper intermediate values of this quantity, when suitable candidate triangles are likely to exist. It is interesting to note in both figures that the average number of relay nodes needed increases with the number of terminal nodes up to the point where $N/A \cdot \pi r^2 \approx 1$: when $r^2/A = (10\%)^2$, this point is at $N \approx 32$, and with $r^2/A = (5\%)^2$ at $N \approx 127$. This is especially true with the two greedy algorithms.

7.   Discussion

We assumed throughout this paper that all the nodes have equal transmission range. It would also be reasonable to assume that the relay nodes can have a larger range when communicating with each other than when communicating with the terminal nodes. It takes only slight modifications to adjust our algorithms to this relaxed assumption.

We also precluded the mobility of terminal nodes in our assumptions. The approach of adding relay nodes in optimized locations has little application if all the terminal nodes tend to move all over the network region. However, by keeping track of the locations of terminal nodes over time, it should be possible to recognize those nodes that are nearly stationary and place relay nodes to connect these nodes. Studying this question is left as further work.

References

[1] F. Aurenhammer. Voronoi diagrams – a survey of a fundamental geometric data structure. *ACM Comput. Surv.*, 23(3):345–405, 1991.

[2] D.-Z. Du and F. Hwang. An approach for proving lower bounds: solution of Gilbert-Pollak's conjecture on Steiner ratio. In *Proceedings of 31st Annual Symposium on Foundations of Computer Science*, volume 1, pages 76–85, Oct. 1990.

[3] M. R. Garey, R. L. Graham, and D. S. Johnson. The complexity of computing Steiner minimal trees. *SIAM J. Appl. Math.*, 32(4):835–859, June 1977.

[4] R. Sedgewick. *Algorithms in C*. Addison Wesley, 1990.

THE CRITICAL NEIGHBOURHOOD RANGE FOR ASYMPTOTIC OVERLAY CONNECTIVITY IN DENSE AD HOC NETWORKS

Sandrine Calomme and Guy Leduc
Research Unit in Networking
Electrical Engineering and Computer Science Department
University of Liège, Belgium
Email: { calomme,leduc} @run.montefiore.ulg.ac.be

Abstract

We define, for an overlay built on top of an ad hoc network, a simple criterion for neighbourhood: two overlay nodes are neighbours if and only if there exists a path between them of at most R hops, and R is called the (overlay) neighbourhood range. A small R may result in a disconnected overlay, while an unnecessarily large R would generate extra control traffic. We are interested in the minimum R ensuring overlay connectivity, the so-called critical R.

We derive a necessary and sufficient condition on R to achieve asymptotic connectivity of the overlay almost surely, i.e. connectivity with probability 1 when the number of overlay nodes tends to infinity, under the hypothesis that the underlying ad hoc network is itself asymptotically almost surely connected.

This condition, though asymptotic, sheds some light on the relation linking the critical R to the number of nodes n, the normalized radio transmission range r and the overlay density D (i.e., the proportion of overlay nodes). This condition can be considered as an approximation when the number of nodes is large enough. Since r is considered as a function of n, we are able to study the impact of topology control mechanisms, by showing how the shape of this function impacts the critical R.

Keywords: ad hoc networks, overlay, connectivity, topology control

1. Introduction

In a previous work, we adopted an overlay approach for the introduction of the active technology in ad hoc networks [Calomme and Leduc, 2004]. The framework proposed allowed active nodes to inject customized routing protocols in the network to communicate all together, or to use any upper-layer active application, in order to improve the communication performance.

More generally, as most application of MANETs involve group communication [Mohapatra et al., 2004] and as grouping behaviour of the mobile users has been observed [Wang and Li, 2002; Tang and Baker, 2000], most wireless ad hoc networks can be seen as composed of one or several communities. The nodes of these communities can be characterized by a common specialized hardware, such as a sensor, or software, such as an active platform, or share a custom routing protocol or application. In all cases, they can use and take advantage of their common enhanced capabilities if and only if they are able to communicate efficiently through the other nodes, that is if and only if they are organized as an overlay.

Overlay advantages come however at the expense of the overlays creation, usage and maintenance, that must be kept moderate. Consequently, a full mesh is probably not the most adapted nor efficient solution for overlay applications. A natural rule of thumb is to admit as overlay neighbours a set of close overlay nodes, the distance measure employed being the number of hops. Two approaches are possible. One can fix the cardinality of the set of neighbours or the maximum number of hops admitted between overlay neighbours. We adopt the latter one. In this case, the maximum distance between two neighbours is an integer value that must be sufficiently high to obtain a connected overlay but as low as possible to limit the amount of messages generated in the network by overlay nodes communication.

The parallel with topology control in ad hoc networks is obvious. To achieve connectivity, each ad hoc node could use its maximum transmission range, in order to reach many neighbours. However, mobile devices have a limited amount of battery power. Moreover, this would create a lot of interferences, reducing the overall capacity of the network. With a homogeneous topology control algorithm, all nodes adopt the same transmitting range value. The critical transmitting range problem consists of determining the minimum value that generates a connected network. We have adopted a similar terminology for our problem: the maximum number of hops allowed between overlay neighbours is called the neighbourhood range and the determination of its best value the critical neighbourhood range problem.

This paper is structured as follows. In Sect. 2, we give an overview on previous related work over the critical transmission range. In Sect. 3, we precisely define the problem studied. In Sect. 4, we present analytical results and discuss some of their practical implications. We then conclude.

2.   Related Work

In many realistic scenarios, node positions are not known in advance. Hence a probabilistic approach is used in every analytical study of the critical transmission range problem.

First studies of graph connectivity were developed in the context of the random graphs theory. A random graph is a graph generated by some random procedure [Bollobas, 1985]. In 1960, Erdos and Rényi [Erdos and Rényi, 1960] showed that for many monotone-increasing properties of random graphs, like connectivity, graphs of a size slightly less than a certain threshold are very unlikely to have the property, whereas graphs with a few more graph edges are almost certain to have it. This is known as a phase transition phenomenon.

In classical random graph models, there is no *a priori* structure. All vertices are equivalent and there is no correlation between different edges existence. In ad hoc and sensor networks, nodes are more likely to be direct neighbours if they are located close to each other. Therefore random geometric graphs are more suited to model them. Random geometric graphs are constructed by placing points at random according to some arbitrary specified density function on a d-dimensional Euclidean space and connecting nearby points [Penrose, 2003]. Some of the geometric random graphs results can be applied in the study of connectivity in ad hoc and sensor networks [Penrose, 1999]. Various transition phenomena can also be observed in geometric random graphs [Krishnamachari et al., 2001]. Monotone properties for this class of graphs have sharp treshold [Goel et al., 2004]. Asymptotically, as the network density tends to infinity, a critical value transmission range can be established [Gupta and Kumar, 1999].

We are not aware of any work related to the critical (overlay) neighbourhood range problem. In the following sections, we define it in more details, and we solve it using known results on the critical transmission range problem cited above.

3.   Problem Definition and Discussion

We are interested in the asymptotic connectivity of overlay graphs built over asymptotically almost surely (a.a.s.) connected basic graphs.

These notions are defined in the following paragraphs. We then discuss the implicit assumptions we make in the problem and model specification.

Basic and Overlay Graphs

Consider an ad hoc network of n nodes, deployed over a square field of unitary area, and where each node is assigned a normalized transmission range of length r. This network is modelled by a random geometric graph denoted $g(n, r)$ which has the following properties.

The vertices of g are uniformly and independently distributed on the unitary square. They can either have been disseminated following the uniform distribution of n points or by a spatial homogeneous Poisson point process of mean n.

There exists an edge between each pair of vertices if and only if the Euclidean distance between them is not greater than r.

Let then $g(n, r)$ be a connected graph, D be a real number with $0 \leq D \leq 1$ and R be an integer with $R \geq 1$.

An overlay graph $G(n, r, D, R)$ denotes a graph with the following properties.

The D parameter represents the overlay nodes density. The number of vertices of G equals the lowest integer above a proportion D of the number of vertices of g. These are randomly and uniformly selected in the vertices set of g, which is called its basic graph.

The parameter R is called the neighbourhood range. There exists an edge between a pair of vertices (v_1, v_2) if and only if the shortest path in g from v_1 to v_2 contains less than or exactly R hops.

In the following, in conjunction with the ad hoc and sensor networks terminology, the vertices of an overlay graph will be referred to as overlay nodes and the vertices of its basic graph as nodes.

Asymptotic Connectivity

Let all graph parameters be a function of the number of nodes. For example, $r(n)$ can be decreasing when n increases, which is a desired behaviour for minimizing the capacity loss due to interferences.

A basic graph can be denoted by $g(n, r(n))$ and an overlay graph by $G(n, r(n), D(n), R(n))$ or $G(g, D(n), R(n))$. We may generally simply write $g(n, r)$, $G(n, r, D, R)$ or, if $g(n, r)$ is given, $G(g, D, R)$.

DEFINITION 1 *A graph is connected asymptotically almost surely (a.a.s.) if and only if the probability that it is connected tends to one as its number of vertices tends to infinity.*

Graph $\mathcal{G}$ is connected a.a.s.
$$\Longleftrightarrow$$
$\lim_{n \to \infty} P[\mathcal{G} \text{ is connected}] = 1.$

Note that for overlay graphs, the vertices are the overlay nodes. This means that $D(n)$ must be such that $\lim_{n\to\infty} D(n)n = +\infty$.

Problem and model discussion

Connected basic graph.   We consider only connected basic graphs. This seems reasonable to us as a disconnected basic graph will not provide connected overlays, whatever the neighbourhood range is, unless all the overlay nodes are concentrated in a connected part of it.

Asymptotics.   Many asymptotic properties of random geometric graphs have been demonstrated [Penrose, 2003]. In particular, we mentioned in Sect. 2 several studies of the asymptotic connectivity of ad hoc networks, while the connectivity probability of a finite network, because of its complexity, has been the subject of very few analytical studies [Desai and Manjunath, 2002].

Our asymptotic results can be seen as approximations of finite (real) networks when the number of nodes is large. They also shed some light on the relation linking n, r, D and R to get a connected overlay.

Network density.   Asymptotically, the model presented induces that the overlay nodes geographical density, i.e. the number of overlay nodes per unit area, tends to infinity. This is why it is only suited to so-called dense networks. There exists a more general model, covering dense and sparse networks, that was introduced in [Santi and Blough, 2003], and for which we present similar results in an extended version of this paper [Calomme and Leduc, 2006].

Homogeneous transmission range assignment.   The transmission range is represented as a function of the number of nodes. This allows us to model a possible topology control protocol running on the ad hoc network, which would reasonably reduce the transmission range as the number of nodes increases, in order to conserve energy and global network capacity. We however implicitly limit ourselves to homogeneous topology control protocols, i.e. protocols which assign the same transmission range to all nodes.

This assumption greatly simplifies further mathematical developments and seems realistic in the context of our study. A common transmission range at each node provides some appealing features [Kawadia and Kumar, 2005]. Moreover, a common power is asymptotically nearly optimal in terms of network capacity [Narayanaswamy et al., 2002].

4.   Mathematical analysis

Known Results on Basic Graphs

Consider a basic graph $g(n, r)$. Let us build a graph $g\prime(n, r\prime)$ that has the same nodes set as g and such that there is an edge between every pair of nodes. Let M_n denote the longest edge length of the minimal spanning tree built on $g\prime$. In [Penrose, 1997], it is demonstrated that the graph $g(n, r)$ is connected if and only if $r \geq M_n$ and

$$\forall \alpha \in R : \lim_{n \to +\infty} P[n\pi M_n{}^2 - \ln n \leq \alpha] = \exp(-e^{-\alpha}) \qquad (1)$$

This implies directly the following theorem.

THEOREM 2 *(Asymptotic connectivity of basic graphs)*
A graph $g(n, r)$ with

$$\pi r^2 = \frac{\ln n + k(n)}{n}$$

is connected a.a.s. if and only if $\lim_{n \to +\infty} k(n) = +\infty$.

The same result was demonstrated by Gupta and Kumar for a uniform distribution of nodes over the unit disk [Gupta and Kumar, 1999].

Overlay graphs study

We begin with a theorem that sets an upper bound on the asymptotic number of hops between any pair of nodes, given the distance separating them and the normalized transmission range used.

THEOREM 3 *(Asymptotic path length)*
Let g be an a.a.s. connected graph and m be a strictly positive integer. Let n_1 and n_2 be two nodes of g. If the Euclidean distance between n_1 and n_2 is strictly less than mr, then there exists a.a.s. a path between them composed of less than or exactly m hops.

The detailed demonstrations of this theorem and of the next one are published in the extended version of this paper [Calomme and Leduc, 2006]. We only draw here the sketch of their proof.

PROOF 4 *(summary) Asymptotic path length*

We use a recurrent approach .
If $m = 1$, then nodes n_1 and n_2 are physical neighbours and the property is valid.
If $m > 1$, then it can be demonstrated that there exists a.a.s. a node n_i such that the distance between n_1 and n_i is strictly less than $(m-1)r$ and

that the distance between n_i and n_2 is strictly less than r. Consequently, the property is valid for any m. □

Using the previous theorem, we can derive the main result of this paper.

THEOREM 5 *(Asymptotic connectivity of dense overlay graphs)*
Consider an overlay graph $G(g, D(n), R(n))$ with

$$\pi(Rr)^2 = \frac{\ln(\lceil Dn \rceil) + K(n)}{\lceil Dn \rceil} \tag{2}$$

Assume $g(n, r(n))$ is a.a.s. connected and $\lim_{n\to+\infty} Dn = +\infty$. G is a.a.s. connected if and only if $\lim_{n\to+\infty} K(n) = +\infty$.

PROOF 6 *(summary) Asymptotic connectivity of dense overlay graphs*

Let $G(n, r, D, R)$ be an overlay graph.
Consider a graph $g\prime(\lceil Dn \rceil, Rr)$ such that the vertices sets of G and $g\prime$ are identical.

As the maximal edge length of G equals Rr, its edges set is included in the edges set of $g\prime$. If $g\prime$ is not connected, then G neither is.

By definition, any edge (n_1, n_2) of $g\prime$ is shorter than or has length Rr. If it is strictly shorter than Rr, then, by theorem 3, this edge also exists in G.
If it has length Rr, then it can be demonstrated that one can find a node n_i such that two edges (n_1, n_i) and (n_i, n_2), each strictly shorter than Rr, belong to G.
Consequently, if there exists a path between two nodes of $g\prime$, there also exists a path between these nodes in G.
If $g\prime$ is connected, then G also is.

Applying Theorem 2 to $g\prime$, we obtain a necessary and sufficient condition for the asymptotic connectivity of G. □

Discussion

The following two corollaries are meant to give an insight about the relationship between the neighbourhood range and the overlay density. Their proof, quite simple, are given in the extended version of this paper [Calomme and Leduc, 2006].

For both of them, we consider an overlay graph $G(g, D, R)$ and make the assumptions that g is a.a.s. connected and that $\lim_{n\to+\infty} Dn = +\infty$.

COROLLARY 7 *If* $DR^2 \geq 1$ *then* G *is a.a.s. connected.*

The sufficient condition $R > \frac{1}{\sqrt{D}}$ shows that a decreasing overlay density does not necessarily make the overlay graph a.a.s. disconnected. We can for example have $D = \frac{1}{\ln n}$ and $R = \sqrt{\ln n}$. It also confirms the intuitive idea that the lower D is, the larger R must be.

The advantage of the previous corollary is that we do not need any information about the basic graph, except that it is a.a.s. connected. However, lower values for the neighbourhood range could be obtained if the relationship existing between n and r is known.

COROLLARY 8 *Let* $\pi r^2 n = \ln n + k(n)$ *with* $k(n) \gg 1$. *Assume* D *is constant and* R *is an integer with* $R \geq 1$.

1 If $k(n) \gg \ln n$, *then* G *is a.a.s. connected for any* R.

2 If $k(n) \geq a \ln n$ *with* $a > 0$, *then* G *is a.a.s connected for any* $R > \frac{1}{\sqrt{D(1+a)}}$.

3 If $k(n) \ll \ln n$, *then* G *is a.a.s. connected if and only if* $R \geq \frac{1}{\sqrt{D}}$.

Concerning a basic graph, a function $k(n)$ that grows quickly just accelerates the convergence of the connectivity probability [Santi and Blough, 2003]. This function has a stronger impact on the neighbourhood range needed for connectivity. For example, for a constant overlay density D, it decides if R can take any value or must be greater than a fixed threshold.

In particular, if the transmission range r is kept constant while the number of nodes grows, we have $k(n) \gg \ln n$ which implies that $R = 1$ is sufficient to obtain an a.a.s. connected overlay. The overlay nodes do not need other intermediary nodes to forward their packet for communicating. The subnetwork composed of the overlay nodes only is a.a.s. connected. In fact, there is no need for building an overlay in this case; the overlay nodes can directly use their own routing protocol, with customized packet format.

Oppositely, if a topology control protocol is used for optimizing the transmission range, $R = 1$ can be too small to make the overlay a.a.s. connected. In this case, the subnetwork composed of the overlay nodes only is a.a.s. disconnected. It is necessary for some overlay nodes to communicate through intermediary non overlay nodes. Overlay techniques are required; the overlay nodes control and data packets must be encapsulated in packets that can be routed by all nodes.

5. Conclusions

We first motivated the study of overlays built over ad hoc networks.

We then presented and analyzed the critical neighbourhood range problem.

In connected networks, as the network gets denser ($n \rightarrow +\infty$), the shortest path between any pair of nodes draws close to the straight line. This sets an upper bound on the number of hops between any pair of nodes, knowing the distance between them and the nodes normalized radio transmission range r.

Thanks to this property, that we called the asymptotic path length theorem, and known work on the critical transmission range problem, one can derive an analytical solution to the critical neighbourhood range problem.

The mathematical condition obtained does take into account the potential use of a homogeneous topology control algorithm and allows the overlay density D to evolve with the number of nodes. In particular, if D diminishes, they show how a compensation in R can keep the overlay still connected.

The analysis of these results provides, among others, the following properties for overlays built on ad hoc networks.

Whatever the characteristics of the underlying network are, an overlay built on an a.a.s. connected network with $DR^2 \geq 1$ is asymptotically almost surely connected.

In many cases, if the relationship between n and r is known, one can determine a lower value than $\lceil \frac{1}{\sqrt{D}} \rceil$ for R, which will still achieve asymptotic overlay connectivity.

For constant D, depending on the network degree of connectivity, the minimal value of R for asymptotic overlay connectivity can either be equal to one, or to a higher fixed threshold, or be an unbounded function of the number of nodes.

In particular, if D and r are kept constant while the number of nodes increases, the overlay nodes can asymptotically use their own routing protocol, bypassing the network routing protocol common to all nodes.

Oppositely, if the transmission range value is optimized, using a topology control protocol for the underlay, the network composed only of the overlay nodes can be a.a.s. disconnected.

Acknowledgments

This work has been partially supported by the Belgian Science Policy in the framework of the IAP program (MOTION P5/11 project) and by the European Commission (IST E-NEXT NoE).

References

Bollobas, B. (1985). *Random Graphs.* Academic Press, London, England.

Calomme, S. and Leduc, G. (2004). Performance study of an overlay approach to active routing in ad hoc networks. In *Proc. of the Third annual Mediterranean Ad Hoc Networking Workshop (Med-Hoc-Net'04)*, Bodrum, Turkey.

Calomme, S. and Leduc, G. (2006). The critical neighbourhood range for asymptotic overlay connectivity in ad hoc networks. To appear in Ad Hoc and Sensor Wireless Networks.

Desai, M. and Manjunath, D. (2002). On the connectivity in finite ad hoc networks. *IEEE Commun. Lett.*, 10(6):437–490.

Erdos, P. and Rényi, A. (1960). On the evolution of random graphs. *Hungarian Academy of Science*, 5:17–61.

Goel, A., Rai, S., and Krishnamachari, B. (2004). Sharp thresholds for monotone properties in random geometric graphs. In *Proc. of the thirty-sixth annual ACM symposium on Theory of computing (STOC'04)*, pages 580–586, Chicago, IL.

Gupta, P. and Kumar, P. (1999). Critical power for asymptotic connectivity in wireless networks. In McEneaney, W.M., Yin, G., and Zhang, Q., editors, *Stochastic Analysis, Control, Optimization and Applications, A Volume in Honor of W. H. Fleming.* Birkhäuser, Boston.

Kawadia, V. and Kumar, P.R. (2005). Principles and protocols for power control in wireless ad hoc networks. *IEEE J. Select. Areas Commun.*, 23(1):76–88.

Krishnamachari, B., Wicker, S., and Bejar, R. (2001). Phase transition phenomena in wireless ad-hoc networks. In *Proc. IEEE Global Conference on Telecommunications (Globecom'01), Symposium on Ad-Hoc Wireless Networks*, San Antonio, TX.

Mohapatra, P., Gui, C., and Li, J. (2004). Group communications in mobile ad hoc networks. *IEEE Computer*, 37(2):52–59.

Narayanaswamy, S., Kawadia, V., Sreenivas, R.S., and Kumar, P. R. (2002). Power control in ad-hoc networks: Theory, architecture, algorithm and implementation of the compow protocol. In *Proc. of European Wireless 2002. Next Generation Wireless Networks: Technologies, Protocols, Services and Applications*, pages 156–162, Florence, Italy.

Penrose, M. (2003). *Random Geometric Graphs.* Oxford University Press, England.

Penrose, M. D. (1997). The longest edge of the random minimal spanning tree. *The Annals of Applied Probability*, 7(2):340–361.

Penrose, M. D. (1999). On the k-connectivity for a geometric random graph. *Random Structures and Algorithms*, 15(2):145–164.

Santi, P. and Blough, D. M. (2003). The critical transmitting range for connectivity in sparse wireless ad hoc networks. *IEEE Trans. Mobile Comput.*, pages 25–39.

Tang, D. and Baker, M. (2000). Analysis of a local-area wireless network. In *Proc. of the Sixth Annual International Conference on Mobile Computing and Networking (MOBICOM'00)*, Boston, MA.

Wang, K. H. and Li, B. (2002). Efficient and guaranteed service coverage in partitionable mobile ad-hoc networks. In *Proc. Annual Joint Conference of the IEEE Computer and Communications Societies (INFOCOM'02)*, New York, NY.

DESIGN OF A FLEXIBLE CROSS-LAYER INTERFACE FOR AD HOC NETWORKS*

Marco Conti, Gaia Maselli, Giovanni Turi
IIT Institute, CNR, Via G. Moruzzi 1, 56124 Pisa, Italy

Abstract   Cross layering has recently emerged as a new trend to cope with performance issues of mobile ad hoc networks. The concept behind this technique is to exploit local information produced by other protocols, so as to enable optimizations and deliver better network performance. However, the need for a new interaction paradigm inside the protocol stack has to face with the legacy aspects of classical architectures (e.g., the Internet), where layer separation allows for easy standardization and deployment. In this paper, we show that cross layering can be achieved maintaining a clean architectural modularity, making protocols exchange information through a vertical interface. Specifically, we present the design of a cross-layer module, and provide a proof of concepts of its "usability" at different layers of the protocol stack, considering two case studies from a design and implementation standpoint.

1.   Introduction

Cross layering is generally intended as a way to let protocols interact beyond what allowed by standard interfaces. This clashes with the design principles of classical protocol stacks. Just to provide an example, the Internet architecture layers protocols and network responsibilities, breaking down the networking system into modular components. The resulting "strict-layered" system is composed by modules that are independent of each other and interact through well-defined (and static) interfaces, located between adjacent layers. Although this design principle brings important benefits in terms of flexibility and maintenance costs, it suffers from several characteristics of wireless networks (e.g., node mobility or power constraints), degrading the overall network performance [1]. Hence, the need of introducing stricter cooperation among protocols belonging to different layers. This last point sets the focus of this pa-

*This work was partially funded by the Information Society Technologies programme of the European Commission, Future and Emerging Technologies under the IST-2001-38113 MobileMAN project, and by the Italian Ministry for Education and Scientific Research in the framework of the FIRB-VICOM project.

per, which aims at investigating cross-layer interactions from an architectural standpoint, in the context of mobile ad hoc networking.

In the ad hoc literature, there are several contributions showing the potential of cross layering for isolated performance improvements [2][3][4][5]. They all focus on specific problems, mainly looking at the joint design of two layers. However, their deployment has to deal with the following issues:

1 *Tight-coupling*: the design of cross-layer optimizations requires direct modification of interfaces, causing the involved protocols to become tightly-coupled, and therefore mutually dependent.

2 *Unbridled stack design*: while an individual suggestion for cross-layer design, in isolation, may appear appealing, combining several of them together could result in a "spaghetti" stack design [6], making architectural maintenance a challenging task. Moreover, an uncontrolled combination of isolated cross-layer optimizations may cause mutual interferences, which could lead single nodes to unstable and degraded behavior, with negative impacts on the entire network.

3 *Correct system implementation*: when introducing new interactions among protocols, special care has to be taken to maintain a correct execution flow, without causing critical problems on the internals of the operating system. In real platforms, network protocols consist of a mixed set of processes executing at both kernel and user levels. For this reason, the implementation of cross-layer interactions should guarantee a correct interleaving of protocols execution, without introducing failure patterns on synchronization and scheduling of local system processes.

This paper addresses cross-layering from an architectural standpoint, providing a basis for tackling the semantic problems of interfering optimizations and correct system implementation. In particular, we claim that new interactions can be realized maintaining the layer separation principle, with the introduction of a cross-layer interface (XL-interface) that standardizes vertical interactions and gets rid of tight-coupling from an architectural standpoint. The key aspect is that protocols are still implemented in isolation inside each layer, offering the advantages of:

- allowing for full compatibility with standards, as the XL-interface does not modify each layer's core functions;

- providing a robust upgrade environment, which allows the addition or removal of protocols belonging to different layers from the stack, without modifying operations at other layers;

- maintaining the benefits of a modular architecture (layer separation is achieved by standardizing the usage of the XL-interface).

Engineering the XL-interface presents a great challenge (Section 2). This component must be general enough to be used at each layer, providing a common set of primitives to realize local protocol interactions (Section 3). To support this novel paradigm, we classified cross-layer functionalities and extended standard TCP/IP protocols in order use them. The result of this effort has been implemented in the $ns2$ Network Simulator (Section 4), realizing a simulative evaluation framework for the usability of the XL-interface at different layers.

2. Architectural Functionalities

We designed the XL-interface with two models of interaction in mind: *synchronous* and *asynchronous*. Protocols interact synchronously when they share private data (i.e. internal status collected during their normal functioning). A request for private data takes place on-demand, with a protocol issuing a query to retrieve data produced at other layers, and waiting for the result. Asynchronous interactions characterize the occurrence of specified conditions, to which protocols may be willing to react. As such conditions are occasional (i.e. not deliberate), protocols are required to subscribe for their occurrences, and then return to their work. The XL-interface is in turn responsible for delivering eventual occurrences to the right subscribers. Specifically, we consider two types of events: *internal* and *external*. Internal events are directly generated inside the protocols. Picking just one example, the routing protocol notifies the rest of the stack about a "broken route" event, whenever it discovers the failure of a preexisting route. On the other hand, external events are discovered inside the XL-interface on the basis of instructions provided by subscriber protocols. An example of external event is a condition on the host energy level. A protocol can subscribe for a "battery-low" event, specifying an energy threshold to the XL-interface, which in turn will notify the protocol when the battery power falls below the given value. Note that the host energy controller simply provides the current battery level value, but it is not in charge of checking the threshold and notify related events.

As the XL-interface represents a level of indirection in the treatment of cross-layer interactions, an agreement for a common representation of data and events inside the vertical component is a fundamental requirement in order to guarantee loosely-coupling. To this end, the XL-interface works with *abstractions* of data and events, intended as a set of data structures that comprehensively reflect the relevant (from a cross-layering standpoint) information and special conditions used throughout the stack. A straightforward example is the topology information collected by a routing protocol. In order to abstract from implementation details of particular routing protocols, topology data can be represented as a graph inside the XL-interface. Therefore, the XL-interface becomes the provider of shared data, which appear independent of its origin, and hence usable by each protocol.

How is protocols internal data exported into XL-interface abstractions? This task is accomplished by using *call-back* functions, which are defined and installed by protocols themselves. A call-back is a procedure that is registered to a library at one point in time, and later on invoked (by the XL-interface). Each call-back contains the instructions to encode private data into an associated XL-interface abstraction. In this way, protocol designers provide a tool for transparently accessing protocol internal data.

3.   Designing the cross-layer interface

In order to give a technical view of the vertical functionalities, we assume that the language used by the XL-interface allows for an object oriented representation of data structures and functions. We adopt the following notation to describe the XL-interface interface:

$$XL\_object.method : (input) \rightarrow (output)$$

As described in the previous Section, the XL-interface does not generate shared data, but simply acts as intermediary. Protocols synchronize on an abstract representation of internal data (namely XL_data) where one *producer* protocol specifies a call-back function to export its private data to the abstract representation.

$$XL\_data.seize : (callback()) \rightarrow ()$$

On the other hand, *consumer* protocols access the shared data with read only permissions, using

$$XL\_data.access : () \rightarrow (abstractData)$$

Going back to the example on network topology data, the routing agent plays the role of the producer protocol, exporting routing tables into an abstract graph representation. Consumer protocols living in the scope of other layers, could gather network topology information calling the *access()* method, which in turn invokes the call-back function registered by the routing agent. This makes the interaction between producer and consumer protocols loosely-coupled, avoiding direct protocol dependencies.

The remaining functionalities of the XL-interface cope with asynchronous interactions. In the case of internal events, the role of the XL-interface is to collect subscriptions, wait for notifications, and vertically dispatch event occurrences to the appropriate subscribers. A protocol *subscribes* for a cross-layer event (namely XL_event) by calling the function

$$XL\_event.subscribe : (handler()) \rightarrow ()$$

Note that the subscriber protocol has to specify a handler function, which will be used by the XL-interface to notify occurrences and triggering event handling. So, subscriber protocols play again the consumer role, while producer protocol *notify* event occurrences by calling

$$XL\_event.notify : () \rightarrow ()$$

The XL-interface is in charge of maintaining a subscription list for each kind of cross-layer event, dispatching occurrences to the correct subscribers.

In the case of external events, the XL-interface must additionally act as event notifier. The idea is that some protocols might be interested in conditions that are not directly verified by other protocols. To this end, subscriber protocols instruct the XL-interface on how to detect the event. The detection rules are embedded in a monitor function, which periodically checks the status of the cross-layer abstractions under inquiry. When the monitor detects the specified condition, the XL-interface dispatches the information to the subscriber protocol. A protocol initiates the *monitoring* of an external event by passing a monitor and a handler function to the XL-interface, through the following method of the target data abstraction

$$XL\_data.setMonitor : (monitor(), handler()) \rightarrow ()$$

The XL-interface serves this call by spawning a *persistent* computation that executes the following steps:

```
while true do
    freshData = XL_data.access()
    if monitor(freshData)
        handler()
    endif
endwhile
```

4.   Using the cross-layer interface

In order to practise the usage of the XL-interface, we realized a simulation framework, based on the Network Simulator $ns2$ (v. 2.27), and a library of objects and abstractions, called ProtoLib, provided by the Naval Research Laboratory (NRL) [7]. The choice of ProtoLib is motivated by its high flexibility. It provides a set of simple, cross-platform C++ classes that allow the development of network protocols and applications. Currently, the ProtoLib supports several real platforms (e.g., Unix and WIN32), as well as the $ns2$ simulation environment. Another important feature is that the ProtoLib package comes with an implementation of Optimized Link State Routing protocol (OLSR), compliant with the latest specification [8]. In the framework resulting from the integration of $ns2$ with the ProtoLib, it was a "natural" choice to

Figure 1. Cross-layer data.   *Figure 2.* Cross-layer events.

place the objects of the XL-interface inside the ProtoLib. We engineered them as abstract classes that other protocols can implement in order to share data and exchange local events. Specifically, we realized interfaces for *XL_Data* and *XL_Event* objects, respectively for sharing protocol internal data (i.e., synchronous interactions) and for subscribing/notifying internal events (i.e., asynchronous interactions). In the following, we briefly describe the functionalities of the new objects:

ProtoXLData This is a generic class (see Figure 1) that identifies internal data *owned* by a protocol and *shared* to the rest of the network stack. It offers methods to declare ownership of the data and to specify a call-back function for "translating" the internal data format used by the owner, in a cross-layer ontology common to the whole stack. Other protocols access instances of this class with read-only permissions.

ProtoXLEvent This is a generic class (see Figure 2) that identifies conditions or events detected internally to the protocol, which may result of interest for the rest of the stack. It offers methods to *subscribe* interest in events derived from this class, as well as to *notify* occurrences of them.

In the following, we present two examples of cross-layer optimization based on the XL-interface. We show interactions involving network, transport and middleware layers, to highlight how the objects of the XL-interface suites different levels of the protocol stack. The two case studies implement their cross-layer interactions by specializing the base objects presented in the previous Section.

4.1   Improving the performance of data transfer

In this Section, we show how the XL-interface has been used to cope with performance issues of TCP data transfer. TCP performance degrades in ad hoc environments due to losses, which are induced by fault conditions (e.g. network partitions, route failures, and misbehaving nodes), and are erroneously interpreted as effects of congestion. To deal with this problem, we introduce a forwarding mechanism able to improve the performance and reliability of data transfer, also in presence of misbehaving (e.g. selfish) nodes, by means

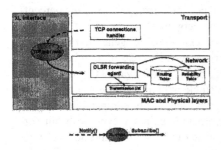

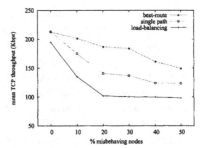

Figure 3.   Cross-layer interaction between the network and the transport layer.

Figure 4.   Mean TCP throughput as function of the percentage of misbehaving nodes.

of a cross-layer interaction between the forwarding and transport agents. This mechanism is based on multi-path forwarding and estimates neighbors reliability according to end-to-end acknowledgments. Specifically, in case of reliable data transfer, TCP acknowledgments are used as delivery notifications. The reception of a TCP ack at the transport layer indicates that the corresponding sent packet has been correctly delivered at destination, and hence correctly forwarded by intermediate nodes. Each node estimates only neighbors' reliability, and uses this index to forward packets on most reliable routes, so as to avoid unreliable paths and minimize congestion events. For further details on the forwarding mechanism we point the reader to [9].

The realization of the forwarding mechanism in our evaluation framework involves the introduction of a class of cross-layer events of type *Recv TCP-ack/nack*, to which the forwarding agent subscribes for notifications coming from a local TCP agent (see Figure 3). Specifically, the TCP agent notifies a TCP-ack event to the forwarding agent whenever it receives a valid acknowledgment. Instead, TCP-nack events are caused by packets retransmissions. An event notification causes the forwarding agent to update the reliability index associated to the neighbor through which the packet passed. The update is positive for TCP-ack and negative for TCP-nack. Reliability indexes are used to send packets on most reliable routes. Specifically, we implemented a forwarding policy which chooses the route with the smallest route-length/reliability ratio, namely *best-route* forwarding. As the simultaneous use of multiple paths (i.e., *load-balancing*) degrades TCP performance [10], we compare our best-route forwarding policy with the conventional case in which packet forwarding is based on single path routing (like in OLSR), where the shortest route is always chosen (i.e., *single path*).

The simulation study investigates TCP performance by varying the percentage of misbehaving nodes. The simulated network is composed of 20 nodes, with 5 active Telnet sessions. Connection endpoints are generated randomly, and each simulated scenario is characterized by an increasing number of misbehaving nodes that cooperate to routing, but do not forward TCP traffic. Figure 4 shows how best-route outperforms single path forwarding whenever misbehaving nodes are present, while the two method are comparable in cooperative networks. Specifically, the performance gain achieved with our forwarding mechanism grows up to 50% in the case of 20% and 30% of misbehaving nodes. Results also confirms the poor performance achieved by the load-balancing policy, that increase the chances of encountering misbehaving nodes.

4.2   Improving the quality of unstructured overlays

In this Section, we show how the XL-interface has been used to improve the performance of Gnutella, a well-known unstructured overlay platform. Although we used Gnutella as a case study, a similar approach could be used for other peer-to-peer (p2p) platforms, so as to make them more reactive and usable in ad hoc environments. Full details about this application of the XL-interface are reported in [11].

By simulating a fully-fledged Gnutella system in ad hoc environments, we identified peer discovery as a critical issue. In summary, discovery procedures based on application layer flooding generate overhead, and decrease the capacity of building the overlay. Moreover, as peer selection is random, Gnutella overlays are significantly sensitive to nodes mobility, and fail to react promptly in scenarios with partitioning or heavy churn rates. Under these observations, we re-designed peer discovery and link selection in order to interact with the routing agent at the network layer. The fundamental idea is to exploit node discovery procedures provided by routing agents, so to jointly perform peer discovery together with gathering topology information. For example, in a proactive routing protocol like OLSR, nodes periodically issue Hello and Topology Control messages, containing information about the neighbors that they currently sense. This information could be enriched with *Optional Information* (OI), containing peer credentials (e.g., IP address and port number of the Gnutella service). This approach saves the network resources consumed by an explicit peer discovery protocol.

We modeled the cross-layer interactions using events between Gnutella peers and OLSR agents (see Figure 5). We initially extended the NRL implementation of OLSR to handle new messages for *optional information*, and afterward specialized two classes of cross-layer events: i) *Spread OI* events, to which routing agents subscribe, receiving notifications from Gnutella peers. These

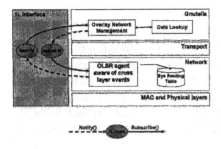

Figure 5. Event-based cross layer interaction for Gnutella peer discovery.

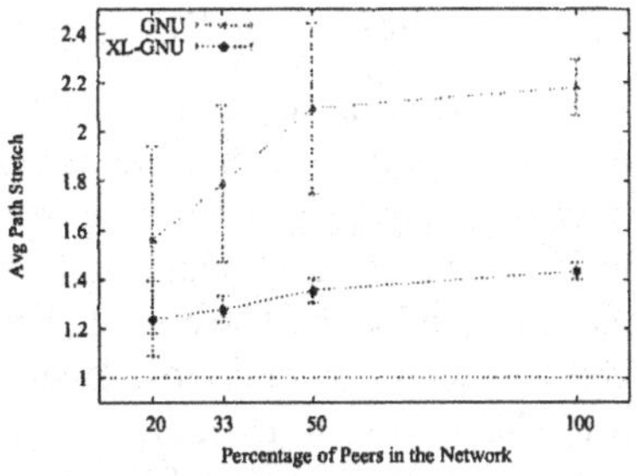

Figure 6. Comparison of the average
path stretch produced by Gnutella and XL-
Gnutella under increasing peer densities.

events are used to ask OLSR agents to advertise local peer credentials around,
along with the next Hello or Topology Control message (see OLSR RFC [8] for
details on the protocol); ii) *Recv OI* events, to which Gnutella peers subscribe,
in order to receive notifications from underlying OLSR agents. These events
are used to notify Gnutella peers about incoming credential advertisements of
remote peers. This allowed us to realize peer discovery by making each peer
periodically advertise its credentials, and reacting to events of advertisements
reception. The overall discovery procedure became simpler and easier to control. On receiving cross-layer events, peers were able to fill up a local table of
advertisement generated by foreign agents. Moreover, as advertisements travel
the network along with routing control packets, it was possible to get accurate
estimates of peers physical distances (in number of hops). This topological
information enriched the advertisement table, and allowed us to play a smarter
overlay formation protocol, introducing a link selection policy based on physical distances. The rational behind was to simply prioritize closer connections
over further ones, with the goal of building an overlay topologically closer to
the physical network. In order to give a flavor of the benefits introduced by the
XL-interface, Figure 6 shows the results obtained by studying the *path stretch*
generated by the legacy and the cross-layer version of the protocol, defined as
the ratio of the number of hops (in the physical network) along the path connecting two peers in the overlay, to that along the direct unicast path. This
metric measures how far (from a topological point of view) the overlay is from
the physical network, and characterizes the overhead induced by the former
on the latter. By configuring an increasing percentage of peers in a network
of fixed size, we observed that cross-layer Gnutella (XL-Gnutella) produces
better path stretches (e.g., respectively 1.35 against 2.1 of legacy Gnutella with
a 50% of peers), exhibiting a stable behavior with smaller variances.

5.   Concluding Remarks

Cross layering represents a trendy solution to overcome performance limitations of mobile ad hoc environments. Current proposals testify the effectiveness of cross-layering in delivering better protocol performances, but they
tackle single cases without prospecting any form of coexistence from an architectural standpoint. The contribution of this paper is the design of an interface
able to support several cross-layer solutions, using common interaction models. This approach decouples interacting entities, and preserves the flexibility
and modularity features of legacy architectures.

In order to evaluate the usability of the proposed interface, we considered
two case studies, verifying that the cross-layer primitives could be used at different layers of the stack, for different purposes. The next step is to engineer
and deploy an implementation of the cross-layer interface on a real platform,
and verify that the interaction primitives guarantee a clean execution pattern,
without introducing mutual interferences.

References

[1] M. Conti, J. Crowcroft, G. Maselli and G. Turi. "A Modular Cross-Layer Architecture for
     Ad Hoc Networks," in *Handbook on Theoretical and Algorithmic Aspects of Sensor, Ad
     Hoc Wireless, and Peer-to-Peer Networks*, CRC Press, July, 2005.

[2] K. Chen, S. H. Shah, and K. Nahrstedt. "Cross-Layer Design for Data Accessibility in
     Mobile Ad Hoc Networks," in *WPC*, vol. 21, no. 1, pp 49-76, 2002.

[3] R. Schollmeier, I. Gruber, and F. Niethammer. "Protocol for Peer-to-Peer Networking in
     Mobile Environments," in *Proceedings of the 12th IEEE ICCCN '03*, Dallas, Texas, USA,
     Oct. 2003.

[4] M. Chiang. "To Layer or not to Layer: Balancing Transport and Physical Layers in Wireless
     Multihop Networks," in *Proceedings of IEEE INFOCOM 2004*, Hong Kong, China, Mar.
     2004.

[5] U. C. Kozat, I. Koutsopoulus, and L. Tassiulas. "A Framework for Cross-layer Design of
     Energy-efficient Communication with QoS Provisioning in Multi-hop Wireless Networks,"
     in *Proceedings of IEEE INFOCOM 2004*, Hong Kong, China, Mar. 2004.

[6] V. Kawadia and P. R. Kumar. "A Cautionary Perspective on Cross Layer Design", in *IEEE
     Wireless Communications*, Feb. 2005.

[7] "PROTEAN Research Group", http://cs.itd.nrl.navy.mil/5522/

[8] T. Clausen and P. Jacquet. "Optimized Link State Routing Protocol (OLSR)", *RFC 3626*,
     Oct. 2003.

[9] M. Conti, E. Gregori, and G. Maselli. "Improving the performability of data transfer in
     mobile ad hoc networks", to appear in the *2nd IEEE SECON '05*, Sept. 2005.

[10] H. Lim, K. Xu, and Mario Gerla. "TCP Performance over multipath routing in mobile ad
     hoc networks", *Proceedings of the 38th IEEE ICC '03*, Anchorage, Alaska, May 2003.

[11] M. Conti, E. Gregori, and G. Turi. "A Cross Layer Optimization of Gnutella for Mobile
     Ad hoc Networks", in *Proceedings of the 6th ACM MobiHoc '05*, Urbana-Champaign,
     Illinois, USA, May 2005.

EMULATION ARCHITECTURE FOR AD HOC NETWORKS

A.Giovanardi
DI, University of Ferrara, Italy
agiovanardi@ing.unife.it

G.Mazzini
DI, University of Ferrara, Italy
gmazzini@ing.unife.it

Abstract   The paper presents an emulation architecture working in the user space useful to implement and test routing protocols for ad hoc networks. The emulator interfaces with the Simple Ad hoc siMulator (SAM) [1], where many routing protocols are present. The novelty with respect to SAM is the possibility to test routing protocols with a real exchange of signaling and data packets between the nodes present in the network. With respect to a live test, the emulator works on hosts connected each other via wired links and the wireless channel is simulated.

Keywords: Emulation, Ad Hoc Networks, Routing Protocols.

1.   Introduction

Ad hoc networks have become an increasingly popular technology in the past few years. In these wireless networks nodes communicate with other nodes in their range and act as forwarders of data from nodes communicating with out-of-range nodes.

Many approaches are possible to test the ad hoc network performance: simulation, live test and emulation. **Simulation** runs a model/representation of the code in a synthetic environment, by imitating the time operations executed by a real system. **Live test** runs the real code in the real environment. **Emulation** is a simulation which involves hardware or firmware components. Simulation can be very slow; the synthetic environment may poorly represent real one. Live tests may only be possible very late in development cycle; it is often difficult or too expensive to create a real test environment of any significant size; real environment tests also tend not to be reproducible. Emulation can give a controlled, reproducible environment for running live code in a lab-environment network. Benefits of network emulation include the ability to expose experimental algorithms and protocols to live traffic loads and to introduce real packet processing times. In many cases, a large number of hosts can be considered without impact on the final cost.

Many simulators (OPNET [2], NS2 [3], GloMoSim [4] and SAM [1]) and emulators ([5] [6] [7]) have been proposed and developed to validate the proposal of new routing protocols for ad hoc networks.

Emulation environments can be classified as follows [6]:

- *Central Control Emulators*: all nodes are connected to a central emulation server. All traffic is directed via that server, which forwards the traffic to the destinations. An example is [7].

- *Simulator Combined Emulators*: also in this case stations are connected to a central server, which decides whether packets get forwarded, delayed or dropped. With respect to the preceding case, the packets do not passes through the server, which simply manage the whole emulation, by simulating radio channel, topology and mobility. An example is [5].

- *Distributed Emulators*: as opposite to the centralized approaches each station acting as mobile node is responsible for directing and forwarding traffic. An example is: [6].

The emulation architectures can be classified also regarding their easy software portability or not. Many of the proposals need the modification of the kernel code of the operating system, or to load suitable kernel modules, with a consequent not easy portability.

In this paper we propose an emulator platform falling in the *Distributed Emulators* category and easy to implement. The architecture is fully distributed: nodes exchange signaling routing packets (according to the selected routing protocol) to update topology knowledge; then, on the basis of the run-time updated routing tables, data packets are transmitted from the source to the destination with hops on intermediated nodes. Nodes are connected via wired links and the wireless channel is simulated. Our implementation is fully developed in the user space (it does not need any change to the kernel code) and uses the libpcap library [8] and the RAW sockets [9].

To easy change the routing protocol to be tested, the emulator interfaces with SAM [1], where many kinds of unicast and multicast ad hoc routing protocols (Dijkstra, Link State, Distance Vector, DSR, AODV, AMRIS, ODMRP, AMRoute) are present. To test the emulator, we have used a simple routing protocol (Link State-LS [10]) by taking into account also the channel impairment. The final performance of the selected routing protocol have been compared with those of SAM.

2. Emulator Architecture

The emulator has been implemented on Linux hosts connected by means of a Fast Ethernet network. The N nodes involved in emulation have routing functions, i.e., can relay packets to other nodes. Each node in the network is identified by a logical number n, where $n \in \{1, \cdots, N\}$. Hosts are involved in many activities (not only emulation); so, a basic real traffic is always present (relative to services and applications such as NFS, DNS, DHCP, multicast and so on). The emulation traffic is composed by signaling broadcast packets (useful to know and update the topology) and by data packets.

The emulation architecture interfaces with SAM, which is a discrete event simulator, composed by the following modules: *Traffic*, dealing with the traffic generation; *Channel*, simulating the radio propagation; *Mob*, dealing with the terminal mobility; *Radio*, simulating the hardware transceiver; *Mac* realizing the Data Link Layer; *Route*, implementing the routing protocols; *Statistics*, collecting statistics results.

Emulator interacts with the *Traffic*, *Channel*, *Mob* and *Route* modules. To have an emulation platform giving results only on the routing protocols without out care of a particular MAC Layer, we have not considered the *Radio* and *Mac* modules used in SAM. This choice is also motivated by the presence of the MAC Layer of the wired system, which could become wireless if the hosts are equipped with wireless cards. So, we have created a suitable EMULA-TOR MAC which is simply performing a transparent interface between network card and Network Layer, making no particular medium access actions. At the Transport Layer, we only consider UDP.

A *Logical Management* block contains scripts able to configure the system. A file named *hosts* contains the MAC and IP addresses of all hosts which could be involved in the emulation. This file is read at the emulation start to perform all socket and network interface operations. Other scripts are able to manage the emulation simultaneously on all hosts, by also collecting and processing information stored in the output files to derive synthetic performance indexes.

An *Input* block is used to set parameters useful for the emulation: the number of nodes; the number of packet generated per host; the parameters to control the network interface; the maximum number of hops; the parameters to manage the network topology, i.e., the virtual host positions; the parameters to control the transmitted power and the propagation channel behavior; the parameters to manage the packet generation; the parameters identifying the routing protocol selected in the emulation.

A *Socket* block manages the frames generation and their insertion on the network, while a *Packet dump & Forwarding* block performs the dump and the relay of the packets. Finally, the *Output/Statistics* block collects parameters of interest to derive the final performance.

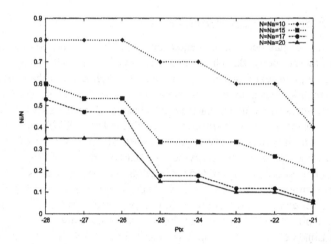

Figure 1. N_i/N as a function of P_{tx}, by varying $N = N_a = 10, 15, 17, 20$.

2.1   Implementation Details

The packets are dumped (captured at the network interface) by using the *libpcap* library [8]: *pcap_open_live()*, opens the network device for packet capture; *pcap_compile()*, sets a packet filter to select the packets useful for the emulation (and to discard any other kind of packets); *pcap_setfilter*, links the packet filter to the socket; *pcap_loop()*, collects and processes packets; *pcap_stats()*, collects statistics on the packet correctly dumped, discharged at the interface or by the kernel.

To insert the Ethernet frames on the network we use the RAW sockets [9], having set ETH_P_ALL as protocol (to send a not well known packet format) and having considered the socket option $IP\_HDRINCL$ to make sure that the kernel knows the header is included in the data, and does not insert its own header (for example an IP header) into the packet before the payload. The broadcast routing signaling packets has been redirected to a MAC address different from the broadcast one, to avoid to flood the network with broadcast packets not interesting for the hosts not involved in the emulation.

The Ethernet frames are composed by an header including: the destination and source MAC addresses; the type field; the numbers identifying the source node n_s and the destination node n_d; the Time To Live (TTL), decreased of 1 at each packet relaying; a timestamp, useful to evaluate the delivery time; the nexthop identifier; the transmission power. To discriminate into the network the packets involved in the emulation from those relative to other applications or protocols, we have identified and selected an ad hoc type field in the Ethernet frame (0x0020). TTL is included into the frame to drop a packet circulating

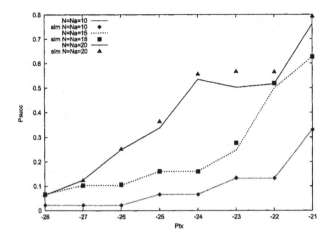

Figure 2. P_{succ} as a function of P_{tx}, by varying $N = N_a = 10, 15, 20$.

into the network indefinitely; furthermore, it is useful to evaluate the total number of hops experimented by a given packet.

To insert data into the frames in a machine-independent fashion, the eXternal Data Representation standard (XDR) [11] has been adopted. XDR is useful for transferring data between different computer architectures, it fits into the ISO presentation layer and support all classic C data types. The frame generation is performed trough the *Traffic* module present in SAM where Poisson, CBR, Isochronous, FTP and Video traffic can be set. By default, the number of active hosts (N_a) is set equal to N, i.e., all hosts are generating traffic.

At the frame born, the source node n_s collects the generation time, to identify the timestamp to include in that frame. Then, n_s searches the nexthop in the path, by applying the rules corresponding to the selected routing protocol. If the nexthop exists (i.e., at least the first relaying node is reachable from the source), n_s creates the frame to send, by setting in the Ethernet header: SA= Source MAC, DA= Nexthop MAC, Type= $0x0020$; and including n_s, n_d, TTL, timestamp, nexthop and transmit power. After the frame creation, n_s sends the frame to the selected interface by using the RAW sockets.

The frame forwarding capability (router functionality) is started on each host and is maintained active until the end of the emulation. When a host captures a frame with type field 0x0020, it can discriminate if this frame is addressed to another node or not. In the first case it does not perform any action; in the last case it processes the frame to establish if it must be forwarded to the next hop or it has reached the final target. The first operation of the frame processing is to identify the source and destination nodes, the TTL

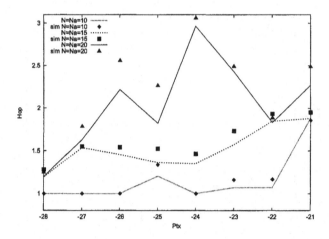

Figure 3.   hop as a function of P_{tx}, by varying $N = N_a = 10, 15, 20$.

and the timestamp (representing the time of frame generation at the source node). Then, also the last node in the path which has relayed the frame is identified (it is often an intermediate node, i.e., not the source node). This permits to evaluate the channel impairment in the last link, and then, according to a received power threshold, to determine if the frame is correctly received or not. If the frame is correct and has not reached the final target, the local node starts the procedures to forward it to the next hop. If the frame is correct and has reached its last destination, the local node processes it to collect performance indexes. Otherwise the frame is dropped. The frame forwarding procedure follows these steps: TTL decrease and control, i.e., $TTL = TTL - 1; if \ (TTL = 0) \rightarrow packet \ expired$; next hop evaluation (applying the rules of the selected routing protocol); frame regeneration with new TTL; packet insertion on the network. When a frame has reached $TTL = 0$ it is dropped and an error message is returned to the output.

3.   Numerical Results

All nodes are involved in the statistics collection: many output files are created, each characterized by a prefix identifying the logical number n of the node. As a consequence of the possible high number of hosts (N) involved in the emulation, the number of output files to be processed could be high. So a suitable post-processing software has been developed to collect : **success probability** (correctly delivered packet fraction), **delivery time** (end-to-end time), **number of hops, number of isolated nodes, energy spent per byte, total energy spent** for each host and the relative average values on the network.

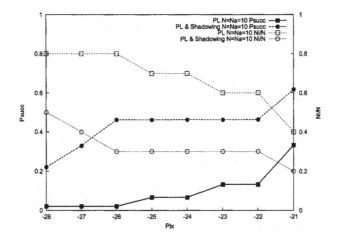

Figure 4. P_{succ} and N_i/N as functions of P_{tx}, with and without shadowing.

We have tested a simple protocol, i.e., Link State (LS) [10], by also verifying the match between emulation and SAM simulation. We consider a wireless fixed scenario with hosts located in a square room with size 10x10m. The propagation channel is characterized by path loss, with exponent $\beta = 2.5$ and reference distance $d_{ref} = 0.2$m. In some cases shadowing has been also taken into account, with log-normal distribution and deviation $\sigma = 6dB$. The transmit power P_{tx} is the same for each host and for each packet sent. The minimum received power is $P_{rx} = -76$dBm. The traffic is Poissonian with average arrival rate $\lambda = 10$packet/s. 5000 packets generated per station have been considered. In the performance evaluation we have varied the number of hosts present into the network and the transmit power P_{tx}. Figures from 1 to 5 show performance indexes representing values averaged on the whole network. Figures 6 and 7 show these parameters for any single host. In figure 1, 2 and 3 we consider only path loss, while in all other Figures the cases with only path loss and with path loss and shadowing are showed.

In Figure 1 the ratio between the number of isolated nodes, N_i, and the total number of hosts present in the network, N, is reported, by varying the transmit power P_{tx} in the range $[-28, -21]$dBm and setting the number of hosts into the network $N = N_a = 10, 15, 17, 20$. The results are only relative to the emulation, since the simulator does not report this information. As expected, N_i/N decreases by increasing P_{tx} and by increasing N, i.e., by increasing the density of host in the network area.

In Figure 2 the average success probability, P_{succ}, i.e., the correctly delivered packet fraction, is reported by varying the transmit power P_{tx} as in Figure

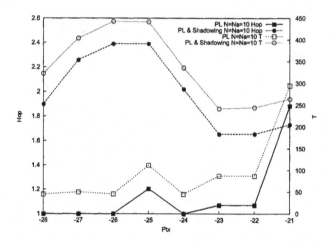

Figure 5.   hop and T as functions of P_{tx}, with and without shadowing.

1 and assuming $N = N_a = 10, 15, 20$. In this case, simulation results are also reported. The results obtained by emulation are depicted with lines, those obtained by simulation with points. We can verify the good match. Furthermore, as expected, by increasing the transmit power, the success probability increases, since the probability to have isolated nodes decreases. By increasing the number of hosts in the network, the effect is similar to a transmit power growth, since the network becomes more dense and then nodes are closer each one (and then more reachable) with higher probability.

In Figure 3 the average number of hops to deliver a packet, *hop*, is reported in the same parameter condition of Figure 2. A quite good match between emulation and simulation can be verified. For high N values, by increasing P_{tx}, *hop* first increases, then decreases, and this general trend is repeated more times. This can be probably explained as follows: at the begin the transmit power growth permits to eliminate zones with isolated nodes (characterized by short path, with few hops), by allowing paths longer, with higher number of hops; then, when the transmit power overcomes a given threshold, some nodes becomes directly reachable (i.e., without need of intermediate node with relaying functions) and then the number of hop decreases. On the other hand, by increasing the number of hosts in the network, the hop number increases and the effect could be similar to that of the initial transmit power growth.

In all Figures presented in the following only emulation results are shown. Furthermore, $N = N_a = 10$ has been assumed. In Figure 4 P_{succ} and N_i/N are depicted as functions of P_{tx}. The cases with and without shadowing are directly compared. We can note the same increasing and decreasing trends

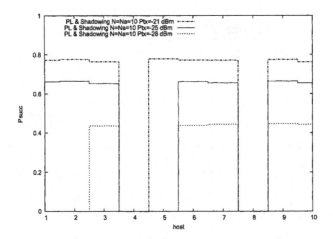

Figure 6. P_{succ} for each generic host, with shadowing.

of P_{succ} and N_i/N with P_{tx} of Figures 1 and 2. Furthermore, we can note the positive effect of shadowing which makes the network more "dense", by mitigating the attenuation effects of the path loss. In particular, shadowing doubles the nodes in visibility and the success probability. In Figure 5 the *hop* number and the final delivery time T (in ms) are reported as functions of P_{tx}, in the same conditions of Figure 4. Shadowing allows paths more long, with higher number of hops (in some cases *hop* doubles its value). This trend is related to the effect explained above (shadowing makes the network more dense); so, a lower number of isolated nodes allows to reach farer hosts, with higher number of hops on intermediate nodes. Note that, a part a scale factor, the delivery time and *hop* trends are quite the same.

Figure 6 shows P_{succ} for each generic host, with shadowing and by varying $P_{tx} = -28, -25, -21$dBm. As expected, by increasing P_{tx} the success probability increases for all hosts. Furthermore, it is possible to note that some hosts can not deliver packets, since they are probably isolated. The number of hosts in this condition decreases with the P_{tx} growth. The behavior depicted in this Figure allows to better understand if the average values depicted above (obtained by also considering unreachable nodes) are really representative or not. The last graph (Figure 7) depicts the number of forwarded packets for each generic host, having considered $P_{tx} = -28, -25, -23, -21$dBm. Note that this parameter increases when P_{tx} increases and that for any different level of transmission power the number of hosts performing routing action is limited (about the half of the hosts involved in the emulation).

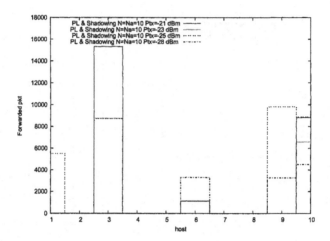

Figure 7.   Number of forwarded packets for each generic host, with shadowing.

Acknowledgments

This work is developed under MURST/MIUR Pattern Project and Regional Insebala Project.

References

[1] P.Bergamo, D.Maniezzo, A.Giovanardi, G.Mazzini, M.Zorzi, "Distributed Power Control for Power-aware Energy-effi cient Routing in Ad Hoc Networks," in Proc. of EW2002, pp. 237-243, Florence, Italy, Feb. 2002.

[2] "OPNET commercial tool", http://www.opnet.com.

[3] "The Network Simulator NS2," http://www.isi.edu/nsnam/ns/.

[4] "GloMoSim," http://pcl.cs.ucla.edu/projects/glomosim/.

[5] K. Fall, "Network emulation in the VINT/NS simulator", in Proc. of IEEE Computers and Communications, 6-8 July 1999, pp. 244-250.

[6] M. Matthes; H. Biehl; M. Lauer; O. Drobnik, "MASSIVE: An Emulation Environment for Mobile Ad-Hoc Networks" in Proc. of Wireless On-demand Network Systems and Services, (WONS 2005), 19-21 Jan. 2005, pp. 54-59.

[7] J. Flynn, H. Tewari, D. O'Mahony, "Jemu: a Real Time Emulation System for Mobile Ad hoc Networks", in Proc. of the First Joint IEI/IEE Symposium on Telecommunications System Reasearch, Dublin, Irelend, Nov. 2001.

[8] S. McCanne, C. Leres and V. Jacobson. libpcap, 1994. ftp://ftp.ee.lbl.gov/libpcap.tar.Z

[9] R. Stevens, "UNIX Network Programming, Volume 1: Networking APIs - Sockets and XTI", 1998, Prentice Hall PTR.

[10] A.S. Tanenbaum, "Computer Networks", Prentice Hall, 1989.

[11] RFC   1014   -   XDR: External   Data   Representation   standard, http://www.faqs.org/rfcs/rfc1014.html.

WIRELESS LOCAL AREA NETWORKS AND MOBILE DEVICES TO ACTUALIZE THE NOTION OF UBIQUITOUS COMPUTING IN LIVING CLASSROOMS
A case study in teaching and learning Astrophysics

Serena Pastore
INAF – Astronomical Observatory of Padova, vicolo Osservatorio 5 – 35122 – PADOVA – ITALY

Abstract: The integration of wireless local area network and wireless mobile devices allows to implement a complete information system able to support everyday activities unobtrusively and seamlessly as the ubiquitous computing paradigm says. Wireless mobile ad hoc networking could be successfully used in the construction of flexible and adaptive information system with no fixed infrastructure and it allows to covers multi-hop scenarios such as m-learning approaches. This paper describes choices and issues encountered in the adoption of wireless technologies as regards standards and topologies in order to realize a wireless network infrastructure suitable for teaching and learning Astrophysics using mobile devices. This study is part of the "Learning form Starlight" project presented by the Italian National Institute for Astrophysics to the Hewlett Packard Philanthropy foundation aiming at introducing in schools a new way of teaching and learning not strictly related to the classroom location context. The realization of this system outlines that the Wi-Fi standard in network deployment has up to now to be preferred to other available wireless technologies for the easiest way of set up connection and use and the possibility to implement different network topologies suitable for m-learning applications.

Key words: wireless local area networks (WLAN), ubiquitous computing, ad-hoc networks, 802.11 standards.

1.   INTRODUCTION

Ubiquitous computing [1] means that the computing system becomes a part of everyday environment, and user's interaction with it is available whenever he/she needs. The achievement of such vision necessarily requires an adequate wireless network infrastructure. Ubiquitous technology is characterized by the attributes of mobility, interconnectivity and context-awareness. Mobility could be realized using devices easily transportable and simple to interact with: challenges are limited graphics capabilities, minimal screen dimensions, memory, disks and battery duration. Interconnectivity should support not only point-to-point connection, but also additional capabilities such as being aware of each other or knowing how to exchange information. The concept of the context aware means the recognition of network, protocol, software, hardware (knows as the resource qualification) when interacting with other devices. A mobile learning[1] environment is an appropriate scenario to put ubiquitous computing into practice since it allows to build a technology-supported classroom environment that is independent by the physical location. The major function of this virtual classroom is to capture and automatically integrate various information of teacher's lecture, including presentation-style lectures, notes, materials, voice and images to form available multimedia courseware so as to facilitate users' access and learning. By using mobile hardware such as handwriting tablets and palms with wireless connectivity, this interactive networked environment enables collaborative learning with groupware functions. The strict integration of mobile devices, wireless communication and network technology allows the utilization of computing power for teacher and students anytime and anywhere and the interconnection with other offering applications and services devices seamlessly.

With the vision to actualize ubiquitous computing in an educational environment, this paper describes the work and the technological solutions adopted in terms of wireless standards and network topologies to implement a wireless information system suitable to enhance teaching and learning Astrophysics in schools of different grades in Italian education. The document finally outlines the main issues encountered in network deployment.

---

[1] Mobile learning (m-learning) is the intersection of mobile computing and e-learning: it's a kind of e-learning independent of location, time or space.

2. BACKGROUND: THE "LEARNING FROM STARLIGHT" PROJECT

The "Learning from Starlight project" was presented by the Italian National Institute for Astrophysics to the Hewlett Packard Philanthropy Foundation [2] with the aim of allowing Italian students to realize that Astrophysics is a science based on observation of signals (light and other electromagnetic waves). The overall goal is to demonstrate that mobile devices and wireless technology could improve learning and teaching. The project was selected by the foundation that granted a package consisting in a consistent number of handled devices such as Personal Digital Assistant – PDAs (HP iPAQ Pocket PC) and notebooks (HP TabletPC) [3] all equipped with a Microsoft Windows[2] environment and wireless adapters for Wi-Fi [4], Bluetooth [5] and infrared connections together with other devices useful for network support (access points, printers, digital projectors).

The project is included in the field of mobile learning [8] by enabling the use of portable computing devices over wireless networks. Mobile computing in education extends learning and teaching activities to spaces beyond the traditional classroom even if teachers and learners gain increased flexibility and new opportunities for interaction also within the classroom itself. This led to a more collaborative environment, more richly contextualized and continuously accessible that is the concept of ubiquitous and pervasive computing. The described case study could give a model for science learning in schools with a better interaction between the education and research environments.

Three classrooms from primary, secondary and high schools[3] have been selected to join in the project allowing also to test the approach to wireless technology and mobile devices on behalf of students of different ages. The learning train consists of three modules: in the first one students follow a course about an astrophysical concept in each classroom, then they attend a set of activities in an Astrophysical research institute to improve their knowledge interacting with astronomers, and later on they done a final summary module.

---

[2] TabletPC is provided with Microsoft Windows XP Tablet PC edition [6] that is a Windows XP Professional enhanced version to exploit the features of this special notebook, while iPAQ uses Microsoft Windows Mobile 2003 for Pocket PC [7] that is a less complex operating system as that used by personal computer.

[3] A primary school ("Scuola Elementare Tempesta") a secondary school ("Scuola Media Peopoli") of Bologna (Italy) and one high school ("Liceo Scientifico Fracastoro") of Verona (Italy) joined in the project. Children were respectively 8, 13 and 18 years old.

3. THE CASE STUDY: A WIRELESS NETWORK INFRASTRUCTURE FOR AN "EXTENDED" ELECTRONIC CLASSROOM

The case study refers to the realization of an environment for learning and teaching activity such a classroom that is extended independently by the physical location: the idea is to apply wireless technology to build a highly interactive and mobile learning system using the mobility and portability features of the devices to allow ubiquitous learning. Students should use mobile devices to learn individually whenever they are and where they want (in classroom or in laboratory at school, at home or in another place such as different rooms of a research environment). They could interact each other in order to realize group work in and outside the school and to refer with the teacher/astronomer providing the didactic content, verifying and monitoring the learning phases. The activities to be deployed in several locations consist for example in reading digitized contents, practicing assignment while teacher assist them with multimedia context such as presentation slides, web pages, videos, online quizzes, e.g.

3.1   Design of the system architecture

According to the requirements[4], each student has two handled devices – a tabletPC and a iPAQ – to participate in learning activities for individual and group-based competition. These devices should interact each others to exchange messages and materials for the group work and in the same time they should be connected to a main computer that acts as a server sharing and providing contents as the figure 1 shows. The device becomes the virtual interactive classroom server (equipped with the Apache HTTP [9] web server) for the activities of keeping records of individual student's learning portfolio and supporting teacher to give feedback to students. Moreover the same server could provide print and monitor functionalities sharing a printer and a digital projector. This interactive system requires the implementation of a wireless LAN (WLAN) [10] to provide location-independent network access over radio waves to all resources and services useful for learning. The connection to Internet through a wired network

---

[4] Learning activities are designed by teachers and astronomers involved in the project: in particular the didactic design and its realization in each classroom has been carried out by Angela Turricchia of the "Planetario – Settore Istruzione – Comune di Bologna" and Maria Antonietta Carrozza of the "Liceo Fracastoro" School of Verona, while in the research institute by astronomers Caterina Boccato, Luca Nobili and Elena Lazzaretto of INAF.

could increase learning train including search for information as one of the teaching activities.

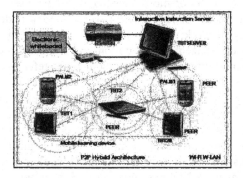

Figure 1. [Network infrastructure for the interactive system: the virtual classroom]

3.2 Technological solutions for wireless network topologies and standards

Basically speaking the effective range or distance reached by the network determines the type of network or standards. Each handled device could use the common wireless technologies: infrared, Bluetooth and Wi-Fi, the friendlier name for the IEEE 802.11b standard. The use of infrared port has been soon abandoned since the requirement of exchanging multimedia context in a fast way and between more devices. Bluetooth and Wi-Fi standards are both used for WLAN deployment suitable for the learning information system since they realize the two topology modes: ad hoc/ MANET [11] or infrastructure mode. The two topologies address different scenarios and system architectures. As regards wireless connectivity, the key difference between the Bluetooth and Wi-Fi standards is the expected operational rate: while operating in the same spectrum and suffering from the same level of interference Bluetooth is a short-range network that offers lower speed (2Mbps), while Wi-Fi is designed to offer full LAN connectivity and support the suite of networking protocols (i.e. TCP/IP) with theoretical 11Mbps of data rate. Moreover Bluetooth technology has a limit in the maximum number of connected devices without an appropriate access point. For these considerations Wi-Fi standard has been chosen to implement the WLAN for learning environment in both the two network topology modes allowing the use of such information system in different physical locations (figure 2).

3.2.1   Wireless ad hoc network topology

The MANET consists of mostly homogeneous wireless links based on standard medium access control (MAC) where mobile nodes dynamically form a temporary network without the use of any existing wired network infrastructure or centralized administration and communicate directly with one another in a mesh to mesh topology (sometimes referred as Independent Basic Service Set – IBSS – topology). Owing to the limited radio propagation range of the wireless devices used, messages among non-neighbor nodes go through multiple intermediate nodes to reach destinations. Because of the multi-hop communication even for short geographical distances and random movement of mobile nodes, applications of ad hoc wireless networks are mainly restricted to small wireless islands which can be useful for intranet applications. Windows XP operating system supports the enabling of wireless of ad-hoc network both for Wi-Fi and Bluetooth technologies. The "Windows Connect Now" technology embedded in Windows XP Service Pack 2 (SP2) allows for creating a wireless network able to connect each network adapter. A pure ad hoc network using Wi-Fi wireless standard has been implemented for the classroom work: a small intranet has been manually created for each of the three classroom with a specific SSID. Within the network it could be possible to enable the ability to share files and directory for each nodes becoming part of a well-defined workgroup. All the devices must have an unique name to be identified and exchange information. The security problem in this deployment, has not be taken in consideration due to the locality of the network in a classroom context. This infrastructure gives the opportunity to exchange contents of all formats and to provide web access to resources: using the Windows network functionalities the tablets' network work well and it is possible to identify each one in the network. Problems arise with iPAQs since their operating system doesn't permit to assign an IP and every device is shown with the generic name "Pocket PC" making impossible their network unique identification. Moreover, the ad-hoc network implementation shown some connectivity issues when all the devices are connected to the wireless network, and obviously performance problems in the simultaneous exchange of multimedia content due to the limited band.

3.2.2   Infrastructure topology: W-LAN with access point

Generally using the infrastructure mode of 802.11 standard (known as Basic Service Set – BSS), devices requires the installation of at least one Access Point (AP) referred to as a base station connected to the wired network. In this context all the communications also those between the nodes occur via the AP. Wireless nodes have to establish a relation of association before the messages exchange: they listen for beacon messages to identify the access points within the range. However if such wireless network are badly designed W-LAN access points can become bottlenecks. In this context an AP could improve data transmission, since all available devices support the 802.11g standard enabling a rate of 54Mbs. This configuration could not be adopted in the school due to the lack of a wired network infrastructure, but only in the research institute where students attend a course's module structured in several activities.

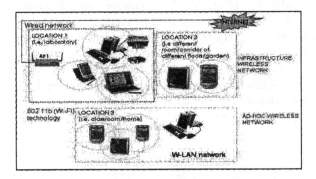

Figure 2. [W-LANs for several physical location in intranet and internet context]

In this location, the existent wireless network is expanded adding multiple APs which are combined into a single sub-network (as in the Extended Service Set – ESS) topology. It has been decided to use the existent WLAN infrastructure, also because since the Wi-Fi standard does not define roaming techniques, there could be problems when roaming users crossed a router boundary between subnets. Adopting DHCP, it is necessary to force users to release IP address as migrate from one subnet to another. A detail plan for installation of these devices is necessary for interference problems, since wireless network and any data transmitted over it employ radio signals and broadcast that extend in all direction. The overlapping problem is solved using different radio channels to boost aggregate throughput and this change has really improve performance issues. Finally as regards security and the three main methods [12] built into 802.11 networks (SSID, MAC address filtering and WEP), the MAC address filtering has been chosen both for the fact that the devices are known at start point and the necessity to don't introduce complexity in the management of the whole network. With this configuration, the wireless network work well and with good performance for all the learning activities done in different rooms of the institute and also outside it (in the garden): this test contribute to really show students and teachers the efficacy of the mobility feature.

3.3   Encountered Issues

The main issues encountered in the network deployment are the following:

- iPAQs problems with inter-connectivity and limited software
- unexpected lost of signal in ad-hoc network topology
- limited band of 802.11b protocol in exchanging simultaneous multimedia context both in ad-hoc and infrastructure mode.

The issue of the iPAQs network unique identification that limits the possibility to control them and to interact directly with tablets, is probably due to the software. A test using tablet's Bluetooth feature and its functionalities (figure 3) permits to assign a unique name for each iPAQ with the paring option, but this connection don't give full control of each student's PDA and could be used only in a limited context such as at home for example.

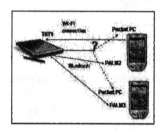

Figure 3. [Issues for recognizing palm in unique way with Wi-Fi connectivity]

Other software problems using devices regard the network file transmission that could not be done using the basic functionality of the iPAQ operating system. Students use normally the "drag & drop" utility also for transferring files and it is difficult for them to follow a set of steps to transfer a single file, such as using the basic procedure. The issue is partially solved by the use of an ftp server installed on the interactive server, but it's on study the way to realize an effective interaction between all these devices. Microsoft Mobile software has the possibility to synchronize remotely the iPAQ with a server using the ActiveSync software, but this option is available only for a limit set of applications (Calendar, Contact or Inbox). The goal is to develop an application able to provide this functionality.

4. CONCLUSIONS

WLAN offers flexibility but the factors implementing a successful wireless network are: user interface, network logon rate, response time, throughput and reliable data delivery. The first test of this W-LAN deployment has demonstrate its effectiveness both in each school than in the research institute environment. The wireless network is up to now widely use in each classroom for learning and teaching activities due also for the easy way of set up and use even if some issues remain regarding performance and a sometime unexpected lost of connectivity. On the other hand the WLAN implemented in the wired infrastructure has permitted to make all the learning/teaching programmed activities with a reliable data delivery and a good response time. The learning modules developed using all formats (e.g video and animation) could permit a really test of the network that had maintained a good performance. To continue the experiment with other schools and make a more direct link between education and research world, it will be necessary to design two different WLAN networks in order to separate the student network by that of researcher and also really face security aspects.

5. ACKNOLEDGMENTS

The author likes to acknowledge HP Philanthropy, the project head Prof. Leopoldo Benacchio, the astronomers Caterina Boccato, Luca Nobili, Elena Lazzaretto of INAF, Angela Turricchia of the "Planetario – Settore Istruzione – Comune of Bologna and Maria Antonietta Carrozza of the Fracastoro School of Verona involved in the project and Roberto Greggio for his help in the testing phase.

6. REFERENCES

[1] Mark Weiser, "The Computer for the Twenty-First Century," Scientific American, pp. 94-10, September 1991
[2] HP Philanthropy, http://grants.hp.com/
[3] HP Tablet PC TC1100 http://h18000.www1.hp.com/products/tabletpc/tc1100/
[4] IEEE Standards Department. IEEE 802.11 standard for wireless LAN, medium access control (MAC) and physical layer (PHY) specifications, 1997
[5] IEEE Standards Department. IEEE Bluetooth standard: Wireless mac and phy specifications for wireless personal area networks (wpans[tm]), 1997
[6]   Windows   XP   Tablet   PC   Home   Page, https://s.microsoft.com/windowsxp/tabletpc/default.mspx

[7]   Windows   Mobile   2003   for   Pocket   PC,
http://www.microsoft.com/windowsmobile/pocketpc/ppc/default.mspx
[8] Mobile Learning and Pervasive Computing, http://www3.telus.net/~kdeanna/mlearning/
[9] The Apache HTTP Server, http://www.apache.org
[10] Wireless LAN (WLAN), http://www.ukoln.ac.uk/public/earl/issuepapers/wireless.html
[11] Mobile Ad-hoc Networks (manet), http://www.ietf.org/html.charters/manet-charter.html
[12]   WLAN   security   measures,
http://www.backupbook.com/02Security/A1WLAN_Security.html

THROUGHPUT ANALYSIS OF AN ALOHA-BASED MAC POLICY FOR AD HOC NETWORKS*

Konstantinos Oikonomou
Department of Informatics and Telecommunications, University of Athens, Greece.
Address: Panepistimiopolis, Ilissia, 157-84, Athens, Greece.
Phone: +30 210 727 5341, Fax: +30 210 7275333
okon@di.uoa.gr

Ioannis Stavrakakis
Department of Informatics and Telecommunications, University of Athens, Greece.
Address: Panepistimiopolis, Ilissia, 157-84, Athens, Greece.
Phone: +30 210 727 5343, Fax: +30 210 7275333
ioannis@di.uoa.gr

Abstract   Re-use of existing widely explored Medium Access Control (MAC) schemes, like the well-known Aloha scheme, is not applicable in ad hoc networks where the transmissions of the users can be normally sensed by only a fraction of the users present in the network. Therefore, *estimations of the network traffic load* are not possible anymore. Here, an *adaptive probabilistic policy* for medium access control in ad hoc networks, inspired by the Aloha paradigm, is proposed and analyzed. Simulation results show that this policy is capable of achieving higher *system throughput* when compared to other policies that have been proposed for ad hoc networks. It is also shown that *mobility* severely impacts the system throughput and therefore, an alternative approach is proposed that reduces the effects of mobility in the expense of the maximum achievable system throughput.

Keywords: Ad Hoc, Aloha, MAC

1.   Introduction

The design of Medium Access Control (MAC) policies in ad hoc networks is challenging due to the idiosyncratic behavior of these networks. Several MAC policies have been proposed, [1], [2], [3], which are based on the CSMA/CA

*This work has been supported in aprt by the E-NEXT research program that is partly funded by the European Commission.

mechanism, including in most of the cases the Ready-To-Send/Clear-To-Send handshake dialogue to avoid the *hidden/exposed terminal* problem. TDMA-based MAC protocols have also been proposed (e.g., [4]) and it has been shown that when an optimal solution is required, the derivation of the *scheduling (time slots* in which a node is allowed to transmit during a *frame*), is an NP-complete problem, similar to the *n*-coloring problem in graph theory, [5], [6]. Consequently, these approaches are *not suitable for ad-hoc networks* where, in general, nodes are moving and therefore, the scheduling needs to be recalculated for all nodes in the network.

TDMA-based MAC policies, which do not require recalculation of the scheduling of the nodes when the *topology of the network* is changing and the *frame size* is significantly smaller than the number of nodes in the network, have already been proposed, [7], [8], [9], [10]. The Deterministic Policy (referred to hereafter as D-Policy) has originally been proposed in [7]. Under this policy nodes are allowed to *transmit only at a (small) subset of the available time slots* carefully selected so that at least one of them be collision free. While the latter results in a guaranteed minimum throughput per node, restricting the transmission opportunities of a node to a (small) subset of the available slots, leads to a fairly low overall system throughput, [10].

Since most of the non-assigned - under the D-Policy - slots may be wasted if other nodes are temporarily idle or move away, it has been proposed in [10] that such slots be utilized *probabilistically*. This is the key idea behind the Probabilistic Policy (referred to hereafter as P-Policy) introduced in [10]. It turns out that the system throughput is (in general) significantly increased under the P-Policy. The higher system throughput under the P-Policy is achieved by *giving access to all nodes to all slots*, with probability 1 if the slot is assigned (under the D-Policy) to a node and with *access probability p* otherwise.

In this paper, an Aloha-based MAC policy is proposed and studied. This new policy assumes the deterministic framework provided by the D-Policy and *adapts* accordingly to the *network traffic load* conditions and the *topology density*. The proposed policy will be referred to, hereafter, as the Adaptive Policy, or A-Policy. The probabilistic transmission attempts introduced under the P-Policy are preserved, the key idea being, behind the A-Policy, transmission attempts with probability 1 after successful transmissions, provided that there are data available. As a result, the utilization of any unused time slots (under the D-Policy and the P-Policy) is further improved, as it is shown in this study.

2.   The Adaptive Policy (A-Policy)

The key idea behind the A-Policy is to utilize further (compared to the P-Policy) the set of unused time slots and at the same time reduce as much as possible any interference caused to other time slots. Exchanging control messages among the nodes, is one possible way to proceed, but this process should be repeated every time the network topology changes and an extra overhead would be introduced.

The A-Policy: Each node u transmits in slot i during frame j, if $i \in \Omega_u$ and transmits with probability $p^j_{i,u \to v}$, if $i \notin \Omega_u$, provided it has data to transmit.

$p^j_{i,u \to v}$ may take two different values, p or 1, depending on the status of the most recent attempt of transmission $u \to v$ in time slot i. The initial value (for the case that no transmission $u \to v$ took place in the past) is set to p. The remaining of this section focuses on the derivation of an analytical expression regarding the *system throughput* under the A-Policy.

3. Simulation Results

In ad hoc networks, nodes are generally moving and it is interesting to examine the system throughput under the A-Policy under certain mobility conditions. Certainly, the D-Policy and the P-Policy are not affected by the movement of the nodes (except when the mobility of the nodes results in a denser topology, [10]) as the A-Policy does. It is already shown that a certain number of frames is required before the system throughput under the A-Policy (P_A) converges to a certain value. If nodes are moving, then the value of $p^j_{i,u \to v}$ will change (initialize and start converging again) by the time node v is not within the transmission range of node u. Obviously, the higher the mobility of the nodes, the more frequent the initializations and the smaller the system throughput under the A-Policy.

In order to demonstrate the aforementioned case using simulation results, nodes "initialize" the corresponding values of $p^j_{i,u \to v}$ after a number of frames equal to parameter *Initialization*. This is depicted in Figure 1. In Figure 1(a), where *Initialization* is set to 100 frames, it can be seen that P_A, for $p = \tilde{p}_{\lambda,\overline{|S|}}$ and $p = 0.01$, begins from 0.1 and 0.08 and converges towards, 0.12 and 0.16, respectively. At frame $j = 100$, both curves return to their initial values and converge again towards 0.12 and 0.16, respectively. Of course this is not the case for the other policies or for P_A for $p = 0.5$ (for the latter case the convergence period is rather small and equal to 2 frames).

In Figure 1(b), *Initialization* is set to 50 frames and it may be observed that P_A, for $p = 0.01$, is not able to reach 0.16 (the system throughput drops down before reaching the maximum achievable value). For smaller values of *Initialization* (5 and 1 in Figures 1(c) and 1(d), respectively), P_A, for $p = 0.5$, remains unaffected, while P_A, for $p = 0.01$, is severely affected. However, it is observed that P_A, for $p = \tilde{p}_{\lambda,\overline{|S|}}$, even though affected by the mobility of the nodes, is equal or slightly higher than P_P.

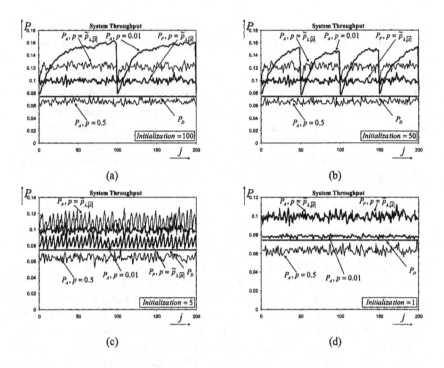

Figure 1.   System throughput, P, simulation results for various values of $Initialization$, as j increases.

4.   Conclusions

Here, a new MAC policy for ad hoc networks, the A-Policy, based on the Aloha paradigm, was proposed and analyzed. It is a simple policy that requires no knowledge of the topology to operate and it is shown that it achieves higher system throughput than other existing policies. The limitations of the A-Policy were also revealed in this work.

The A-Policy is suitable for ad hoc networks, since it is a simple policy to be implemented, it does not introduce any extra control overhead and the system throughput is largely increased compared to other policies (under certain conditions studied in this work). Even for the case of highly-mobile environments, an eloquent choice of the access probability p determines a certain lower bound for the system throughput, equal to the maximum system throughput under the P-Policy. However, the possible unfair treatment of some nodes in the network has to be taken into account with respect to the desired system throughput.

References

[1] IEEE 802.11, "Wireless LAN Medium Access Control (MAC) and Physical Layer (PHY) specifications," Nov. 1997. Draft Supplement to Standard IEEE 802.11, IEEE, New York, January 1999.

[2] P. Karn, "MACA- A new channel access method for packet radio," in ARRL/CRRL Amateur Radio 9th Computer Networking Conference, pp. 134-140, 1990.

[3] V. Bharghavan, A. Demers, S. Shenker, and L. Zhang, "MACAW: A Media Access Protocol for Wireless LAN's," Proceedings of ACM SIGCOMM'94, pp. 212-225, 1994.

[4] R. Nelson, L. Kleinrock, "Spatial TDMA, A collision-free Multihop Channel Access Protocol," IEEE Transactions on Communications, Vol. COM-33, No. 9, September 1985.

[5] A. Ephremides and T. V. Truong, "Scheduling Broadcasts in Multihop Radio Networks," IEEE Transactions on Communications, 38(4):456-60, April 1990.

[6] G. Wang and N. Ansari, "Optimal Broadcast Scheduling in Packet Radio Networks Using Mean Field Annealing," IEEE Journal on Selected Areas in Communications, VOL. 15, NO. 2, pp 250-260, February 1997.

[7] I. Chlamtac and A. Farago, "Making Transmission Schedules Immune to Topology Changes in Multi-Hop Packet Radio Networks," IEEE/ACM Trans. on Networking, 2:23-29, 1994.

[8] J.-H. Ju and V. O. K. Li, "An Optimal Topology-Transparent Scheduling Method in Multihop Packet Radio Networks," IEEE/ACM Trans. on Networking, 6:298-306, 1998.

[9] Z. Cai, M. Lu, C. N. Georghiades, "Topology-Transparent Time Division Multiple Access Broadcast Scheduling in Multihop Packet Radio Networks," IEEE Transactions on Vehicular Technology, Vol. 52, No. 4, July 2003.

[10] K. Oikonomou and I. Stavrakakis, "Analysis of a Probabilistic Topology-Unaware TDMA MAC Policy for Ad-Hoc Networks," IEEE Journal on Selected Areas in Communications (JSAC), Special Issue on Quality-of-Service Delivery in Variable Topology Networks, Vol. 22, No. 7, September 2004, pp. 1286-1300.

[11] N. Abramson, "The Aloha System - Another Alternative for Computer Communications," Proc. Fall Joint Comput., AFIPS Conf., p. 37, 1970.

[12] K. Oikonomou and I. Stavrakakis, "Load Analysis of Topology-Unaware TDMA MAC Policies for Ad-Hoc Networks," Quality of Future Internet Services (QoFIS), 29 September - 1 October, 2004, Barcelona, Spain.

PERFORMANCE EVALUATION OF BROADCASTING PROTOCOLS FOR AD HOC AND SENSOR NETWORKS

Hong Guo[1], François Ingelrest[2], David Simplot-Ryl[2], and Ivan Stojmenović[1]

[1] *Computer Science, SITE. University of Ottawa, Canada.*
hguo023yahoo.ca, ivan@site.uottawa.ca

[2] *IRCICA/LIFL, University of Lille 1, France. INRIA futurs, POPS research groups.*
Francois.Ingelrest@lifl.fr, David.Simplot@lifl.fr

Abstract   Many broadcasting protocols for ad hoc and sensor networks have been proposed. Multipoint relay (MPR) and dominating set (DS) schemes can effectively improve the efficiency while providing reliable broadcasting. The neighbor elimination scheme (NES) can improve any broadcasting protocol as an added feature. We evaluate the performance of MPR (source dependent), MPR-DS (source-independent MPR), and DS-based protocols. We add NES to these schemes separately and evaluate the performance of the resulted protocols. As a result, DS-NES appears to be the most robust, taking all measurements and parameters into acount, because it remains competitive under all scenarios, and has significant advantages over MPR-DS-NES in dynamic scenarios, and over MPR-NES when the broadcast message is not very large, because MPR has overhead in packet lengths.

1.   Introduction

Ad hoc and sensor networks are two kinds of wireless networks operating without infrastructure, relying on hosts for communication tasks. Among the common problems found in these two kinds of networks is broadcasting, which can be used for route discovery for example. It is a well-known *one-to-all* communication task, where one host u whishes to send a given set of data to all the other ones. Since normally the source node is not within transmission radius to all the recipient nodes, many hosts will have to act as routers for the task to be achieved. The easiest way is to have all nodes act as routers and retransmit the messages at least once to their neighborhood: this is a protocol known as *blind flooding*. In networks which are not sparse, it generates a lot of collisions that could possibly prevent the broadcasting from being correctly performed. Moreover, significant energy is consumed by the redundant messages. A number of other schemes have been proposed to replace blind flooding, and they can be classified in different categories: simple flooding, probability based, area based and neighbor knowledge methods.

In this paper, we aim at evaluating the performances of protocols from the fourth category only. Indeed, for the existing probability and area based protocols, the performances of the protocols are closely related to the predetermined parameters and thresholds for which the best values may depend on network conditions. Moreover, they are not reliable as illustrated by [Stojmenović et al., 2001]. The reliability of a broadcasting protocol refers to the capability of reaching all the nodes in the network when considering a collision free environment. Neighbor knowledge methods normally provide reliable broadcasting, and can be further divided into self-pruning and neighbor-designating methods, according to whether a node makes a local decision to retransmit a broadcast packet or is told by the upstream sender (either via the packet or via a previously sent control packet) whether it needs to retransmit the packet. We may also refer to these two types of methods as source-dependent and source-independent methods. From these two behaviors, we chose the *multipoint relay protocol* (MPR) proposed by [Qayyum et al., 2002] and the *generalized self-pruning rule* presneted by [Dai and Wu, 2003] as they are both efficient and representative. A variant combining MPR and dominating sets, namely MPR-DS proposed by [Adjih et al., 2005], is also studied. Secondly, by adding the neighbor elimination scheme studied by [Peng and Lu, 2000] and by [Stojmenović et al., 2001] to the above mentioned schemes, we are able to illustrate that it improves the performance of any broadcasting protocol as added feature.

The remainder of this paper is organized as follows: in the next section, we provide the definitions needed by our network model, while in Sec. 3 are provided the technique, algorithms and procedures used in our simulations, as well as the assumptions made for our experiments and the obtained results. We finally conclude in Sec. 4 and provide some directions for future research.

2.   Preliminaries

We represent an ad hoc network by a graph $G = (V, E)$ where V is the set of nodes and $E \subseteq V^2$ is the set of edges that gives the available communications: (u, v) belongs to E means that v is a physical neighbor of u, i.e. u can directly send a message to v. Let us assume that the maximum range of communication, denoted by R, is the same for all vertices and that $d(u, v)$ is the Euclidean distance between u and v. The set E is then defined as follows:

$$E = \{(u, v) \in V^2 \mid d(u, v) \leq R\}.$$

So defined graph is called the *unit graph*, with R as its transmission radius. Each node $u \in V$ is assigned a unique value to be used as an *identifier* (id), so that the identifier of u is denoted by id(u). We also define the neighborhood set $N(u)$ of a vertex u as:

$$N(u) = \{v \mid (u, v) \in E\}.$$

The size of this set, $|N(u)|$, is also known as the degree of u. The density of the graph is the average degree for each node. Note that (u, u) is not in E.

The distance between two nodes is measured in term of *number of hops*, which is simply the minimum number of links to cross from a source node to a destination one.

Nodes in a broadcasting protocol may require various neighborhood information. The protocols considered in this article require 2-hop topological information at each node. It may be obtained by two rounds of 'HELLO' messages, to send information about itself to neighbors, and to send collected information about its neighbors so that each node can acquire 2-hop knowledge. One of the selected protocols, MPR-DS, requires the third round of 'HELLO' messages, so that each node can inform all its neighbors about forwarding decisions, which are used later when a broadcasting task emerges.

Extended literature review and more explanations on our simulations design can be found in [Guo et al., 2005].

3. Performances Evaluation

In our research, the experiments were carried out in two phases: in the first one, the performance of the basic MPR, CDS and MPR-DS schemes were evaluated. In the second one, we added a NES to these algorithms and evaluated the performance of the resulting methods. We used random uniform unit disc graphs to model ad hoc and sensor networks, and considered only connected topologies. We adopt certain assumptions to appropriately define the area of our study. These assumptions can be summarized as follow:

- An ideal MAC protocol (no collision) is used, and nodes are static. Thus, any effect that mobility may have is avoided: because of localized algorithms being applied, it is assumed that relative positions of nodes do not change (sufficiently to impact the performance) while broadcasting.

- There is only one broadcasting task at a time in the network and no other message traffic exists. We thus avoid the impact of collisions, believing that a protocol with a lower overhead on one broadcasting task reduces collision impact on other tasks and is thus expected to perform better if collision were added.

- There is synchronization among the transmissions, channel is time-slotted and each transmission takes one slot.

- Each time a node transmits a packet, all its 1-hop neighbors receive it.

- While a node transmits, none of its neighbors up to 2-hop are transmitting. This assumption was used to eliminate the problem of interference when a node receives two radio transmissions at the same time by two of its neighbors, which are not neighbors themselves.

We used the rule by Dai and Wu to compute CDS's. We define the priority of a node with a record key = (degree, id): nodes compare their degrees first and the node with the higher degree has greater chances of being in the connected dominating set. In case of ties, the node with the highest id has priority to be selected. We used the same priority for MPR-DS and the enhancement by Wu.

We call a node that is in multipoint relay set or in connected dominating set a relay candidate. There are two factors that a relay candidate c needs to consider before it relays the broadcast packet when using NES: timeout and forwardingList. Upon the first reception of the broadcast packet, c sets up timeout = (1/numberCoverd, id), where numberCovered is the number of 1-hop neighbors who have not received the packet after the same transmission. In case of ties, the node with the lowest id will rebroadcast the packet first. The forwardingList, at first, contains all 1-hop neighbors of c. For each reception of the packet, c eliminates from the forwardingList all neighbors receiving the packet from the same transmission. If c gets a packet from one of its neighbors after its first reception, it may need to adjust its original timeout when the number of uncovered neighbors changes. When timeout expires, c will rebroadcast the packet if its forwardingList is not empty. When adding a neighbor elimination scheme within a multipoint relaying broadcasting protocol, instead of letting all existing MPR's compute their own MPR's, we decided that only the MPR's which relay the packet to their neighbors carry out further computation. That means, if a MPR v has an empty forwarding list, v will not rebroadcast the packet and thus will not compute its own MPR's.

We first measure the percentage of re-transmitting nodes (PRN). To do this, the number of nodes that rebroadcasts the message is counted, and compared to the total number of nodes. Fig. 1 illustrates the simulation results. Subfigure 1(a) indicates that MPR has a lower ratio compared to DS and MPR-DS. However, each message in MPR is of longer size and therefore the selection of method with lowest overall packet size depends on the size of broadcast packet with respect to the size of neighbor's id. DS and MPR-DS behave equally well. This observation is consistent with results by [Adjih et al., 2005].We observe that the neighbor elimination scheme has improved DS and MPR-DS significantly, but does not seem to have a significant impact on MPR when the

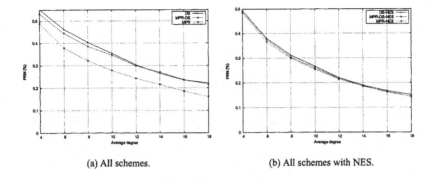

(a) All schemes.   (b) All schemes with NES.

Figure 1.   PRN versus average degree.

average node degree is less than 10 and only does trivial improvement to MPR for $d > 10$. It is interesting to note that after adding the neighbor elimination scheme, three new protocols behave almost equally well.

Our result reveals that all algorithms depend on the density of the network. In sparse networks, more nodes need to rebroadcast in order to reach all the nodes in the network. As the density increases, proportionally fewer nodes rebroadcast. This observation differs from the result by [Stojmenović et al., 2001], where it has been observed that the ratios appear to be relatively stable with respect to degree d. We argue that our result is more reasonable because when the degree d increases, the number of neighbors covered by one transmission increases, consequently the number of retransmissions needed to cover a certain number of nodes ($n = 100$ in our case) decreases.

We also measure the number of nodes that each transmission covers. In fact this number is the number of 1-hop neighbors of each transmitting node. An average value on all the transmitting nodes is computed and compared with other methods. In Fig. 2(a) and 2(b), it is observed that NFN increases with respect to the average node degree d for all the methods. This was predictable as theoretically the NFN is closely related to d. DS has shown superiority over MPR and MPR-DS while DS-NES performs a little better than MPR-NES and MPR-DS-NES. Recall that in MPR, a node is chosen to be a multipoint relay because it covers a maximal number of un-covered neighbors. Although this number relies on the node degree to a certain extent, a node which covers the most uncovered neighbors will not necessarily have the highest degree in its neighborhood. However in DS, nodes with higher degrees have a higher priority to be in the connected dominating set. This is also true for MPR-DS most of the time. Notwithstanding the previous statement, in MPR-DS, a node with the highest degree in its neighborhood but without being an intermediate

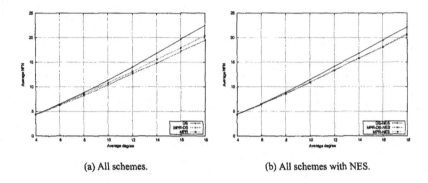

(a) All schemes.   (b) All schemes with NES.

Figure 2.   NFN versus average degree.

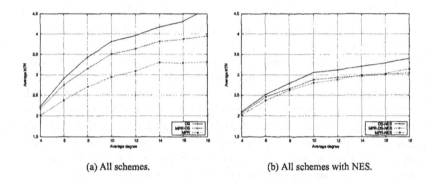

(a) All schemes.   (b) All schemes with NES.

Figure 3.   NTN versus average degree.

node cannot be in the connected dominating set. Ergo, there is the possibility that node with highest degree is not selected for both MPR and MPR-DS. Consequently, DS has a larger coverage per transmission.

The neighbor elimination scheme does not have significant impact on the average number of nodes covered by each transmitting nodes. This demonstrates that the neighbor elimination scheme improves the broadcasting protocols by reducing redundant retransmissions.

We now give results concerning the number of times each non-transmitting node receives the message, noted NTN. From Fig. 3, we observe that, in sparse networks, non-transmitting nodes get less redundant messages. While the degree d increases, each node receives more copies of the same message. The neighbor elimination scheme effectively reduces the redundancy in the network.

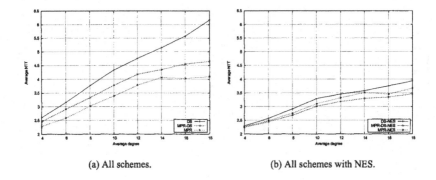

(a) All schemes. (b) All schemes with NES.

Figure 4. NTT versus average degree.

Fig. 3 presents the measured NTN for all methods under consideration. We see that MPR has a better performance than DS and MPR-DS (each node receiving fewer copies of the same packet), while MPR-DS lies in-between DS and MPR. From 3(b), we observe that after adding the neighbor elimination scheme, the three methods tend to have similar performances. The neighbor elimination scheme reduces NTN, thus reducing the traffic in the network. This improvement is more obvious for DS and MPR-DS protocols. In these two methods, on average, NTN has been reduced by 0.5 to 1 in dense networks (when $d = 8$). But, MPR-NES still has slightly better performance than DS-NES and MPR-DS-NES overall.

We now give results about the number of times each transmitting node receives the message, noted NTT. An observation similar to NTN can be obtained for NTT from Fig. 4. That is, there is less redundancy in sparse networks than dense networks. Recall that with the average degree d increases, fewer nodes retransmit the message. However, the number of times each node, transmitting or non-transmitting, receives the same message increases. This can be explained by the increased coverage of each transmission. According to our observations, it appears that the transmitting nodes receive more copies of the same message than non-transmitting nodes. Once again, we notice that the neighbor elimination scheme improves DS and MPR-DS more than on MPR. In fig. 4, MPR exhibits the best performance on NTT. DS has the most redundancy on transmitting nodes. With the help of neighbor elimination scheme, MPR-DS-NES outperforms MPR-NES and DS-NES for most d values, as indicated in 4(b).

We finally consider the overhead brought by MPR scheme in the size of broadcast messages by including ids of relays in these messages. The other

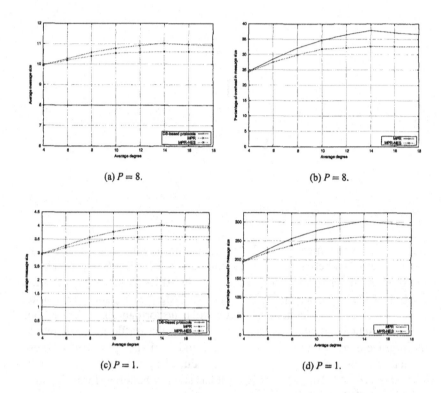

(a) $P = 8$.   (b) $P = 8$.

(c) $P = 1$.   (d) $P = 1$.

Figure 5.   Average message size and overhead in message size for MPR scheme.

schemes, based on CDS, do not need to forward additional information within the broadcast packet. Let the unit packet size be equal to the size of the id of one neighbor in the forwarding list. Let p be the size of broadcast message in such units. Each MPR message is of different length, which is $p + s$, s being the number of neighbors in forwarding list, while dominating set approaches need p size for each message. We give in Fig. 5 the comparison between the different schemes for $p = 1$ and $p = 8$. We first measured the average size of each message being transmitted, and the percentage of overhead in the size of the transmitted message. We can observe that the overhead brought by the inclusion of ids of relays can be rather huge if the original size is small. For $p = 8$ in 5(a) and 5(b), the overhead ranges from 25% to 40% for densities between 4 and 18, while for $p = 1$ in 5(c) and 5(d), it ranges between 200% and 300%, compared to dominating set based approaches.

To complete the study of message overhead, we then measured the message dilation, as the ratio of overall message sizes transmitted by given protocol

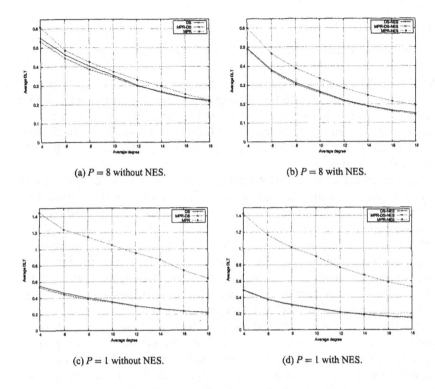

(a) $P = 8$ without NES.

(b) $P = 8$ with NES.

(c) $P = 1$ without NES.

(d) $P = 1$ with NES.

Figure 6. Average dilation for the miscellaneous schemes.

with respect to the overall message size used in blind flooding solution. The latter is np, where n is the number of nodes in the network. We thus give in Fig. 6 the value of this ratio for the values $p = 1$ and $p = 8$. It confirms that for small value of p, the overhead brought by the inclusion of MPR relays is rather huge, while the two schemes based on CDS are very near from each other.

We can infer that CDS-based schemes are superior to MPR scheme when p has a small value, because of the significant overhead (and consequently the number of collisions at the MAC layer) in MPR, while the difference will become negligible for higher values of p (for example when broadcasting large files).

An interesting observation is that the notable improvement on MPR, by adding the neighbor elimination scheme, starts at $d = 10$. This happens because in sparse networks more relaying nodes need to rebroadcast to reach isolated neighbors.

4.   Conclusion

We have seen that the NES can enhance the performances of all the protocols as an added feature, especially in dense networks. The notable improvement on MPR starts at $d = 10$: in sparse networks, more relaying nodes need
to relay to reach isolated nodes. Examples are the neighbors of a node with
degree one, and such nodes are more likely to exist in sparse networks than in
dense ones. NES improves DS and MPR-DS protocols more significantly than
MPR, revealing that source-independent protocols benefit more from NES than
source-dependent ones.

Among all the schemes, MPR-NES appears to require the least number of
retransmissions, but the advantage is not major. However, this is balanced by
the increased size of messages, which can cause more collisions and requires
more energy. For smaller packet sizes, CDS-based protocols appear superior:
MPR-DS-NES protocol performs slightly better than DS-NES. However, it
requires a third round of HELLO messages, and is therefore inferior in dynamic networks. It appears that pure DS-based methods approaches are overall winning ones, remaining competitive under all scenarios and having huge
advantage in dynamic networks or with smaller packets.

All algorithms depend on the density of the network: in sparse ones, more
nodes need to relay to reach all the nodes but as the density increases, proportionally fewer nodes need to rebroadcast while the number of times each node,
transmitting or not, receives the same message increases. Transmitting nodes
receive more copies of the same message than non-transmitting ones for all d
values.

References

[Adjih et al., 2005] Adjih, C., Jacquet, P., and Viennot, L. (2005). Computing connected dominated sets with multipoint relays. *Ad Hoc & Sensor Wireless Networks*, 1(1 – 2):27 – 39.

[Dai and Wu, 2003] Dai, F. and Wu, J. (2003). Distributed dominant pruning in ad hoc networks. In *Proceedings of the IEEE International Conference on Communications (ICC'03)*,
Anchorage, Alaska.

[Guo et al., 2005] Guo, H., Ingelrest, F., Simplot-Ryl, D., and Stojmenović, I. (2005). Performance evaluation of broadcasting protocols for ad hoc and sensor networks. Technical
report, INRIA.

[Peng and Lu, 2000] Peng, W. and Lu, X. (2000). On the reduction of broadcast redundancy in
mobile ad hoc networks. In *Proceedings of the ACM MobiHoc 2000*, Boston, USA.

[Qayyum et al., 2002] Qayyum, A., Viennot, L., and Laouiti, A. (2002). Multipoint relaying
for flooding broadcast messages in mobile wireless networks. In *Proceedings of the Hawaii
International Conference on System Sciences (HICSS'02)*, Big Island, Hawaii.

[Stojmenović et al., 2001] Stojmenović, I., Seddigh, M., and Zunic, J. (2001). Dominating
sets and neighbor elimination-based broadcasting algorithms in wireless networks. *IEEE
Transactions on Parallel and Distributed Systems*, 13(1):14 – 25.

MOBILITY-AWARE ADAPTIVE COUNTER-BASED FORWARDING ELIMINATION TO REDUCE DATA OVERHEAD IN MULTICAST AD HOC ROUTING*

Carmen M. Yago Sánchez, Pedro M. Ruiz, and Antonio F. Gómez Skarmeta
Dept. of Information and Communication Engineering, University of Murcia,
Campus de Espinardo, 30100 Murcia, Spain
{carmen,pedrom,skarmeta}@dif.um.es

Abstract   Most of the previous efforts regarding multicast routing in MANETs, have been devoted to the provision of low-control overhead protocols, being able to maximize the packet delivery ratio. In multicast routing, the non-optimality of the forwarding structure can also lead to transmission of additional data packets (compared to the minimum required). We call those additional data packets data-overhead. In this paper, we present a counter-based forwarding elimination scheme, being able to reduce that overhead depending upon the mobility of the nodes. Our results show that this approach is able to enhance the bandwidth consumption of mesh-based multicast ad hoc routing protocols while maintaining nearly the same packet delivery ratio.

Keywords: ad hoc, routing efficiency, multicast, data overhead.

1.   Introduction and Motivation

Nowadays mobile and wireless technologies are responding to the necessity of communicating everyday and everywhere without restrictions. In this atmosphere, ad-hoc networks, the infrastuctureless wireless networks, are gaining momentum. These networks are creating a big interest due to the variety of applications they have in different environments, for example rescue operations, battlefields, or communication between home automation devices.

There is also a manifest interest in allowing these networks to make use of multicast communication. Several routing protocols have been developed to route multicast traffic. These protocols are basically grouped into three

*This paper has been partially funded by the Spanish MCYT by means of the SAM (TIC2002-04531-C04) project, and the "Ramon y Cajal" workprogramme and also by the "Consejeria de Trabajo, Consumo y Politica Social de la Region de Murcia" and the European Social Fund by means of the "Integrated Operacional Programme for the Region de Murcia 2000-2006".

categories [Cordeiro et al., 2003]: stateless multicast like DDM, tree based protocols like MAODV or AMRIS and mesh based protocols like ODMRP or CAMP. There are also some hybrid approaches like AMRoute. Stateless multicast protocols are oriented to small groups. Tree based protocols do not have this restriction but they usually have problems with high mobility networks. In that case, they are outperformed by mesh based protocols which introduce more redundancy and alternate paths.

Mesh based approaches seem to be a good way to route multicast traffic in ad hoc networks, however they produce a considerable overhead. This overhead has two causes: firstly, the instability of the network makes it necessary to flood control messages periodically. Secondly, there is data overhead. Data overhead is a consequence of the non-optimality of multicast trees and meshes. Multicast meshes provide robustness but also cause forwarding nodes to redundantly transmit the same message in the same area. Then, as defined in [Ruiz and Gómez-Skarmeta, 2004] this data overhead consists of the data messages unnecessarily transmitted due to the redundancy of the mesh. In addition, provided that data traffic rates are higher than control packet rates, data overhead becomes the main source of sub-optimality of routing protocols, producing excessive bandwidth consumption, increased link-layer contention, and most of the issues associated to blind flooding [Ni et al., 1999].

Ruiz [Ruiz and Gómez-Skarmeta, 2004] showed that the problem of computing the minimal data-overhead multicast tree is an NP-complete problem. So, an approximation algorithm is necessary to limit the number of data messages delivered into the network.

Several algorithms and protocols have been developed to limit the number of messages flooded or multicasted into the network. These proposals can be basically grouped into two categories [Yi et al., 2003], topology based approaches and heuristic based approaches. The former refers to the use of topological information to reduce the number of nodes which can retransmit a message for example neighbour-topology-based schemes such as self-pruning [Lim and Kim, 2000] and multipoint relay MPR [Laouiti et al., 2001] or hierarchical approaches such as Domain-Based [Gui and Mohapatra, 2004] and Overlay-Driven hierarchical multicast. The latter, rather than reducing the number of nodes which can retransmit, allows every node which is in charge of forwarding the message to decide, using a heuristic, whether to retransmit it or not; for example in [Ni et al., 1999] three schemes are defined to reduce the Broadcast Storm Problem in flooding: counter-based, distance based and probabilistic.

We consider a heuristic approximation algorithm based on the idea that limiting the number of redundant data messages without pruning multicast meshes will improve the efficiency whilst keeping the robustness. Within the heuristic category we encounter the counter-based algorithm particularly remarkable due to its performance, its ease of calculation and low resources consumption.

This algorithm not only is useful to deal with overhead in flooding but also to make the nodes belonging to the mesh reduce the data overhead.

It is based on the "expected additional coverage" concept [Ni et al., 1999]. Every time a message is retransmitted by a node it covers an area in which the message can be heard. Then the "expected additional coverage" is the new area that would be covered for the first time if the node retransmitted the message. This area gets smaller every time a node listens to the message it has to retransmit because part of it is already covered by the message heard.

The counter-based algorithm proposes that a message must not be retransmitted if the host has heard it C times before (from now on C is called the threshold value), when the "expected additional coverage" becomes too small.

Using this counter-based approach, the threshold value C has to be carefully chosen and it has to be a trade off between the performance of the protocol and the reduction of the overhead. A greater threshold provides better performance, but also higher overhead. Moreover, when the links are instable the number of messages heard has less significance because the instability of the links may have prevented the other nodes in the area from receiving the message. This might be solved by using a greater fixed threshold C, but then the message saving would decrease with the consequent increment of the overhead and its problems.

Due to these disadvantages, we consider the traditional counter-based scheme can be improved by making the threshold C dependant on the local network conditions. To do this, we need a representative and distributed metric which tells the node about the stability of the network around it.

Based on this, we propose here a method to reduce the data overhead in mesh based protocols: the mobility-aware counter-based algorithm. It is a new adaptation of the counter-based algorithm which adapts itself to network conditions using a new mobility metric which fits the requirements detailed above. This metric, the modal link duration interval, is based on the stability of the links and allows the node to be aware of its local network conditions.

This paper is organized as follows, in the next section we propose the mobility-aware counter-based algorithm, our adaptation to multicast of the counter-based mechanism. In Section 3 we present and evaluate the results of the simulation. Finally, the conclusions are provided in the last section.

2.   Mobility-aware Counter Scheme

As we have seen before, counter-based mechanisms [Ni et al., 1999], based on the "expected additional coverage" concept have been revealed as a good approach to reduce the redundancy in flooding. We use a similar approach for dealing with data overhead reduction. Below, we define our proposed metric, and afterwards we will describe our proposed approach.

Modal link duration interval (MLD) mobility metric

We have chosen a metric based on the link duration [Boleng et al., 2002] which is a good indicator for protocol performance. The link duration metric fits many of our requirements: it is distributed and reflects network conditions. But if a few nodes behave very differently from the rest, the average may not reflect the behaviour of the majority of the network. We desire a metric which reflects the behaviour of the majority of the forwarder neighbours, hiding the distortion produced by "rebel" nodes. Thus, instead of the mean, we have adopted a modal interval of the average link duration of every forwarder neighbour.

The way we compute the metric is the following: firstly, we split the set of real numbers into intervals (for example, due to the heuristic function proposed the x axis has been split into three intervals). Secondly, for a period of time T, every node computes the average link duration LD_f with each forwarder neighbour it has. In order to compute if the links are up or down, the period of time T is divided into k timeslots whose size t has to be long enough to allow the node to receive at least one message from every neighbour (this happens at least every periodic flooding timeout). Then, the average link duration for each forwarder node f in a period of time T, LD_f, is defined as:

the $h(i)_f$ function determines if the link with f is alive in the timeslot i.

$$h(i)_f = \begin{cases} 1 \text{ if the node has heard a message from f} \\ 0 \text{ otherwise} \end{cases} \tag{1}$$

Ch_f calculates how many times the link goes up in the period T.

$$Ch_f = \begin{cases} \sum_{i=1}^{i=k-1} \overline{h(i)} * h(i+1) \text{ if } h(1) = 0 \\ 1 + \sum_{i=1}^{i=k-1} \overline{h(i)} * h(i+1) \text{ if } h(1) \neq 0 \end{cases} \tag{2}$$

Then LD_f is calculated by dividing the time in which the link with node f is alive over the times the link goes up in the period T:

$$LD_f = \begin{cases} \sum_k h(i)_f \text{ if } Ch_f = 0 \\ \frac{\sum_k h(i)_f}{Ch_f} \text{ if } Ch_f \neq 0 \end{cases} \tag{3}$$

Thirdly, every computed LD_f belongs to an interval from the set previously defined in the first step, then, modal link duration interval MLD is the interval to which the greatest number of LD_f belongs.

In order to adapt the metric asymptotically to the changing network conditions, the T period has a window structure computing the metric every t time units.

This metric gives the node an idea of what is happening with the majority of the nodes in the neighbourhood, what is happening in the area it is in. For example, if MLD is higher, the network around is basically stable, no matter if there are a few nodes with low stable links or they are moving together in the same direction.

The Mobility-aware Counter-based Algorithm

The mobility-aware counter-based algorithm used to reduce data overhead in mesh based protocols is built around the basic counter algorithm. This mobility-aware counter-based algorithm is only executed by the nodes belonging to the mesh because they are in charge of forwarding the data messages and consists of two processes working concurrently: the first computes the value of the threshold C as a function of MLD, $C = CC(MLD)$, whereas the second applies the counter-based approach. Fig. 1 shows how the mobility-aware counter-based algorithm works and we have chosen a function $C = CC(MLD)$ based on the following heuristics:

- If the value of MLD is low, the node itself has not been able to establish stable links with other nodes. Probably, when it is going to resend the message, the links with the intended receivers will be broken. For this reason, it will only retransmit the message if it has heard it very few times, to deal with the possibility that there are hardly any nodes in the area able to forward the message.

- If the value of MLD is medium, the node is in a network where a great number of the nodes are able to set links of a moderate duration. A medium value of C helps to cover the expected area.

- If the value of MLD is high, the network is basically stable: there are few changes, so a low threshold should be enough.

3. Simulation Results

The data overhead reduction mechanisms presented above are going to be applied to a multicast routing protocol to test if they really assess the performance of the proposed approach. We have chosen ODMRP because it is a well known mesh based protocol and offers a good performance when compared with other multicast routing protocols [Lee et al., 1999].

To simulate our mobility-aware counter scheme we have considered the following time ranges:

- MLD is the interval $[0, 21)$: it has a low value. Then C is low, and we considered low $C = 2$. According to [Boleng et al., 2002] links

```
mainLoop()
{
    msg = receiveMessage();
    if(msg.isDuplicate() == false)          /* Event handler called when
    {                                            timer expires for message
        msg.setCounter(1);                       'msg' */
        msg.setTimer(random(0,..           timerExpired(msg)
    tmax));                                {
        msg.startTimer();                      C=CC(MLD);
    }                                          if(msg.getCounter() == C)
    else                                           msg.discard();
    {                                          else
        if(msg.timerExpired() == false)            msg.retransmit();

        msg.incrementCounter();            }
    }
    ...
}
```

Figure 1.   Pseudocode for the mobility-aware counter-based algorithm

with a lifetime lower than 20 seconds lead to a poor performance of the protocols.

- MLD is the interval $[21, 75)$: it has a medium value. Then C is medium and we considered medium $C = 3$.Links which last more than 75 seconds are highly stable links when dealing with the instability of ad-hoc networks.

- MLD is the interval $[75, \infty)$: it has a high value. Then C is low, and we considered low $C = 2$.

The period of time T in which the MLD is calculated is 90 seconds which we consider a good value to capture both long and short lived links. The MLD is computed every 3 seconds because that is the flooding timeout. We have chosen $C = 3$ as the medium value because according to [Ni et al., 1999], the additional expected coverage is about 10%.

For simulating we have used the NS-2 [Ns] network simulator version 2.1b8 with the multicast extensions developed by the Rice University Monarch Project [Mon].

The simulated scenario consists of 100 mobile hosts randomly distributed over an area of 1600x1200m. The radio channel capacity for each mobile node is 2 Mb/s, using the IEEE 802.11b DCF MAC layer and a communication range of 250 m. Each one of the approaches has been evaluated over the same pre-generated set of 330 scenarios with varying mobility speed and traffic loads. Mobile nodes move using a Gauss-Markov model [Camp et al., 2002] with a maximum speed of 0, 5, 10, 15, and 20 m/s. Ten different traffic loads where tested consisting of 1, 2, and 4 CBR sources for the same multicast group, and a varying number of receivers, 5, 15, and 30.

Performance Metrics

To assess the effectiveness of the different mechanisms, we have used the following performance metrics:

- Packet delivery ratio. Defined as the number of data packet successfully delivered over the number of data packets generated by the sources.

- Normalized packet overhead. Defined as the total number of control and data packets sent and forwarded normalized by the total number of packets successfully delivered.

- Forwarding efficiency. The average number of times that a multicast data packet was forwarded by the routing protocol. This metric represents the efficiency of the underlying forwarding structure.

- Average delivery delay. For each receiver, the average delay of all packets received is computed. Then the average delivery delay is the mean of all of these averages.

Analysis of the Results

We have simulated three approximations of the counter-based scheme: two with fixed threshold values of C=2 and C=3 respectively and one with our mobility-aware counter approach. Their results have been compared with the results offered by the ODMRP protocol. Fig. 2 to fig. 7 show the results with 15 receivers and 1, and 4 sources as a function of the maximum speed of the nodes. The increment of the number of sources implies the increase of both the traffic and the density of the forwarder nodes.

Fig. 2 and fig. 6 show the packet delivery ratio (PDR). In all simulations, the fixed threshold $C = 2$ offers an insufficient PDR: almost always under 95%. This is because having fewer retransmissions affects the network connectivity. Regarding the other approaches, counter-based schemes have worse PDR than ODMRP in sparse networks. This is because the mesh has not enough redundancy; this situation gets worse as speed increases because there are more link breakages and there are no alternative paths. As the network becomes denser, counter-based mechanisms offer a higher PDR and with $C = 3$, the speed only causes a slight drop. However, our mobility-aware counter scheme gets a higher PDR when the speed is higher than 10 m/s. This is because our scheme adapts itself to higher speeds.

Fig. 3 and fig. 7 show the normalized overhead. In all cases, the use of counter-based schemes reduces considerably the overhead, obtaining the higher saving when more redundancy is in the network. Our mobility-aware counter scheme provides better savings than $C = 3$ but worse than $C = 2$ (when compared with ODMRP the saving is between 27% and 56%). It also provides better overhead reduction when the mesh is denser. However, unlike fixed threshold approaches, there is a variation with the speed of the nodes: the saving is better in low mobility environments where the links are stable. This is because our scheme detects the stability of the network, and hence it can provide better savings.

Fig. 4 and fig. 8 show the forwarding efficiency (FEF). It is observed that the number of times a packet has to be forwarded experiments an important decrease compared with ODMRP when using counter-based schemes. This is because they prevent the nodes from retransmitting unnecessary broadcasts. Results are similar to those for overhead, and our mobility-aware counter scheme provides lower FEF than $C = 3$ but greater than $C = 2$.

Fig. 5 and fig. 9 show the average delivery delay. Here, all counter-based schemes present similar results higher than the ones presented by ODMRP. This is because ODMRP always follows a shortest path tree approach, but when using a counter-based approach the path that a message follows from its source to its destination does not have to be the shortest one, since there are nodes which do not retransmit.

Summing up, these graphs show that counter schemes can be applied successfully to multicast mesh based protocols. In general, all the adaptations save overhead and obtain a better forwarding efficiency, getting better results in environments where the density of forwarder nodes is higher. Regarding our mobility-aware counter scheme, its performance can be situated into both thresholds: it usually offers an acceptable PDR (near the PDR of the $C = 3$ approach) with a better forwarding efficiency and overhead reduction. The overhead curve is nearer $C = 2$ (whose performance has resulted insufficient) when the mobility is low because links last more time and it is nearer $C = 3$ when the mobility is high because of link breakages. The best performance is when the mobility is low but not completely static, in which it offers really better PDR than $C = 2$ but the overhead saving is almost the same.

4.   Conclusions

The alternative paths grant robustness to multicast mesh based protocols at the expense of adding redundant data transmissions. Providing more efficiency to data dissemination has to be done while keeping the robustness. To address this question we have made the mesh nodes use the counter-based algorithm to decide whether to forward or not. This approach has proven to be a good solution to reduce data overhead while maintaining the performance. However, this approach is based on a fixed threshold value: if this value is low, the algorithm provides better savings at the expense of performing worse, and vice versa. For this reason we have proposed in this paper an adaptive variant of this approach. The proposed mobility-aware counter-based mechanism obtains

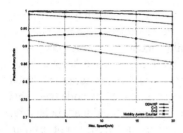

Figure 2. PDR with 1 source and 15 receivers.

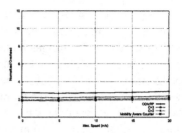

Figure 3. Overhead with 1 source and 15 receivers.

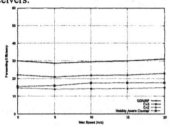

Figure 4. FEF with 1 source and 15 receivers.

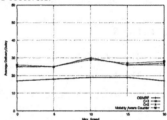

Figure 5. Average Delivery Delay with 1 source and 15 receivers.

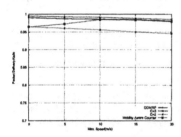

Figure 6. PDR with 4 sources and 15 receivers.

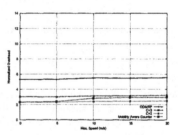

Figure 7. Overhead with 4 sources and 15 receivers.

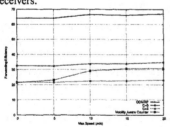

Figure 8. FEF with 4 sources and 15 receivers.

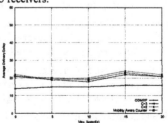

Figure 9. Average Delivery Delay with 4 sources and 15 receivers.

good performance as high thresholds do, but has better efficiency in terms of bandwidth consumption. Using the mobility-aware counter-based mechanism, every forwarder node changes its threshold value according to the stability of the network around it. To allow the node to realize the network conditions, the algorithm uses a new metric, the modal interval of the link duration, which gives the modal interval of the average duration of the links the node has. This gives the node an idea of how the majority of the nodes around it are behaving. Using our mobility-aware counter-based mechanism, the mesh is not pruned, and as a consequence, its robust structure is preserved. The good performance of the protocol is kept and the overhead is reduced up to a 56%.

References

[Ns]   The Network Simulator Ns-2.

[Mon]   The Rice University Monarch Project.

[Boleng et al., 2002] Boleng, J., Navidi, W., and T.Camp (2002). Metrics to enable adaptive protocols for mobile ad hoc networks. In *Proc. of the International Conference on Wireless Networks (ICWN '02)*, pages 293–298.

[Camp et al., 2002] Camp, T., Boleng, J., and Davies, V. (2002). A survey of mobility models for ad-hoc network research. *Wireless Communications and Mobile Computing (WCMC): Special issue on Mobile Ad Hoc Networking: Research, Trends and Applications*, 2(5):483–502.

[Cordeiro et al., 2003] Cordeiro, C. Moreis, Gossain, H., and Agrawal, D. P. (2003). Multicast over wireless mobile ad hoc networks: present and future directions.

[Gui and Mohapatra, 2004] Gui, C. and Mohapatra, P. (2004). Scalable multicasting in ad hoc networks. In *IEEE INFOCOM*.

[Laouiti et al., 2001] Laouiti, A., Qayyum, A., and Viennot, L. (2001). Multipoint relaying: An efficient technique for flooding in mobile wireless networks. In *35th Annual Hawaii International Conference on System Sciences (HICSS'2001)*. IEEE Computer Society.

[Lee et al., 1999] Lee, S. J., Gerla, M., and Chiang, C.C. (1999). On demand multicast routing protocol. In *Proc. of the IEEE WCNC'99*, pages 1298–1302.

[Lim and Kim, 2000] Lim, H. and Kim, C. (2000). Multicast tree construction and flooding in wireless ad hoc networks. In *Proc. of the 3rd ACM international workshop on Modeling, analysis and simulation of wireless and mobile systems*, pages 61–68.

[Ni et al., 1999] Ni, S.Y., Tseng, Y.C., Y.S., Chen, and Sheu, J.-P. (1999). The broadcast storm problem in a mobile ad hoc network. In *Proc. of Int'l Conf. Mobile Computing and Networking (MOBICOM)*, pages 151–162.

[Ruiz and Gómez-Skarmeta, 2004] Ruiz, P. M. and Gómez-Skarmeta, A. F. (2004). Mobility-aware mesh construction algorithm for low data overhead in multicast ad hoc routing. *Journal of Communications and Networks (JNC)*, 6(5):331–342.

[Yi et al., 2003] Yi, Y., Gerla, M., and Kwon, T. J. (2003). Efficient flooding in ad hoc networks: a comparative performance study. In *Proc. of the IEEE International Conference on Communications (ICC 2003)*.

SUPPORTING MULTICAST IN AD-HOC NETWORKS IN A HOTSPOT CONTEXT

Andreas Kassler[1], Susana Sargento[2], Adel Ben Mnaouer[3], Chen Lei[3], Pedro Neves[2], Rui L. Aguiar[2], Pedro M. Ruiz[4]

[1]Karlstad University, Sweden; [2]Instituto de Telecomunicações, Universidade de Aveiro, Portugal; [3]Nanyang Technological University, Singapore; [4]University of Murcia, Spain

Abstract: This paper discusses the usage of Ad-Hoc technologies as "hotspot extension" mechanisms. We propose a hybrid network where 802.16 links are used for providing high-bandwidth access, and local distribution is performed by Ad-Hoc network nodes, thus covering arbitrary areas around the 802.16 stations, which might be connected to the Internet. We evaluate the performance of the system and its efficiency in providing QoS in multicast connections. We propose two extensions of the ODMRP and MAODV routing algorithms by augmenting them with a zone routing behavior, thus producing two new hybrid multicast routing algorithms: ZODMRP and ZMAODV. The simulation results show that ZODMRP provides the highest packet delivery ratio and lowest delay without introducing large overhead.

Key words: Multicasting; Hybrid MANET; Internet Connectivity; Hotspots.

1. INTRODUCTION

Ad-Hoc networks have gone through large developments over the last years. Researchers have investigated aspects of routing, multicasting, QoS and security in these networks. Currently, Ad-Hoc is reaching a stage where they can support the mixing of different services in order to provide an infrastructure useful for the common user. One such service is the basic network connection. Future users will be permanently connected, not only to their local environment, but also to the overall Internet. The "hotspot" concept is a clear indication of this trend, with more and more access points available for public usage. With the increased desire to be always connected, this concept will be certainly enlarged to an "extended hotspot" concept. The idea is to increase the range of hotspots through the automatic creation of Ad-Hoc networks based on connections to nodes increasingly nearer the hotspot range. We propose such a hybrid network where 802.16 links [1] [2] are used for providing high-bandwidth access, and local distribution is performed by multi-hop Ad-Hoc networks using IEEE 802.11. This allows for the covering of arbitrary areas around the 802.16 stations. Recent announcements of intrinsic laptop support for both 802.11 and 802.16 technologies [2], and the proposals of incentive-based charging schemes for Ad-Hoc networks [3], make this scenario quite feasible in the near future.

The paper discusses this scenario and analyzes multicast services on this environment. We discuss the usage of MAODV (Multicast Ad-Hoc On-demand Distance Vector protocol) and ODMRP (On-Demand Multicast Routing Protocol) and variants to provide multicast support. The smooth integration of these different protocols and proposed evolutions will be presented. Furthermore, the adequate mapping of multicast requirements in the distribution 802.16 technology will also be discussed.

This paper is organized as follows. In section 2 the proposed overall network architecture is presented. Section 3 addresses the multicast mapping into 802.16 technologies. Multicast proposals in Ad-Hoc networks and their integration are described in section 4. Simulation results are presented in Section 5. Finally, Section 6 reports the main conclusions.

2.   NETWORK ARCHITECTURE

We propose to use 802.16 as an extension of access networks, providing high bandwidth access between the terminals and wired access network, and then extend this access by the creation of Ad-Hoc networks over 802.11. This situation can appear either with operator-owned hotspots or with dynamic situations, where 802.16/11-enabled users act as the gateway between the telecommunications operator and the other users (see Figure 1). The access router can be directly connected to the 802.16 base station (BS). As a broadband wireless access technology, 802.16 is intended to be used as a bridging solution between the access network and the backhaul wireless access technologies. Each one of these 802.11 Ad-Hoc networks is connected to the 802.16 technology through the (eventually fixed) subscriber station (SS) units. Each Ad-Hoc node is connected to the access point through a multi-hop path composed by mobile nodes in the Ad-Hoc network.

In the uplink direction, the subscriber stations must forward the traffic to the base station in an on-demand basis, depending on the used uplink scheduling service. The mesh topology allows subscriber stations to communicate directly between them, avoiding forwarding all of its traffic to the base station. The purpose of this network is to be able to deliver and support any type of services and applications, as audio and video conferencing and streaming, to the end users, located in any hotspot network connected to the Internet through broadband wireless. Since the access network is composed by wired and fixed network, 802.16 network and wireless Ad-Hoc network, these networks need to be closely integrated.

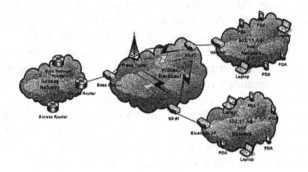

Figure 1. Network Architecture

3. IEEE 802.16 MULTICAST

While in 802.16 networks broadcast management and data connections are supported, there is no explicit multicast data transport connection defined. Instead, a range of connections is defined for multicast polling. These connections are used for the SSs to join multicast polling groups. Concerning multicast data transport connections, although there is no dedicated connection, it is possible to have a multicast connection for data.

The process for setting up a multicast connection is as follows. The BS should have information on the mobile nodes joining a multicast group. This can be provided by e.g. the access router which is then responsible to setup a multicast group inside the 802.16 network. The BS starts to create and associate a unicast transport connection with a specific SS. Then, this same connection is associated with all the SSs that belong to the multicast group. With this process, when multicast traffic is sent on this connection, all the SSs that belong to the multicast group are able to listen to this traffic. Inside Ad-Hoc networks, Ad-Hoc multicast routing protocols, as MAODV or

ODMRP, are used to manage the multicast groups. An 802.16 multicast connection is only required if the multicast nodes belong to different SSs.

4.   AD-HOC MULTICAST INTEGRATION

In multicast communications a source is sending only one packet with a group address as a destination. The network will be in charge of replicating that packet only when necessary to make it reach all destinations. The classical IP multicast protocols used in the Internet consists of the Internet Group Management Protocol (IGMP) [4] for group membership (or its IPv6 variant MLD) in combination with an IP based multicast routing protocol like Protocol Independent Multicast - Sparse Mode (PIM-SM) [5]. Because of Ad-Hoc network specific problems like frequent topology changes, unreliable links, battery constraints and limited capacity of mobile nodes, standard internet multicast routing protocols, introducing high overhead in maintaining efficient multicast delivery structures, do not perform well regarding scalability and performance in Ad-Hoc networks, especially when trees need to be re-organized frequently due to mobility. The benefits of multicast include the lower bandwidth consumption and increased scalability which makes support of multicast essential in Ad-Hoc networks.

4.1   Multicasting in Ad-Hoc Environments

Specific multicast routing protocols have been designed for Ad-Hoc networks, which can be classified according to the placement of the multicast delivery structure. In addition to pure flooding, which leads to a very high overhead in Ad-Hoc networks, we can distinguish between tree, mesh and location based multicast routing mechanisms. AMRoute [6], AMRIS [7], or MAODV [8] delivery structure is tree based. ODMRP [9] and CAMP [10] are mesh based. The motivation for mesh based approaches is due to the problems with tree-based approaches in the presence of mobile nodes because tree-structures are fragile and need to be frequently readjusted when connectivity changes. Using delivery meshes that span all multicast group members, multiple links do exist which provides redundancy to route breaks caused by mobility of nodes. In location-based multicasting (e.g. [11]), location information is used to define group membership and distribute multicast traffic.

Traditional (multicast) routing protocols for Ad-Hoc networks have not been designed to interoperate with fixed networks due to several reasons: The addressing architecture is different in Ad-Hoc networks, in which host-based routes are commonly used and addressing structure is flat compared to a hierarchical structure in the internet. In the Internet, two nodes sharing the same network part of their IP addresses are assumed to be in the same link, which is not necessarily the case in multi-hop networks. Classical internet multicast protocols offer superior performance in fixed networks than pure Ad-Hoc solutions, which are designed for frequent topology change. Due to these reasons, it is hard to design a multicast protocol that works efficiently in the Ad-Hoc part while still being able to interoperate with the fixed network. Therefore, it is desirable to design inter-working between Ad-Hoc and internet multicast protocols to achieve the best performance. Very little efforts, if any, have been started to provide multicasting in such hybrid Ad-Hoc networks, see e.g. [12], [13], and those approaches present severe limitations in terms of functionality and generality.

4.2   Integration of MANET with the public Internet

In our scenario, where Ad-Hoc networks are connected through 802.16 with the internet, it is required to interoperate with a fixed IP network and support standard-IP multicast sources or receivers, and then, several extensions are required. These extensions must be designed in such a way that they are compatible with the standard IP Multicast mode, and they must allow standard IP nodes to take part in multicast communications without requiring any change. Therefore, an Ad-Hoc multicast routing protocol should support IGMP as a means to interoperate both with access gateways and standard IP nodes. In addition, the 802.16 BS must be enabled to setup a multicast group inside the 802.16 network, which requires information about what members of which multicast group are attached to what 802.16 SS.

We propose that all nodes in the Ad-Hoc fringe situated just one hop away from the gateway (denoted as Multicast Internet Gateways - MIG - in the Multicast MANET Routing Protocol – MMARP – [14] terminology) notify the access routers about the group memberships within the Ad-Hoc fringe. Any node within the Ad-Hoc fringe may become a MIG at any time if that node receives IGMP reports from multicast routers in the access network, because IGMP messages are sent with TTL=1. This requires in our architecture that the 802.16 network does not change the TTL of IGMP messages. This mechanism allows the multicast Ad-Hoc routing protocol to work with any IP multicast routing protocol in the access network and, therefore, it shields the multicast Ad-Hoc routing protocol operation from the protocols performing the intra-domain or inter-domain multicast routing. Therefore, MIGs must periodically advertise themselves to all other Ad-Hoc nodes as default multicast gateway to the fixed network. Ad-Hoc nodes can determine if they have to advertise themselves as MIG by receiving IGMP queries from the access router attached to the 802.16 BS. Such advertisement messages broadcasted from MIGs inform intermediate Ad-Hoc nodes about the path towards multicast sources in the access network, and thus the global internet. When such an advertisement reaches a receiver or neighbor of a receiver of a multicast group within the Ad-Hoc part, this node has to initiate a joining process using the multicast Ad-Hoc routing protocol towards the MIG. Once the MIG receives the request from an Ad-Hoc node to join, it sends an IGMP Report towards the access router thus updating group membership information. This ensures that IP multicast data from sources in the fixed network reach the destinations within the Ad-Hoc network. Also, the access router then notifies the 802.16 BS, which then sets up the multicast group within the 802.16 network to forward traffic to the correct 802.16 SS and thus to the proper Ad-Hoc island.

If an Ad-Hoc node is becoming a multicast source, it triggers the creation of a multicast distribution structure (tree or mesh) depending on the routing protocol in use. If the MIGs become aware of new multicast sources in the Ad-Hoc island, they notify the access routers about this information by sending IGMP reports towards the access router.

4.3   Design of new Multicast Routing Protocols

When all MIGs join multicast sources located in the MANET, this will result in high overhead. Therefore, we have to limit the control and data overhead of routing protocols. Combining the Zone Routing with reactive protocol features to form new hybrid protocols is expected to achieve good performance. Also, it has already been shown in [8] and [9] that MAODV and ODMRP present good performance. Therefore, our objective is to extend MAODV and ODMRP with a proactive behaviour.

The new hybrid protocol contains reactive and proactive (based on zone routing) elements. In the proactive mode, each node in the Ad-Hoc part of the network constructs and maintains a zone around it with a pre-configured zone radius. Each node thus maintains a zone routing table (ZRT) to record the multicast information of the nodes in its zone by periodically broadcasting an update packet. The time-to-live (TTL) value of the packet is set to the pre-configured zone radius. Each update packet includes multicast information of the source node (the node which is sending the update packet) to distribute information about the source node sending the update packet to members within its zone. In this way, any node receiving such an update packet knows immediately to which multicast groups a specific source node belongs. If such neighbours receive join requests for a specific multicast group, they can immediately determine to which source node to forward such a request. For MAODV, the update packet includes multicast group addresses that the source node belongs to, multicast group leader address, and the multicast group sequence number. For ODMRP, it includes multicast group addresses that the source node belongs to. When an Ad-Hoc node within the zone receives the update packet, it records all information in that packet, keeping the ZRT up-to-date by periodic broadcast. Also, we modify the way MAODV and ODMRP send out a join request. The resulting two protocol variants are described as ZMAODV and ZODMRP, respectively.

Sending RREQ in ZMAODV: When a node needs to send a RREQ, it first looks up the zone routing table to see whether there are nodes in the zone that belong to the multicast group the node intends to join. If there are, it compares other information, for example, multicast group sequence number and multicast group leader address, to ensure that the information recorded in the zone routing table is fresh. If there are still some nodes in the zone, the source node unicasts a RREQ to the nearest node and waits for the reply. If there are no nodes, the source broadcasts a RREQ (with TTL = zone radius). Only border nodes will handle the RREQ and all other nodes in the zone propagate the RREQ to border nodes. When a border node receives RREQ, it looks up its ZRT and continues the path finding procedure until some nodes belonging to multicast group receive the RREQ. That node will then generate a RREP and send it to the source node following the reverse path.

Sending Join Query in ZODMRP: The procedure sending Join Query in ZODMRP is similar to the procedure of sending RREQ in ZMAODV. The difference is when a node finds other nodes in its zone belonging to the multicast group. In this situation it does not only unicasts the Join Query to the node with the shortest path, but to all nodes belonging to the multicast group. This helps to build up the forwarding group as a mesh.

5. EVALUATION OF ZMAODV AND ZODMRP

We used GloMoSim [15] to compare the performance of ZMAODV and ZODMRP with MAODV and ODMRP. We distribute in total 50 Ad-Hoc nodes running 802.11 within an area of 1000x1000 m. Radio propagation range for each node is set to 250 m and channel capacity is 2 Mbps. Each simulation is executed for 500s of simulation time, which corresponds to a typical time required for video news consumption within a hotspot. We assume the MANET to be the bottleneck and not the 802.16 backhaul network. We use constant bitrate UDP sources emulating typical audio and video streams. For audio, we use 240 byte packets, sent out every 30 ms at a total bitrate of 64 kbps. For video, we use 1500 byte packets, sent out every 80 ms at a total bitrate of 150 kbps. We select one node (mobility=0m/s) to be the access point towards the 802.16 access network. This node receives traffic from three (two audio and one video) other multicast sources and forwards it to the 802.16 access network. In addition, this node also multicasts two audio and one video stream that it receives from the 802.16 network towards the Ad-Hoc nodes. We use the following performance metrics to compare the performance of the multicast protocols: *packet delivery ratio*, which determines the effectiveness of the protocol (for interactive audio, packet delivery ratio must approach one for high quality experience), *average packet delay* and *protocol overhead*. Each node moves constantly with a randomly generated speed and moving directions are randomly selected. Nodes reaching the simulation boundary bounce back and continue to move. Although there are other mobility models available (like e.g. group mobility model), the random mobility model was selected as it stresses the routing protocols. Two different scenario setups are used. In the first setup we are interested in the protocol performance depending on the multicast group size. Here, we fixed the mobility of the nodes at 5 m/s and vary the group size between 5 and 25 members in steps of 5. In the second scenario, we fixed the multicast group size to 10 and vary the mobility of the nodes from 0 to 30 m/s in steps of 5 m/s.

Figure 2 shows packet delivery ratio as a function of terminal speed. ODMRP shows good performance compared to MAODV even under high mobility. This is due to the mesh topology: the chances of packet delivery are high even if primary route is no longer available. ZODMRP outperforms ODMRP and ZMAODV performs better than MAODV, as the proactive zone feature helps to recover broken links. This is mostly visible at high mobility for ZMAODV. More packets are dropped in the direction towards the 802.16 network (denoted as at AP) as traffic is concentrated around the AP which leads to high collision ratio. Here, also the Z-variant outperforms the standard protocols and performance improvement is best for the ZMAODV when compared to MAODV at high mobility.

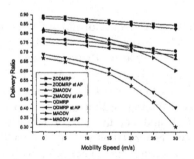

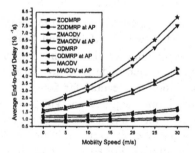

Figure 2. Delivery Ratio (mobility speed)   *Figure 3.* Average Delay (mobility speed)

Figure 3 shows the average packet delay as a function of terminal speed. This is important in order to evaluate the suitability with respect to QoS provisioning. Again, ZODMRP outperforms ODMRP, which is better than ZAODV and AODV. Here, the performance degradation at high mobility is severe for MAODV (150 ms at 0 m/s compared to 420 ms at 30 m/s) and ZMAODV. However, the delay for ZODMRP is nearly constant and below 100 ms even at high mobility, due to the intrinsic back-up routes provided by the mesh. Again, performance is significantly lower in direction towards the access point for all protocol variants.

Regarding protocol overhead, we have analyzed the number of data packets transmitted per number of data packets delivered to the destination, as a function of terminal speed. Both ZODMRP and ODMRP have highest number of transmissions (around 3 data packets transmitted per received data packet) due to the mesh structure exploiting multiple redundant routes. MAODV has higher overhead (around 2.3 packets) compared to 2.2 packets), especially for mobility higher than 15 m/s than ZMAODV.

Concluding the analysis, we consider that the variants including the zone routing features are superior in providing QoS to the standard multicast routing protocols, when connecting Ad-Hoc islands to infrastructure based networks and thus to the internet. The performance increase is especially visible when comparing ZMAODV with MAODV. However, when considering QoS provisioning under the aspect of terminal mobility, ZODMRP is the method of choice.

6. CONCLUSION

We have presented a proposal for the integration of Ad-Hoc islands with infrastructure-based networks for providing multicast operations for users across both domains. The proposed scheme has interesting applications in hotspots' design and extensions thereof. This approach enables a seamless integration of wireless MANs and LANs with the public Internet, providing a common multicast framework. We have proposed and evaluated two new hybrid protocols ZODMRP and ZMAODV (based on the ODMRP and MAODV protocols) that were built using the zone routing concept. Extensive simulations of these protocols, and their original counterparts, revealed the superiority of the ZODMRP in providing predictable QoS guarantees for multicast sessions spanning over dissimilar and interconnected networks, without imposing higher overhead.

Our future work concentrates on exploiting Ad-Hoc mechanisms inside the 802.16 network, especially in the case of mobile and meshed 802.16 networks and evaluating the overhead of the announcement of default routes for the Ad-Hoc nodes. With respect to multicast routing in Ad-Hoc networks connected to the internet, we are working towards more realistic mobility models applicable to public hotspot environments. We will also consider other performance metrics like the connectivity of clients and delay for a user to connect to multicast sources located in the internet or Ad-Hoc fringe.

ACKNOWLEDGEMENT

The work described in this paper is partly based on results of IST FP6 Integrated Project DAIDALOS and "Ramon y Cajal" workprogramme.

REFERENCES

[1] IEEE 802.16-REVd/D2-2003, "IEEE Draft for Local and Metropolitan Area Networks – Part 16: Air Interface for Fixed Broadband Wireless Access Systems", November 2003.
[2] Carl Eklund, Roger B. Marks, Kenneth L. Stanwood and Stanley Wang, "IEEE Standard 802.16: A Technical Overview of the Wireless MAN Air Interface for Broadband Wireless Access", IEEE Communications Magazine, June 2002.
[3] B. Lamparter, et al, "Charging Support for Ad Hoc Stub Networks", In Elsevier Journal of Comp. Com. Special Issue on Internet Pricing and Charging, Elsevier Science, Aug. 2003.
[4] Fenner, W., Internet Group Management Protocol, Version 2. RFC 2236, 11/ 1997.
[5] Estrin, D. et. al., "Protocol Independent Multicast Sparse Mode (PIM-SM): Protocol Specification." RFC 2362, June 1998.
[6] E. Bommaiah, M. Liu, A. McAuley, R. Talpade, "Ad-Hoc Multicast Routing Protocol", Internetdraft, Aug. 1998.
[7] C. Wu, Y. Tay, C. Toh, "Ad-Hoc Multicast Routing Protocol utilizing Increasing id-numbers (AMRIS): functional specification", Internet-draft, November 1998.
[8] E.M. Royer and C.E. Perkins, "Multicast Ad-Hoc On-Demand Distance Vector (MAODV) Routing," Internet-Draft, draft-ietf-manet-maodv-00.txt, July 2000.
[9] Y. Yi, S. Lee, W. Su, and M. Gerla, "On-Demand Multicast Routing Protocol (ODMRP) for Ad-Hoc Networks," Internet-Draft, draft-yi-manet-odmrp-00.txt, March 2003.
[10] J. J. Garcia-Luna-Aceves and E.L. Madruga, "The Core-Assisted Mesh Protocol," IEEE JSAC, Aug. 1999, pp. 1380–94.
[11] Y. Ko, N. Vaidya: "Geocasting in Mobile Ad-Hoc Networks: Location-Based Multicast Algorithms", Technical Report TR-98-018, Texas A&M University, September 1998.
[12] C. Jelger, T. Noel: "Unicast and Multicast Gatewaying in IPv6 Ad-Hoc networks", https://safari-rnrt.rd.francetelecom.com/Public/workshop_safari_2004/.
[13] W. Ding, "Multicast Routing in Fixed Infrastructure and Mobile Ad-Hoc Wireless Networks with a Multicast Gateway", Carleton University, Ontario, Canada, July 2002.
[14] P. Ruiz et al., "The MMARP Protocol for Efficient Support of Standard IP Multicast Communications in Mobile Ad-Hoc Access Networks". In proc. of the IST Mobile & Wireless Comm. Summit 2003, June 2003.
[15] GloMoSim: A Scalable Simulation Environment for Wireless and Wired Network Systems. http://pcl.cs.ucla.edu/projects/glomosim/.

A LIGHTWEIGHT CLUSTERING ALGORITHM UTILIZING CAPACITY HETEROGENEITY

Nicklas Beijar[1], Raimo Kantola[1], and Jose Costa-Requena[2]

[1]*Helsinki University of Technology, Espoo, Finland, {Nicklas.Beijar,Raimo.Kantola}@hut.fi;*
[2]*Nokia Mobile Phones, Helsinki, Finland. Jose.Costa-Requena@nokia.com*

Abstract: This paper describes an algorithm for clustering an ad hoc network, in which the devices have highly varying resources. Such a heterogeneous ad hoc network is formed when wireless and fixed consumer devices like laptops, personal data assistants, cellular phones and servers automatically interconnect. The aim of clustering is twofold: to reduce broadcast traffic, which is typical to ad hoc routing protocols, and to concentrate traffic to devices with more available resources and less mobility. Further, the clustering process identifies nodes that are suitable for service provision. The algorithm is lightweight as it operates with a single periodically sent message. We provide simulation results that show the performance of the algorithm.

Key words: clustering; mobile ad hoc network; virtual backbone

1.   INTRODUCTION

Ad hoc networks are wireless networks established on temporary basis between a set of mobile nodes. The key feature of an ad hoc network is that there is no infrastructure; hence, there are no wired links and other fixed equipment. Data transmission is based on multi-hop routing, i.e. nodes act as routers by forwarding traffic of other source-destination pairs. Numerous routing protocols have been proposed for ad hoc networks. These can be divided into proactive and reactive protocols. Both approaches utilize flooding for distributing topological information: proactive protocols distribute information about topology changes by broadcasting to all nodes, and reactive protocols broadcast route requests. Several papers[1-5] have shown that the flooding traffic can be reduced by minimizing the number of nodes participating in broadcasting. This can be achieved with clustering or with a virtual backbone spanning the network. The control information is then only forwarded by selected nodes, such as cluster-heads and gateway nodes, or nodes belonging to the virtual backbone.

In scenarios including consumer devices, it can be assumed that a wide range of different types of devices are part of the ad hoc network. The devices have different amounts of available resources, e.g. memory, battery and processing power, and they have different mobility patterns. In this paper, we assume an ad hoc network consisting of commercially available devices of widely different type. Roughly, we can group the devices into two main categories: (i) highly mobile devices with low resources, such as personal data assistants (PDAs) and mobile phones, and (ii) devices with low mobility and high capacity, such as laptops, servers and access points.

Information about the available resources of a device can be reduced into a *preference value* using a *preference function*. Fundamentally, the preference function calculates the preference value by summing the weighted values of battery power, available memory, CPU resources, administrative preference, etc. Both control traffic and packet transmission should prefer a path consisting of nodes with a high amount of available resources. The preference function should additionally observe the level of mobility. Low mobility increases the preference value, while high mobility decreases it.

This paper presents an algorithm for clustering a network and forming a spanning virtual backbone by loosely interconnecting clusters. The aims of the algorithm are (i) to utilize the diversity in resources and mobility among nodes, (ii) to be very lightweight and adapt quickly to changes, and (iii) to provide a platform for service discovery. The protocol uses only a single Hello message for constructing the clusters and connecting them into a virtual backbone, consisting of nodes with relatively high preference.

2.   NETWORK MODEL

We represent an ad hoc network using an undirected graph $G = (V, E)$, where V is the set of nodes and E is the set of edges in the graph. The distance $D(v,w)$ between two nodes v and w is the lowest number of edges on a path from v to w. The ith neighborhood $N_i(v)$ of a node v is the set of nodes $N_i(v) = \{w \mid w \in V, D(v,w) \leq i\}$. The ith deleted neighborhood $N'_i(v)$ of node v is the set of nodes $N'_i(v) = N_i(v) \ / \ \{v\}$. The nodes in the 1st deleted neighborhood $N'(v) = N'_1(v)$ are said to be the direct neighbors of v. We denote the number of direct neighbors with $|N'(v)|$ and call it the degree of the node. We assume that the nodes in the network share the same communication channel. Every node is assumed to have an identical omnidirectional radio transmitter and receiver, so that a message transmitted by a node is received by every node within a fixed radio-range with the radius Z. Links are assumed bi-directional. A node operating in promiscuous mode is able to receive transmissions directed to other nodes than itself provided that the sender is within radio-range. If the network is partitioned, the clustering algorithm operates separately in each partition, and these are automatically combined as the partitions unite.

3. OBJECTIVE

Each node has a *preference* value, $P(v)$, which indicates the node's suitability as a backbone node. The preference can be calculated based on the stability and resources of the node using a *preference function* used by all nodes in the network. The determination of the preference function is out of the scope of this paper. Generally, a stable node (whose neighbors do not frequently change) with low velocity and high resources should have a high preference value. The algorithm categorizes nodes into three colors, $C(v) \in$ *{white, green, black}*, depending on the node's function in the network. *White* nodes are isolated nodes that have no neighbors within radio-range. *Black* nodes are the most stable and resource-rich nodes in the network. The aim is to keep the highest preference nodes as black nodes. *Green* nodes are nodes that have at least one black node as a neighbor. These have the lowest resources and their participation in message forwarding is minimized. The set of black nodes is denoted $V_{black} = \{v \mid v \in V, C(v) = black\}$. Correspondingly the sets of green, and white nodes are denoted V_{green}, and V_{white}, respectively. The colors are ordered so that black is higher than green, and green is higher than white. In addition to the color, a node can have an additional role: a black node can act as a *cluster-head* and both a green and a black node as a *bridge*.

Every node v has an unique address, which we denote $A(v)$. Further, every node v belongs to a *cluster*, $\pi(v)$, which can contain a variable number of nodes. The cluster is identified with the address of its *cluster-head* $\lambda(\pi)$, which is the node with the highest preference of the nodes in the cluster. The distance $hdist(v)$ from a node to its cluster-head is measured in hops. In addition to the color and the cluster, the algorithm assigns every node a *dominator*, $dom(v)$. The dominator can be any of the direct neighbors of the node, or the node itself: $dom(v) \in N_I(v)$.

When a node receives updated neighborhood information through a Hello message, it re-selects its dominator, its color and its cluster so that the following objectives are satisfied. Firstly, a node must always have a dominator, which is either a direct neighbor or the node itself. In the selection, the color order is the primary selection criteria and the preference the secondary selection criteria. Hence, if there are black nodes in the first neighborhood $N_l(v)$ of node v, then the black node w with the highest $P(w)$ is selected as $dom(v) = w$. If there are no black nodes in $N_l(v)$, the green node w in $N_l(v)$ with the highest $P(w)$ is selected. If there are no green nodes, the white node with the highest preference is selected. We denote this combination of color order and preference value as the (color, preference)-order. The reason for first observing the color is to improve stability of the backbone. The link between a node and its dominator is called a *dominator link*. The node w that has selected node v as its dominator $(dom(w) = v)$ is called a *dominatee* of node v. A node can have zero or more dominatees but only one dominator.

The color of a node is determined by the neighboring nodes. A node v is white if it has no direct neighbors, i.e. $N'(v) = \varnothing$. If some direct neighbor w has selected v as its dominator $(dom(w) = v, w \in N_l(v))$, then the color of v is black. Thus, all dominators are black. Note that the node is also black if it has selected itself as its dominator. If v has neighbors, but none of them has selected v as its dominator, the color of v is green. Consequently, all dominators are black and other connected nodes are green. A node that has selected itself as its dominator takes its own address as its cluster identifier. It becomes the cluster-head of its cluster. In practice, this indicates that it has the highest (color, preference) value within its first neighborhood. Otherwise, the node joins the cluster of its dominator, and obtains the cluster identifier from the Hello message of the dominator.

The black nodes form a backbone within the cluster. Black nodes have the locally highest preference value. Since the preference value represents the resources and stability of the node, black nodes are suitable for distributing and storing information. The cluster-head can easily be located by following the path of dominator links. Hence sending a message to the local head can be implemented as the process of repeated forwarding of the message to the dominator until the head is reached. Because the cluster-head has the highest preference in the cluster, and because of the simple locating, it is suitable for storing persistent information related to the cluster.

The size of the cluster is determined probabilistically. The geographical size of a cluster is limited if the preference value is uncorrelated to the node's location in the network. However, with certain node placements it is possible to create a cluster encompassing all nodes in the network, and the cluster size is practically unlimited. Although these cases are improbable in a real scenario, we propose a method for limiting the cluster size: A node only considers a neighbor eligible as its dominator if the neighbor's distance to the cluster-head $hdist(v)$ is smaller than a given threshold, called the *cluster* *radius limit, R_{max},*. Otherwise, it chooses the dominator from the remaining nodes (including itself).

4. CONTROL MESSAGES

The algorithm uses a single control message. The *Hello Message* is periodically sent to all direct neighbors. The message sent by node v contains the fields $\{A(v), C(v), P(v), dom(v), \pi(v), hdist(v), dv(v)\}$. The fields $A(v)$, $C(v)$, $P(v)$, $dom(v)$, $\pi(v)$ are the address, color, preference, dominator and cluster identifier of the node, respectively. The field $hdist(v)$ is the distance from the node to its cluster-head. The field $dv(v)$ is a distance vector table, as will be described later.

Every node maintains a neighbor table N_v containing the information received in Hello messages from its direct neighbors. When a Hello message is received, the contents is inserted into N_v. Entries in the neighbor table time out if not refreshed after a specified time, whereas they are removed. Because a Hello message is required in most routing protocols, the clustering does not add message overhead, but only increases the Hello message size.

5. CLUSTERING ALGORITHM

When a node v powers on, it sets its color $C(v) = white$, its dominator $dom(v) = A(v)$ and its cluster $\pi(v) = A(v)$. It starts sending and receiving Hello messages. A node continuously listens to Hello messages received from neighboring nodes, and builds up and maintains the neighbor table N_v. When a Hello message is received, the information in the Hello message is added to or updated in the neighbor table. Additionally, the timer for the specific neighbor is restarted. If a Hello message has not been received within a specific timeout period, the entry is removed.

An *attribute determination procedure* is invoked (i) after each received Hello message and (ii) if a neighbor entry times out. The procedure has two phases. It first determines the dominator and cluster (phase 1), and then the color (phase 2) of a node. We provide two versions of the first phase.

When node v performs the determination procedure, it includes every node w of the neighbor table for which *hdist(w)* is less than the cluster radius limitation (R_{max}) in its dominator-candidate list $(E(v))$. In our first version of this phase, also the node v itself is included:

$$E(v) = \{w \mid w \in N_1(v), hdist(w) < R_{max}\}$$

In the second version, the node v is included only if it is the dominatee of some direct neighbor:

$$E(v) = \begin{cases} \{w \mid w \in N_1(v), hdist(w) < R_{max}\} & , if \; \exists u \in N_1'(v) : v = dom(u) \\ \{w \mid w \in N_1'(v), hdist(w) < R_{max}\} & , otherwise \end{cases}$$

The rest is identical for both versions. From the dominator-candidates, it selects the node w with the highest (color, preference) order as its dominator:

$$dom(v) = w : w \in E(v) \quad so \; that$$
$$\forall u \in E(v) : C(w) \geq C(u) \vee (C(w) = C(u) \wedge P(w) \geq P(u))$$

After that, it updates its cluster and head-distance attributes:

$$\pi(v) = \begin{cases} A(v) & , if \; dom(v) = v \\ \pi(dom(v)) & , if \; dom(v) \neq v \end{cases}$$
$$hdist(v) = \begin{cases} 0 & , if \; dom(v) = v \\ hdist(dom(v)) + 1 & , if \; dom(v) \neq v \end{cases}$$

The second phase checks the $dom(u)$ of every direct neighbor u and updates the color $C(v)$.

$$C(v) = \begin{cases} black, if \; \exists u : u \in N_1'(v) : dom(u) = v \\ green, if \; |N_1'(v)| > 0 \vee \forall u : u \in N_1'(v) : dom(u) \neq v \\ white, if \; |N_1'(v)| = 0 \end{cases}$$

6.   CONNECTING CLUSTERS

The described algorithm connects the nodes within a cluster with a backbone. However, the backbone does not connect the clusters. The nodes connected by dominator links therefore form a forest consisting of one tree for each cluster. In this section we present an approach that obtains routes to neighboring clusters without permanently connecting them. Instead it connects a temporary *bridge* between two neighboring clusters.

A node learns through the Hello messages to which cluster each of its direct neighbors belongs. For neighbors in a different cluster than itself, the node also knows the distance to the respective cluster-head since the Hello message contains the *hdist* field. A routing table entry is created for each neighboring cluster and the node with the lowest cluster-head distance becomes the next hop to this cluster. The distance to the neighboring cluster is set as the cluster-head distance plus one. This favors routes leading close to the center of the cluster. In case of equal cluster-head distance, the next hop with the highest preference is selected. A distance vector with entries for all neighboring clusters is included in the Hello message.

The distance vector information is progressed toward the cluster-head in the dv field of the Hello messages. A node stores the distance vectors received from a dominatee in its routing table. For each cluster, it selects the neighbor with the lowest distance to the cluster as the next hop. In case of equal distance, the neighbor with the highest preference is selected. Because there is a strict hierarchy within the cluster, distance vector loops cannot appear. Eventually, the cluster-head has routing table entries to all neighboring clusters. A path is available from the cluster-head to each neighboring cluster since every intermediate node has a next hop entry to the given cluster. This mechanism enables sending messages between neighboring clusters through a cluster-head. The route follows the backbone, and consequently consists of nodes with high preference. There may be one or two green nodes acting as bridge nodes between two neighboring clusters.

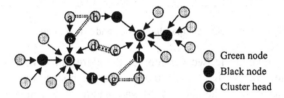

Figure 1. Example of connecting clusters with bridges

Figure 1 illustrates two neighboring clusters connected with bridges. Node a and node c both have selected node b as its bridge to the neighboring cluster, and node b has selected c. Node d and node e have selected each other. Node g has selected node i, while node i and node h both have selected node g. The cluster-heads have selected node d and node e.

7. SIMULATION

In order to observe the cluster formation and its performance, we performed a series of simulations. We based the simulation on a topology simulator[6] implemented in the Python[7] language. A Hello message is received error free by all nodes within the radio-range Z of the sender, and lost by all other nodes. Only network layer functionality is implemented, as we assume that the physical layer operates at a much faster time scale than the network layer. The Hello interval was 1 s and the Hello timeout was 2 s.

Initially the nodes are randomly distributed in the 1000 x 1000 m roaming area. The random waypoint mobility model[8] is used. A node selects a random destination and a speed between 1 m/s and a maximum speed, and moves towards the destination. When the destination is reached, the node pauses for a time randomly chosen between 0 s and 100 s. Five runs of 600 s each were performed for each set of parameters, and the results were averaged. In the simulations presented in this paper, the nodes were assigned a fixed randomly generated preference value.

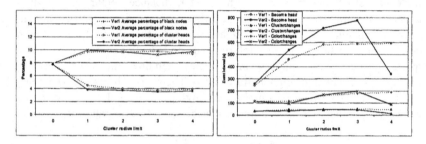

Figure 2. Influence of algorithm version and cluster radius limit

First we compared the two versions of the algorithm. The cluster radius limit parameter was varied, while the number of nodes was 100 and the radio-range was 300 m. The node speed was randomly chosen between 0 and 10 m/s (36 km/h). Figure 2a shows the average percentage of black nodes and cluster-heads for both versions of the algorithm. The number of cluster-heads is equal to the number of clusters since each cluster has exactly one cluster-head. The reason for using the second version is to reduce the number of redundant cluster-heads. As expected, the second version has fewer cluster-heads, but the difference is marginal. The number of black nodes is in practice similar for both versions. Figure 2b shows the average time between color changes, cluster changes and head-selection for the same simulation. A higher value represents more stability. The average interval $\overline{T}$ is calculated as $\overline{T} = (NT)/N_e$, where N_e is the measured number of events, N is the number of nodes, and T is the simulation time. We see that the changes to become cluster-heads are more infrequent in the second version. The intervals of color and cluster changes are similar in both versions. Because of the ability to form larger clusters and the increased stability of cluster-heads, we will use the second version in further simulations.

In the simulation we varied the cluster radius limit parameter. Some applications and routing protocols may perform better in small clusters. We can see that the largest difference is between values 0 and 1 of the parameter.

When the parameter is 0, all black nodes are cluster-heads and the curves coincide. When the parameter is 1, the number of cluster-heads is halved but some more black nodes are required. Higher values of the parameter have minimal influence on the color distribution. However, stability increases until the maximum at the parameter value 3 and then dramatically decreases. A reason is that a node can keep the same dominator longer as the cluster radius limitation does not force it to change. After a certain distance, mobility causes long branches to break more frequently. We will use a cluster radius limit of one in further simulations.

The influence of node density can be tested by either varying the radio-range or the number of nodes in a fixed size network. As a measurement of density, we use the average number of nodes within the radio-range of a node, i.e. the average degree Δ. Denoting the number of nodes in the network with N, the roaming area size with A and the radio-range of a node with Z, the theoretical average degree Δ_t can be calculated as $\Delta_t = (N/A) \pi Z^2$.

Figure 3a shows the percentage of white, green and black nodes when the radio-range is increased from 50 m to 350 m. There are 50 nodes in the network of size 1000 x 1000 m. Because the radio-range Z is increased linearly, the average degree increases exponentially ($\Delta_t \sim Z^2$). The node speed is uniformly random between 0 and 20 m/s (72 km/h).

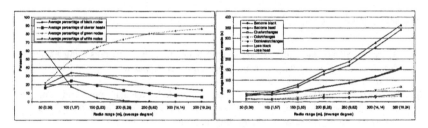

Figure 3. Influence of density on node type distribution (a) and event intervals (b)

For each parameter of Z, five 600 s simulations were run and the results were averaged. As Figure 3a shows, the percentage of green nodes and the percentage of black nodes decrease as the density increases. White nodes have no neighbors and their existence indicate a too low density, especially for radio-range of 150 m and less ($\Delta_t < 4$). The fraction of black nodes is less than 30% in most connected networks and less than 20% in dense ($\Delta_t > 10$) networks. In dense networks, about half of the black nodes are cluster-heads. Figure 3b shows the average interval between various events. We can see that nodes change their dominator at a rate that is relatively independent of the node density (15 – 25 s). Black nodes remain black long – in most connected networks over one minute despite the high mobility. Cluster-heads are stable, with a change interval of over 3 minutes in dense networks.

8.   CONCLUSIONS

The simulations give a rough estimation about the performance of the clustering algorithm. Because of paper length limitations, only some simulations were presented. We can see that the algorithm is able to reduce the number of nodes that participate in broadcasting. By allowing an additional layer of black nodes in addition to the cluster head, the stability can be increased. The clustering algorithm has a low overhead with a single periodically sent Hello message. The proposed algorithm creates a clustering structure that respects the different resources of the nodes. It allows concentration of traffic and service provision to nodes with more resources.

ACKNOWLEDGEMENTS

This work has been partly supported by the European Union under the E-Next Project FP6-506869, and by the European Commission under the IST-2001-38113 MobileMAN project. The work has also been partly supported by the TES and Sonera foundations.

REFERENCES

1.   B. Das, R. Sivakumar, and V. Bharghavan, Routing in ad hoc networks using a spine, in *Proceedings of Sixth International Conference on Computer Communications and Networks*, 1997, pp. 34-39, September 1997
2.   R. Sivakumar, B. Das, and V. Bharghavan, The Clade Vertebrata: Spines and routing in ad hoc networks, in *Proceedings of the Third IEEE Symposium on Computers and Communications*, 1998, ISCC '98, pp. 599-605, June-July 1998
3.   Jie Wu, and Hailan Li, On calculating connected dominating set for efficient routing in ad hoc wireless networks, in *Proceedings of the 3rd international workshop on Discrete algorithms and methods for mobile computing and communications*, August 1999
4.   Stojmenovic, M. Seddigh, and J. Zunic, Dominating sets and neighbor elimination-based broadcasting algorithms in wireless networks, in *IEEE Transactions on Parallel and Distributed Systems*, Volume 13, Issue 1, pp. 14-25, January 2002
5.   Srivastava, R. K. Ghosh, Cluster based routing using a k-tree core backbone for mobile ad hoc networks, in *Proceedings of the 6th international workshop on Discrete algorithms and methods for mobile computing and communications*, September 2002
6.   Simple Network Layer Simulator for Ad-Hoc Networks, http://www.netlab.hut.fi/tutkimus/MobileMan/snelsan/
7.   http://www.python.org/
8.   R. Giovanni, S. Paolo, An analysis of the node spatial distribution of the random waypoint mobility model for ad hoc networks, in *Proceedings of the second ACM international workshop on Principles of mobile computing*, pp. 44-50, October 30-31, 2002

OLSR TREES: A SIMPLE CLUSTERING MECHANISM FOR OLSR

Emmanuel Baccelli
Hipercom Project, INRIA Rocquencourt
78153 Le Chesnay Cedex, FRANCE
Emmanuel.Baccelli@inria.fr

Abstract   The main ad hoc routing protocols that were proposed generally provide only flat networks. However the Internet has always been of a hierarchical nature, for scalability and manageability reasons. This paper therefore introduces a simple mechanism providing dynamic clustering with OLSR, one of the MANET routing solutions, chosen for its ease of integration in the Internet infrastructure. This clustering can have many different applications. This work describes how it can be used to provide hierarchical routing with OLSR. However, it is not limited to this use.

Keywords: Mobile Ad Hoc Networks, Clustering

Introduction

While the main ad hoc routing solutions OLSR [1], AODV [6], DSR [8], and TBRPF [7] generally provide only flat routing, the Internet has always been hierarchical in nature. Hierarchy was introduced as a tool to cope with scalability problems, concerning both routing and managing administratively. Indeed, having several levels of hierarchy limits the growth of the routing information needed in the biggest routers in the Internet. Hierarchy enables this growth to be only logarithmic with respect to the size of the network, instead of linear. And on the other hand, when an organization grows in size, hierarchy and clustering have obvious advantages in terms of management in general. Issues due to scalability have not been entirely resolved with the main solutions that were proposed (see [1] [6] [7] [8] [2]). However, MANET routing is in dire need to address these issues, as it suffers from what is also its advantage: native mobility disturbing the Internet architecture, and decentralized wireless access incurring a lack of bandwidth limiting its flat growth.

OLSR [1], the most popular solution easily integrated in the Internet infrastructure, is no exception to this fact. This work therefore presents a mechanism providing dynamic clustering in an OLSR network, based on a technique close to the tree clustering described in [3]. This clustering can be used for different purposes: (i) to enable hierarchical routing, or (ii) to create relatively natural regions for some administrative purpose such as address (auto)configuration, security, or any other purpose needing a dynamic partitionning of the network.

The remainder of this paper is organized as follows. The next section will briefly overview OLSR, essentially very close to the widely used routing protocol OSPF [9] [10]. The clustering mechanism will then be detailed in the context of an OLSR network. And finally an application of the clustering mechanism to hierarchical routing with OLSR will be exposed, before we conclude on the matter.

1.   OLSR Protocol Overview

In this section we essentially outline OLSR, keeping in mind our goal: to design a clustering mechanism that integrates in the OLSR framework as a simple extension. For further details on OLSR, or on its performance characteristics, see [1] and [4].

As a proactive link-state routing protocol, OLSR employs the periodic exchange of control messages in order to accomplish topology discovery and maintenance. This exchange results in a topology map being present in each node in the network, from which a routing table can constructed.

Basically, OLSR employs two types of control messages: HELLO messages and TC messages. HELLO messages have local scope and are exchanged periodically between neighbor nodes only, essentially tracking the status of links between neighbors. On the other hand, TC messages have larger scope and are emitted periodically to diffuse link-state information throughout the entire network.

This operation of diffusing a message to the entire network – also called flooding – is optimized in OLSR with a mechanism called MPR-flooding (see [5] for more details on this OLSR-specific technique). This optimization reduces drastically the cost of performing a flooding operation, through having each node select a minimal set of "relay nodes" (called MPRs), responsible for relaying flooded packets. As shown in Fig. 1, from the local point of view of a node flooding a packet – *i.e.* the center node in the figure – this corresponds to only the minimal number of neighbors (the black nodes) relaying the broadcast, instead of basically all the neighbors.

Figure 1. Multipoint Relays of a node. A node (the center black node) floods a message that is forwarded only by the neighbors it has selected as its MPRs (the other black nodes). The range of the neighborhood of the node is depicted by the circle.

OLSR control traffic is transmitted in an unified packet format: this allows messages to be piggybacked together, therefore optimizing the number of transmissions overall. The OLSR packet format is shown in Fig. 2. As seen in in this figure, a packet is a collection of messages, each with individual headers. This allows the individual treatment (including flooding behavior) of each message. See [1] for further details. Note that this unified format also allows extensions to easily take advantage of the MPR flooding mechanism.

2.   OLSR Tree Formation and Maintenance

The base is to pragmatically and yet optimally identify the root of trees, in other words the heads of the clusters. This must be done in a dynamic fashion, as well as the tree formation that is induced by these choices.

Taking advantage of local maximum connectivity, *i.e.* nodes that feature the most neighbors are designated cluster heads. This mechanism initially forms trees in the following way: each node selects as parent its *preferred neighbor*. A node's preferred neighbor is the neighbor which has the maximum *degree* (number of neighbors). A node which is a local maximum degree-wise (all its neighbours have lower degree) is then the *root* of its tree. Ties are broken with the classical highest ID criteria.

```
 0                   1                   2                   3
 0 1 2 3 4 5 6 7 8 9 0 1 2 3 4 5 6 7 8 9 0 1 2 3 4 5 6 7 8 9 0 1
+-+-+-+-+-+-+-+-+-+-+-+-+-+-+-+-+-+-+-+-+-+-+-+-+-+-+-+-+-+-+-+-+
|          Packet Length          |      Packet Sequence Number    |
+-+-+-+-+-+-+-+-+-+-+-+-+-+-+-+-+-+-+-+-+-+-+-+-+-+-+-+-+-+-+-+-+
|  Message Type |     Vtime       |         Message Size           |
+-+-+-+-+-+-+-+-+-+-+-+-+-+-+-+-+-+-+-+-+-+-+-+-+-+-+-+-+-+-+-+-+
|                          Originator Address                      |
+-+-+-+-+-+-+-+-+-+-+-+-+-+-+-+-+-+-+-+-+-+-+-+-+-+-+-+-+-+-+-+-+
|  Time To Live |  Hop Count   |      Message Sequence Number      |
+-+-+-+-+-+-+-+-+-+-+-+-+-+-+-+-+-+-+-+-+-+-+-+-+-+-+-+-+-+-+-+-+
|                                                                  |
:                          MESSAGE                                 :
|                                                                  |
+-+-+-+-+-+-+-+-+-+-+-+-+-+-+-+-+-+-+-+-+-+-+-+-+-+-+-+-+-+-+-+-+
|  Message Type |     Vtime       |         Message Size           |
+-+-+-+-+-+-+-+-+-+-+-+-+-+-+-+-+-+-+-+-+-+-+-+-+-+-+-+-+-+-+-+-+
|                          Originator Address                      |
+-+-+-+-+-+-+-+-+-+-+-+-+-+-+-+-+-+-+-+-+-+-+-+-+-+-+-+-+-+-+-+-+
|  Time To Live |  Hop Count   |      Message Sequence Number      |
+-+-+-+-+-+-+-+-+-+-+-+-+-+-+-+-+-+-+-+-+-+-+-+-+-+-+-+-+-+-+-+-+
|                                                                  |
:                          MESSAGE                                 :
|                                                                  |
+-+-+-+-+-+-+-+-+-+-+-+-+-+-+-+-+-+-+-+-+-+-+-+-+-+-+-+-+-+-+-+-+
:                                                                  :
                               (etc)
```

Figure 2.   Generic OLSR packet format. Each packet encapsulates several control messages into one transmission.

The network is then viewed as a *forest*, *i.e.* a collection of logical trees, as described in [3], where this mechanism is used for flooding following the branches of the trees. In this paper, we on the other hand use the clustering produced by the trees, shown in Fig. 3.

In order to enable OLSR nodes to form and maintain trees, OLSR nodes periodically exchange so-called Branch messages (in addition to usual OLSR messages). Typically a Branch message will be piggy-backed with a Hello message and have the same 1 hop scope. This approach is most scalable, since light, local and non-centralized. With a Branch message a node specifies information such as its identity (the *Node ID* field), the tree it belongs to (the *Tree ID* field) and its parent in the tree (the *Parent ID* field). The format of these messages is shown in Fig. 4. The *Depth* field indicates the distance of the node to the root. The format also reserves room for eventual extensions with the *Reserved* field, unused and zeroed out, for now. Note that the IDs of the nodes are generally the IP addresses of the nodes.

3.   Hierarchical Routing with OLSR Trees

One application of the tree structuring described above can be the introduction of hierarchical routing in OLSR, using the dynamic clustering defined by the trees. The following sections briefly describe a way to achieve that when the tree structures are in place. Note that, as mentionned in the introduction, there

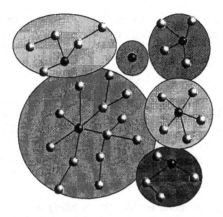

Figure 3. Tree clustering. Roots are shown as black nodes, and branches of the trees are shown as plain links between nodes. Links that are not branches are dashed. One tree is reduced to its root, as it is disconnected from any other node.

```
 0                   1                   2                   3
 0 1 2 3 4 5 6 7 8 9 0 1 2 3 4 5 6 7 8 9 0 1 2 3 4 5 6 7 8 9 0 1
+-+-+-+-+-+-+-+-+-+-+-+-+-+-+-+-+-+-+-+-+-+-+-+-+-+-+-+-+-+-+-+-+
|                            Node ID                            |
+-+-+-+-+-+-+-+-+-+-+-+-+-+-+-+-+-+-+-+-+-+-+-+-+-+-+-+-+-+-+-+-+
|                           Parent ID                           |
+-+-+-+-+-+-+-+-+-+-+-+-+-+-+-+-+-+-+-+-+-+-+-+-+-+-+-+-+-+-+-+-+
|                    Tree ID   (Root Node ID)                   |
+-+-+-+-+-+-+-+-+-+-+-+-+-+-+-+-+-+-+-+-+-+-+-+-+-+-+-+-+-+-+-+-+
|  Depth  |                      Reserved                       |
+-+-+-+-+-+-+-+-+-+-+-+-+-+-+-+-+-+-+-+-+-+-+-+-+-+-+-+-+-+-+-+-+
```

Figure 4. OLSR Branch message format.

may be other applications that may benefit from using this clustering, and even, other ways to use OLSR trees for hierarchical routing.

3.1 Routing within Tree Scope

Within a tree, OLSR operates as if there was no tree, except for the following points:

1 Messages coming from a neighbor that is not in the same tree are generally not considered and not forwarded.

2 The root of a tree has the special additional role of being responsible for the communication of the tree with the rest of the MANET.

3 A node in contact with another tree must inform its own tree and especially its root.

In the following, we will describe how the restriction to tree scope is done, and how the root performs its special role. Note that routing within a tree is identical to routing with regular OLSR, and that the only difference stands in routing outside the tree.

Flooding within Tree Scope.   MPR selection is unaltered by the use of trees: MPRs are selected as if there were no trees. The MPR mechanism is local and therefore very scalable. What is less scalable is the diffusion by all the nodes in the network (no hierarchy) of all the link state information (i.e. TC messages).

Addressing this, the tree mode enables the flooding of TC messages by any node in a tree to be restricted to that tree. In other words: TC messages originated and flooded inside a tree remain inside this this tree i.e. they are not forwarded nor considered outside the tree: they are not forwarded beyond this tree. This is done via usual MPR flooding, with an additional rule: A node will not forward a message coming from a neighbor from another tree, except if

1 It is selected as MPR by this neighbor, AND

2 It is the first time it receives this message, AND

3 It has another neighbor that is in the same tree as this neighbor.

This rule ensures the MPR flooding will be complete inside the tree. In order to make sure that the MPR flooding completeness is not broken since MPR selection does not take into account tree segregation, border nodes just outside the tree may relay messages between two different neighbors from the same tree (different from the border node's tree).

Leaf Nodes.   A node in contact with another tree (a node that has one or more neighbors that are not in the tree) must inform its tree and especially its root node. For each other tree this node reaches to, it can inform its tree with a so-called Leaf message specifying the roots of the other trees and its estimation of the distance between the roots (i.e. the sum of its depth in its tree and the depth of its neighbor in its own tree). The node will periodically flood this Leaf message throughout the tree, unless it has already received another Leaf message advertizing the same tree with a shorter distance estimation (and this information is still fresh enough). This way, the root and the other nodes in the tree are informed of the paths leading to any neighbor tree, and these are shortest available paths through the trees, from root to root.

```
0                   1                   2                   3
0 1 2 3 4 5 6 7 8 9 0 1 2 3 4 5 6 7 8 9 0 1 2 3 4 5 6 7 8 9 0 1
+-+-+-+-+-+-+-+-+-+-+-+-+-+-+-+-+-+-+-+-+-+-+-+-+-+-+-+-+-+-+-+
|                            Node ID                          |
+-+-+-+-+-+-+-+-+-+-+-+-+-+-+-+-+-+-+-+-+-+-+-+-+-+-+-+-+-+-+-+
|                   Advertized Neighbor Tree ID               |
+-+-+-+-+-+-+-+-+-+-+-+-+-+-+-+-+-+-+-+-+-+-+-+-+-+-+-+-+-+-+-+
|  Distance   |                  Reserved                     |
+-+-+-+-+-+-+-+-+-+-+-+-+-+-+-+-+-+-+-+-+-+-+-+-+-+-+-+-+-+-+-+
```

Figure 5.   OLSR Leaf packet format.

Leaf messages are typically piggybacked with TC messages inside a tree and share the same scope, *i.e.* tree-scope. Their format is shown in Fig. 5. They include information such as the identity of the advertizing node (the *Node ID* field), the identity of the advertized tree (the *Advertized Neighbor Tree ID* field), or the estimated distance between the root of the tree and the root of the advertized tree (the *Distance* field).

3.2   Communication with Other Trees

OLSR routing and MPR flooding being restricted to a tree, something special must be done in order to distribute routing information MANET-wide, from tree to tree. This is the additional task of the root of a tree. In order to address this task, the root basically operates OLSR at a higher level: over the super-topology formed by the roots of trees throughout the MANET. At this level, each tree, embodied by its root, behaves as if it were a single OLSR node: a super node. Similarly to regular OLSR, these super nodes (i.e. the roots) periodically send Super-Hellos, and Super-TCs. These super-messages are the only messages to be forwarded outside a tree. This is described in the following.

Super Messages.   Super messages are identical to regular messages except that they feature an additional IP address in their header that indicates the next super-hop (the next root to reach). The essential difference with regular OLSR messages stands in the fact that super-messages are routed and use OLSR-established paths inside each tree, instead of being simply flooded. With hierarchical routing in place, these messages are the only messages that are forwarded outside tree scope, therefore featuring MANET scope. The format is shown in Fig. 6. All the fields are as specified in [1], except that the *Message Type* field is set to a special value indicating a super message, and the fact that the header of the message (actually the beginning of the super-message) is

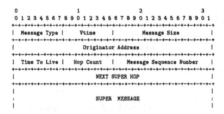

Figure 6.   OLSR Super packet format.

completed with an additional IP address specifying the next super-hop.

Super Hello Messages.   The root periodically sends a Super-Hello message to all the other roots it knows of via Leaf messages. Super-Hellos are unicasted and use the shortest root-to-toot paths advertized by the Leaf messages and OLSR routing/forwarding inside each tree. This way, as in OLSR, roots are informed of their super-neighborhood and can perform super-MPR selection. Super Hellos only have one super-hop scope (they are not forwarded further than the neighbor roots).

Super-Hellos are similar in functionality and format to regular Hellos messages, except they also feature the next super-hop in their header (as mentionned above). Nodes use this IP address to route the message from root to root.

Super TC Messages.   In addition to Super-Hellos, the root periodically sends a Super-TC message that is super-flooded (concurrent unicasts using Super-MPR and the shortest root-to-root OLSR paths) to all the roots in the network. Note that Super-TC messages therefore have a scope that is bigger than one super-hop since they are forwarded way beyond neighbor roots: throughout the whole MANET. This way, roots are informed of the whole super-topology formed by the roots.

Super-TC messages are similar in functionality and format to regular TC messages, except they also feature the next super-hop in their header (as mentionned above). Subsequent roots update this field in order to achieve super-MPR flooding over the super-topology. The format is specified in the last section.

Super HNA Messages. Super-HNA messages are also periodically super-flooded by each root to all the other roots in the MANET. With the generation of a Super-HNA message, a root summarizes the link state information its cluster encompasses. This way, roots are aware of the link state information of the other trees.

Super-HNA messages are similar in functionality and format to regular HNA messages, except they also feature the next super-hop in their header (as mentionned above). They are generally piggy-backed with the generated Super-TCs. Note that it can actually be envisionned to collapse Super-TCs and Super-HNAs in only one message type that would accompish both functionalities. It was not presented here for purposes of simplicity in explaining OLSR over the super-topology.

Routing Beyond Tree Scope. Being in possession of MANET-wide information with Super-HNA and Super-TC messages, a root node will then be able to route beyond tree scope. It will therefore advertise the default route inside its tree and traffic with outside the tree will transit via the root.

4. Conclusion and Future Work

Addressing the lack of alternatives to flat networking in the main MANET routing solutions, this paper presents a dynamic clustering mechanism for OLSR [1], one of these solutions, chosen for its particular ease of integration within the Internet infrastructure. This is indeed the goal with the introduction of hierarchy in ad-hoc networking: facilitate the integration of MANETs in the Internet architecture, and address scalability issues within MANETs – issues that are left to be completely resolved with the main solutions that are proposed (i.e. OLSR [1], AODV [6], DSR [8], and TBRPF [7]). The clustering can be used for different purposes such as routing, or administrative purposes that could benefit from the dynamic partitionning of the network into relatively natural regions. These purposes include, but are not limited to, address autoconfiguration and security. In this paper, an application of the clustering mechanism is described in order to introduce hierarchical routing with OLSR. Future work will tackle using the clustering mechanism for other applications in large MANETs such as: address autoconfiguration mechanisms, distributed security authorities and group management, and other ways to use hierarchical routing, including mechanisms using clustering to provide more stability in face of mobility.

References

[1] T. Clausen, P. Jacquet, A. Laouiti, P. Minet, P. Muhlethaler, A. Qayyum, L. Viennot, "Optimized Link State Routing Protocol," RFC 3626, http://ietf.org/rfc/rfc3626.txt, 2003.

[2] S. Corson, J. Macker, "Mobile Ad hoc Networking (MANET): Routing Protocol Performance Issues and Evaluation Considerations," RFC 2501, http://ietf.org/rfc/rfc2501.txt, 1999.

[3] Navod Nikaein, Houda Labiod, Christian Bonnet, "DDR - Distributed Dynamic Routing Algorithm for Mobile Ad hoc Networks," MobiHOC Proceedings, 2000.

[4] T. Clausen, P. Jacquet, L. Viennot, "Comparative Study of Routing Protocols for Mobile Ad-hoc NETworks," Proceedings of IFIP Med-Hoc-Net 2002, September 2002.

[5] A. Qayyum, L. Viennot, A. Laouiti, "Multipoint Relaying: An Efficient Technique for Flooding in Mobile Wireless Networks," INRIA Research Report RR-3898, March 2000.

[6] C. E. Perkins, E. M. Royer, S. R. Das, RFC 3561: "Ad Hoc On-Demand Distance Vector Routing." Internet Engineering Task Force, Request For Comments (experimental), July 2003.

[7] R. Ogier, F. Templin, M. Lewis, RFC 3684: "Topology Dissemination Based on Reverse-Path Forwarding." Internet Engineering Task Force, Request For Comments (experimental), February 2004.

[8] D. Johnson, D. Maltz, Y. Hu, draft-ietf-manet-dsr-10.txt: "The Dynamic Source Routing Protocol for Mobile Ad Hoc Networks." Internet Engineering Task Force, Internet Draft (Work in Progress), July 2004.

[9] J. Moy, "OSPF version 2," Internet Engineering Task Force RFC 2328, http://ietf.org/rfc/rfc2328.txt, 1998.

[10] C. Adjih, E. Baccelli, P. Jacquet, "Link state routing in wireless ad-hoc networks", MILCOM 2003 - IEEE Military Communications Conference, vol. 22, no. 1, pp. 1274-1279, Oct. 2003.

ASYNCHRNOUS ARCHITECTURE FOR SENSOR NETWORK NODES

Aurélien BUHRIG, Marc RENAUDIN, Dominique BARTHEL
TIMA Laboratory, CIS group, Grenoble, France {Aurélien.Buhrig, Marc.Renaudin}@imag.fr
France Telecom R&D - Meylan – France – Dominique.Barthel@francetelecom.com

Abstract: We present an asynchronous software and hardware architecture specifically
            suited for wireless sensor network nodes. To reduce power consumption
            and/or increase performances, some blocks go into hardware. The whole
            system is modelled using a unique asynchronous HDL before being
            partitioned. The software part that is executed on an asynchronous processor is
            then scheduled using a quasi-static scheduling and operates in an event-driven
            way with reactive hardware through an interface controller. We use an
            asynchronous analog to digital converter combined to a new approach in the
            non-uniform signal processing theory to obtain an entire event-driven
            platform. The use of asynchronous hardware allows to efficiently design a
            fine-grained dynamic power consumption control mechanism controlling V_{dd}
            (digital voltage scaling) and V_{bb} (bulk biasing) in order to manage the
            speed/power consumption trade-off and to go in a low-power idle mode state
            with very few static leakage. Finally, to increase the lifetime of the nodes,
            some scavenging techniques are added.

Key words: sensor network node, architecture, asynchronous, low-power, event-driven,
            high level description, modeling.

1. INTRODUCTION

Ambient intelligence is getting more and more importance in nowadays life and addresses a large panel of applications. This intelligence is closely linked to the sensing of the environment that leads to the design of sensor platforms that can be connected into wireless ad hoc networks. The possible applications of sensor networks are numerous. Among them: home humidity and temperature monitoring, seismic sensing in harsh environment, movement detection and localization for the consumer electronic and military purpose, analysis of chemical substance in a natural environment, and so on.

Ad hoc networks, due to their intended support of "no-limit" infrastructure-less communication, pose many significant new challenges in comparison with traditional wireless networks. The improvements in microelectronic technologies have made possible the design of small and less consuming systems on chip, but the autonomy of such devices is still a key issue. Indeed, these nodes are expected to sense the environment, compute data and perform wireless communications while consuming as little energy as possible, potentially under some application-imposed real-time constraints. They have a limited embedded energy that consists in a traditional battery to which it is possible to add a renewable energy source (coming from vibrations[1], solar radiations [2] or RF power [3]).

In this context, energy saving is critical to operate the sensor network for a long period of time. This work aims at minimizing this power consumption at the node-level and we present in this paper our vision of such an ultra low-power platform in which both software and hardware are designed in an asynchronous and totally event-driven way to maximize the lifetime of the nodes. As there is no switching activity when the circuit does not require to perform any operation and since they allow easier dynamic power management and are able to respond very quickly, asynchronous circuits are ideal for sensor networks in which most of the time is spent waiting for events on the radio interface, sensor or even timeouts from a standalone timer.

In this paper, we give a new vision of the co-design of the hardware/software architecture of sensor network nodes. This vision lies in the adoption of a fully asynchronous event-driven system, especially well suited to design for ultra low power. The nodes of the sensor network are asynchronous systems (clock-less) in which all the processing chain, software and hardware processes are event-driven.

The whole system is modeled using a single language or at least a single representation. This common description, which is at the moment Petri Nets, can be simulated and analyzed to allow an efficient co-design and an efficient generation of the interfaces.

In order to save even more energy, a fine-grained power consumption management is adopted. For confidentiality purpose, a low-power cryptography operator can be used. Finally, if some applications require dynamic hardware reconfiguration, the use of asynchronous FPGA is considered.

2. CLASSICAL SENSOR NETWORK OS COMPARISON AND LIMITATION

2.1 TinyOS vs general-purpose OS

An important problem to cope with is to make code execution efficient by minimizing the operating system (OS) overhead without removing traditional wireless-sensor network features. Traditional general-purpose multitasking embedded OS were originally developed for the PC platform and have been adapted to embedded systems. Those OS, even the most embedded ones, are too general-purpose to be efficient and the context switching generates expensive overhead that is tolerable for a fast and unlimited energy PC platform or a powerful embedded processor but is not acceptable for ultra low power embedded platforms.

A very interesting way to solve this problem is approached with TinyOS developed at UC Berkeley [4]. TinyOS is a reactive OS that does not target a broad range of general applications but only specific tasks for sensor networks. It can be described as follow: external events that occur on the RF or sensor interface propagate upward from the lowest layers till they are handled by the upper ones in an asynchronous way between the different blocks.

A performance and power consumption comparison between TinyOS and the general-purpose operating system eCOS [5] is reported in [6]. The result is that the use of TinyOS drastically reduces power consumption and improves performances. Some features (such as virtual memory, dynamic memory allocation, etc.) that are useless for sensor networks are not implemented.

2.2 Limitations

The TinyOS architecture is good at reducing power consumption. However we here–after highlight some important limitations of TinyOS [6]:
- It would be advantageous for power consumption and/or performance to implement some components of the application into hardware
- Those components could execute specific tasks whereas in TinyOS and traditional operating systems all tasks go into software
- There is no way to dispatch software tasks onto different resources
- There is no global power-control mechanism; implementing dynamic voltage scaling is a good way to reduce power consumption while meeting the performance constraint but is hardly possible with TinyOS.

- Some events can be lost during treatment if the event queue is full.

2.3   Approach adopted

2.3.1   Overview

In our approach, we want to keep the advantages of TinyOS without its drawbacks. In particular, we think that a major feature is to implement some parts of the system into hardware. For example, if a CRC or a Viterbi operator is needed to encode and decode messages, it is advantageously integrated into hardware in order to reduce the power consumption that would be engendered by the numerous computations performed by the processor to execute equivalent software.

Furthermore, due to the reactive nature of the desired operating system and applications, one expects the hardware part to be event-driven. Therefore, we implement it using the asynchronous technology [7], also known for its low-power consumption. The choice for this technology is detailed in the next section and requires dedicated hardware/software interfaces.

Finally, we add a global power-control mechanism, supported by a power management unit implemented in software and hardware. This power management is flexible enough to be applied at different granularity levels according to the hardware processes and the node architectures.

2.3.2   Asynchronous technology

As mentioned previously, it is advantageous to implement some parts of the system in hardware. We have chosen the asynchronous technology for two main reasons.

Firstly, the asynchronous technologies allow an important power consumption reduction. Indeed, asynchronous systems do not use any clock and the synchronization between the different asynchronous operators is performed by a request/acknowledgment protocol (handshaking protocol) implemented locally as shown in Figure 1. Consequently, only the parts of the circuit performing an operation have an activity. The rest of the circuit consumes very little energy (only static leakage) and are immediately woken-up when an event occurs on its inputs.

Figure 1. Asynchronous principle

Secondly, due to the reactive nature of the software, it is interesting to go further with the asynchronous architecture so that the whole system behaves in a totally event-driven way. With such an architecture, an event (from the radio interface for instance) will propagate between different asynchronous blocks regardless of the software or hardware nature of the crossed blocks. This communication type requires specifying a communication interface between software and hardware. This interface is not as complex as an interface between synchronous hardware and event-driven software.

2.3.3 Communications

The synchronous and asynchronous notions can be tricky and depends on the context. Indeed, these notions apply at different levels (hardware technology, communication specification, communication implementation). At hardware technology level, an asynchronous system is a clock-less system where the synchronization between two asynchronous blocks is performed as mentioned previously. Figure 2 shows the four phases protocol.

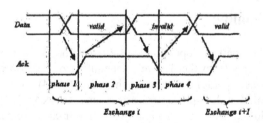

Figure 2. Four phases protocol

Therefore, in asynchronous technology, since both communicating processes exchange information using requests and acknowledgements, both are synchronized and hence the asynchronous hardware implements a synchronous communication.

3.   SOFTWARE ARCHITECTURE

3.1   Modelling of the whole system and partitioning

Both software and hardware have an identical asynchronous event-driven architecture and this is very interesting to model the whole system and to abstract the implementation of the processes. At top level, the system is designed using a single concurrent description model. At the moment, this description is done with an asynchronous HDL, the CHP (Communicating Hardware Processes [8], derived from the CSP [9]). This HDL being not very convenient to describe software and another description language capable of being translated into Petri Nets will be used in the future.

The concurrent description of the system is then automatically translated into Petri Nets [10] and each concurrent process of the high level description is translated into a Petri Net.

The complete description of the system is obtained by the composition of the Petri Nets of every top level processes are composed at the communication level.

Once the system is described, the partitioning can occur according to some criteria such as performance, power consumption (that can be simulated and analyzed with adequate tools such as TAST [11] using the Petri Net representation of the system) or modularity.

Finally, the software part is scheduled, whereas the hardware parts are synthesized into gates using appropriate tools [11].

3.2   Scheduling

An important part of operating system overheads and hence power consumption comes from the dynamic scheduling of the software tasks. In dedicated software operating systems such as TinyOS [4], or in hardware OS parts implemented in low-power processors such as SNAP [12] or bitSNAP [13], the scheduling is ensured using a FIFO. In our case, we have chosen to implement a static scheduling to cope with this problem. This scheduling is found using an algorithm whose core is based on the algorithm proposed in [14] and applied to the Petri Net model of the whole system. The limitations of the algorithm proposed in [14] is that the communications cannot be probed and are implemented with infinite FIFO. Our method does support probing operation and does not assume infinite memory communication channels.

4.   HARDWARE FEATURES

4.1   CPU

As seen before, asynchronous hardware has an event-driven architecture that allows the system to be clock-less and to reduce power consumption. The class of asynchronous circuit we use to design the nodes is Quasi Delay Insensitive (QDI) circuits. A QDI circuit behaves correctly regardless of the delay of the gates and wires under the weak assumption of *isochronic fork*. A fork (a wire that connects a sender to several receivers) is *isochronic* when the delays between the sender and the receivers are about the same. This architecture is data-driven. In other words, the asynchronous block is asleep when no data comes in. As soon as a data is present on its input, the hardware wakes up.

The processing unit is not defined yet. Enhanced versions of the asynchronous 8-bit microcontroller MICA [15] or the 16-bit processor ASPRO [16, 17] can be used as well as an asynchronous 32-bit RISC processor currently under development. The data width can be selected to enable the best power consumption/computational power trade-off for a given sensor network.

4.2   Power management

A different way to make power savings is to use dynamic voltage scaling (DVS) to control power consumption at run time. With synchronous circuits, decreasing the voltage makes the signal transition slower to establish and hence imposes a decrease of the clock frequency. Changing the clock frequency introduces delay overhead due to the synchronization of the *phase lock loop* (PLL) and extra power consumption. With asynchronous circuits, modifying the voltage does not introduce any overhead. The speed of the circuit changes on its own since the circuit behavior is not sensitive to the rising and falling times of the signals (delay insensitivity).

So it is easy to add to the processor a hardware part that smoothly manages power consumption. This power manager is able to increase or decrease the supply voltage (V_{dd}) of one or several parts of the system according to the performances required. With the evolution of the technologies, a more and more important part of the power consumption is due to static leakage. To reduce the static leakage, we use a technique called "back biasing" which consists in biasing the bulk to affect the transistors threshold V_T [18]. The bulk biasing is a feature that is integrated to the power management unit. Therefore this unit is able to control V_{dd} and V_{bb} to reduce power consumption, and this at different granularity levels. In practice, the software is controlling the power management unit in order to optimize the speed/power

According to the application, it is possible to define different policies. For instance, if the node has to perform real time operation, one chooses the power management to enable the application to meet the real time constraints. On the contrary, if the node must have the longest lifetime as possible, the speed will be chosen according to the power consumption and the remaining battery energy.

4.3   Hardware-Software Interface

A controller is designed to operate correctly between software and hardware tasks. This *Hardware-Software Interface* (HIS, Figure 3) will manage communications between hardware and software in order to prevent the microprocessor from being interrupted by each hardware bloc that would generate software handler calls and extra power consumption. This controller wakes up the microprocessor when a desired hardware event income.

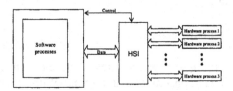

Figure 3. Hardware Software Interface Scheme

4.4   Signal processing chain – AADC

A new approach in the signal processing which leads to a significant energy saving is to use an asynchronous analog to digital converter (AADC) [19]. This one takes samples only if the sensed physical characteristic changes more than a predefined quantum. The samples and the date are saved altogether. This enables a saving on samples. Then a non uniform sampling theory [20] is applied to the samples to take advantage of the AADC. Such a converter is hence totally data driven.

As for the performances of such a method, for the same number of points, the processing of the measures needs more computations than a traditional ADC with classical signal theory. Nevertheless, since these computations are performed on a smaller set of points, the computational complexity is globally reduced. In comparison with traditional synchronous ADC on a voice signal application, the computational complexity is reduced by one order of magnitude by using asynchronous processing chain with non uniform sampling theory [20].

5. CONCLUSION AND FUTURE WORK

This paper presents an entire event-driven platform for sensor networks. This platform aims at drastically reducing power consumption thanks to the reactivity of every parts of the system, from the analog to digital converter to the radio frequency interface and through a data-driven asynchronous processor executing software processes that communicates with hardware with an interface controller (HSI). This platform is able to operate in a large range of power supply making possible a fine-grained power consumption management by controlling the voltage and the bias of the bulk.

Now, the asynchronous platform is specified and a first prototype is being designed. Our future works will focus on the design of CAD tools in order to describe the whole using system level language or model. Those CAD tools will have to integrate features to help the designers to co-design the system at best, taking into account the required performances and power consumption.

Future work will also focuses on the modeling of performance requirement of the software tasks after the scheduling in order to know statically the speed the system needs at runtime. This aims at controlling dynamically the voltage supply of the CPU according to its orders (expressed in MIPS) using a feedback system [21].

ACKNOWLEDGMENT

This work is partially supported by France-Telecom R&D department.

REFERENCES

1 S. Meninger, J. O. Mur-Miranda, R. Amirtharajah, A. Chandrakasan, and J. Lang, "Vibration-to-electric energy conversion," presented at International Symposium on Low Power Electronics and Design, San Diego, California, USA, 1999.
2 B. A. Warneke, M. D. Schott, B. S. Leibowitz, L. Zhou, C. L. Bellew, J. A. Chediak, J. M. Kahn, B. E. Boser, and K. S. J. Pister, "An autonomous 16 mm3 solar-powered node for

distributed wireless sensor networks," presented at Sensors'02, Orlando, Florida, USA, 2002.

3   A. Bayrashev, A. Parker, W. P. Robbins, and B. Ziaie, "Low frequency wireless powering of microsystems using piezoelectric-magnetostrictive laminate composites," presented at 12th International Conference on Transducers, Solid-State Sensors, Actuators and Microsystems., Boston, USA, 2003.

4   TinyOS Group, "TinyOS tutorial," 2003.

5   RedHat, "eCOS."

6   S. F. Li, R. Sutton, and J. M. Rabaey, "Low Power Operating System for Heterogeneous Wireless Communication Systems," presented at PACT 01, Barcelona, Spain, 2001.

7   M. Renaudin, "Asynchronous Circuits and Systems : A Promising Design Alternative," in *Microelectronic Engineering*, vol. 54, 2000, pp. 133-149.

8   A. Martin, "Programming in VLSI: from communicating processes to delay-insensitive circuits," in *Developments in concurrency and communication.* Boston, MA, USA: Addison-Wesley Longman Publishing Co., Inc., 1991, pp. 1-64.

9   C. A. R. Hoare, "Communicating Sequential processes," *Communication of the ACM*, vol. 21, pp. 666-677, 1978.

10 M. Renaudin and A. Yakovlev, "From Hardware Processes to Asynchronous Circuits via Petri Nets: An Application to Arbiter Design," presented at Workshop on Token Based Computing, Bologna, Italy, 2004.

11 K. Slimani, Y. Rémond, G. Sicard, and M. Renaudin, "TAST profiler and low energy asynchronous design methodology," presented at International Workshop on Power And Timing Modeling Optimization and Simulation, Santorini, Greece, 2004.

12 V. Ekanayake, C. Kelly, and R. Manohar, "An Ultra-low-power Processor for Sensor Networks," presented at Eleventh International Conference on Architectural Support for Programming Languages and Operating Systems, Boston, USA, 2004.

13 V. Ekanayake, C. Kelly IV, and R. Manohar, "BitSNAP: Dynamic Significance Compression For a Low-Energy Sensor Network Asynchronous Processor," presented at Eleventh IEEE International Symposium on Asynchronous Circuits and Systems, New York City, USA, 2005.

14 J. Cortadella, A. Kondratyev, and L. Lavagano, "Quasi-static scheduling for concurrent architectures," presented at Third International Conference on Application of Concurrency to System Design (ACSD'03), Guimarães, Portugal, 2003.

15 A. Abrial, J. Bouvier, M. Renaudin, P. Senn, and P. Vivet, "A New Contactless Smartcard IC using an On-Chip Antenna and an Asynchronous Micro-controller," presented at ESSCIRC'00, Stockholm, Sweden, 2000.

16 M. Renaudin, P. Vivet, and F. Robin, "ASPRO : an Asynchronous 16-bit RISC Microprocessor with DSP Capabilities," presented at ESSCIRC, Duisburg, Germany, 1999.

17 M. Renaudin, P. Vivet, and F. Robin, "ASPRO-216: A Standard-Cell Q.D.I. 16-Bit RISC Asynchronous Microprocessor," presented at 4th International Symposium on Advanced Research in Asynchronous Circuits and Systems, San Diego, California, USA, 1998.

18 E. Labonne, G. Sicard, and M. Renaudin, "Dynamic Voltage Scaling and Adaptive Body Biasing Study for Asynchronous Design." Grenoble: TIMA - INPG, 2004.

19 E. Allier, G. Sicard, L. Fesquet, and M. Renaudin, "A new class of Asynchronous A/D Converters Based on Time Quantization," presented at ASYNC'03, Vancouver, 2003.

20 F. Aeschlimann, E. Allier, L. Fesquet, and M. Renaudin, "Asynchrounous FIR filters: Towards a new digital procession Chain," presented at ASYNC'04, 2004.

21 D. Rios, A. Buhrig, and M. Renaudin, "Power Consumption Reduction using dynamic control of Microprocessor performance", presented at PATMOS, Leuven, Belgium, 2005.

EVALUATING FAULT TOLERANCE ASPECTS IN ROUTING PROTOCOLS FOR WIRELESS SENSOR NETWORKS

Daniel F. Macedo[1], Luiz H. A. Correia[1,2], Aldri L. dos Santos[1,3],
Antonio A. F. Loureiro[1], José Marcos S. Nogueira[1]*, and Guy Pujolle[4]

[1] *Federal University of Minas Gerais, Brazil*

[2] *Federal University of Lavras, Brazil*

[3] *Federal University of Ceará, Brazil*

[3] *University Paris 6, France*

{damacedo,lcorreia,aldri,loureiro,jmarcos}@dcc.ufmg.br, pujolle@rp.lip6.fr

Abstract   Fault tolerance is an essential requirement in the design of protocols and applications for Wireless Sensor Networks (WSNs) since communication and hardware failures are frequent. In this paper we studied the resilience of routing protocols for continuous data dissemination WSNs in face of faults. The main causes of silent failure are presented and classified, including security attacks. An evaluation of routing protocols shows that failures under a large region of the network are the most damaging. We also show how routing protocols may save energy by temporarily turning off disconnected nodes.

Keywords: Wireless sensor networks, fault tolerance, routing

1.   Introduction

Wireless Sensor Networks (WSNs) consist of a large number of sensor nodes, composed of processor, memory, battery, sensor devices and transceiver. These nodes send monitoring data to an access point (AP) responsible for forwarding data to the users [1]. Unlike traditional ad hoc networks, in general it is not possible to replace or recharge node batteries due to the number of nodes deployed or inhospitable environmental conditions. Hence, energy conservation is a critical factor in WSNs.

---

*In sabbatical period at universities of Evry and UPMC/Paris6/LIP6, France.

WSNs are propitious to failure due to events such as node destruction, link quality degradation, among others. Since those networks may be employed in hostile environments, nodes can fail due to landslides, floods or other natural agents. Failures also occur in the communication due to changes in weather or movement of objects near the nodes, or due to malicious agents. Thus, protocols and applications must be developed with fault tolerance in mind.

Data flow in WSNs usually follows a pattern, since data is preprocessed locally and then sent to the AP. This data flow can be categorized according to its frequency [2]. In *event-driven networks*, communication is sporadic, occurring only when an event of interest is detected. In *continuous dissemination networks*, nodes periodically send data to the AP. In those networks it is possible to build a "map" of the current state of the environment, which can be later used to study time and space variations in the observed phenomena. Due to the intrinsic differences in traffic, routing protocols are usually designed to operate on a single network class. Continuous dissemination networks tend to employ proactive protocols, while in event-driven networks routes are build only when an important event is detected. The same fact occurs with fault-tolerance mechanisms.

In this paper we study the performance of routing protocols for continuous dissemination networks in faulty scenarios, where *silent* faults occur. The main causes of failure are presented and then categorized. Next, a performance evaluation through simulation was performed for three routing protocols. This text is organized as follows. Section 2 presents the related work. Section 3 presents an overview of the protocols evaluated. Section 4 describes and categorizes the main causes of silent failures in WSNs. This categorization is then used to evaluate three routing protocols in section 5. Finally, section 6 draws the conclusions and future work.

2.   Related Work

Avizienis et al. present a taxonomy of failures, which also encompasses security issues [3]. Hollick et al. present the challenges of fault tolerant systems for WSNs, ad hoc networks and cellular networks, and list the requirements which should be met by fault-tolerant protocols [4].

Fault tolerance in protocols for WSNs has been widely studied. The first protocols developed [5] were concerned with failures caused by energy depletion, increasing the life time of a node by distributing the energy spent among nodes. Other protocols were designed to be resilient against node failures. Those protocols send multiple copies of data among different routes, thus increasing the probability of correct reception. Ganesan et al. [6] showed that partially disjoint routes are as effective as totally disjoint routes, although spending less energy to be established.

Since the cost of maintaining multiple routes is significant, some protocols define only one high-quality route. De Couto et al. presented a modification to DSR which calculates the reliability of a route [7]. Nodes always choose the route with the best quality, thus increasing the probability of a successful delivery.

Given the occurrence of a failure, it is necessary to identify an alternative route. Vieira et al. proposed two protocols to mitigate failures due to energy depletion [8]. In the first algorithm, the AP notifies nodes to modify its routes whenever a failure occurs. In the second, nodes build a list of "second-best routes". Upon the detection of a failure, one route in this list is selected to become the default route.

3. Evaluated Protocols

We evaluate the performance of three routing protocols for continuous dissemination networks. Those protocols were selected because they provide different levels of fault tolerance.

TinyOS Beaconing is a protocol used in the Mica Motes platform [9]. This protocol periodically creates a minimum distance tree rooted at the AP. Only nodes with good link quality are used to route messages. TinyOS Beaconing was not designed with fault tolerance mechanisms, although the periodic recreation of routes provides some degree of fault tolerance.

Boukerche et al. proposed a routing algorithm, called EAD (*Energy-Aware Distributed routing*), which creates a routing tree that maximizes the number of leaf nodes [10]. Leaf nodes, which do not need to send messages, turn their radios off in order to extend network lifetime. The protocol also uses backoff timers based on current node energy for decreasing collision probability. As in TinyOS Beaconing, EAD uses periodic reconstruction of routes to provide fault-tolerance. In EAD, however, traffic is concentrated in a few nodes, hence failures in those nodes will be more severe than in "ordinary" nodes.

The PROC (*Proactive ROuting with Coordination*) protocol was developed with the goal of reducing energy consumption and increasing network lifetime [11]. PROC creates a routing tree, called *backbone*. The structure of the backbone is influenced by the application, which defines which nodes are more suitable to route data. The protocol provides fault tolerance using link layer acknowledgments. Whenever the number of data packets not acknowledged reaches a certain threshold, PROC selects a new route. As in EAD, the failure of *backbone* nodes will be severe. The proactive probe of nodes using link layer acknowledgments, though, mitigates this issue.

4.   Failure in WSNs

This section identifies the main causes of silent communication failures in WSNs. We assume that protocols perform their functions correctly, and all messages are correctly received. The following failures were identified:

Atmospheric phenomena – Several environmental conditions such as humidity, temperature, among others, modify signal propagation. As weather is constantly changing, communication quality varies with time.

Mobile sources of interference – Other devices operating at similar frequencies or even vehicles, animals and humans may interfere with communicating nodes.

Natural disasters – Sensor nodes may be deployed outdoors or in disaster locations, thus being exposed to landslides, floods and earthquakes. Those events may cause massive destruction of sensor nodes by permanently damaging hardware components.

Accidental breakage – Sensor nodes can be accidentally destroyed, for example due to animals trampling over nodes, or falling trees.

Processor crashes – The application may contain programming errors, which might lead the processor to crash situations. To avoid such situations, microcontrollers reboot if a software malfunction occurs. Thus, nodes will be unavailable for a finite amount of time.

Malicious failures – WSNs are prone to malicious failures due to security attacks caused by an outsider or by a corrupted node. This article does not evaluate security protocols. Some security attacks can be partially mitigated with the use of fault tolerance techniques [12]. We use fault tolerance techniques to avoid the following denial of service attacks: interference attacks, collision attacks, and sinkhole attacks.

Energy depletion – Energy depletion may generate communication failures. Usually, batteries will not be replaced, since WSNs are employed in harsh environments, or the number of nodes deployed makes battery replacement a daunting task. Our study does not encompass energy-related failures, since those are very difficult to model.

Failure Grouping

The failures described above were characterized according to common characteristics. This characterization, summarized in Table 1, aids the performance evaluation presented in section 5. Failures are grouped according to persistence and extension:

Persistence – Indicates if a node will resume correct operation after its failure (*transient failures*), or if the node will fail indefinitely (*permanent failures*) [3]. From a routing perspective, transient failures occur when nodes are out of service for a few minutes, while in permanent failures nodes are out of service for hours.

Extension – Relates to the number of failed nodes. Failures can be *isolated* (only one node fails) or *grouped* (various nodes in a region fail).

Table 1. Failure characterization, divided by their causing agents.

Cause of failure	Persistence	Extension
Atmospheric phenomena	permanent	grouped
Mobile sources of interference	transient	isolated
Natural disasters	permanent	grouped
Accidental breakage	permanent	isolated
Processor crashes	transient	isolated
Interference attacks	permanent	grouped
Collision and sinkhole attacks	both	isolated

5. Evaluation

The three protocols were implemented in the simulation environment NS-2 [13]. The application simulated has traffic characteristics similar to the sensor network deployed in Great Duck Island [14]. In this network each sensor sends a data message of 36 bytes of size every 70 seconds.

The medium access control protocol (MAC) employed is a modified version of the IEEE 802.11 protocol, which emulates the behavior of the standard MAC protocol in TinyOS [9]. The route recreation interval used for EAD and TOSB (a simplified version of TinyOS Beaconing without link quality estimators) was 120s, while for PROC this interval was set to 180s, as empirically determined in [11].

The simulated network consists of 150 nodes deployed in a square area, measuring 70m on each side. The AP is located at the corner of the area. The network operates without failures for 1500s. After that, a failure occurs, and the simulation continues for 1500s. In the scenarios where isolated failures occur, failed nodes are randomly selected. In the grouped and permanent scenario, a central point is defined, and all nodes within a given radius of this point fail. All results are the mean values of 33 simulations, plotted with 95% confidence intervals.

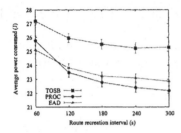

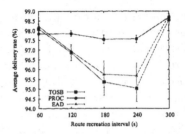

Figure 1. Average power consumed vary- *Figure 2.* Average delivery rate varying
ing the route recreation interval.   the route recreation interval.

Transient and Isolated Failures

The routing recreation interval affects the degree of fault tolerance,
since protocols rely on route reconstructions to recover from failures. In
this scenario 20 nodes fail for 120s. In the first set of simulations we
varied route recreation intervals from 60 up to 300s. Figure 1 shows
that nodes consume more energy when route updates are frequent. The
average delivery rate, shown in Figure 2, decreases for larger route recreation intervals. This reduction is subtle in PROC, since this protocol
identifies failed routes earlier using probes. All protocols recover from
failure within 200s. Average delivery rates increase for 300s recreation
intervals, since network load decreases, and less packets are dropped due
to full packet queues. Latency decreased for all protocols as route recreation intervals increased, since there was a lower load on the network.

Next, we evaluated how failure time affects the performance of the
protocols. PROC presented higher delivery rates (around 0.5% higher),
as shown in Figure 3. Periodic routing recreation guaranteed good fair
tolerance for EAD and TOSB, since both showed delivery rates slightly
lower than PROC's. The amount of energy consumed decreased with
longer failures, since nodes had to route less data. PROC was the
most energy-efficient protocol, consuming 22J of energy, while EAD and
TOSB consumed 4% and 14% more energy than PROC, respectively.

Finally, we varied the number of failed nodes from 25 up to 100 nodes.
All protocols behave similarly in this scenario. The proactive mechanism
in PROC allowed this protocol to recover from failures faster than the
other protocols evaluated, providing a 0.5% increase in average delivery
rates. Since simulation time is significantly bigger than the failure time,
the gains obtained by proactive probing of nodes are not significant in
the final average delivery rate. Average latency and hop count were not
affected, but average energy consumption decreased, since less messages
were sent as more nodes failed. Figure 4 shows the average energy con-

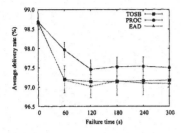
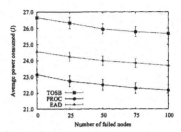

Figure 3. Average delivery rate varying the time of failure.

Figure 4. Average power consumed varying the number of failed nodes.

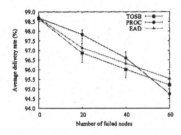
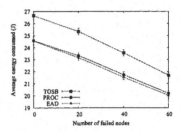

Figure 5. Average delivery rate varying the number of failed nodes.

Figure 6. Average power consumed in permanent and isolated failures.

sumption. Overall, transient and isolated failures are not severe, since nodes easily find new routes.

Permanent and Isolated Failures

In this scenario we evaluate the impact of permanent and isolated failures. We varied the number of failed nodes from 20 up to 60 nodes. As in the previous scenario, all protocols recovered their routes within 200s, though in this scenario the throughput drops after the failure, since failed nodes permanently stop sending data. The average hop count decreased slightly, around 0.1 hops for each 20 failed nodes. Average latency showed a small variation, showing that the traffic reduction compensated the increase in average route lengths. The average delivery rate decreased with the number of failed nodes, as shown in Figure 5.

Compared to transient and isolated failures, permanent and isolated failures allow nodes to save more energy (Figure 6), since the network produces less data. Permanent and isolated failures are more severe than transient and isolated failures, since the former imposes greater degradations at node's average delivery rate and average energy consumption.

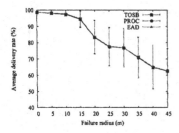 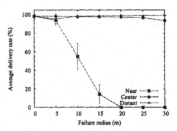

Figure 7. Average delivery rate in per- *Figure 8.* Average delivery rate for fai-
manent and grouped failures.   lures in different sections of the network.

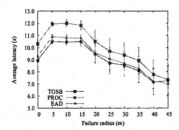 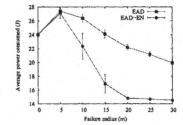

Figure 9. Average latency in permanent *Figure 10.* Average power consumed
and grouped failures.   with energy-saving schemes.

Permanent and Grouped Failures

This scenario evaluates the severity of permanent and grouped failures. The failure radius varied from 5 up to 40m. The average delivery
rate drops up to 9% as failure radius increases (Figure 7). The confidence
interval is up to 5%, showing that the delivery rate varies significantly
in each simulation. This is caused by network partitions, as supported
by Figure 8. The "Near" curve shows the delivery rate for failures near
the AP, the "Center" curve shows results for failed nodes in the center of the network, and the "Distant" shows failures at the edge of the
network. Failed nodes near the AP substantially degrade the average
delivery rate, while failed nodes at the edge of the network are harmless.

To recover from a group of failed nodes, routes must avoid the failed
region, increasing the average hop count and average latency, as shown in
Figure 9. For failures of radius over 20m, average latency and hop counts
decrease, since partitions occur more frequently, and only connected
nodes near to the AP are able to send their packets successfully.

Since network partitions cannot be avoided, as nodes are unable to
route through them, routing protocols should adopt energy conservation

measures in the disconnected nodes. Figure 10 compares the performance of EAD with EAD-EN, an improved version of EAD which turns off the radio of disconnected nodes. Node disconnection in EAD-EN is detected if a node does not receive routing messages for a period of two route recreation intervals. Figure 10 shows that, for failures near the AP, EAD-EN consumes from 16% up to 33% less energy when compared to the original EAD.

6.   Conclusions and Future Work

Wireless Sensor Networks are employed in harsh environments, hence those networks are prone to failures. Sensor nodes must adapt to the environmental conditions to provide a service within the expected quality of service requirements. Thus, nodes must have effective routes even in the presence of failures and security attacks. In this article we characterized the main causes of silent failures in WSNs, and evaluated the performance of routing protocols based on this characterization.

Results showed that transient and isolated failures, and permanent and isolated failures are mitigated with the periodic recreation of routes. Permanent and grouped failures are much more severe, since those failures may partition the network. Fault tolerance algorithms must employ more aggressive approaches near to the AP, since failures in this region may severely degrade the performance of the entire network. Upon shutting down disconnected nodes, significant energy savings can be achieved in situations were a prolonged failure partitions the network.

Fault tolerance can be improved with the design of failure assessment mechanisms. Such scheme would allow early detection or even forecasting of failures, providing means to readily recover from faulty operation. As future work we will study how quality of service parameters are affected by failures.

Acknowledgments

The development and studies described in this article were completed as part of Sensornet project (http://www.sensornet.dcc.ufmg.br), funded by CNPq/Ministry of Science and Technology/Brazil. Some scholarships were given by CAPES/Ministry of Education/Brazil.

References

[1] I. F. Akyildiz, W. Su, Y. Sankarasubramaniam, and E. Cayirci. A Survey on Sensor Networks. *IEEE Communications*, 40(8):102–114, 2002.

[2] Linnyer Beatrys Ruiz, Antonio A. F. Loureiro, and Jose Marcos Nogueira. Functional and information models for the MANNA architecture. In *GRES03 - Col-*

loque Francophone sur la Gestion de Reseaux et de Services, pages 455–470, February 2003.

[3] Algirdas Avizienis, Jean-Claude Laprie, Brian Randell, and Carl Landwehr. Basic concepts and taxonomy of dependable and secure computing. *IEEE Trans. Dependable Secur. Comput.*, 1(1):11–33, 2004.

[4] Matthias Hollick, Ivan Martinovic, Tronje Krop, and Ivica Rimac. A Survey on Dependable Routing in Sensor Networks, Ad hoc Networks, and Cellular Networks. In *Proceedings of the 30th IEEE EUROMICRO Conference 2004*, pages 495–502, Rennes, France, September 2004.

[5] Jamal N. Al-Karaki and Ahmed E. Kamal. Routing techniques in wireless sensor networks: a survey. *IEEE Wireless Communications*, 11(6):6–28, 2004.

[6] Deepak Ganesan and Ramesh Govindan and Scott Shenker and Deborah Estrin. Highly-Resilient, Energy-Efficient Multipath Routing in Wireless Sensor Networks. *SIGMOBILE Mob. Comput. Commun. Rev.*, 5(4):11–25, 2001.

[7] Douglas S. J. De Couto, Daniel Aguayo, John Bicket, and Robert Morris. A high-throughput path metric for multi-hop wireless routing. In *Proceedings of the 9th ACM International Conference on Mobile Computing and Networking (MobiCom '03)*, San Diego, California, September 2003.

[8] Marcos Augusto M. Vieira, Luis Filipe M. Vieira, Linnyer Beatrys Ruiz, Antonio Alfredo F. Loureiro, Antônio O. Fernandes, José Marcos S. Nogueira, and Diógenes Cecílio da Silva Jr. Como Obter o Mapa de Energia em Redes de Sensores Sem Fio? Uma Abordagem Tolerante a Falhas. In *Anais do 5o. Workshop de Comunicação sem Fio (WCSF)*, pages 183–189, 2003.

[9] Philip Levis, Sam Madden, Joseph Polastre, Robert Szewczyk, Kamin Whitehouse, Alec Woo, David Gay, Jason Hill, Matt Welsh, Eric Brewer, and David Culler. TinyOS: An operating system for wireless sensor networks. In W. Weber, J. Rabaey, and E. Aarts, editors, *Ambient Intelligence*. Springer-Verlag, New York, NY, 2004.

[10] Azzedine Boukerche, Xiuzhen Cheng, and Joseph Linus. Energy-aware data-centric routing in microsensor networks. In *Proceedings of the 6th international workshop on Modeling analysis and simulation of wireless and mobile systems*, pages 42–49. ACM Press, 2003.

[11] Daniel F. Macedo, Luiz H. A. Correia, Aldri L. dos Santos, Antonio A. Loureiro, and José M. Nogueira. A pro-active routing protocol for continuous data dissemination wireless sensor networks. In *10th IEEE Symposium on Computer and Communications (ISCC)*, June 2005.

[12] Anthony D. Wood and John A. Stankovic. Denial of service in sensor networks. *Computer*, 35(10):54–62, 2002.

[13] NS-2 simulator. http://www.isi.edu/nsnam/ns/, January, 2005.

[14] R. Szewczyk, J. Polastre, A. Mainwaring, and D. Culler. Lessons from a sensor network expedition. In *Proceedings of the First European Workshop on Sensor Networks (EWSN)*, pages 307–322, January 2004.

SERVICE DISCOVERY PROTOCOL IN PROACTIVE MOBILE AD HOC NETWORKS

Mª Isabel Vara[1], Jose Mª Cabero[1], Jose Luis Jodrá[2] and Jose Oscar Fajardo[2]

[1]*Fundación Robotiker, Parque Tecnológico de Zamudio, edificio 202, 48170 Zamudio;* [2]*UPV-EHU University, Alameda Urquijo s/n, 48013 Bilbao*

Abstract: This paper proposes a service discovery protocol for discovering and advertising services in a proactive ad hoc network. The protocol we have defined is piggybacked into the OLSR protocol. We define a new message type into OLSR called Service Discovery Message (SDM) for both advertisement and discovery of services. The advertisement frequency and advertisement lifetime are user-controlled parameters, so that they can be modified depending on the user requirements. Each node maintains a service cache to store information about its own services, and the services each device discovers in the network. We also present simulation results of our protocol and show that the service discovery protocol defined here achieves much efficiency in discovering services, while it introduces practically no packet overhead compared to the basic OLSR protocol.

Key words: Ad hoc networks; OLSR protocol; Service Discovery.

1.   INTRODUCTION

Service discovery enables users, network devices and applications to seek out and find other users, networks devices and applications, in a friendly and easy way. There are some implementations that take this into account: *Service Location Protocol (SLP)* [1] of IETF, Sun's *Jini*[2], Microsoft's *Universal Plug and Play (UpNP)*[3] and Bluetooth's *Service Discovery Protocol (SDP)* [4]. However, most of them are only suitable for traditional fixed IP based networks.

The main focus of this paper is to present a service discovery protocol integrated into OLSR[5] protocol, to support service discovery and advertisement in ad hoc networks.

OLSR is a proactive[6] protocol. Proactive protocols attempt to periodically evaluate all available routes within a network, so that when a packet needs to be forwarded, the route is already known and can be used immediately. The reason for integrating service discovery with a proactive routing protocol is that, this way the network efficiency increases because, the same routes we use to discover available paths for transmiting data information, are used as well for service discovery.

2.   SERVICE DISCOVERY MECHANISM

The design of the OLSR protocol[5] helps us to add extensions to the protocol through the addition of new messages types. We have defined a new message type into OLSR called *Service Discovery message (SDM)*. Figure 1 illustrates the message format:

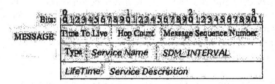

Figure 1. SDM packet format

The *Time To Live* field determines the number of hops the message can travel. This let us save more bandwidth than with a standard broadcast-based solution. The *Hop Count* field contains the number of hops a message is attaining. The *Type* indicates whether the message is an adverstisement or a query request. The *LifeTime* field indicates the time the service advertisement will be available for the rest of the nodes. Finally, the *SDM_INTERVAL* is a parameter that indicates how often an advertisement message is transmited. It is an user configurable parameter, so depending on the working environment this parameter could be higher or smaller. The smaller it is the more overhead it will be introduced into the network.

2.1   Service cache

Service cache enables devices to store their local and foreign services. Each node, when receiving an advertisement, stores the service information in the service cache in the room fitted-out for that purpose.

The cache size will increase with the number of services. Once the cache is full, the first entries to be discarded will be the ones with the lowest remaining *LifeTime*. Also the entries with the lifetime expired will be automatically removed.

2.2 Service advertisements

Every *SDM_INTERVAL* each node will send a new message with the update services. In case there are no new services available the node will not piggyback the message into the OLSR header. The way a node verifies whether it hosts new services or not is by checking the number of entries it has in its local cache where it stores its local services.

Any mobile device hearing this advertisement and interested in the services will store them in its service cache.

It is possible that two different nodes advertise the same service. As the service cache of each device is finite, before storing the services, a node that receives it will first check whether the service offering has been already advertised by another node. If so, it will discard the advertisement.

2.3 Service discovery

The format of the service discovery message is the same as that of the service advertisement, which is illustrated in Figure 1.

MPR nodes will forward the request. A node receiving the request will check whether the service wanted match one of the ones that it supports and it will make a replay. Before, it will wait for a random time to verify whether there is already a reply message from other node. If affirmative, it ignores the service query message. This way the protocol avoids multiple reply copies of the same service being sent at the same time to save network bandwidth. Otherwise, it fills in the fields of the SD message such as Time to Live, Server Address, Service Port, Protocol Type, and the Option field.

3. SIMULATION RESULTS

3.1 Simulation environment

The ns-2[7] simulation tool is used to evaluate the protocol. In the simulations, each mobile node changes its location within the subnet based on the random-waypoint[8] model. In ns-2, the Distributed Coordination

Function (DCF) of IEEE 802.11 for wireless LANs is used as the MAC layer protocol.

The simulated network is comprised of 50 nodes. Each scenario runs for 900 seconds. We use 3 different SDM frequency values: 0,5s, 1,5s and 2,5s.

3.2 Simulation results

We study for various SDM frequency intervals the traffic overhead in packets per second. In the following figure we show the overhead introduced by the SDM messages embedded in the OLSR protocol:

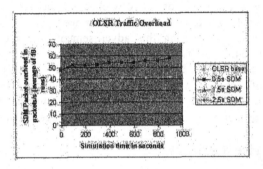

Figure2. SDM packet overhead in the network (in packets/s)

We can observe that the traffic overhead generated by the SDM messages when we advertise them for different frequencies is practically the same as in the basic OLSR protocol. Thus, we can conclude that the traffic overhead introduced with our service discovery proposal is not significant and it can be applied as a generic service discovery mechanism with the OLSR protocol and a mobile environment.

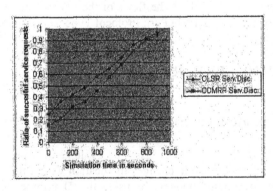

Figure3. Ratio of successful request

Regarding the ratio of service requests, in the figure above are depicted the results we have obtained.

We have compared the results with the service discovery mechanism over the reactive protocol ODMRP. From the figure we conclude that the service discovery made over the proactive protocol is more effective than the one over a reactive protocol, in terms of response time in service requests. The reason is that in a proactive protocol we have more knowledge or "world-view" of the network, and the routes for transmitting the packages are known in advance.

4. CONCLUSION AND FUTURE WORK

In this paper, we propose a service discovery mechanism for proactive ad hoc networks, based on the OLSR routing protocol. The service discovery information is piggybacked in the OLSR protocol as a new message type called SDM.

The simulation results have shown that the proposed mechanism is valid for ad hoc mobile networks. We are currently checking how the protocol behaves when the service cache is full, how it deals with the unavailability of services and false service discoveries. In a second phase of our project we will consider security aspects in the protocol.

REFERENCES

1. E. Guttman, C. Perkins, J. Veizades, and M. Day, "Service Location Protocol, Version 2", RFC 2608, June 1999.
2. Edwards and T. Rodden. Jini Example by Example. Prentice Hall PTR, June 2001.
3. John. UpnP, Jini and Salutation- A Look at some popular Coordination Frameworks for Future Network Devices. Technical report, California Software Labs, 1999.
4, Bluetooth Specification Part E. Service Discovery Protocol (SDP). http://www.bluetooth.com, November 1999.
5. T. Clausen and P.Jacquet "Optimized Link State Routing Protocol (OLSR". RFC 3626, IETF Network Working Group, October 2003.
6. http://www.ietf.org/html.charters/manet-charter.html, work in progress.
7. The Network Simulator ns-2 Homepage. http://www.isi.edu/nsnam/ns.
8. David B. Johnson and David A. Maltz, Dynamic Source Routing in ad hoc Wireless Networks, in Mobile Computing, edited by Tomas imielinski and Hank Korth, Chapter 5, pages 153-181, Kluwer Academic Publishers, ISBN:0792396979, 1996.

AUTONOMOUS RECONFIGURATION BY INNOVATION OF DIFFUSIONS

A Distributed Decision-Making Framework for Multi-State Mobile Ad Hoc Networks

Timothy K. Forde, Linda E. Doyle and Donal O' Mahony
Centre for Telecommunications Chain-Value Research (CTVR)
University of Dublin, Trinity College, Dublin 2, Ireland.

Abstract   The spatially and temporally diverse nature of ad hoc networks strongly suggests the development of a sophisticated multi protocol network-layer that should enable the ad hoc network's nodes to dynamically change the routing protocol as networking scenarios demand. In short, the routing protocol is to be considered a system variable. However, the autonomous reconfiguration of such a dependent variable is a non trivial task in the challenging environment of a realistically modelled open, mobile, wireless ad hoc network. We present a novel framework that builds on the social science theory of diffusion of innovations, a theory which describes a flexible decision-making model. This concept enables the development of an autonomous reconfiguration protocol which addresses the constraints imposed by the mobile ad hoc networking system model.

Keywords: Distributed Reconfiguration, Autonomic Computing

Introduction

Ad hoc routing protocols are at the core of ad hoc networks allowing remote nodes to communicate on a peer to peer basis [1], [2], [3]. It is well established in the literature that a one size fits all approach with regard to the choice of optimum routing protocol does not suffice [4]. Rather, in keeping with the distributed and ad hoc nature of these networks, it is preferable to design a system that allows nodes to dynamically configure and utilise the most suitable ad hoc routing protocol [5], [6]. Divergent network scenarios, as exemplified by node mobility, node density and traffic loading, demand networking protocols which are tailored to their requirements. To this end, we propose a flexible and reconfigurable network-layer which has access to a suite of fully distributed ad hoc routing protocols, each protocol addressing a different subset of the set of possible networking scenarios. The routing protocol is a dependent component of the network-layer, i.e. for neighbouring nodes to facilitate communication on a multi-hop peer to peer basis they must operate the same routing protocol. We present a reconfiguration framework that enables the nodes to autonomously and collaboratively choose their network-layer routing protocol having regard to the prevailing network conditions. The decision framework is based on the social science theory of the diffusion of innovations [7]; its design being tightly constrained by the limited applicability of distributed consensus algorithms in an asynchronous message passing system [8].

1.   Network-Layer Reconfiguration

Framework Objectives.   A reconfiguration framework must allow the network, as constituted by autonomous nodes, to react to changes in the network conditions by suitably reconfiguring the network-layer. However, a network is a distributed system; distributed with regard to both its computing architecture and with regard to its physical scope. The geographical spread of an ad hoc network lends itself to the presence of conflicting networking conditions in different areas of the network. Furthermore, robust ad hoc networks employ distributed routing protocols [1], [2], [3] which have been optimised to minimise overhead and to maximise throughput. This inherent network-layer optimisation should not be diminished by the introduction of ancillary network-layer protocols. Also, the reconfiguration protocol should not be reliant on the explicit services of the core network-layer routing protocols as this would introduce a cyclic dependency.

Realistic System Model.   In designing a robust network-layer protocol, the traits of a realistically modelled open, mobile, ad hoc network should be borne in mind. Among these traits number the *routing protocol signalling profile*, the *node-to-node link quality* and the *autonomy of the nodes' mobility*. In sum, the ad hoc network can be viewed as a distributed system of nodes which communicate over unreliable message passing channels, the structure of which is subject to dynamic, autonomous change.

2.   Decision-Making: Difficulties in Ad Hoc Networks

The reconfiguration of the network-layer's routing protocol is a multilateral choice; no single node has innate authority to make a unilateral decision in a fully distributed system in which there are likely to be divergent systems views. The literature on distributed consensus protocols, which is the discipline concerned with the reaching of agreement among remote processes [9], identifies the limits within distributed agreement is possible. The applicability of such protocols is system dependent, varying over a combination of fault, communication, transmission, message ordering and processor assumptions [8]. Any other agreement problem may be shown to be at least as hard as distributed consensus [10]. Fischer, Lynch and Patterson proved the impossibility of distributed consensus under certain conditions [11], showing that deterministic distributed consensus is impossible in an asynchronous message passing system if even one process crashes; a crashing process is the simplest form of system failure. To circumvent this result certain remedies, such as the use of failure detectors [12], have been proposed.

Despite the difficulties of reaching consensus in an asynchronous message-passing system, such as a mobile ad hoc network, distributed consensus has found its way in to the ad hoc networking community through group membership (GM) schemes which enable spontaneous communities to cooperate at application level. Briesemeister et al. [13] suggest a scheme which is based on the notion of local GM. The authors argue that a service designed for mobile ad hoc networks should be partitionable as disconnections may occur frequently. Their localised GM scheme allows an unbounded number of processes to exist, i.e. it allows for an open network. The localised GM service is built around a neighbourhood service that employs a failure detector-like heartbeat mechanism. The heartbeat operates in an asymmetric manner so that neighbouring processes do not have to have to share a symmetric link. The application described in [13] illustrates the narrow scope within which consensus has been applied to mobile ad hoc networking systems, thus far.

A solution to the issue of terminating the decision-making process within the context of a mobile wireless ad hoc network has been presented in [14] which describes an address auto-configuration scheme which adapted the Ricart Agrawala mutual exclusion algorithm for a multi-hop ad hoc network. The scheme uses a soft-state approach, allowing a node to take an address while the mutex-based allocation process is ongoing. If the attempted allocation is denied to the node, or if the node does not receive a confirmation message within a fixed period, then the node relinquishes the address. Termination of the process is thus guaranteed in the presence of lost or delayed confirmation messages.

3. Diffusion of Innovations: Societal Reconfiguration

Since the mobile ad hoc network consists of autonomous nodes with varying networking experiences (i.e. link properties, degree of connectedness, and observation of prevailing networking conditions), it is useful to categorise these different types of ad hoc nodes with respect to the part that they would play in the reconfiguration decision making process. To this end, we present a discussion of pertinent elements of the social science concept of diffusion of innovations [7]; a tractable model on which to base a robust reconfiguration framework. A simple example of this concept is the adoption of the QWERTY keyboard standard over the ergonomically superior DVORAK keyboard.

Innovation Decision Process.   The innovation decision process is the process through which an individual or Decision Making Unit (DMU) passes from first knowledge, or awareness, of an innovation to forming an attitude towards the innovation, to deciding to adopt or reject it, to implementation of the new idea, and to confirmation of this decision. As the process happens over time, the five steps in the process are individually conceptualised as; *knowledge, persuasion, decision, implementation* and *confirmation*. **Knowledge** is the first stage in the innovation-decision process. It occurs when a DMU is exposed to the innovation's existence. **Persuasion** occurs when the DMU forms a favourable or unfavourable attitude towards the innovation. Individuals seek reinforcement from personal connections and consider the innovation in light of their current situation. As the innovation carries a degree of risk, individuals want to know that their thinking is in line with that of their peers so that it reduces uncertainty about the innovation. During this stage the adoption or rejection of an innovation is not a foregone conclusion. **Decision** occurs when the DMU engages in activities that lead to either the adoption or rejection of the innovation. DMUs or individuals will often trial an innovation on a probationary period at this stage as part of the decision to adopt. However, in many cases it is not possible to trial the innovation alongside the status quo and so the innovation must either be accepted or rejected in its totality. **Implementation** occurs when a DMU puts the innovation into use. This stage normally follows directly after the decision stage within a short period of time. The innovation finally loses its distinctive quality as the separate identity of the new idea disappears. **Confirmation** then occurs when a DMU seeks reinforcement of an innovation that has already been made, but the unit may reverse the decision if it is exposed to conflicting messages about the innovation. In essence, the innovation-decision process is a continual and cyclical process in which the system will look for another innovation if it fails to receive reinforcement about the most recently adopted innovation.

Innovation Decision Actors.   The theory goes on to provide useful characterisations of the actors in the innovation-decision process using ideal types. The most popular classificatory principle is based on the innovativeness of the DMU. The literature describes innovativeness as the degree to which an individual or DMU, e.g. a node, is relatively earlier in adopting new ideas than other members of the system. Five adopter categories are defined; *innovators, early adopters, early majority, late majority* and *laggards*. **Innovators** are generally active information seekers about new ideas. They have a high degree of exposure to pertinent information and are eager to try new ideas. The innovator has the important role of acting as the gatekeeper that controls the introduction of innovations to other individuals. **Early adopters** (EA) have the largest degree of persuasive opinion leadership in most social systems; in terms of communication sources, they are localites, i.e their outlook is parochial, based on local observations. Early adopters have a high degree of connectedness and make reasoned, evidence -based decisions. The early adopter has to be more judicious in its innovation-decisions in order to continue to command the respect of others. They decrease local uncertainty about an innovation by adopting it and conveying messages to other near peers by means of interpersonal networks, i.e. neighbour-to-neighbour connections. The **early majority** (EM) forms a bridge between the early adopters and the late majority. They may deliberate over the adoption of the innovation for a relatively longer period than either the innovator or the early adopter. The early majority do not lead opinion as the early adopter does, but through frequent interaction with their peers, they tend to follow the early adopters. They are crucial in terms of tipping the balance within a society towards adoption of the innovation. They provide interconnectedness between groups of early adopters. The late majority adopt an innovation after the average member of the social system has already done so. The **late majority** (LM) are often forced to adopt the innovation as a result of economic necessity and increasing social pressures. The late majority, being sceptical, wait until most of their social system have already adopted, i.e. the late majority are more influenced by peer pressure than the utility of the innovation. **Laggards** (LD), as the name suggests, are the last in a social system to adopt an innovation. They have no opinion leadership qualities and are very local in outlook; in fact many are near isolates in social networks. The point of reference for laggards is the past; their decisions are made in terms of what has been done in previous generations.

Individual Thresholds.   An interactive innovation is one for which the utility of the innovation rises as the number of near peer adopters also rises. Individuals are likely to watch the other members of their group in an effort to discern what the group choice may be. The outcome for the group then turns on each member watching what the other members do. A threshold is the number of other individuals who must have adopted an innovation before a given individual will follow. For the diffusion of an innovation, a threshold is reached when an individual is convinced to adopt as a result of knowing that some minimum number of other individuals in the system have also adopted. So, the reaching of systemic critical mass turns on the local actions of individuals with respect to their own thresholds.

4.   A Self-Stabilizing Network-Layer

The reconfiguration protocol is supported by a self-stabilizing multi-protocol network-layer built on our communication stack DAWN, the Dublin Ad Hoc Wireless Network [15]. DAWN is a real ad hoc network testbed that facilitates experimentation with ad hoc networks on all levels from the application-layer to the physical-layer. At the network-layer of our communication stack, protocols can be dynamically started up or closed down at runtime, i.e. the state of the node, vis-à-vis its routing protocol, can be configured on the fly. The multi protocol network-layer currently allows a node to use AODV [1], DSR [2] or OLSR [3]. This network-layer also incorporates an ancillary self-stabilising configuration initialisation and conflict resolution protocol [16]. It also incorporates network observation tools that use local information similar to allow nodes to share external-state vectors (ESVs) describing their own neighbourhood observations.

5.   The Reconfiguration Framework

The protocol operates in three stages; the Persuasion Stage, the Decision Stage and the Implementation Stage. The Reconfiguration Decision Protocol (RDP) extends and modifies elements of the innovation-decision process for the task at hand. The RDP uses a two phase decision-making approach in which nodes are continually in the process of making a soft-state decision and are occasionally asked to make a hard state decision. The component is completely distributed, relying on opportunistic communication between nodes. Even though the system characteristics exacerbate the conditions which underlie the premise for the FLP impossibility result [11], a degree of local decision-making is possible, as exemplified by the local GM scheme [13] and by [14]. The use of such soft-state decisions allows for a more flexible decision-making model. The proposed RDP modifies the general layout of the innovation-decision process format. The distributed consensus model and the innovation-decision model are both triggered when a proposal is made to the system by a single node. In the consensus model the next step generally involves consultation with every other node in the system concluding in a clear termination of the process. In the innovation-decision model, a system of individuals progress from first knowledge though to the persuasion, decision and implementation stages before seeking confirmation of their decision; the confirmation stage may lead to a replacement discontinuance if the DMU is dissatisfied with the innovation. In contrast, the RDP starts in the consultation stage without any proposal being made; we term this the RDP's Persuasion Stage. The knowledge stage is not necessary in this system as the routing protocols are not true innovations; each node is already aware of the protocols. Instead, the system may be seen as one in which three protocols have been innovated and the nodes are continually seeking to confirm that their current choice is optimal for the given network conditions.

The Persuasion Stage involves a continuous process of passive observation and analysis. Each node makes soft-state decisions which are based only on passively received information and which may change as that information grows stale and expires. If the nodes manage to sustain a soft-state decision for a time, without altering it, they enter the Decision Stage followed immediately by the Implementation Stage. The Implementation stage completes an execution of the reconfiguration decision protocol and the nodes then re-enter the Persuasion Stage to begin evaluating the networking conditions again.

There are two other general points which should be noted at this stage. Firstly, due to the impossibility of knowing what constitutes the *entire* network in an ad hoc setting, the reconfiguration happens within a region of the network, i.e. a group of nodes that are sufficiently connected to organise themselves using the network-layer's self-stabilizing configuration conflict resolution protocol [16]. Secondly, the RDP employs small reconfiguration beacons which are appended to all packets that are issued by a node in the course of operating the primary network-layer protocols, i.e. they are opportunistically broadcast. The RDP simply queues its current beacon pending signalling activity by a primary protocol - it never actively issues packets itself.

The Persuasion Stage.   It is during the execution of this stage of the protocol that each node decides which protocol suits it, based on the node's knowledge of its local network state. Each node makes decisions based only on information passively received from neighbouring nodes; there is no handshaking. The persuasion stage of the innovation-decision process is concerned with nodes forming an opinion about an innovation; they are either in favour of the innovation or against it. Analogously, nodes in a region of an ad hoc network are continuously engaged in forming an *opinion* about their preferred ad hoc routing protocol. A node's preferred choice at any given time amounts to a soft-state decision; the node's hard-state decision is reflected in its current working routing protocol. A node's soft-state decision may be in agreement with its current hard-state decision, i.e. its current network-layer configuration. The differentiation of DMUs in the innovation-diffusion process extends to the ad hoc networking context with regard to the nodes involved in the RDP. The notions of Early Adopter, Early Majority, Late Majority and Laggard Nodes are introduced into the RDP to define the decision models used by nodes in the Persuasion Stage. There are no Innovator Nodes as the concept of a knowledge stage does not transfer to this setting. Nodes make their soft-state decisions based on a series of rules that relate to their classifications which are closely analogous to their innovation-decision counterparts. Each node changes the decision-making rules that it uses based on the network observations available to it and its knowledge of the decisions of its neighbours. While it is preferable to make a decision based on evidence alone (i.e. EA), nodes are also enabled to make decisions that are influenced by the choices of their neighbours (i.e. EM and LM). For the purpose of clarity note that a node referred to as an Early Majority (EM) Node, for example, is an ad hoc node that has made its decision based on EM decision rules. Both the EM node and the LM nodes' decisions are subject to the control of individual thresholds which dictate how easily persuaded a node can be. For instance an EM node may be required to have a majority of its neighbours as EA nodes before it adopts their decision whereas an LM node may have lower threshold that allows it to adopt the most popular decision that its neighbours have declared. The value to which the thresholds are set dictates the ease with which nodes can agree to reconfigure themselves. Setting the threshold too high would require a high degree of homogeneity within the network whereas lessening the threshold would allow change to occur in more heterogeneous environments. Finally, some other nodes in the system are bound to find themselves with poor connections to the main network partition. These nodes collate observation data that is inconsistent with their neighbours' data and cannot form a decision using one of the above mentioned models. Instead, these LD nodes make no decision. They will follow whatever decision is made by other nodes, if a decision is made.

The reconfiguration beacon has two fields; the Decision field, i.e. which protocol the node prefers, and the Decision Type field which indicates which decision model the node used to arrive at the soft-state decision. The Decision Type field may have the following values; EA, EM, LM, LD and HS (Hard State). The Laggard value indicates that the node could not make a decision and the Hard State value is used to enforce a decision at the Decision Stage.

Each node records information received from neighbours regarding their ESV data and soft-state decision choices in its neighbourhood table. The neighbourhood table is a constituent element of any network-layer's routing protocol; it lists those nodes which to which at least an incoming asymmetric link exists. Entries are added to the table, refreshed and removed in accordance with the techniques associated with the routing protocol in use. Nodes periodically evaluate their recorded observations in order to arrive at a soft-state decision using rules based on the decision hierarchy. This hierarchy places the Early Adopter decision, which is based on network observations alone, at the top and the Laggard decision at the bottom. Each decision is based on the information that is available to the node when it executes an evaluation round. Initial Early Adopter decisions, i.e. the first decisions that can be made in system, are made on the basis of a node's observation that its network observations match those of its neighbouring nodes, which leads them to have a common preferred choice of ad hoc routing protocol. The aim of the reconfiguration protocol is to allow nodes to loosely exchange network observations and soft-state decisions that reflect the underlying heterogeneity or homogeneity of their experiences. If the networking conditions are such that neighbouring nodes do not have a common experience of the network, then those nodes will not progress the RDP towards a hard-state decision.

Flushing Stale Data.   The accuracy of a node's neighbourhood table varies from routing protocol to routing protocol. A neighbour will only persist in an OLSR cache for a short time before it is expunged or refreshed, whereas a DSR cache is much slower to expunge data. However, the RDP is not concerned with the validity of routing information; it will not be attempting to make use of the out going links. The RDP is only concerned with the associated neighbour entry information such as the ESV data and soft-state-decision data, to provide it with a view of the local network's conditions as seen by neighbouring nodes. If the information persists in the neighbourhood table due to the routing protocol's timeout mechanisms, the RDP may use very stale observation data if it uses every entry in the neighbourhood table with equal weighting. To the RDP, neighbouring nodes are simply a timed series of data sources, nothing else, and it can employ a suitable filter, e.g. an EWMA filter, to place greater weight on the most recently received data and to diminish the effects of data that has not been refreshed.

The Decision and Implementation Stages.   The RDP progresses to the Decision Stage when an EA node has been advocating the same decision for a defined period of time. By choosing appropriate time to sustain the EA decision, the RDP can be allowed to progress rapidly through the persuasion stage or it can be made to move slowly towards the Decision Stage. The decisive Early Adopter Node issues a reconfiguration beacon with the Hard State in the Decision Type field. Each receiving neighouring node that has made the same soft-state decision, regardless of how it made the decision, adopts the hard-state decision by changing its protocol. Those nodes then continue to beacon that hard-state decision for a set time. Nodes that are not sufficiently connected are corrected by the configuration conflict resolution protocol [16].

6.   Conclusions

Given the diverse nature of an ad hoc network it is not a trivial task to enable distributed reconfiguration in a realistically modelled system. We have proposed a novel reconfiguration framework that enables nodes of varying network experiences to collaboratively reconfigure themselves notwithstanding the harsh, yet necessary, conditions that we have imposed. The framework is robust and very low cost, extending the concept of diffusion of innovation to the mobile ad hoc networking domain within the bounds defined by the literature on distributed consensus. While this framework has been developed for use at the network-layer, the design conditions that were imposed on it make it suitable for use at the MAC layer or physical layer.

References

[1]   C. E. Perkins and E. M. Royer, Ad-hoc On-Demand Distance Vector Routing, Second IEEE Workshop on Mobile Computing Systems and Applications, 1999, 25-26 Feb. 1999, Pages: 90 -100.

[2]   D.B. Johnson and D.A. Maltz, *Dynamic Source Routing in Ad Hoc Wireless Networks*, In Mobile Computing, edited by Tomasz Imielinski and Hank Korth, Kluwer Academic Publishers, 1996, Pages: 153-181.

[3]   T. Clausen, P. Jacquet, A. Laouiti, P. Minet, P. Muhlethaler, A. Qayyum, L. Viennot, *Optimized Link State Routing Protocol*, IETF MANET Working Group, December 2002.

[4]   D.D. Perkins, H.D. Hughes and C.B. Owen, *Factors Affecting the Performance of Ad Hoc Networks"*, Proceeding of the IEEE International Conference on Communications 2002, Vol. 4, Pages: 2048-2052.

[5]   J. Boleng, W. Navidi and T. Camp, *Metrics to Enable Adaptive Protocols for Mobile Ad Hoc Networks*, Proceedings of the International Conference on Wireless Networks, June 24 - 27, 2002, Pages: 293-298.

[6]   M. Frodigh, S. Parkvall and C. Roobol, *Future-Generation Wireless Networks*, IEEE Personal Communications, Vol: 8 Issue: 5, Oct. 2001, Pages: 10 -17.

[7]   E.M. Rogers, *Diffusion of Innovations*, 4rd Edition, Free Press, London.1996.

[8]   J. Turek and D. Shasha, *The Many Faces of Consensus in Distributed Systems*, IEEE Computer, Volume: 25, Issue: 6, June 1992, Pages: 8 - 17.

[9]   H. Attiya and J. Welch, *Distributed Computing: Fundamentals, Simulations and Advanced Topics*, McGraw-Hill Publishing, England, 1998.

[10]   R. Guerraoui and A. Schiper, *Consensus: The Big Misunderstanding*, 6th IEEE Workshop on Future Trends of Distributed Computing Systems, Tunis, Tunisia, October 29 - 31, 1997.

[11]   M.J. Fischer, N.A. Lynch and M.S. Paterson, *Impossibility of Distributed Consensus with One Faulty Process*, Journal of the ACM, Vol. 32, No. 2, April 1985, Pages: 374-382.

[12]   T.D. Chandra and S. Toueg, *Unreliable Failure Detectors for Reliable Distributed Systems*, Journal of the ACM, Volume: 43, Issue: 2, March 1996, Page: 225

[13]   L. Briesemeister and G. Hommel, *Localized Group Membership Service for Ad Hoc Network*, International Conference on Parallel Processing Workshops, August 18 - 21, 2002, Vancouver, B.C., Canada, Page: 94.

[14]   S. Nesargi and R. Prakash, *MANETconf: Configuration of Hosts in a Mobile Ad Hoc Network* , Proceedings of the Twenty-First Annual Joint Conference of the IEEE Computer and Communications Societies., Volume: 2 , 23-27 June 2002, Pages: 1059 -1068.

[15]   D. O'Mahony and L.E. Doyle, *An Adaptable Node Architecture for Future Wireless Networks*, in Mobile Computing: Implementing Pervasive Information and Communication Technologies, Kluwer series in Interfaces in OR/CS, Kluwer Academic Publishers, 2002, Pages: 77-92.

[16]   T.K. Forde, L.E. Doyle and D. O'Mahony, *Self-stabilizing Network-Layer Auto-Configuration for Mobile Ad Hoc Network Nodes*, in Proceedings of the IEEE International Conference on Wireless and Mobile Computing, Networking and Communications (Wimob 2005), 22 - 24 August 2005, Montreal, Canada.

PREFIX CONTINUITY AND GLOBAL ADDRESS AUTOCONFIGURATION IN IPV6 AD HOC NETWORKS
*Short version**

Christophe Jelger[†]
Computer Networks Research Group - University of Basel
Bernoullistrasse 16, CH-4056 Basel, Switzerland
Christophe.Jelger@unibas.ch

Thomas Noël
Louis Pasteur University (Strasbourg) - LSIIT - UMR 7005 CNRS-ULP
Boulevard Sebastien Brant, 67400 Illkirch, France
noel@dpt-info.u-strasbg.fr

Abstract

Ad hoc networks are formed by the spontaneous collaboration of wireless nodes when no networking infrastructure is available. When communication to the Internet is desired, one or more nodes must act as gateways for the ad hoc network. In this case, global addressing of ad hoc nodes is required. This article presents a protocol which can be used by an ad hoc node to dynamically select a gateway and create an associated IPv6 global address. The core of our proposal is the concept of *prefix continuity*. By building and maintaining a forest of logical spanning trees, our proposal ensures that there exists, between a node A and its gateway G, a path of nodes such that each node on this path uses the same prefix P as the node A and its gateway G. This concept results in an organized ad hoc network, in the sense that sub-networks (with respect to prefixes) are automatically created and dynamically maintained when multiple gateways are available. Moreover, the concept of prefix continuity ensures that each sub-network forms a connected graph of nodes which all use an identical prefix. In contrast to traditional wired networks, this feature is not trivial in ad hoc networks.

* The initial (long) version of this paper, as originally submitted and accepted for the MedHocNet'05 workshop, is available at http://cn.cs.unibas.ch/pub/
[†] Part of this work was carried out during the tenure of an ERCIM fellowship (see http://www.ercim.org for details).

1.   Introduction

In contrast to current wireless networks, ad hoc networks require no pre-existing infrastructure to exist. Because of the inherent limited propagation range of radio transmissions, ad hoc nodes must collaborate to forward (and route) packets within such a spontaneous multi-hop network. Moreover, nodes have to face unpredictable topological changes, which makes routing a challenging task in an ad hoc network. A growing issue with ad hoc networking is Internet connectivity. There is indeed an increasing deployment of community-based *mesh networks* [Draves et al., 2004] [V. Bahl (organizer), 2004], which currently rely on protocols developed for ad hoc networks. For such *species* of ad hoc networks, to be connected to the Internet is of major importance in order to offer Internet services (e.g. email, web access, etc) to their users. Being connected to the Internet requires that each node in the network must have a topologically correct global address in order to be natively reachable from outside the ad hoc network (i.e. without any network address translation mechanism).

In this paper, we present a protocol that can be used to configure the nodes of an IPv6 ad hoc network with a globally routeable address. Our proposal builds a forest of logical spanning trees, where each tree if formed by nodes that share a common global network prefix. As in classical IPv6 wired networks, gateways are responsible for prefix announcement. An inherent feature of our proposal is *prefix continuity*: it ensures that there exists, between a node A and its gateway G, a path of nodes such that each node on this path uses the same prefix P as the node A and its gateway G. When multiple (different) prefixes are available, this concept results in an organized ad hoc network, in the sense that sub-networks (with respect to prefixes) are automatically created and dynamically maintained when multiple gateways are available. As a result, each subnetwork is a connected graph of nodes which all use an identical prefix. In contrast to previous work, prefix continuity is the core element of our proposal.

Following this introduction, we present in Section 2 some of the related proposals. In Section 3 we present our approach and also introduce the concept of prefix continuity in an ad hoc network. We then describe in Section 4 the three algorithms used by an ad hoc node to choose its gateway and its associated prefix. We finally conclude the paper.

2.   Related Work

The particular nature of ad hoc networks makes it impossible to use the IPv6 mechanisms used in wired networks in order to propagate prefix information, mainly because they have been designed to work on a shared broadcast link. To overcome this situation, Weniger *et al.* [Weniger and Zitterbart, 2002]

[Weniger, 2005] have proposed to modify the stateless address autoconfiguration (SAA [Thomson and Narten, 1998]) mechanism used in IPv6 networks, and the duplicate address detection (DAD) procedure of the SAA protocol. The interesting point of these proposals is that they try to re-use the protocols designed for classical IPv6 networks. However, the SAA and DAD protocols are inherently mal-adapted to ad hoc multi-hop networks, mainly because their efficiency and simplicity are based on the fact that they have been designed for networks that have a unique layer-3 link. For ad hoc networks, we believe that the use of such techniques should be avoided.

Wakikawa *et al.* [Wakikawa et al., 2002] have proposed a reactive method that can be used with any kind of routing protocols. With their proposal, an ad hoc node broadcasts a request to obtain a prefix with global scope. This request propagates within the entire ad hoc network and eventually reaches a gateway. The gateway replies to the originator of the request with a message which contains the prefix. The node receiving this information creates a global address and adds a particular entry in its routing table. Xi *et al.* [Xi and Bettstetter, 2002] extended this model with proactive features (i.e. the periodical transmission of prefix information), and with the possibility for an intermediate node to respond to request messages. These two papers also consider the use of Mobile IPv6 [Johnson et al., 2004] to maintain connections at the transport layer. However, these existing proposals do not consider the unpredictable topological changes that occur in an ad hoc network, in the sense that they do not specify how the prefix information is updated (or changed) over time, a crucial consideration with ad hoc networks.

Our work differs from previous work as follows. First, we define *prefix continuity* as the core element of our proposal. For various reasons detailed later, this feature is highly relevant for the management and daily operation of ad hoc networks. Prefix continuity also prevents node isolation (i.e. after a network partition a node cannot reach its gateway) and avoids the use of an IPv6 routing header (as in other proposals). Second and in contrast with some previous work, our method supports multiple gateways which may announce different global prefixes. And third, this work aims to propose a method that is independent of the underlying routing protocol, as our proposed method can be used with both proactive and reactive routing protocols.

3. Protocol Operation and Prefix Continuity

This section introduces the concept of prefix continuity, and the hop-by-hop propagation technique used to disseminate the control messages that contain gateway and prefix information. We also give some implementation details related to the operation of IPv6.

3.1   Prefix continuity

The core feature of our proposal is what we have already defined as *prefix continuity*. Our proposal ensures that any node A that selected a given prefix P has at least one neighbor with prefix P on its path to the selected gateway G. Recursively, this feature thus ensures that there exists between A and G, a path of nodes such that all the nodes on this path use the same prefix P and gateway G as the node A. Prefix continuity is a inherent consequence of the propagation technique presented in Section 3.2. This technique leads to the creation of a forest of logical spanning trees which are dynamically maintained and updated when unpredictable topological changes occur. Each logical tree is rooted at a gateway, and it is formed by nodes which all use the global network prefix advertised by the gateway. Note that we use the term *logical* tree since the real physical topology of a sub-network is not necessarily a tree: the tree is only used to propagate the prefix information. Note that routing among two nodes of the ad hoc network is still done via a shortest path derived by the routing protocol used in the MANET. Figure 1 shows an ad hoc network with (a) and without (b) prefix continuity. There are 3 gateways, and each color corresponds to a given network prefix. Arrows indicate the orientation of the trees.

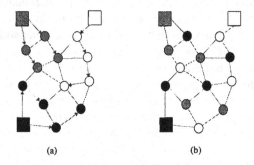

(a)   (b)

Figure 1.   Ad hoc network with (a) and without (b) prefix continuity

A first advantage of prefix continuity is that a node does not need to add an IPv6 routing header in the packets it sends to correspondants located outside the ad hoc network (as in [Wakikawa et al., 2002]). This is because the default route of a node points to its parent in the tree, which necessarily uses the same gateway (recursively, the packet will reach the gateway via nodes that share the same network prefix). Without prefix continuity, a node must indeed specify via which gateway its packets must go through in order to avoid ingress filtering. Our proposal is also natively robust to network partitionning and it does not require any special mechanism in order to handle such situations. If a network partition occurs and if a node becomes isolated from its current gateway, it will quickly receive control messages from a new gateway and will eventually acquire a new global address.

Another advantage of prefix continuity is that it establishes a logical organization within an ad hoc network, i.e. the network becomes divided in sub-networks, each being formed by a contiguous gathering of nodes using the same prefix. This is particularily attractive for network providers that want to deploy specific applications that are meaningless in the absence of sub-networks (e.g. supervision/management systems, billing/accounting, on-demand/pay-per-view multicast streaming).

3.2 Forwarding/propagation of prefix information

Our proposal relies on a periodical hop-by-hop exchange of information between each node and its directly connected neighbors. Each gateway is responsible for sending periodical information in order to notify nodes in the ad hoc network about its existence and the prefix it uses. Such messages are denoted GW_INFO (GateWay INFOrmation), and each message contains:

- the distance (in hops) at which the sender is from the gateway

- the global address of the gateway and the length (in bits) of the prefix part of this address

- a sequence number used to disregard outdated information

- an optional DNS server address

This information subsequently propagates in a hop-by-hop manner. Depending on the network topology and on the number of gateways, each node may receive multiple GW_INFO messages. In short, each intermediate node selects the most appropriate information from one of its neighbors which becomes what we define as its *upstream neighbor*. The algorithms used to select the upstream neighbor are detailed in sections 4. The physical interface from which GW_INFO messages sent by the upstream neighbor are received is called the *upstream interface*.

A GW_INFO message must always be sent with a hop limit of 1. Therefore the initial GW_INFO message sent by a gateway is only received by its directly connected neighbors. Also the initial *distance to the gateway* information sent by a gateway must be zero. When a node has selected its upstream neighbor, it immediately forwards an updated version of the GW_INFO message sent by its upstream neighbor (the information sent by other neighbors than the upstream neighbor is not propagated). The updated message must also be sent with a hop limit of 1. The *distance to the gateway* must be increased by one. All other fields of the forwarded message remain unchanged. The prefix information contained in an initial GW_INFO message (sent by a gateway) is therefore propagated in a hop-by-hop manner among a subset of nodes of the ad hoc network which have decided to use this prefix and gateway. This method of propagation naturally leads to prefix continuity, and to the creation of a logical tree for each prefix. In a topology where multiple gateways and prefixes are present, our proposal leads to the creation of a forest of logical trees.

The propagation technique is illustrated by Fig. 2. There are two gateways G1 and G2 with the respective prefixes P1 and P2. Arrows emanating from a node indicate a GW_INFO message, the number represents the value of the *distance to the gateway* information and the color indicates the carried prefix. For clarity, many GW_INFO messages are not represented. It can be seen on the figure that each gateway announces a distance equal to zero. Nodes A and C therefore select the gateway G1 as their upstream neighbor. They in turn send their GW_INFO messages with a distance field set to one. Note that, for example, node A also receives the GW_INFO messages sent by node C but does not use them as the distance field is greater than the one it uses (i.e. from G1). Node D is the only node at equal distance of both gateways, it therefore has to arbitrarily select one of the two prefixes. In this example, because it selected C as its upstream neighbor, node D will not forward the GW_INFO messages sent by nodes E and F.

3.3   Integration with routing protocol

In this paper we present our proposal as a stand-alone mechanism which can be used in parallel with any ad hoc routing protocol. It is however important to node that our proposal can be integrated in the operation of the routing protocol

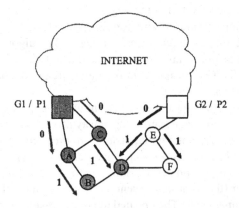

Figure 2.   Hop-by-Hop propagation of GW_INFO messages

used in the ad hoc network. For example, if our proposal is integrated as part of the operation of a proactive routing protocol, it can benefit from the mechanisms used by such a routing protocol to maintain a view of its neighborhood (i.e. exchange of HELLO messages). Moreover, GW_INFO messages can be combined with messages sent by the routing protocol (e.g. in messages used to disseminate topological information). With reactive routing protocols, our proposal can simply be added to the normal operation of the routing protocol. We have for example integrated our proposal in an IPv6 version of the OLSR routing protocol. This version is currently available for the Linux operating system (see http://www-r2.u-strasbg.fr/~frey/safari/autoconf.html).

3.4 Implementation issues and DAD procedure

In this section we give some details about implementation issues since we have implemented our address autoconfiguration mechanism on the FreeBSD and Linux operating systems. First, GW_INFO messages are sent with a link-local source address and the destination address is ff02::1 (all nodes). The fields *prefix length* and *gateway address* are used to derive the gateway's prefix. The prefered prefix length is 64 bits. Finally, *sequence numbers* are used to avoid the propagation of outdated messages and to detect the loss of messages.

Once it has selected its upstream neighbor, a node generates its IPv6 global address with the prefix and prefix length contained in the GW_INFO message sent by its upstream neighbor. With proactive routing protocols, the node also creates a default routing table entry with its upstream neighbor as next hop. Note that the default route entry does not prevent direct routing between ad hoc nodes, as there should be a host entry (i.e. /128) in the routing table for each ad hoc node, even for nodes that use a different prefix. With reactive routing protocols, the GW_INFO information is not used to add a default route towards the gateway. We indeed believe that the reactive nature of such protocols avoids the need of keeping a default route which, by nature, prevents such a protocol from being reactive (the gateway of a node can reply to route requests for destinations outside the ad hoc network).

As stated earlier, the prefered prefix length should be 64 bits. If the prefix length advertised by a gateway is shorter than 64 bits, it must be padded with zeros until it reaches a length of 64 bits. To create an IPv6 global address with SAA, a node normally appends the EUI-64 (Ethernet Unique Identifier) of the upstream interface to the prefix sent by the upstream neighbor. This normally relies on the verification, via a duplicate address detection (DAD) procedure, of the uniqueness of the EUI-64. As mentioned earlier, traditional DAD cannot be used in ad hoc networks, and therefore either a specific DAD mechanism must be used, or the probability of an address collision should be null. In fact, the probability of an IPv6 address collision is already extremely low when EUI-64 are used since they are based on EUI-48 (e.g. Ethernet MAC addresses) which are supposed to be unique. To furthermore reduce the probability of an address collision when generating an EUI-64 from an EUI-48, we propose to replace the added **ff:fe** 16-bit pattern by a randomly generated 16-bit number. It means that in the very rare case where two nodes have a common EUI-48, they will generate a 64-bit host identifier with a collision probability of 1/64536 (1.5e-5). As a result, we think that it is unnecessary to add the overhead and the complexity occured by a DAD procedure.

4.   Upstream neighbor selection

We propose three different algorithms in order to select a prefix/gateway pair. The first algorithm ensures that a node always selects the closest gateway, whatever prefix it uses. We call this algorithm the *distance* algorithm. In contrast, the second and third algorithms ensure that a node keeps its current prefix as long as it has neighbors with the same prefix, whatever distance it is from its current gateway. If a node becomes isolated (in the prefix sense), it is allowed to acquire a new prefix. We therefere call these two algorithms the *stability* algorithms. The difference between the two *stability* algorithms is in the way they select a new prefix (and upstream neighbor).

We also consider that the global address acquired by an ad hoc node should be used as the Mobile IPv6 [Johnson et al., 2004] care-of address of the node. MIPv6 is used with mobile nodes to maintain connections at the transport layer. Each change of global address in the ad hoc network will therefore trigger the sending of at least one binding update message.

To maintain prefix continuity, each node must ensure that it does not become isolated from other nodes which share the same prefix. Each node thus permanently checks its neighborhood in order to detect the loss of neighbors which share the same prefix. To do so, each node maintains a list of its current neighbors, whatever prefix they use. Neighbors are discovered via the reception of the GW_INFO messages they send. When a node receives a GW_INFO message from a node that is not yet in its neighbors list, it adds this node to its neighbors list, records the sequence number of the GW_INFO message and starts a timer associated to the entry. Upon expiration of the timer associated to it, an entry is removed from the neighbors list. When a node receives a GW_INFO message from a node that is already in its neighbors list, it restarts the timer associated to the entry if the sequence number is greater than the one recorded for this neighbor. Note that we assume that all wireless links are bi-directional.

4.1   The distance algorithm

This algorithm is very simple: a node simply chooses as its upstream neighbor the node that advertises the shortest distance to a gateway. The main advantage of this algorithm is therefore that the path between a node and its gateway is a topological shortest path. Moreover, in particular circumstances, this algorithm can also lead to the creation of well-balanced sub-networks, in the sense that all sub-networks will have an equal size (statistically speaking). This is for example the case if the area formed by the gateways is symmetrical, and if the ad hoc nodes are uniformly distributed in this geographical area. This is because each node selects the closest gateway. If we assume that the radio characteristics are similar for each ad hoc node, the distance in hops between two nodes in the network is indeed strongly linked to the geographical distance that separates them. The main drawback of this algorithm is that a node may frequently change its global address as topological changes occur. In particular, the distance algorithm does not prevent a node from joining a new sub-network even if the node still has neighbors which are in its previous sub-network.

4.2   The stability algorithms

We have proposed two alternative algorithms whose objective is to maximize the time during which a node keeps its current global address. In other words, with these algorithms a node remains a member of its current sub-network as long as possible, i.e. until it cannot find an upstream neighbor that uses the same network prefix. In practise, a node ignores GW_INFO messages sent by neighbors of a different sub-network as long as it has neighbors from its own sub-network, i.e. as long as there exists a path of nodes using its current prefix between itself and the gateway. In contrast to the previous algorithm, the distance to the gateway is no longer the main criteria when selecting an upstream neighbor. However, a node must select its upstream neighbor in order to find the shortest possible path to its current gateway. The path between a node and its gateway is therefore a shortest path within the sub-network, but it might not be a topological shortest path. For example in Fig. 1(a), the leaf node of the white sub-network/tree has a 4-hops path to its gateway. This path is the shortest path with respect to the sub-network, but it is not a topological shortest path (i.e. 3 hops via the light-grey node above it). For example, if the distance algorithm was used, the leaf node of the white sub-network would decide to join either the light-grey or the dark-grey sub-network as in both cases there is a closer gateway (i.e. 3 hops).

The two stability algorithms behave differently when a node becomes isolated from its current subnetwork. With the first variant named *stability-nowait*, the node selects as its new upstream neighbor the first node from which it receives a GW_INFO message. The node discards it previous global address and creates the new global address with the new prefix. With the second variant called *stability-slow-start*, the node will first gather neighboring information during a short amount of time (e.g. 3 seconds, hence its name *slow-start*). The idea is to select the upstream neighbor among a large set of neighbors in order to increase the probability to remain a member of the new subnetwork as long as possible. Note that the node also selects its new upstream neighbor such that it finds the shortest possible path to a gateway. The main advantage of the two stability algorithms is that they minimize the number of prefix changes. This greatly reduces the overhead induced by the sending of MIPv6 binding update messages when a node changes its global address. The main drawback of these algorithms is however that the path between a node and its gateway is not necessarily a shortest-path (with respect to the entire topology). However, within a sub-network, this path will always be a shortest-path.

5.   Conclusions

In this paper, we have presented an address autoconfiguration scheme for IPv6 ad hoc networks. The core of our proposal is the concept of *prefix continuity*, which ensures that there always exists a path between a given node and its gateway such that all nodes on this path share the same network prefix. Moreover when there exist multiple gateways, our protocol builds and maintains a forest of logical spanning trees, where each tree if formed by nodes that share a common global network prefix. This concept results in an organized ad hoc network, in the sense that sub-networks (with respect to prefixes) are automatically created and dynamically maintained when multiple gateways are available.

References

Draves, R., Padhye, J., and Zill, B. (2004). Routing in Multi-radio, Multi-hop Wireless Mesh Networks. In *Proceedings of ACM Mobicom 2004*. Philadelphia, PA, USA.

Johnson, D., Perkins, C., and Arkko, J. (2004). RFC-3775 - Mobility Support in IPv6.

Thomson, S. and Narten, T. (1998). RFC-2462 - IPv6 Stateless Address Autoconfiguration.

V. Bahl (organizer) (2004). Wireless Community Mesh Networks - Hype or the Next Big Frontier? In *Panel Discussion at ACM Mobicom 2004*. Philadelphia, PA, USA.

Wakikawa, R., Malinen, J., Perkins, C., Nilsson, A., and Tuominen, A. (2002). Internet Connectivity for Mobile Ad hoc Networks. *Wirel. Comm. and Mobile Computing*, 2(5):465–482.

Weniger, K. (2005). PACMAN: Passive Autoconfiguration for Mobile Ad hoc Networks. *IEEE JSAC*, 23(3):507–519.

Weniger, K. and Zitterbart, M. (2002). IPv6 Autoconfiguration in Large Scale Mobile Ad-Hoc Networks. In *Proceedings of European Wireless Conference 2002*. Florence, Italy.

Xi, J. and Bettstetter, C. (2002). Internet Connectivity for Mobile Ad hoc Networks. In *Proceedings of 3GWireless*. San Francisco, CA, USA.

ADAPTIVE REAL-TIME VBR VIDEO TRAFFIC PREDICTOR FOR IEEE 802.15.3 WIRELESS AD HOC NETWORKS

Yi-Hsien Tseng,[1] Eric Hsiao-Kuang Wu,[2] and Gen-Huey Chen[1]

[1]*Department of Computer Science and Information Engineering, National Taiwan University, Taipei, TAIWAN*
[2]*Department of Computer Science and Information Engineering, National Central University, Chung-Li, TAIWAN*

Abstract   This paper proposes a new real-time video traffic predictor to meet increasing consumer demand for a high speed high performance wireless broadband network. It analyzes the behaviors and the problems of previous adaptive LMS-type predictors using fixed step size in detail and then proposes an adaptive predictor using variable step size for predicting bandwidth requirement of real-time VBR videos. The proposed adaptive predictor has better ability for handling scene changes and needs not change its parameters for different VBR videos. The simulation shows that the performance of the proposed adaptive predictor is better or near the optimal performance of previous adaptive LMS-type predictors using fixed step size.

Keywords: Dynamic bandwidth allocation, traffic prediction, adaptive LMS algorithm

1.   Introduction

The IEEE 802.15.3[1] standard is designed to connect about 200 wireless devices and the existing standard 2.4 GHz PHY is up to maximum data rate of 55M bits/sec. Moreover, the IEEE 802.15 Task Group 3a (IEEE 802.15.3a) is underway to standardize an UWB [6] PHY with a range of data rates between 110 and 480M bits/sec. The new UWB PHY of the IEEE 802.15.3 is ideal for allowing multiple wireless devices to exchange multimedia traffics such as video, audio and digital images.

In addition to high data rates, the IEEE 802.15.3 standard also includes all functionalities needed for reliable QoS. The IEEE 802.15.3 MAC protocol uses TDMA to allocate channel time among devices in order to prevent conflicts and only provides new channel time allocations for a connection if enough bandwidth is available. The elementary topological unit for the IEEE 802.15.3 MAC layer is a piconet, which is a wireless ad hoc data communications system in essence. There are a number of independent data devices (DEVs) contained in a piconet that are allowed to exchange frames directly with each other.

The master/slave relationship was adopted for these DEVs; a particular DEV, named piconet coordinator (PNC), acts as the master and the others are slaves. The PNC is also responsible for admission control and channel time allocation. Timing for a piconet is realized by superframes whose three parts are Beacon, CAP and CTAP. When a DEV intends to transmit data, it has to send a request message to the PNC first. The PNC then decides whether the request can be accepted or not according to the available channel time in the superframe. If accepted, the PNC will allocate enough channel time for the DEV and announce this allocation in the next beacon.

Because the bandwidth in the IEEE 802.15.3 WPANs can be allocated on demand, dynamic bandwidth allocation during the lifetime of a connection should be considered, especially for variable bit rate (VBR) video connection. Since the peak-to-mean ratio of a VBR video is usually high, constant bit rate (CBR) channel allocation which satisfies peak rate requirement often leads to low channel utilization. In contrast, if the channel allocation is not served at a rate close to peak rate, large delays, large queues and packet losses will occur. Therefore, it is important that DEVs should have ability to predict the band-width requirement of future superframes in order to support real-time VBR videos.

A dynamic allocation scheme with a novel VBR video traffic predictor is necessary in order to utilize channel efficiently and guarantee the QoS require-ment of real-time VBR videos at the same time. By allocating bandwidth equal to the predicted value, only the errors of prediction need to be buffered. Thus, higher channel utilization, small buffers and small delays can be achieved if the prediction is accurate enough.

Several papers which deal with multimedia traffic prediction had been pro-posed. We simply classify these works into two categories. The first one is model-type prediction [10], [16], [17] which deals with the development of stochastic source models and adopts these models to predict. These models has the ability to capture both the short-range dependent (SRD) and long-range dependent (LRD) [15]. Since VBR videos have been shown that it has a self-similar characteristic [9], these stochastic source models can be used for accu-rate prediction if the parameters of the models were estimated correctly.

Another class of multimedia traffic prediction is adaptive least mean square (LMS) type prediction [2], [5], [12], [14].The adaptive LMS algorithm is well known for its simplicity. Moreover, the adaptive LMS-type prediction neither does require prior knowledge of the video statistics nor does assume stationary. Therefore, they are fit for on-line VBR video prediction for the IEEE 802.15.3 devices.

However, adaptive LMS-type predictions using fixed step size [13] perform bad performance while scene changes occur. This paper analyzed the effects of scene change on the prediction errors in the adaptive LMS-type prediction which adopts fixed step size. Moreover, this paper proposes an adaptive VBR video predictor based on a variable step-size LMS algorithm [11] in order to overcome the problem of scene change.

The proposed predictor performs much better performance while scene change occurs. Furthermore, instead of the fixed step-size adaptive LMS-type predictor which is hard to determine the optimal parameters for different VBR video traffics in advance, the proposed adaptive predictor adjusts its step size automatically according to the statistics of different VBR video traffics. And the computational complexity of the proposed predictor is also low. By above reasons, the proposed predictor not only satisfies the low-cost requirement of the IEEE 802.15.3 devices but also produces good performance for predicting VBR videos.

The rest of this paper is organized as follows. Related work is introduced in next section. The proposed adaptive VBR video predictor is addressed in Section 3. Analysis and simulation results are shown in Section 4. Finally, this paper concludes with some remarks in Section 5.

2. Related Work

There were several papers which deal with traffic prediction proposed in recent years. We simply classify these works into two categories: statistical model-type prediction and adaptive LMS-type prediction. For the first category, the fractional autoregressive integrated moving average (F-ARIMA) [7] model is the most popular one. The F-ARIMA is a self-similar [15] model which has the ability to capture both the SRD and LRD characteristics. It also has been shown that VBR video traffic has a self-similar characteristic [9]. Therefore, the F-ARIMA model is useful for a VBR video traffic predictor.

All parameters of F-ARIMA model should be estimated from the historical traffic data before starting to predict. This causes the bottleneck of computation, especially for the low-cost IEEE 802.15.3 devices. Furthermore, the performance of model-type prediction depends on the parameters of the model can be estimated accurately. It requires large traffic data to estimate the parameters precisely. Therefore, the model based prediction does not suit for bandwidth prediction for real-time VBR videos.

The second category is the adaptive LMS-type prediction. The adaptive LMS algorithm has been wide used in many domains due to its simplicity and relatively good performance. Moreover, the adaptive LMS-type prediction does not require any prior knowledge of the video statistics and does not assume video contents to be stationary. Thus, it well suits for bandwidth prediction for on-line real time VBR videos which can be non-stationary. A pth order k-step linear predictor has the form as:

$$\widehat{x}(n+k) = \sum_{i=0}^{p-1} w_n(l)x(n-l) = W_n^T X(n) \tag{1}$$

The k-step linear predictor estimates $x(n+k)$ using a linear combination of the current and previous values of $X(n)$. In an adaptive LMS algorithm, W_n is the time varying coefficient vector obtained by minimizing the mean square error. The initial vector W_0 can be assigned any value and W_n is updated using the recursive equation as:

$$W_{n+1} = W_n + \mu e(n)X(n) \tag{2}$$

Since it is difficult to select the proper value of μ to guarantee convergence, the normalized LMS (NLMS) is often used in practice. The NLMS is a modification of LMS algorithm where the update equation is changed as:

$$W_{n+1} = W_n + \frac{\mu e(n)X(n)}{\|X(n)\|^2} \tag{3}$$

The NLMS will converge in the mean [13] if $0 < \mu < 2$. Large μ causes a faster convergence and quicker response to statistic change. However, after convergence, misadjustment is larger. In contrast, the use of a small μ results in a slower convergence with smaller misadjustment. It is a tradeoff.

[2] proposed a dynamic bandwidth allocation using the NLMS predictor with the fixed value of μ to support real-time VBR video under RCBR network service model. [5] adopted the fixed step-size NLMS predictor for traffic management of ATM networks. [12] proposed method based on a scene change identification to improve the forecasting performance. They made $X(n)$ to forget historical data while scene changes occur and still used fixed step size.

[14] proposed a scene change indicator for real-time VBR MPEG videos and dynamically controlled the step size μ between two values: $\mu_{default}$ and STEP_JUMP $\times \mu_{default}$. STEP_JUMP is a constant. A scene change is recognized by indicator as:

$$\frac{|e(n)|}{\sum_{i=n-k}^{n} x(i)l(k+1)} > Threshold \tag{4}$$

The step size μ is increased to STEP_JUMP times $\mu_{default}$ when a scene change is detected. In contrast, the step size is returned to the initial default value if the normalized prediction error is less than or equal to the threshold value.

Unlike [14] whose step size of μ is determined by indicator using experienced values of STEP_JUMP, Threshold and the default value $\mu_{default}$, this paper adopts a variable step size LMS algorithm [11] to control the step size for handling scene changes and needs not to determine the value of μ in advance. The performance of the proposed predictor is better than the other LMS-type predictors which use fixed step size.

3. Proposed NLMS Adaptive Predictor

This paper proposes an adaptive predictor based on the variable step size LMS (VSSLMS) algorithm proposed in [11]. This section introduces to the VSSLMS algorithm first and then describes our modification to the VSSLMS algorithm in order to obtain better performance for predicting different VBR videos.

The VSSLMS algorithm adjusts the step size by the square of the prediction error. The motivation of the VSSLMS algorithm is that a large prediction error will cause the step size to increase to provide faster tracking, whereas a small prediction error will result in a decrease in the step size to obtain smaller misadjustment.

The VSSLMS algorithm is the same as the LMS algorithm except the step size of the VSSLMS is updated dynamically. The step-size update equation is expressed as:

$$\mu_{n+1} = \alpha\mu_n + \gamma e^2(n) \qquad (5)$$

where $0 < \alpha < 1$, $\gamma > 0$, and μ_{n+1} is set to μ_{max} or μ_{min} when it falls above or below these upper bound and lower bound, respectively. The constant μ_{max} should be chosen to ensure that the MSE of the VSSLMS algorithm remains bounded and is normally selected near the point of instability of fixed step-size LMS algorithm to provide the maximum possible convergence. The constant μ_{min} is chosen as a compromise between the desired level of steady-state misadjustment and the required tracking capability. Usually, the value of μ_{min} is near the one of μ that would be chosen for the fixed step-size algorithm. The parameter α is selected from the range (0, 1) in order to provide exponential forgetting. The parameter γ controls the convergence time and the level of misadjustment. The value of γ is usually small. The additional computational overhead of the VSSLMS algorithm is one update for μ value at each iteration, so that the computational complexity is also low.

The prediction error is large while a scene change occurs and the value of μ should be larger during scene changes. Therefore, the VSSLMS algorithm can meet our requirements for predicting VBR videos. For practical uses, we adopt the NLMS algorithm instead of the LMS algorithm, so our modified algorithm of the VSSLMS one is called the VSSNLMS algorithm. The weighted vector W_{n+1} update equation of VSSNLMS algorithm is the same as one of the NLMS listed in (3). For an one-step predictor, the value of $x(n + 1)$ is not available to calculate $e(n)$ at time n. Thus, $e(n-1)$ is instead of $e(n)$ and the step-size update equation of the VSSNLMS algorithm should be changed as:

$$\mu_{n+1} = \alpha\mu_n + \gamma e^2(n-1) \tag{6}$$

By the properties of the NLMS algorithm, the VSSNLMS algorithm will converge in the mean if $0 < \mu_{min} < \mu_{max} < 2$. However, in theory of [3], the value čg= 1 for the NLMS algorithm provides the fastest convergence, whereas the step size of the NLMS algorithm needs to be considered smaller in practice [4]. By experiments, we set the value $\mu_{max} = 0.5$ in the beginning of prediction. The value of μ_{min} is chosen as 0.1 for smaller misadjustment while there is no scene change occurs.

The value of γ is set to 1×10^{-8} to detect scene changes properly. Too large value of γ causes the value of μ to be increased even through there is no scene change. On the contrary, too small value of γ can not make predictor response to scene changes. The optimal value of is varied by video videos with different autocorrelations. Since the autocorrelation of a real-time VBR video can not be known in prior, it is difficult to determine the optimal value of α before predicting. However, the effect on performance by different values of α is small. By our experiments, the optimal values of α for simulated traces fall in the range from 0.93 to 0.99. The VSSNLMS predictor chooses $\alpha = 0.96$ for simulations.

4.   Analysis and Simulation Results

This section analyzes the order selecting strategies of the VSSNLMS predictor as well as shows the ability of the VSSNLMS predictor for handling scene changes first. And then we compare the performance between the fixed step-size NLMS predictor and the VSSNLMS predictor by simulations using the MATLAB. The optimal values of step size and the optimal orders using by the fixed step-size NLMS predictor for different VBR videos are listed in Table 1. These values were obtained by exhausting search and will be used for comparison.

Unlike the order of the NLMS algorithm varied with different autocorrelations of VBR Videos, the VSSNLMS algorithm provided better performance while the order is increased. Figure 1 shows that both the MSE of the "Soccer" and the one of the "Parking Cam" are decreased while the order is increased. Figure 1(a) shows the performance of predicting the "Soccer" is not obviously promoted when the order is increased in excess of 23, whereas Figure 1(b) shows the performance of predicting the "Parking Cam" is not obviously promoted when the order is increased in excess of 6.

Therefore, there is no confusion for the VSSNLMS to determine the order (i.e. the larger order is, the better performance is). However, the computational

Table 1. Optimal value of μ and order for NLMS algorithm

Trace	Subsequence	μ	Order	Trace	Subsequence	μ	Order
Jurassic	I	0.01	2	Soccer	I	0.07	2
Park I	P	0.02	3		P	0.03	2
	B	0.03	3		B	0.04	2
Silence of	I	0.22	15	The	I	0.07	2
The	P	0.06	3	Firm	P	0.05	12
Lambs	B	0.16	15		B	0.04	2
Parking	I	0.47	11	Lecture	I	0.39	10
Cam	P	0.21	15	Room	P	0.27	15
	B	0.19	8	Cam	B	0.28	15

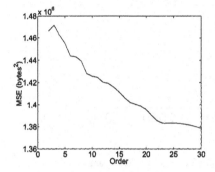

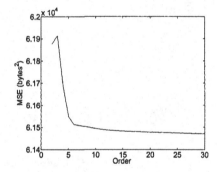

Figure 1(a). Performance of the VSSNLMS predictor with increased order (Soccer)

Figure 1(b). Performance of the VSSNLMS predictor with increased order (Parking Cam)

complexity of the VSSNLMS algorithm depends on the order. Too large order causes higher computational complexity of the VSSNLMS algorithm. By experiment, the order = 12 is good enough for most cases and we adopt order = 12 for comparison.

We compare the ability of handling scene changes between the VSSNLMS algorithm and the NLMS algorithm (with $\mu = 0.47$ and $\mu = 0.01$) for the case of predicting the "Parking Cam". The order used by the NLMS algorithm is 11 and the results is depicted in Figure 2. It shows that the VSSNLMS algorithm has better ability for handling scene changes. And the VSSNLMS algorithm can achieve smaller misadjustment if there is no scene change. A scene change occurred from the frame 2030. The prediction errors of the VSSNLMS algorithm can converge to steady state with the fastest speed. Also, the prediction errors of the VSSNLMS algorithm are smaller than the other two instances in steady state.

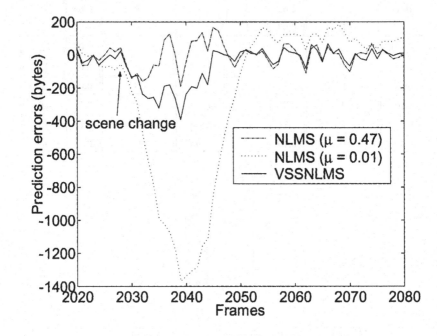

Figure 2.   Comparison of the ability for handling scene change

Finally, the comparisons of performance for predicting I-frames, P-frames and B-frames of all MPEG-4 video traces are shown in Table 2. Smaller MSE (bytes^2) indicates better performance and the ratio is defined as that the MSE of the VSSNLMS algorithm divided by the one of the NLMS algorithm. The parameters used by the VSSNLMS algorithm have been discussed in Section 3. The parameters used by the NLMS algorithm are listed in Table 1. The performance of the VSSNLMS predictor is compared with the optimal performance of the NLMS predictor.

The results in Table 2 show that the performances of the VSSNLMS predictor are better or close to the optimal performances of the NLMS predictor. It means that the VSSNLMS algorithm with fixed values of parameters can obtain good performance for most VBR videos with difference statistics and does not need any prior knowledge of VBR videos. Therefore, the VSSNLMS predictor is suitable for the prediction of real-time VBR videos.

Table 2. Performance comparison for NLMS AND VSSNLMS

Trace	Subsequence	NLMS (MSE)	VSSNLMS (MSE)	Ratio
Jurassic	I	6.7995×10^5	7.4378×10^5	1.094
Park I	P	9.3774×10^5	9.5932×10^5	1.023
	B	3.1501×10^5	3.3754×10^5	1.072
Soccer	I	1.5527×10^6	1.4495×10^6	0.934
	P	1.3397×10^6	1.3179×10^6	0.984
	B	3.8252×10^5	3.7135×10^5	0.971
Silence	I	1.2415×10^6	1.0353×10^6	0.834
of The	P	9.9232×10^5	8.9586×10^5	0.903
Lambs	B	4.1607×10^5	3.8041×10^5	0.914
The	I	3.1928×10^5	2.9656×10^5	0.929
Firm	P	4.6159×10^5	4.6378×10^5	1.005
	B	4.5939×10^4	4.3917×10^4	0.956
Parking	I	6.1875×10^4	6.1545×10^4	0.995
Cam	P	8.4472×10^4	1.0586×10^4	1.253
	B	7.035×10^4	7.9874×10^6	1.135
Lecture	I	2.5206×10^4	2.3031×10^4	0.914
Room	P	2.4951×10^4	2.178×10^4	0.873
Cam	B	1.5203×10^4	1.4246×10^4	0.907

5. Conclusion

This paper proposed the VSSNLMS predictor which can overcome the problems caused by the fixed step-size LMS-type predictor. The VSSNLMS is based on a variable step-size LMS algorithm which controls step size dynamically by the square of the prediction error. The simulations showed that, without any prior determination of the parameters of the VSSNLMS predictor, the performances of the VSSNLMS predictor are almost better or close to the optimal performances of the fixed step-size LMS-type predictor for the predictions of different VBR videos. Moreover, since the computational complexity of the VSSNLMS predictor is low and the parameters of the VSSNLMS predictor need not be changed for different VBR videos, the VSSNLMS predictor can be implemented in the low-cost IEEE 802.15.3 devices to require predictive bandwidth for different real-time VBR videos.

Acknowledgments

This work was supported by the MediaTek Inc. under the project "Wireless Communication Systems".

References

[1] IEEE standard 802.15.3: Wireless Medium Access Control (MAC) and Physical Layer (PHY) Specifications for High Rate Wireless Personal Area Networks (WPANs), Inst. Elec. Electron. Eng., New York, USA, 2003.

[2] A. M. Adas, "Using adaptive linear prediction to support real-time VBR video under RCBR network service model," *IEEE/ACM Transactions on Networking*, vol. 6, pp. 635-644, 1998.

[3] B.Widrow and S. D. Stearns, *Adaptive Signal Processing*. Englewood Cliffs, NJ: Prentice-Hall, 1985.

[4] D. P. Mandic, "A generalized normalized gradient descent algorithm," *IEEE Signal Processing Letters*, vol. 11, pp. 115-118, 2004.

[5] G. Chiruvolu, R. Sankar and N. Ranganathan, "Adaptive VBR video traffic management for higher utilization of ATM networks," it ACM SIGCOMM Computer Communication Review, vol. 28, pp. 27-40, 1998.

[6] J. Foerster, E. Green, S. Somayazulu and D. Leeper, "Ultra-wideband technology for short- or medium-range wireless communications," *Journal of Intel Technology*, 2nd quarter, 2001.

[7] J. Hosking, "Fractional differencing," it Biometrika, vol. 68, pp. 165-176, 1981.

[8] M. Reisslein et al., "Traffic and Quality Characterization of Scalable Encoded Video: A Large-Scale Trace-Based Study," Arizona State University, Dept. of Elect. Eng., Tech. Rep., Dec. 2003. Video traces available from http://trace.eas.asu.edu.

[9] M. W. Garrett and W. Willinger, "Analysis, modeling and generation of self-similar VBR video traffic," *ACM SIGCOMM Computer Communication Review, Proceedings of the conference on Communications architectures, protocols and applications*, vol. 24, pp. 269-280, 1994.

[10] N. Sadek, A. Khotanzad, and T. Chen, "ATM dynamic bandwidth allocation using F-ARIMA prediction model," *Proceedings of The 12th International Conference on Computer Communications and Networks*, pp. 359-363, 2003.

[11] R. H. Kwong and E. W. Johnston, "A variable step size LMS algorithm," *IEEE Transactions on Signal Processing*, vol. 40, pp. 1633-1642, 1992.

[12] S. Feng, and R. Sankar, "Limitation of and improvement to linear prediction and smoothing-based bandwidth allocation for VBR traffic," *Proceedings of IEEE GLOBE-COM '99*, vol. 1A, pp. 209-213, 1999.

[13] S. Haykin, *Adaptive Filter Theory*. Englewood Cliffs, NJ: Prentice-Hall, 1991.

[14] S. J. Yoo, "Efficient traffic prediction scheme for real-time VBR MPEG video transmission over high-speed networks," *IEEE Transactions on Broadcasting*, vol. 48, pp. 10-18, 2002.

[15] W. E. Leland, M. S. Taqqu, W. Willinger and D. V. Wilson, "On the self-similar nature of Ethernet traffic (extended version)," *IEEE/ACM Transactions on Networking*, vol. 2, pp. 1-15, 1994.

[16] Y. Shu, Z. Jin, J. Wang and O. W. W. Yang, "Prediction based admission control using FARIMA models," *Proceedings of IEEE ICC 2000*, vol. 3, pp. 1325-1329, 2000.

[17] Y. Shu, Z. Jin, L. Zhang, L. Wang and O. W. W. Yang, "Traffic prediction using FARIMA models," *Proceedings of IEEE ICC'99*, vol. 2, pp. 891-895, 1999.

AN EFFICIENT PROACTIVE RSA SCHEME FOR LARGE-SCALE AD HOC NETWORKS

Ruishan Zhang and Kefei Chen
Department of Computer Science, Shanghai Jiaotong University
{zhang-rs,kfchen@sjtu.edu.cn}

Abstract   In this paper, we present an efficient proactive threshold RSA signature scheme for large-scale ad hoc networks. Our scheme has two advantages. Firstly, the building blocks of the whole scheme are proven secure. Secondly, the whole scheme is efficient.

Keywords: Ad hoc networks, Threshold signature, Proactive secret sharing, RSA

Introduction

Proactive threshold signature is very important to tolerate a more powerful, mobile adversary [OY][HJKM].Large-scale ad hoc networks have hundreds or even thousands of network nodes. Generally, all network nodes have shares of the secret key (private key), and only a small number of nodes could be corrupted. That is, n is very large and far larger than t. Most current proactive RSA schemes are not designed for this purpose [FGMYa][FGMYb][Rab]. To the best of our knowledge, the only proactive RSA scheme is URSA [LKZL]. Unfortunately, the scheme has proved faulty [JSY].

In this paper, we present an efficient proactive threshold RSA signature scheme for large-scale ad hoc networks. Our scheme includes four protocols: the key distribution protocol, the signature generation protocol, the share refreshing protocol and the share distribution protocol. Our scheme has two advantages. Firstly, the building blocks of the whole scheme are proven secure. Secondly, the whole scheme is efficient. The efficiency of our scheme is approximate to that of the scheme of Wong et al.

In our scheme,an ad hoc network consists of $P_1, P_2, ..., P_n$ nodes . There are two types of nodes: R (refreshing) nodes and S (signing) nodes. There are $2t + 1$ R nodes, which perform the share refreshing protocol. All nodes are S nodes, which perform signing operations.

The remaining paper is organized as follows. The initial key distribution protocol, the share refreshing protocol, the share distribution protocol and the

> Input: secret key $d_i \in Z_{\phi(N)}$,N,g,n,t, RIDList, PIDList
> 1. Choose and hand P_i $d_i \in_R [-nN^2, nN^2]$ for $i \in RIDList$, set $d_{public} = d - \sum d_i$.
> 2. Compute and broadcast the witness $w_i = g^{d_i} mod N$ for $i \in RIDList$.
> 3. Share the value d_i using the sharing Z_n-VSS on input d_i, N,g,n,t, RIDList, PIDList.

Figure 1.   Initial key distribution

signature generation protocol are presented in Section 1,2,3,4 respectively. In Section 5, some discussions are given.

1.   Initial key distribution

The key distribution protocol is used to distribute the initial secret shares to $2t + 1$ R nodes. Before distributing the secret key, we assume that a set-up process has been carried out in which the RSA key generation took place and the RSA key pair has been computed. Denote the public key by (e, N) where $N = pq$ and p, q are primes of the form $p = 2p' + 1$,$q = 2q' + 1$ and p',q' themselves prime. The private key is d where $ed \equiv 1 mod\phi(N)$. In addition, an element g of high order is chosen as $g = g_0^{L^2}$ where g_0 is an element of high order and $L = n!$. As shown in Figure 1, the protocol consists of three steps. First, the private RSA key d is shared by generating additive secret shares $d_i$such that $d = d_{public} + \sum_j d_j$. Then, the witnesses for the additive shares are generated in the second step. Finally, each additive share is backed-up using a protocol Z_n-VSS, which is depicted in Figure 2. Here polynomial secret shares of the additive share are sent to $4t+2$ nodes, of which $2t+1$ nodes are R nodes, the other nodes $2t + 1$ are one-hop or two-hop neighbors. Note that not d_i , but $d_i L^3$ is shared in Z_n-VSS. After the initial key distribution protocol, every party achieves their polynomial shares of $d_i^{poly} = \sum f_j(i,0)$ of $(d - d_{public})L^3$, where d_j is shared by $f_j(x,y)$. Here $(d - d_{public})L^3$ is shared by $F(x,y) = \sum f_j(x,y)$, where $F(x,0) = \sum f_j(x,0)$. We call $F(x)$ Joint-Z_n-VSS. For differentiation, we call d_i^{poly},d_i the polynomial secret share and the additive secret share, respectively. After the initial key distribution protocol, a group of $2t + 1$ nodes within one-hop or two-hop distance hold the polynomial secret shares of the secret key. (RIDList, PIDList are R node ID list and node ID list of $2t + 1$ nodes within one-hop or two-hop distance).

The details of Z_n-VSS are shown in Figure 1. In sharing stage, the dealer computes a two-dimensional sharing of the secret $s \in [-nN^2, nN^2]$ by choosing a random bivariate polynomial $f(x,y)$ of degree at most t with $f(0,0) = SL^3$. It commits to $f(x,y) = \sum_{j,l=0}^t f_{jl}x^j y^l$ by computing a matrix $C =$

Input: secret value $s \in [-nN^2, -nN^2]$ and N,g,n,t , RIDList, PIDList
Sharing steps:
1.The dealer chooses $f_{00}, f_{01}, ..., f_{t-1t}, f_{tt} \in [-nL^3N^3, nL^3N^3]$ and $L|f_{00}, f_{01}, ..., f_{t-1t}, f_{tt}$, then defines $f(x,y) = \sum_{j,l=0}^{t} f_{jl}x^j y^l$ with $f_{00} = 0$.
2. Compute $a_i(y) = f(i,y), b_i(x) = f(x,i)$ for $i \in (RIDList \cup PIDList)$, and $C_{iy} = g^{f_{iy}} mod N$ for $i,y \in [0,t]$.
3. Hand node P_i the polynomial $a_i(y), b_i(x)$ and broadcast C_{iy} for $i,y \in [0,t]$.
Verification steps:
1. Node P_i use $verify-poly(a,i,C)$ $verify-poly(b,i,C)$ to verify if $a_i(y), b_i(x)$ is correct. If the verification fails, P_i requests that the dealer make $a_i(y), b_i(x)$ public.
2. The dealer broadcasts all polynomial requested in the previous step. If the dealer fails to do so, he is disqualified.
3. Node P_i carried out the verification of Step 1 for all public polynomial. If the verification fails, the dealer is disqualified.

Figure 2. Z_n-VSS

$\{C_{jl}\}$ with $C_{jl} = g^{f_{jl}} mod N$ for $j,l \in [0,t]$. Then the dealer sends to every node P_i the share polynomials and broadcast the commitment matrix C. When node P_i receives $a_i(y), b_i(x)$ and C, it use $verify - poly(a,b,i,C)$ to verify if $a_i(y), b_i(x)$ are correct. If the verification is ok, P_i computes and keeps $a_i(0) := f(i,0)$ as its share. The reconstruction stage is straightforward and omitted.

In Z_n-VSS, $verify-poly(a,b,i,C)$, $verify-point(\alpha,\beta,i,m,C)$, $verify-share(\sigma,m,C)$ are employed to verify that the given polynomial, the given point and the given share are correct.

The message complexity and the communication complexity is $O(t^3)$ and $O(t^5 k)$ (k is the security parameter), respectively.

2. Share refreshing

The essence of the share refreshing protocol is that each party splits his additive-share d_i into sub-shares d_{ij} which sum up to d_i , and gives each party P_j such a sub-share d_{ij}. The details are shown in Figure 3, including seven steps. The message complexity and the communication complexity of protocol are $O(t^3)$ and $O(t^5 k)$, respectively.

3. Share distribution

In the share distribution protocol, S nodes obtain their secret shares from their neighbors. First, those $2t + 1$ nodes, which have been refreshed in the

---

Public information: N,g,n,t and w_i (for $i \in RIDList$), RIDList, PIDList

Input of party P_i : secret share d_i such that $g^{d_i} = w_i$

1. Party P_i randomly chooses $d_{ij} \in_R [-N^2, N^2]$ for (for $j \in RIDList$), set $d_{i,public} = d_i - \sum d_{ij}$, computes and broadcast $g_{ij} = g^{d_{ij}} mod N$.

2. P_i sends to P_j the value d_{ij} .

3. Verification of distribution of proper share size and public commitments: P_j verifies that $d_{ij} \in [-N^2, N^2]$ and $g_{ij} = g^{d_{ij}} mod N$ if not then he requests that d_{ij} be made public and set g_{ij} to g raised to this public value.

4. If P_i does not cooperate in Step 3 then d_i is reconstructed.

5. Verification that the sub shares in fact sum up to the previous share of P_i : P_j verifies that $w_i = g^{d_{i,public}} \prod g_{ij} mod N$ if not then d_i is reconstructed.

6. P_i computes his new share d_i^{new} and shares it. This results in a value g^{sL^3} where s is the secret that shared.

7. If P_i fails to share his secret or $(g^{d_i^{new}})^{L^3} \neq g^{sL^3} mod N$ then each party P_j exposes d_{ij} . If P_j fails to expose d_{ij} , then d_j is reconstructed by all parties.

Figure 3.   Share refreshing

share refreshing protocol, update the shares of their neighbors. Then their neighbor nodes update other nodes in a diffused way. A node can obtain his share polynomial from his $2t + 1$ neighbor nodes by interpolating. Each local member P_r sends a message containing point $a_i(r), b_i(r)$ to node P_i . Then P_i interpolates its polynomial $a_i(y), b_i(x)$ and obtains $a_i(0)$ as its share. The message complexity and communication complexity of the whole scheme are $O(t)$ and $O(tk)$, respectively.

4.   Signature generation

A signature share on a message m is generated as follows. Let H and be a hash function. The signature share of P_j consists of $x_i = x^{4Ld_i^{poly}}$. Suppose we have valid shares from a set of I parties, where $I = \{P_1, P_2, ..., P_{t+1}\}$. Before combining shares, we define $\lambda_{i,j}^I = L \dfrac{\prod_{P_{j'} \in I/\{P_j\}} i-j'}{\prod_{P_{j'} \in I/\{P_j\}} j-j'} \in Z$ for any $P_i \in [1, n]/I$ and $j \in I$. Clearly, these values are integers. From the Lagrange interpolation formula, we have $LF(i) = \sum \lambda_{i,j}^I F(j)$. Then we compute $y' = x^{4L^4 d_{public}} x_1^{\lambda_{0,1}^I} ... x_{t+1}^{\lambda_{0,t+1}^I} mod N = x^{4L^4 d} mod N$ such that $y'^e = x^{4L^4} mod N$. Since e is a prime and larger than n, $gcd(4L^4, e) = 1$. Applying the extended Euclidean algorithm on e and $4L^4$ to compute a and b such that $4L^4 a + eb = 1$, then we achieve signature $y = y'^a x^b$ of the message m such that $y^e \equiv x mod N$

. The message complexity and the communication complexity are $O(t), O(tk)$, respectively.

5. Discussions

The initial key distribution protocol is carried out at the onset of the system to distribute shares to $2t + 1$ R nodes. The share refreshing protocol is carried out to update the old shares of $2t + 1$ R nodes at the beginning of the every phase. After the initial key distribution or the share refreshing protocol, the share distribution protocol is performed to distribute secret shares to all other nodes. After nodes obtain their secret shares, they can employ these secret shares to perform signing using the signature generation protocol. As we point out in Section 1, the only proactive RSA scheme for large-scale ad hoc networks is the URSA scheme. However, URSA is insecure. Compared to URSA, our scheme is proven secure. Furthermore, the efficiency (the message complexity and the communication complexity) of our scheme is approximate to that of URSA. Due to space limitation, we only give some brief discussions. Both signature generation are based on polynomial secret shares, so the efficiency is similar. Our share distribution protocol is more efficient than that of URSA. The share refreshing protocol and the initial key distribution protocol of URSA are more efficient than ours.

References

R. Ostrovsky and M. Yung. How to withstand mobile virus attacks. In Proc. 10th ACM Symposium on Principles of Distributed Computing (PODC), pages 51-59, 1991.

A. Herzberg, S. Jarecki, H. Krawczyk, and M. Yung. Proactive secret sharing or how to cope with perpetual leakage. In Advances in Cryptology CRYPTO '95 (D. Coppersmith, ed. Springer.). 963:339-352, 1995

Danny Dolev and H. Raymond Strong. Authenticated algorithms for byzantine agreement. SIAM J. Computing, 12(4), 1983.

Y. Frankel, P. Gemmell, P. D. MacKenzie, and M. Yung. Optimal-Resilience Proactive Public-Key Cryptosystems. In Foundations of Computer Science FOCS'97, pages 384-393, 1997.

Y. Frankel, P. Gemmell, P. D. MacKenzie, and M. Yung. Proactive RSA. In Proc. of Crypto'97, pages 440-454, 1997.

T. Rabin. A simplified approach to threshold and proactive RSA. in Proc. CRYPTO '98, pp. 89-104, Springer, 1998.

Haiyun Luo, Jiejun Kong, Petros Zerfos, Songwu Lu, and Lixia Zhang. URSA: Ubiquitous and Robust Access Control for Mobile Ad Hoc Networks, IEEE/ACM Transactions on Networking (ToN), pp.1049 - 1063,12(6),2004.

Stanislaw Jarecki, Nitesh Saxena, and Jeong Hyun Yi. Cryptanalyzing the Proactive RSA Signature Scheme in the URSA Ad Hoc Network Access Control Protocol. In ACM Workshop on Security of Ad Hoc and Sensor Networks (SASN), October 2004.

HYBRID KEY MANAGEMENT FOR MOBILE AD HOC NETWORKS

David Sanchez Sanchez, Heribert Baldus
Philips Research Laboratories, Weisshausstrasse 2, Aachen, Germany
david.s.sanchez@philips.com, heribert.baldus@philips.com

Abstract: Many public key infrastructure (PKI) approaches have been proposed in the recent years to secure mobile ad hoc networks (MANETs). We present a new hybrid key management infrastructure, which combines the concepts of PKIs for MANET with trusted-third-party based infrastructures. In our hybrid approach, the underlying PKI is merely used to set-up initial trust of nodes in a MANET, and, thus, generate a random trust graph connecting all the nodes of the MANET. Then, MANET nodes cooperate to securely distribute trust information and symmetric keys to other nodes through the shortest trust path. The hybrid key management infrastructure enables the same security services as a normal PKI yet key establishment and node-to-node authentication, as demonstrated by our performance analysis, is substantially improved in terms of computational and communication efficiency. We also discuss the security level of the hybrid approach.

1. INTRODUCTION AND MOTIVATION

MANETs are wireless ad hoc networks increasingly deployed for multiple *civilian* applications. Key management is paramount for enabling security in MANETs.

In this paper, we propose a new hybrid key management infrastructure for MANETs, which perfectly trades off security and efficiency, by setting a middle point between the two general key management infrastructures, i.e. PKI and TTP based. PKIs[1,13] enable confidentiality, integrity, authentication and non-repudiation services in a very flexible way. However, existing proposals[2,6-8,15,18] for MANET do not offer optimal performance. Trusted-third-party (TTP) based infrastructures[1,13] enable confidentiality, integrity and authentication services in a performance efficient manner.

However, applying the TTP concept to MANETs is not straightforward because MANETs lack of security servers.

The remainder of this paper is organized as follows. In Section II, we review relevant related work. In Section III, we describe the hybrid key management infrastructure for MANETs. The performance and the security level of the hybrid approach are assessed and compared with related work in Section IV and Section V, respectively. Finally, Section VI concludes this paper.

2.   PUBLIC KEY INFRASTRUCTURES FOR MANET

A very simple PKI can be enabled with an offline CA[17]. This approach provides nodes with one or more digital certificates in a bootstrapping phase. Afterwards, the MANET nodes can establish keys, authenticate and even sign messages using their private/public key pairs, without the need to contact the CA anymore. However, node revocation is not possible without further control mechanisms.

Many papers address the use of threshold cryptography to distribute PKI certification authority (CA) functionalities to n MANET nodes denoted servers[3-6]. The CA private key is divided into n shares using $(n, t+1)$ threshold cryptography and, then, distributed among the n servers. A number $t+1$ of partial signatures are needed in the generation of new certificates. Then, this approach increases security robustness and availability in the presence of security attacks from malicious nodes and compromised nodes.

Capkun et al.[2] propose a fully self-organized PKI for MANETs that allows users to generate their public/private key pairs and to issue certificates to other users. Revocation of nodes is also enabled. Their proposal is similar to the concepts of key generation and certificate issuing of PGP[14,13]. PGP's web-of-trust model defines different trust levels (complete, marginal and notrust) for public keys, i.e. for what and how much a node is trusted.

A number of proposals[6-8,18] exploit the clustering infrastructures of some MANETs to propose self-organized or distributed PKIs. Cluster heads are generally nodes with higher computational capability, which play the role of a (distributed) CA. They issue, renew and revoke public key certificates to MANET nodes within the same cluster. Additionally, different cluster heads can coordinate to build a MANET-wide PKI.

Martucci et al.[15] propose a PKI-based security architecture for small and medium-sized MANETs. MANET nodes must obtain valid trust information and public keys from the CA before they can join and communicate in the MANET.

3. HYBRID KEY MANAGEMENT

3.1 Assumptions

We assume a wireless MANET composed of self-organized mobile nodes and without online access to any fixed network infrastructure. Sporadically new nodes join or leave the MANET. Typical MANET devices, considered in this paper, are PDAs, mobile phones, and embedded systems in portable devices. These devices have moderate computing power and storage resources as well as limited battery power life. Nodes are capable of computing public key operations to the cost of a significant downside effect in their performance.

We target civilian applications in which devices are carried/wore or placed around human users, i.e. nodes are not generally left unattended, and, then the risk of node compromise by an attacker is very low. Misbehaving users may try to fake information in their behalf or in behalf of their "mates". They may also not cooperate. Furthermore, an attacker may exploit the vulnerabilities of wireless transmissions to anonymously eavesdrop, modify, replay or inject bogus messages.

For the descriptions in the rest of the paper, we assume a MANET with P nodes. We use A, B, W, V, Y, X and Z to refer to some generic nodes of the MANET.

3.2 System Bootstrapping

We assume the existence of a MANET PKI[2,6-8,15,17,18] underlying the hybrid key management infrastructure. The PKI provides each MANET node X with a public key certificate, which digitally binds its identity with the corresponding public key. The certificate may additionally include the level of trust TL_X in the public key of node X (This is of special relevance in PKIs based on web-of-trust models[2,14]). Furthermore, other operations of the PKI such as certificate renewal and revocation may be enabled. Trust information related to a node may be dynamic[15] and evolve throughout MANET lifetime.

3.3 Trusted Portal Establishment

In joining the MANET, each node V arbitrarily selects another node Y from the ones present at the MANET. Then, both nodes mutually authenticate by using their certified public keys. This mutual authentication establishes a bi-directional trust relationship between both nodes, which is required for "Nodes Trust and Key Establishment".

Assume that, from a MANET with nodes A, B, V, W, X and Z, node Y selects node X as its initial trusted node. In future communications, Y will use X as a portal to address other nodes of the same MANET securely and efficiently. Therefore, we call X a *Trusted Portal* (TP) for Y. In the following we use TP-X to denote "*node X serving as TP*".

In a hybrid key management infrastructure, with a very simple underlying PKI, all the MANET nodes may have associated the same level of trust. Thus, in such case, all of them can serve as TPs. Conversely, in others, only nodes with special permissions may be allowed to serve as TPs. Finally, with web-of-trust models based PKIs, a node may need to possess a sufficient level of trust to be accepted to act as TP. For instance, using PGP's terminology[14], node X can act as TP if and only if its public key is associated a *complete* trust level.

A node Y, whose current TP is *TP-X*, must establish a new TP, when node X quits the MANET.

3.3.1   Trusted Portal Domain

Because each and every node of a MANET must follow the "TP Establishment" process and TPs are randomly selected, more than one node may establish initial trust with the same node X. We define as TP-X domain the group of MANET nodes associated to TP-X and, from now on, use D_{TPX} to denote TP-X domain. For instance, in Figure 1, domain D_{TPX} includes Y and W (which are depicted as TP-Y and TP-W because they also have respective TP domains) as trusted nodes of TP-X. TP-X is the domain administrator of its own domain D_{TPX}.

3.3.2   Generation of MANET Trust Graph

A consequence of the "TP Establishment" process is that one or more TPs are randomly set in the MANET. Because these TP nodes are selected randomly, a random trust graph connecting different nodes in the MANET is generated. Figure 1 shows an instance of a trust graph formed with nodes A, B, W, V, Y, X and Z.

We can guarantee the continuous existence of a random trust graph without isolated cycles under the following two conditions. First, each and every node of the MANET must *dynamically* initialize trust with an own selected TP, i.e. a node repeats the "TP Establishment" process in joining the MANET and when its TP disappears. Second, a node, which is serving as TP in the moment it selects its own TP, must choose as TP a node not included in its TP domain or sub-domains (e.g. in Figure 1, *TP-Y* cannot select nodes *V* or *Z* as TP). If this condition cannot be satisfied for a node (e.g. *X* in Figure 1), then such node should not select any TP.

It is easy to see that at the end of the above process, two arbitrary TPs are interconnected by either a direct trust relationship or by a set of indirect ones. Additionally, a trusted path of TPs interconnects two arbitrary nodes in different TP domains.

Figure 1. Random Trust Graph

3.3.3 Trust Initialization Protocol

Assuming that node *X* is not included in *TP-Y* domain or sub-domains, the following protocol enables *Y* to establish *X* as its TP:

$$Y \rightarrow X: \; TP\_Service\_Request \qquad\qquad (1)$$

$$TP\text{-}X \leftrightarrow Y: \; PKC \; challenge\text{-}response \; authentication \qquad (2)$$

$$TP\text{-}X \rightarrow Y: \; TP\_Service\_Accept, \; K\{S_{Y,TPX}, T\} \qquad (3)$$

In message (1), *Y* requests a TP service to node *X*. In (2), assuming that node *X* is cooperative, *X* and *Y* mutually authenticate using certified public keys and agree in a session key *K*. In (3), *TP-X* sends to *Y* a long-term shared symmetric key $S_{Y,TPX}$ encrypted and integrity-protected with *K* and a timestamp *T*. Finally, *Y* sets *TP-X* as its TP and, similarly, *X* sets *Y* as one of its trusted nodes.

In the rest of the paper, we will use the term TP-shared-key and the notation $S_{node,TP}$ to refer to a long-term symmetric key $S_{node,TP}$ shared between a node and its TP or to any of the keys k_i derived from it, interchangeably. For instance, in the protocol above $S_{Y,TPX}$ is the TP-shared-key between *Y* and *TP-X*.

3.4   Nodes Trust And Key Establishment

TPs can be used as *ad hoc* TTPs to distribute keys and related trust information within the MANET. The first instance is when two arbitrary nodes *V* and *Z* of the same TP domain want to establish a shared key K_{VZ}. In such a case, their TP, e.g. *TP-Y* on Fig. 1, acts as a TTP providing them of the shared key K_{VZ}. Similarly, a common TP can vouch for nodes in its TP domain. For instance, *TP-Y* can associate V's identity to the symmetric key K_{VZ} distributed to Z and Z's identity to the symmetric key K_{VZ} distributed to V. In some trust models this information may be sufficient to enable key establishment and mutual authentication of nodes V and Z. In web-of-trust models, *TP-Y* additionally includes *recommendation values*, which enable both nodes V and Z to respectively evaluate the level of trust that *TP-Y* has on their communication partner.

These concepts can be easily extended to several TP domains. An arbitrary *TP-Y* can delegate to its parent TP, *TP-X*, to vouch and distribute keys in D_{TPY} related to *TP-X* trusted nodes. In this manner, different TPs cooperate to securely distribute shared keys and/or vouch for nodes in different TP domains.

3.4.1   Trust And Key Distribution Protocol

In this section we describe the TKD protocol, a protocol to distribute trust and keys across TP domains (It can also be applied for intra-TP-domain trust and key distribution by considering just *one* intermediary TP below):

$$V \rightarrow \text{TP-Y}: S_{V,TPY}\{KeyReq\ (ID_W,\ ID_V),\ T_1\} \qquad (1)$$

$$\text{TP-Y} \rightarrow \text{TP-X}: \ S_{Y,TPX}\{KeyReq\ (ID_W,\quad ID_V), \qquad (2)$$

$$\text{TP-X} \rightarrow W: S_{W,TPX}\{K_{V,W},\ ID_V,\ T_3\},\ ticket_V \qquad (3)$$

$$W \rightarrow V: ticket_V \qquad (4)$$

In step (1), node V requests *TP-Y* a key for W. This message is encrypted under $S_{V,TPY}$ to guarantee the confidentiality of the process as well as the anonymity of *TP-Y* and of the involved nodes V and W. To protect against message replay and modification attacks, the messages must be additionally integrity protected, e.g. by including message authentication codes (MAC) as well as timestamps T_1, T_2 and T_3.

In (2), *TP-Y* decrypts message (1) and obtains the included timestamp T_1. *TP-Y* computes a *Delegation Key* K_{TPYdel} by applying a pseudorandom function F with $S_{V,TPY}$ and T_1 as inputs, i.e. $K_{TPYdel} = F(S_{V,TPY},\ T_1)$. With K_{TPYdel}, *TP-Y* delegates to other TPs to vouch for V and distribute keys associated to V's identity in their domains. Note that the *Delegation Key* also enables other TPs to communicate securely with V (see further steps below). *TP-Y* constructs message (2) by including K_{TPYdel} and V's key request. It then encrypts message (2) using the *TP-shared-key* with *TP-X* (the next TP in the trust path), i.e. $S_{Y,TPX}\{KeyReq(ID_W, ID_V), K_{TPYdel}, T_2\}$. *TP-Y* sends to *TP-X* message (2). In this manner, V's key request is forwarded to a TP in a different domain.

In (3), decryption of message (2) with $S_{Y,TPX}$ transmits to *TP-X* (*W*'s TP) *TP-Y*'s trust in ID_V. *TP-X* randomly generates a new shared key $K_{V,W}$ for *V* and *W*. *TP-X* encrypts $K_{V,W}$ and ID_V using its *TP-shared-key* with *W*, i.e. $S_{W,TPY}\{K_{V,W}, ID_V, T_3\}$. *TP-X* also creates a *ticket* for *V* secured with K_{TPYdel} containing $K_{V,W}$ and ID_W, i.e. $ticket_V = K_{TPYdel}\{K_{V,W}, ID_W, T_3\}$. *TP-X* sends to *W* message (3).

In (4), node *W* forwards $ticket_V$ to *V*. Finally, *W* obtains $K_{V,W}$ by decrypting message (3) with $S_{W,TPX}$. In parallel, *V* obtains $K_{V,W}$ by decrypting message (4) with K_{TPYdel}.

For simplicity' sake we have assumed above a simple underlying PKI trust model. In PKI web-of-trust models, the messages of the TKD protocol additionally include *recommendation values* $R_{target}^{voucher}$ on the identities of the participant TPs and end nodes.

4. PERFORMANCE ANALYSIS

In this section we analytically study the performance efficiency of the hybrid key management infrastructure and demonstrate its improved performance for MANET applications by comparing with PKIs.

To avoid impersonation or man-in-the-middle attacks, two arbitrary nodes *V* and *W*, which want to establish a key K_{VW}, need to, respectively, also assess the authenticity of the node they are establishing the key with[1]. This can be achieved in PKIs by using an X.509 strong two-way authentication protocol with key establishment (a similar protocol is included within the SSL/TLS protocol suite). In the hybrid case, nodes use TKD protocol to establish a key.

For simplicity's sake, in the following sections we assume that every MANET node holds a public key certificate signed by a common CA and the corresponding CA public key. For evaluating the hybrid approach, we further assume a MANET with *P* nodes, from which *N* act as TPs. We use N_{AV} to denote the average number of intermediary TPs in the shortest trust path between any pair of MANET nodes.

4.1 Communication Cost

In this section, for simplicity's sake, we assume a small or medium sized MANET where MANET nodes are in direct wireless range of each other.

Let us compare the TKD and the X.509[1] protocols. The following formulas quantify the bandwidth used by each protocol:

$$BWCost^{X.509} = 2 \times (Cert + 2 \times T_i + ID + Sign + RSAEnc)$$

$$BWCost^{TKD} = (N_{AV} + 3) \times TKDMessage$$

Let us use N_{BWEQ} to denote the average number N_{AV} of TPs for which $BWCost^{X.509} = BWCost^{TKD}$. Then, for $N_{AV} < N_{BWEQ}$, hybrid key management enabled trust and key establishment outperforms PKI. For instance, in a MANET application using public key certificates of 256 bytes (just including a public key and a digital signature of 1024 bits), timestamps of 8 bytes, symmetric keys of 128 bits and the cipher AES-128, N_{AV} should be lower than $N_{BWEQ} = 32$.

The number N_{BWEQ} can be used as an additional parameter to control the maximum number N of TPs in a MANET with P nodes, such that $N_{AV} \leq N_{BWEQ}$. For instance, by using Doyle and Graver[19] formula for average path length, in a worst-case scenario where the N TPs are subsequently disposed on a simple trust path and each TP domain contains in average $(P - N)/N$ NTP nodes, $N \leq 3N_{BWEQ}$.

4.2   Computational Cost

The following formulas quantify the computational overhead incurred by the X.509[1] and TKD protocols, respectively: requires two nodes V and W to compute four signature verifications, two signature generations, two public key encryptions and two private key decryptions. Then:

$$CCost^{X.509} = 6 \times RSASigVer + 4 \times RSASigGen$$

$$CCost^{TKD} = (N_{AV} + 2) \times AESEnc + (N_{AV} + 2) \times AESDec$$

We have developed a testing environment using Microsoft® CryptoAPI 1.0[9] and Szymon Stefanek's AES C++ Class[10] on an iPaq Pocket PC with ARM SA1110 CPU at 206 MHz to measure the cost to compute typical RSA public key and AES symmetric key operations. Let us use N_{CEQ} to denote the number of TPs for which $CCost^{X.509} = CCost^{TKD}$. The TKD protocol outperforms the X.509 for a number N_{AV} of TP nodes lower than $N_{CEQ} = 7700$ TPs. As demonstrated with our communication cost analysis, in normal MANET applications, the average number N_{AV} of intermediate TP nodes between two arbitrary nodes V and W is much lower than 7700.

5. SECURITY ANALYSIS

In MANET applications where the risk of node compromise is very low or null, the major security risks are imposed by the open nature of wireless MANETs.. In this case, the hybrid key management infrastructure offers perfect security because all the messages are protected with confidentiality and integrity mechanisms. In some other applications attackers may compromise nodes and then use them to attack the MANET by faking trusted identities or issuing false keys and recommendations. In applications where devices are owned by different administrative entities some nodes may misbehave by not cooperating. These kind of attacks are common in security solutions based on node trust and cooperation[2,14], and, particularly, also in the hybrid approach. However, the security robustness of the hybrid approach can be improved by further applying other mechanisms such as reputations[11], by minimizing the average number of intermediate TP nodes to reduce the risk that an attacker is among them, or, even, by allowing the formation of isolated trust graph cycles (to the cost of decreased trust graph connectivity), and by allowing nodes to establish multiple TPs (to the cost of increased computational overhead).

6. CONCLUSIONS

In this paper, we have presented a hybrid key management infrastructure for MANETs, which combines the concepts of PKIs with TTP-based infrastructures. In our hybrid approach, an underlying PKI is merely used to set-up initial trust of nodes in a MANET. This trust initialization method generates a random trust graph connecting all the nodes of the MANET. Then, the nodes of the shortest trust path connecting two end nodes can cooperate to securely distribute trust information and symmetric keys to the end nodes.

We have demonstrated that the hybrid approach enables key establishment and node-to-node authentication with a substantial improvement in terms of computational efficiency and communication efficiency in respect to current PKI solutions for MANETs. We have also discussed the security level of the hybrid approach and compared with other trust and cooperation based approaches.

7.   REFERENCES

1.   A. J. Menezes, P. C. Van Oorschot, S. A. Vanstone. Handbook of Applied Cryptography. CRC Press. 1996.
2.   S. Capkun, L. Buttyan and J.-P. Hubaux. Self-Organized Public-Key Management for Mobile Ad Hoc Networks. IEEE Transactions on Mobile Computing, vol. 2, n° 1, pp. 52-64. 2003.
3.   L. Zhou and Z. J. Haas. Securing Ad Hoc Networks. IEEE Network Magazine, vol. 13, no.6, 1999.
4.   H. Luo and S. Lu. Ubiquitous and Robust Authentication Services for Ad Hoc Wireless Networks, Technical Report TR-200030, Dept. of Computer Science, UCLA, 2000.
5.   H. Luo, P. Zerfos, J. Kong, S. Lu and L. Zhang. Self-Securing Ad Hoc Wireless Networks. 7th International Symposium on Computers and Communications. 2002.
6.   M. Bechler, H.-J. Hof, D. Kraft, F. Pählke and L. Wolf. A Cluster-Based Security Architecture for Ad Hoc Networks. IEEE Infocom 2004.
7.   E. C. H. Ngai, M. R. Lyu. Trust- and Clustering-Based Authentication Services in Mobile Ad Hoc Networks. ICDCSW'04 Workshops - W4: MDC. 2004.
8.   L. Venkatraman and D. P. Agrawal. A Novel Authentication Scheme for Ad hoc Networks. WCNC 2000, pp. 1268-1273, vol.3.
9.   The MSDN Library. http://msdn.microsoft.com/library/default.asp.
10. The Rijndael Page. http://www.esat.kuleuven.ac.be/~rijmen/rijndael/.
11. P. Michiardi and R. Molva. Core: A Collaborative Reputation mechanism to enforce node cooperation in Mobile Ad Hoc Networks. Communication and Multimedia Security Conference. 2002.
12. A.B. MCDonald and T.F. Znati. A Mobility-Based Framework for Adaptive Clustering in Wireless Ad Hoc Networks. IEEE JSAC, 1999.
13. C. Kaufman, R. Perlman and M. Speciner. Network Security: Private Communication in a Public World. Prentice Hall PTR, 2002.
14. Network Associates, Inc. An Introduction to Cryptography.
15. L. Martucci, C. Schweitzer, Y. Regina Venturini, T. C. Carvalho, W. Ruggiero. "A Trust-Based Security Architecture for Small and Medium-Sized Mobile Ad Hoc Networks". The Third Med-Hoc-Net Workshop, 2004.
16. K. Hoeper and G. Gong. Models of Authentication in Ad Hoc Networks and Their Related Network Properties. Technical Report, University of Waterloo, CACR 2004-03.
17. S. Capkun, J.-P. Hubaux and L. Buttyan. Mobility helps security in ad hoc networks. In Proc. MobiHoc'03, 2003.
18. M. Elhdhili, L. B. Azzouz, F. Kamoun. A Totally Distributed Cluster Based Key Management Model for Ad Hoc Networks. The Third Med-Hoc-Net Workshop. 2004.
19. J.K. Doyle and J.E. Graver. Mean distance in a graph. Discrete Mathematics Vol. 17, Issue 2, pp. 147-154. 1977.

DESIGN AND OPTIMIZATION OF REPUTATION MECHANISMS FOR CENTRALIZED CLUSTERED AD HOC NETWORKS

Spyridon Vassilaras, Dimitrios Vogiatzis and Gregory S. Yovanof
Athens Information Technology, Markopoulo Ave., PO. Box 68, 190 02, Peania, Athens, Greece, e-mail: {svas, dvog, gyov}@ait.edu.gr

Abstract: In this paper, we present and analyze a reputation scheme aiming at reinforcing node cooperation in clustered Mobile Ad hoc Networks with centralized control. The main goal of this scheme is to differentiate between intentional misbehavior and apparent failure to cooperate due to wireless channel conditions or mobility. To this end, a statistical decision method based on the notion of a random walk is employed. Selecting the optimal parameters for this random walk is investigated in the context of time dependent events. Special care has been given to issues such as probability of detection of a misbehaving mobile node, probability of falsely accusing a legitimate node due to non-intentional failures to cooperate and fast detection of misbehaving nodes in the light of time varying behavior of such nodes.

Key words: Ad hoc networks, MANETs, Cooperation Enforcement, Misbehavior Detection, Reputation Mechanism, Random Walk.

1.   INTRODUCTION

The correct execution of network functions in *Mobile Ad hoc Networks* (MANETs) relies on the cooperation of the individual nodes that constitute the network. Malicious *Mobile Nodes* (MNs) that intentionally fail to execute their part of a network protocol in order to cause damage and selfish MNs that do not cooperate in order to save precious resources (such as battery power) can severely disrupt proper network operation. Thus providing incentive mechanisms that will convince selfish MNs to cooperate and detection mechanisms that will identify malicious MNs and isolate them from the network is a critical issue, which has received considerable attention recently from the research community ([1]-[10]).

In the literature of node cooperation enforcement, the proposed solutions can be subdivided into two main categories: *trade based* schemes and *reputation based* schemes (see [1] for a more rigorous taxonomy of incentive schemes). In trade based schemes, a node that provides some service to a peer node (e.g., packet forwarding) is rewarded by either another immediate service in exchange or some monetary token that he can later use to buy services from another node (e.g., [2]-[4]). In reputation based schemes each node keeps a reputation metric for other nodes he deals with and provides services only to nodes that exhibit good reputation (e.g., [5]-[10]).

In all reputation based mechanisms for cooperation enforcement, each node in the network performs two distinct functions: rating the behavior of neighboring nodes and using these ratings to adjust his own behavior towards them. Rating the conformance of neighboring nodes to a given network protocol is an operation that depends on the specific protocol and network architecture. For instance, in single channel MANETs rating the packet forwarding service provided by a node's neighbors is simply performed through monitoring of the common channel. However, in clustered MANETs which use different channels in each cluster and bridge nodes to relay packets between clusters (such as Bluetooth scatternets) a node cannot receive the transmissions of all of his neighbors. Hence, a different technique for rating the forwarding services provided by them is needed. Similarly, rating the conformance to a neighborhood discovery protocol or a Medium Access protocol is fundamentally different than rating packet forwarding.

On the other hand, a cooperation reinforcing reputation mechanism can be easily adapted to use such behavior ratings independently of the rated service. A crucial task for this mechanism is to distinguish between perceived and actual non-cooperative behavior. For example, a MN might receive a bad cooperation rating because of wireless link failure or mobility. Misbehaving MNs might also choose to misbehave in a probabilistic way in order to evade detection. If erroneously perceived misbehavior is permitted with a certain probability, then detecting intentional misbehavior boils down to an estimation problem.

In this paper, we are investigating reputation mechanisms that use cooperation ratings to identify malicious and selfish MNs in a special kind of MANETs: Clustered mobile Ad hoc networks which operate under the coordination and supervision of a central entity. The problem of estimating the probability with which a MN misbehaves is analyzed for both time dependent and independent non-cooperative behavior. The design goal is to maximize the probability of detection of misbehaving MNs while keeping the probability of falsely accusing legitimate MNs to a minimum.

The rest of the paper is organized as follows: In Section 2, a brief description of the Centralized Clustered Ad hoc network architecture is provided. In Section 3, we develop a general framework for detecting non-cooperative behavior and introduce a reputation scheme for distinguishing between erroneously perceived misbehavior and malicious or selfish behavior of mobile nodes. Finally, Conclusions are presented in Section 4.

2.   CENTRALIZED CLUSTERED MOBILE AD HOC NETWORKS

Current user needs and modern multimedia network applications require high bit rates for data transfer. Existing WLAN technologies though, like IEEE 802.11 or HIPERLAN/2 (HL/2) cannot always meet these high data rate requirements due to the nature of the wireless channel. A typical case describing this situation is in hotspot areas, where a large number of users with high traffic needs are in the transmission range of each other. To increase the total capacity of such networks, a clustered mobile ad hoc architecture can be used. In such a setting, a specific set of MNs that are closely located and want to exchange data, are organized into a cluster. Each cluster operates in a different frequency channel to avoid interference with neighboring clusters. Through the use of power control, MNs limit their transmissions to a shorter range. Thus the network is capable of accommodating more users within the same area and transmissions inside a cluster can achieve higher bit rates. Communication between MNs that belong to different clusters is achieved with the help of *Forwarding Nodes* (FNs). FNs are MNs which belong simultaneously to two adjacent clusters and serve as bridges to forward data packets among them. A FN is able to communicate in both communication channels, but at any given time he is only capable of being tuned in one of the two clusters.

The decisions about cluster formation, including assigning FNs, are made by a central entity, commonly known as the *Access Point (AP)* or *Central Controller (CC)*. Thus, the AP assumes the role of the coordinator of the system, having under its supervision the MNs of all clusters. In order to discriminate between pure Ad hoc clustered networks, from this point on we will be referring to this type of networks as Centralized Clustered Mobile Ad hoc Networks. A typical example of such type of systems is the *Centralized Ad hoc Network Architecture (CANA)* (see [11], [12] for more details). Other network architectures that uses centralized control to assist in Ad hoc network formation are described in [13] and [14]. Under this schemes, heterogeneous Ad hoc networks are formed under the central supervision of a cellular network infrastructure. All the above architectures assume that the central authority can communicate control information directly to the MNs via wireless links. Hence the need of creating an Ad hoc network is not generated by the fact that the MNs are outside of the transmission range of the AP; multihop communication is employed in order to achieve higher capacity and centralized control helps in the network set-up and operation.

MN mobility and changing communication needs dictate a dynamic cluster formation algorithm. Network topology information is gathered by the AP during a *Neighborhood Discovery (ND)* operation, which is performed repeatedly in certain time intervals, in order to adapt to dynamic network conditions. ND takes place in a predefined channel where all MNs exchange messages at a shorter transmission range, in order to identify their one hop neighbors. When a broadcast *'NextND Phase'* message sent by the AP is received by the MNs, they all enter the ND phase and send *'hello messages'* in specific time slots assigned by the AP (so that collisions do not occur). Then each MN sends to the AP a *Neighbors list,* each row of which is filled with the source MAC address of a 'hello message' it has received and the quality of reception (link status). Based on input from all MNs, the AP then decides on the exact cluster topology and communicates it to the MNs.

3.   REPUTATION BASED COOPERATION REINFORCEMENT

The AP is considered to be a trusted entity, adopting thus the role of the security manager in the network. In fact the AP is believed to be the only trusted device in the network; all the MNs may constantly or occasionally misbehave, drop packets, misroute data packets, try to mislead the AP regarding the network topology, etc.

The key mechanism for addressing these issues is a node reputation mechanism implemented by the AP. The goal of this mechanism is to keep track of misbehaving MNs so that they can be isolated from the network and penalized appropriately. In order to distinguish between perceived (e.g., due to wireless link failure or mobility) and actual non-cooperative behavior, the AP can observe each MN for a large period of time and compare their behavior to the expected behavior of a well-behaving node. One common way of keeping track of a MN's long term behavior is by assigning to it a reputation metric which will be reduced if the node is suspected to have misbehaved and increased otherwise. A set of such reputation metrics can be maintained for each MN, to track different kinds of misbehavior. If one of these metrics falls below a given threshold, the node is considered misbehaving. This way, not only nodes that exhibit consistent misbehavior, but also nodes that misbehave with a certain probability will get detected. Although this scheme is popular in the literature ([5], [6], [10]), it has not been, to the best of our knowledge, analyzed quantitatively. In the remainder of this paper we model the evolution of a reputation metric in time as a random walk process and investigate appropriate selection of this random walk's parameters.

3.1   The reputation metric as a random walk process

Let as denote by $r_i^j(k)$ the value of the i-th reputation metric of the j-th MN at time k. All metrics should be initialized at some positive value a_i, i.e. $r_i^j(0) = a_i > 0$, $\forall i, j$. Time is considered to be discrete and independent for each reputation metric; for each event that can contribute positively or negatively to the reputation metric r_i^j, its associated k is increased by one. Therefore after the k-th 'event' we have:

$r_i^j(k) = r_i^j(k-1) + \Delta r_i^j(k)$ with:

- $\Delta r_i^j(k) = -1$, if a suspicious event occurs and
- $\Delta r_i^j(k) = b_i$, otherwise.

If the i-th reputation metric of a node becomes smaller than or equal to 0, this node is considered to have performed a type-i protocol attack. Clearly, each random process $\{r_i^j(k)\}$ is a random walk in which the event of a node getting accused for misbehavior is a threshold crossing event [15]. For a well-behaving node, we expect suspicious events (also known as false positives) of different types to occur in a variety of time patterns; false positives of a certain type might be i.i.d., whereas false positives of another type might exhibit strong time dependencies.

Let us first consider the case where false positives are i.i.d. with probability P_{loss}. Then $\{r_i^j(k)\}$ for a well-behaving node is a random walk with i.i.d. steps. Assuming that we can estimate P_{loss} with a reasonable accuracy[1] we want to set the parameters of the random walk in such a way that the threshold crossing probability (i.e., the probability of wrongly accusing a well behaving node) does not exceed a very small value P_{wrong}. A logical choice for the value of b_i is:

---

[1] In any case, a conservative estimate of P_{loss} can be used instead, e.g., the upper end of a 99% confidence interval.

$$b_i = \frac{P_{loss}}{1 - P_{loss}} \tag{1}$$

which results in a zero drift random walk by making the mean value of the per step change in the reputation metric equal to 0. It is well known that a zero drift random walk with infinite horizon will eventually cross any finite threshold with probability 1. To avoid this, we can select an appropriate window size n, and update the reputation metric for k>n, as follows:

$$r_i^j(k) = r_i^j(k-1) + \Delta r_i^j(k) - \Delta r_i^j(k-n)$$

An upper bound to the threshold crossing probability for a random walk in a finite horizon is given by (see [15]):

$$P_{good}(r_i^j(k) \leq 0) \leq \exp[n\gamma(\theta^*) - \theta^* \cdot a_i] \tag{2}$$

where θ^* is the minimizing θ in $\min_{\theta \geq 0}[n\gamma(\theta) - \theta \cdot a_i]$, $\gamma(\theta) = \ln E[\exp(-\theta \cdot \Delta r_i^j(k))]$ and a_i the initial value of r_i^j.

3.2   Dealing with time dependent suspicious events

In the case of time dependent suspicious events there exist generalizations of Eq. 2 for several classes of random processes. A simple case is when the time dependence of false positives can be modeled as a Markov chain process with two states (state 0 corresponds to a suspicious event and state 1 to normal operation) and transition probability matrix $P = \begin{bmatrix} P_{00} & P_{01} \\ P_{10} & P_{11} \end{bmatrix}$.

Then, $\{r_i^j(k)\}$ is a Markov modulated random walk in which the upper bound to the 0 crossing probability in a finite horizon n is given by Eq. 2 with (see [15]):

$$\gamma(\theta) = \ln \rho \left(\begin{bmatrix} P_{00} e^\theta & P_{01} e^{-b_2\theta} \\ P_{10} e^\theta & P_{11} e^{-b_2\theta} \end{bmatrix} \right)$$

where $\rho(A)$ denotes the largest eigenvalue of matrix A.

In order to illustrate the applicability of these theoretical results, we provide the following example: Assume that the transition probability matrix for the false positives process has been estimated to be $P = \begin{bmatrix} 0.6 & 0.4 \\ 0.005 & 0.995 \end{bmatrix}$ and the marginal probability of a well behaving node to be in the apparent misbehavior state $p_0 \approx 1.23 \cdot 10^{-2}$. For zero mean increments we set $b_i = \dfrac{p_0}{1 - p_0} = 0.0125$. Then requiring the upper bound in Eq. 2 to be equal to $P_{\text{wrong}} = 10^{-3}$, we calculated the values of a_i for window sizes of n=1,000, 5,000 and 25,000 respectively. Using these parameters, we ran simulations to estimate the actual probability of ruin of a well behaving node in a time period of length n. The results are shown in Table 1. They show that in all three cases the actual probability of ruin is indeed lower than its theoretical upper bound (by an order of magnitude). At this point we should stress the obvious fact that the cumulative probability of ruin in a growing number of successive sliding windows tends to 1 for any value of P_{wrong}. For example, the cumulative probabilities of ruin, for the above mentioned window sizes and random walk parameters, in a total time period of 100,000 events were estimated experimentally and the results are given in Table 1.

Table 1. Actual probabilities of ruin of a well behaving node for different window sizes and constant P_{wrong}

N	1,000	5,000	25,000
a_i	39.09	71.61	144.65
P_{ruin} prior to n	$9.9 \cdot 10^{-5}$	$1.2 \cdot 10^{-4}$	$1.4 \cdot 10^{-4}$
P_{ruin} prior to 100,000	$4.6 \cdot 10^{-2}$	$1.5 \cdot 10^{-2}$	$2.5 \cdot 10^{-3}$

Table 2. Actual probabilities of ruin of a well behaving node for different window sizes and constant P_{wrong} / n

N	1,000	5,000	25,000
P_{wrong}	10^{-5}	$5 \cdot 10^{-5}$	$2.5 \cdot 10^{-4}$
a_i	55.24	88.76	159.76
P_{ruin} prior to n	$8.4 \cdot 10^{-7}$	$5.4 \cdot 10^{-6}$	$3.5 \cdot 10^{-5}$
P_{ruin} prior to 100,000	$4.6 \cdot 10^{-4}$	$6.6 \cdot 10^{-4}$	$7.5 \cdot 10^{-4}$

An alternative empirical approach to selecting the parameter a_i for different values of n would be to fix the ratio P_{wrong} / n aiming at approximately equal cumulative probabilities over a longer period of time. By requiring $P_{\text{wrong}} / n = 10^{-8}$ and repeating the same procedure as above, we obtained the results shown in Table 2. Note that all probabilities of ruin prior to n are smaller than the respective P_{wrong} and that all probabilities of ruin prior to 100,000 are smaller than $100{,}000 \cdot P_{\text{wrong}} / n = 10^{-3}$.

Then, using the parameters shown in Table 1 (for fixed P_{wrong} over different n), we calculated the probability of ruin of a malicious node which misbehaves with probability P_{mal} (and independently of previous behavior) when in state 1. The results are plotted in Figure 1. We observe that as the window size increases, a malicious node gets detected with probability approaching 1 for lower values of P_{mal} when P_{wrong} is kept constant. This is a direct result of the fact that the accuracy of any estimation (and our ability to make estimation based decisions) improves as the sample size increases.

On the other hand, if a well behaving node suddenly turns malicious and misbehaves with a relatively high P_{mal} (so that the probability of ruin is close to 1 for two window sizes $n_1 < n_2$) this change in behavior will most probably get detected sooner if the sliding window with the smaller size is used. Take for example the case where $P = \begin{bmatrix} 0.7538 & 0.2462 \\ 0.0538 & 0.9462 \end{bmatrix}$, $p_0 = 0.1793$, $P_{\text{wrong}} = 10^{-2}$, and a malicious node exhibits $P_{mal} = 0.02$ for $t \leq 1200$ and $t > 3000$ and $P_{mal} = 0.2$ for $1200 < t \leq 3000$. In Figure 2 we plot the probability of this node getting detected in a sliding window of size n as time progresses for different values of n. It can be seen that a sliding window of a smaller size reacts faster to this sudden change of behavior.

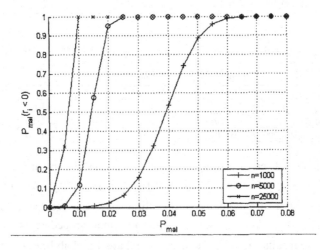

Figure 1. Probability of a malicious node getting detected as a function of his misbehavior probability, for n=1,000, 5,000 and 25,000

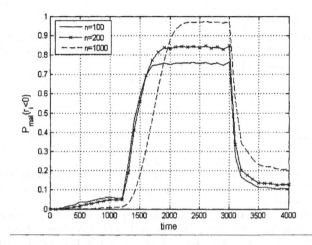

Figure 2. Probability of a malicious node with changing behavior getting detected for different window sizes

4.   CONCLUSIONS

In this paper, we have investigated a cooperation enforcement scheme based on scalar reputation metrics and performed a quantitative analysis on methods for selecting step sizes and threshold values. We have treated the evolution of the reputation metric over time as a stochastic process. Both time dependent and independent stochastic models have been considered and the results have been evaluated with simulation experiments. Our work has shed some new light into the issue of detecting malicious behavior with certain probability while keeping the probability of wrongfully accusing a well behaving node below a given upper bound. We have also studied the effect of using different window sizes for the detection of malicious behavior. The trade-off between detecting nodes that misbehave with lower probabilities but reacting more slowly to changes in the behavior as the window size increases has been illustrated.

Although our cooperation reinforcement mechanism has been designed for clustered Ad hoc networks with centralized supervision, the issue of appropriately selecting the parameters of a reputation scheme (initial value/ruin threshold, step value and sliding window size) is not different regardless of this scheme being distributed or centralized. Thus, the introduced random walk model for the reputation metric and the associated parameter selection technique can be applied to distributed reputation mechanisms for pure Ad-hoc networks, as well.

5.   REFERENCES

[1] P. Obreiter, J. Nimis, "A Taxonomy of Incentive Patterns - the Design Space of Incentives for Cooperation", Technical Report Nr. 2003-9, May 21, 2003, http://www.ipd.uka.de/DIANE/en/index.html

[2] L. Buttyan, J.P. Hubaux, "Stimulating Cooperation in Self-Organizing Mobile Ad Hoc Networks", ACM/Kluwer Mobile Networks and Applications, Vol. 8, No. 5, October 2003

[3] N. Salem, et al., "A Charging and Rewarding Scheme for Packet Forwarding in Multi-hop Cellular Networks", MobiHoc'03, June 2003, Annapolis, Maryland, USA

[4] S. Zhong, J. Chen, and R. Yang, "Sprite: A Simple, Cheat-proof, Credit-based System for Mobile Ad-hoc Networks," In IEEE INFOCOM, San Francisco, USA, 2002. IEEE Press.

[5] S. Marti, et al., "Mitigating Routing Misbehavior in Mobile Ad Hoc Networks", Proc. ACM Int'l Conf. Mobile Computing & Networking, Mobicom 2000

[6] S. Bansal and M. Baker, "Observation-Based Cooperation Enforcement in Ad hoc Networks," Research Report cs.NI/0307012, Stanford University, 2003.

[7] P. Michiardi, R. Molva , "Analysis of Coalition Formation and Cooperation Strategies in Mobile Ad hoc Networks", Ad-hoc Networks Journal (Special Issue), Elsevier, 2003

[8] S. Buchegger, J. Y. Le Boudec, "Performance Analysis of the CONFIDANT Protocol (Cooperation Of Nodes - Fairness In Dynamic Ad-hoc NeTworks)", Proceedings of MobiHoc 2002, Lausanne, June 2002, pp. 226-236.

[9] S. Buchegger, J.Y. Le Boudec, "The effect of rumor spreading in reputation systems for mobile ad-hoc networks," In WiOpt'03: Modeling and Optimization in Mobile Ad Hoc and Wireless Networks (2003).

[10] H. Miranda and L. Rodrigues. "Preventing Selfishness in Open Mobile Ad Hoc Networks," .In Proceedings of the International Workshop on Mobile Distributed Computing (MDC), pages 440–445, Providence, Rhode Island USA, May 2003. IEEE. (Proceedings the 23rd International Conference on Distributed Computing Systems Workshops).

[11] K. Oikonomou, A. Vaios, S. Simoens, P. Pellati, I. Stavrakakis, "A Centralized Ad-Hoc Network Architecture (CANA) Based on Enhanced HiperLAN/2," 14th IEEE PIMRC 2003, Beijing, China, September 7-10, 2003.

[12] S. Vassilaras, D. Vogiatzis, T. Dimitriou, G. Yovanof, "Security Considerations for the Centralized Ad-Hoc Network Architecture", IEEE Int'l Workshop on Ad-Hoc Networks (IWWAN'04), Oulu, Finland, June 2004.

[13] M. Danzeisen, et al., "Heterogeneous Network Establishment Assisted by Cellular Operators", 5th IFIP TC6 Int'l Conference on Mobile and Wireless Communication Networks, Singapore, October 2003.

[14] B. Bhargava et al. "Integrating Heterogeneous Wireless Technologies: A Cellular Aided Mobile Ad Hoc Network (CAMA)," Mobile Networks and Applications 9, 393–408, 2004 Kluwer Academic Publishers.

[15] R.G.Gallager, "Discrete Stochastic Processes", Kluwer Academic Publishers.

"DIRECTION" FORWARDING FOR HIGHLY MOBILE, LARGE SCALE AD HOC NETWORKS

Mario Gerla[1], Yeng-Zhong Lee[1], Biao Zhou[1], Jason Chen[1], Antonio Caruso[2]
[1]*University of California, at Los Angeles Computer Science Department;* [2]*Institute of Sciences and Technologies Information, ISTL, National Research Council, Reasearch Area of San Catalado – Pisa, Italy*

Abstract: In this paper, we present a novel packet forwarding scheme for wireless ad hoc networks --- "Direction" Forwarding (DFR). Popular routing protocols such as DSDV and AODV use "predecessor" based forwarding, namely, the packet is forwarded to the predecessor on the shortest path from the destination, as advertised during the last update. Predecessor forwarding may fail in large scale networks where the routing update rate must be reduced by the need to maintain link O/H below reasonable levels. However, if nodes are mobile, routing table entries may become "stale" very rapidly. DFR is designed to overcome the "stale" routing table entry problem. When the routing update arrives, the node remembers not only the predecessor delivering the update, but also the update "direction" of arrival. When a packet must be forwarded to destination, it is first forwarded to the node ID found in the routing table. If the node has moved and ID forwarding fails, the packet is "direction" forwarded to the "most promising" node in the indicated direction. At first glance, DFR seems to combine the features of table based routing and geo-routing. However, direction forwarding differs from geo-routing in that the direction is learned from the routing updates, instead of being computed from the destination coordinates. Thus, DFR does not require destination coordinates, a global coordinate system, or a Geo Location Server. In the paper we show the application of DFR to a scalable routing scheme, LANMAR. Through simulation experiments we show that DFR substantially enhances LANMAR performance in large, mobile network scenarios.

Key words: Wireless Networks; MANET; routing; Geographic Routing Protocol; Location System; mobility; scalability

This work was supported in part by the ONR "MINUTEMAN" project under contract N00014-01-C_0016, and in part by NSF "WHYNET" project under contract CNS-0335302.

1.   INTRODUCTION

Ad hoc wireless networking technology has been gaining increasing visibility and importance in distributed applications that can not rely on a fixed infrastructure but require instant deployment and easy reconfiguration. These networks are typically characterized by limited bandwidth, limited radio range, high mobility and high bit error rate (BER). These characteristics pose challenges to the design and implementation of MANET (Mobile Ad Hoc Net) routing protocols and have motivated extensive research in this area over the past few years.

One of the most challenging research areas that have recently emerged in the design of MANETs is in fact scalability; in particular, scalability of the routing protocols. Conventional proactive routing protocols, such as DSDV [11] and Fisheye [10], rely on periodic exchanges of routing information. They do not scale well because they propagate routing information of all nodes throughout the entire network. With mobility, more frequent updates are required to keep the information up to date, thus producing a large amount of control overhead. In a large scale mobile environment, on-demand routing protocols such as AODV [12] and DSR [6], which generate routing overhead only when there is data traffic to send, and thus have been traditionally considered more suitable for ad hoc wireless networks, also tend to cause heavy overhead due to the large-scale flood search triggered by motion. In the case of 100 nodes and 40 sources with uniform traffic patterns, results have shown that both DSR and AODV generate more routing overhead than actual throughput [3][5].

An important class of MANETs finds applications in disaster recovery, civilian emergencies and battlefield operations. These networks tend to grow large, involving up to thousand nodes. Thus, scalability becomes a critical design issue, especially when combined with high node mobility. Recently some efforts have been made to improve the scalability of ad hoc routing protocols. One technique is to utilize geographical information such as in LAR [8] and GPSR [7], which try to utilize geographic information (typically from GPS) to achieve scalability. Such position based routing protocols use physical location information about the participating nodes to make decisions on how to route packets. Traditional techniques such as Link State routing have also been retrofitted for scalability. Link State routing algorithms generally use flooding to distribute network topology information, leading to significant control traffic overhead that reduces the bandwidth available for application data. In order to reduce the control overhead in presence of mobility, recent extension of Link State have explored group mobility patterns such as in the LANMAR scheme [13][14].

In this paper we introduce DFR (Direction Forwarding) [15] to overcome the "stale" next hop problem. Suppose our ad hoc network is equipped with a geo coordinate system, either a global system (e.g., GPS) or a localized system (e.g., virtual coordinates locally computed via trilateration). When the routing update arrives, the node remembers not only the predecessor, but also the "direction" from which the update arrived. When a packet must be forwarded to destination, it is first forwarded to the node ID found in the routing table. If the node has moved and ID forwarding fails, the packet is "direction" forwarded to the" most promising" node in the indicated direction. If the network is sufficiently dense, direction forwarding will recover from most ID forwarding failures.

In the remainder we report on the extension of LANMAR [4] using DFR. The version of DFR used in conjunction with LANMAR is rather sophisticated as it takes advantage of the Link State (Fisheye) local routing procedure of LANMAR. We note however that a basic version of DFR can be retrofitted in any Distance Vector scheme, including On Demand vector schemes such as AODV.

The rest of the paper is organized in the following way. In section 2, we present the protocol DFR routing scheme in details. Intensive performance evaluations are presented in section 3 and then we present conclusions in section 4.

2.   "DIRECTION" FORWARDING PROTOCOL

2.1   Direction forwarding computation

In direction forwarding we apply the Distance Vector concept, and each intermediate node selects the predecessor with minimum hop distance. The main difference: the intermediate node saves not only the ID, but also the "direction" to the predecessor on the path. If there is only one update with minimum hop distance to the destination, the direction to the predecessor is also the "direction" of the destination.

2.1.1   Computation of the direction to the predecessor

The computation of the direction implies that a node knows the coordinates of a predecessor. Once a node receives an update for a destination with min hop distance from a neighbor as a predecessor, the node simply reads the GPS coordinates in the packet header or consults a cache named "Neighbor coordinates cache" to get the coordinates of the predecessor. If GPS is not available, a virtual coordinate system is used. The

Neighbor coordinates cache is maintained with information extracted from local routing update packets. The "direction" to the predecessor is computed based on the node's current coordinates (X_1, Y_1) and the predecessor coordinates (X_2, Y_2). From elementary geometry we get:

$$r = \sqrt{(X_2 - X_1)^2 + (Y_2 - Y_1)^2}$$

$$\theta = \tan^{-1}(\frac{Y_2 - Y_1}{X_2 - X_1}) \qquad\qquad (1, 2)$$

In this polar coordinate space the node is at the origin point. The radial coordinate r is the distance from the node to the predecessor and the polar angle θ is the radian from the x-axis that is used as the direction of the predecessor node.

2.1.2   Update the direction to a destination

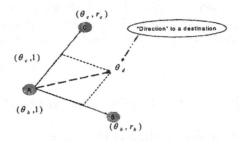

Figure 1. Computation of the "direction"

A node may receive more than one distance vector update packet from different "predecessors" with same hop distance and sequence number for the same destination. Thus, we need to aggregate the updates to get an accurate direction of the destination. To illustrate the procedure, in Figure 1, first, node A gets a distance vector update from node B for destination D and computes the forwarding direction θ_b by using the equation (1, 2). Later, node A gets another update from node C and computes a new forwarding direction θ_c. The two directions can be combined by using the addition of unit vectors $(\theta_b, 1)$ and $(\theta_c, 1)$ leading to:

$$\theta_d = \frac{\theta_b + \theta_c}{2}$$

Here, order of addition does not matter since unit vectors are used to combine the "directions". If a distance vector update packet with a new sequence number or same sequence number but smaller hop distance to the destination is received, the direction of the destination will be reset.

2.2 Packet Forwarding Procedure

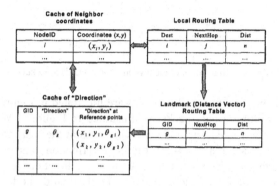

Figure 2. Illustration of the cache and routing tables

In this subsection, we describe in detail the routing tables and caches maintained at each node and the procedure of data packet forwarding. After DFR computation is performed, each node will have one neighbor coordinates cache, one "Direction" cache, and two routing tables (local and Landmark). The neighbor coordinates cache keeps the coordinates of all its neighbors within its scope as discovered by the local link state routing protocol. The "Direction" cache keeps the direction to all remote nodes (i.e. Landmarks) computed from DV update and from neighbor coordinates cache. This cache is refreshed and its entries are expired after a pre-specified timeout. The refresh time of these entries is related to the mobility of the neighbors. If the nodes seldom change their position, long refresh time can be used, the "Direction" cache is not so frequently refreshed. The two routing tables - Local proactive and Landmark- provide complete routing information i.e., "direction" to all destination nodes. The local routing table is built by the local scoped proactive routing protocol (e.g. Fisheye in our implementation). It provides the exact routing information to any nodes within the local scope of current node. The landmark distance vector routing table contains routing information to all landmark nodes as discovered through propagated landmark distance vectors.

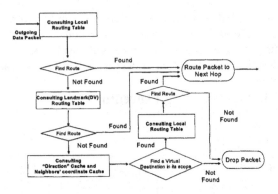

Figure 3. Illustration of the procedure to route data packets

The two caches and two routing tables are illustrated in Figure 2, and the procedure for routing a data packet is illustrated in Figure 3. When a data packet needs to be routed, the node will first consult the local routing table as it provides accurate and up-to-date routing information to nearby nodes. If a route is found and the next hop is along the "direction" to the packet destination, the packet is routed directly. If the destination node is a remote node not in the local routing table, the node then checks the DV routing table for an available next-hop for the destination node. If a next-hop exists, then the packet is routed towards the landmark node of that group via the landmark routing table. Once the packet reaches the remote group, it will then be forwarded via the local routing table either by that landmark node or any other node in the same group. If there is no next-hop for the destination, then the "direction" cache is used for forwarding the packet.

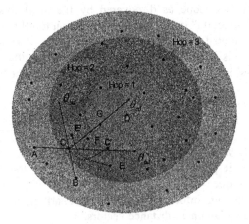

Figure 4. "Direction" Forwarding method

Most geo-routing protocols select the most forward node within radius (MFR) closest to the packet's destination as a next hop. In DFR, the selection of the most forward node along the "direction" to the destination may lead to a loop. Consider the situation in Figure 4. Suppose node A has data packets destined for node D. Now, the predecessor of node A, C has moved to C'; note that C was also the predecessor of node B. Node A finds that node B is the most forward node according to DFR direction, and transmits to B. Once the data packet is received at node B, node B computes the "directional" next hop to D and sends the data packets back to node A. Thus, a loop is formed between node A and node B. To avoid such loops, we have modified our scheme for finding the next "direction" hop by using a "virtual destination" method. Basically, we do "look ahead" i.e., we look at the direction computed by the predecessor in the previous hop. When Node A gets a distance vector routing update from a predecessor, say node C, node A consults the Cache of Neighbor Coordinates to get node C's current location and saves the location as a reference point. Also, node A saves the "previous hop" direction to destination D that was computed at the predecessor node C (the information is piggybacked in the distance vector update packet from C). In Figure 4 that would be the direction from C to G. When a next-hop to destination D is needed at node A, first, node A finds a 2-hop neighbor as a "virtual destination" which is the most forward node originating from the reference point (i.e. location of C) in the direction from C to D. Then, node A uses the virtual destination to find a next-hop to the destination by consulting its local routing table. If more than one reference point exist (i.e., other predecessors besides C), node A computes a virtual destination for each reference point. Then node A selects an optimal virtual destination that is the most forward node within radius among all computed virtual destinations. Back to the example in Figure 4, the virtual destination from A is node G, and the next hop is node E'. Directional forwarding will fail when there is no neighbor left in the desired direction. This occurrence however is unlikely if the network is reasonably dense and a node has at least six neighbors on average.

3. PERFORMANCE EVALUATION

3.1 Simulation Environment

We use QualNet® simulator [1], a packet level simulator to evaluate the proposed DFR routing scheme. The main purpose is to verify its scalability and flexibility in various scenarios. In our simulations, standard IEEE 802.11 radios are adopted with a channel rate of 2Mbps and transmission range of

367 meters. Randomly generated UDP based Constant Bit Rate (CBR) traffic is used for evaluation. The CBR traffic pairs are spread randomly over the network. The number of source-destination pairs is varied in the simulations from 20 pairs to 80 pairs thus varying the offered traffic load. The size of data payload is 512 bytes and the inter-arrival time of the data packets on each source/destination connection is 1 second to model an interactive environment. The routing protocol selected for comparison is the original LANMAR routing, which has been proved to deliver outstanding performance in large scalable MANETS [13][14].

3.2   Comparison with Original LANMAR

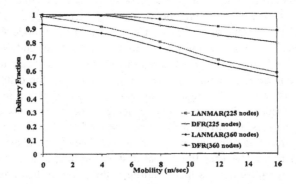

Figure 5. Delivery ratio vs. speed (including packets lost due to disconnected destination)

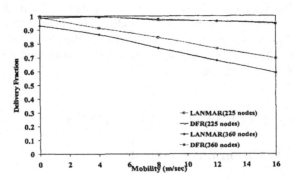

Figure 6. Delivery ratio vs. speed (excluding packets lost due to disconnected destination)

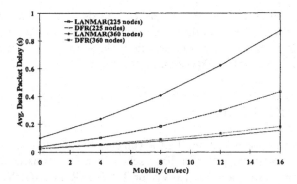

Figure 7. Average data packet delay vs. speed

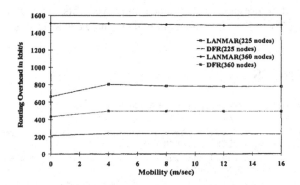

Figure 8. Routing overhead(per node) vs. speed

In this set of experiments, we investigate the scalability of the DFR scheme under various network sizes and movement speeds. We fix the number of CBR pairs as 40 per experiment. We run simulations with two different network sizes (225 nodes and 360 nodes) to see the impact of size on performance. For the larger network size, we keep the network field size as 2250 by 2250 meters. The simulation results are presented from Figure 5 to Figure 8.

First, let us compare Figure 5 and Figure 6. In Figure 5, there is no distinction between packet delivery failure due to routing failure and topology disconnection. The latter clearly is not the responsibility of routing. We have run another experiment in which for each packet dropped by the simulator, we have checked whether the destination was connected or not, and have not counted the drop in the latter case. The results in Figure 5 show, when the network disconnected cases are discounted, that DFR is above 95% delivery even for 15 m/sec speeds. This is an enormous improvement with respect to the conventional LANMAR that delivers only 60% in a 225 node topology! Remarkable is the lower delay (see Figure 7) due to lower overhead (see Figure 8).

4.   CONCLUSIONS

In this paper we have identified a vulnerability to high motion in the conventional "predecessor forwarding" scheme used in virtually all popular routing schemes, such as Distance Vector, LANMAR and AODV. We have proposed a more robust forwarding scheme called DFR (Direction Forwarding), which is based on direction of arrival (of the updates) rather than on predecessor ID. We have tested the new scheme on LANMAR and have reported impressive performance improvements. The delivery ratio jumps from 60% to 95% in a moderately dense network at 15 m/s.

REFERENCES

[1]   Qualnet simulator. Available at http://www.qualnet.com.

[2]   T. Clausen and P. Jacquet. Optimized link state routing protocol (OLSR). RFC 3626, Oct. 2003.

[3]   S. R. Das, C. E. Perkins, and E. M. Royer. Performance comparison of two on-demand routing protocols. Proceedings of IEEE INFOCOM'00, Mar. 2000.

[4]   M. Gerla, X. Hong, and G. Pei. Landmark routing for large ad hoc wireless networks. Proceeding of IEEE GLOBECOM 2000, Nov. 2000.

[5]   A. Iwata, C.-C. Chiang, G. Pei, M. Gerla, and T.-W. Chen. Scalable routing strategies for ad-hoc wireless networks. IEEE Journal on Selected Areas in Communications (JSAC), 17(8), Aug. 1999.

[6]   D. B. Johnson and D. A. Maltz. Dynamic source routing in ad hoc wireless networks. Mobile Computing, edited by T.Imielinski and H. Korth, Chapter 5, 1996.

[7]   B. Karp and H. T. Kung. GPSR: Greedy perimeter stateless routing for wireless networks. Proceedings of ACM Mobi-Com'00, Aug. 2000.

[8]   Y. B. Ko and N. H. Vaidya. Location-aided routing (LAR) in mobile ad hoc networks. Proceedings of ACM/IEEE MOBICOM98, Oct. 1998.

[9]   R. Ogier, F. Templin, and M. Lewis. Topology dissemination based on reverse-path forwarding (TBRPF). Internet Draf draft-ietf-manet-tbrpf-11.txt, Oct. 2003.

[10]   G. Pei, M. Gerla, and T. W. Chen. Fisheye state routing in mobile ad hoc networks. Proceeding of ICDCS 2000 workshops, Apr. 2000.

[11]   C. Perkins and P. Bhagwat. Highly dynamic destinationsequenced distance-vector routing (DSDV) for mobile computers. Proceeding of the ACM SIGCOMM'94, Sep. 1994.

[12]   C. E. Perkins and E. M. Royer. Ad-hoc on-demand distance vector routing. Proceedings of IEEE WMCSA'99, Feb. 1999.

[13]   G. Pei, M. Gerla and X. Hong, "LANMAR: Landmark Routing for Large Scale Wireless Ad-Hoc Networks with Group Mobility," in Proceedings of IEEE/ACM MobiHOC"00, Aug. 2000.

[14]   X. Hong, M. Gerla, Y. Yi, K, Xu, and T. Kwon, "Scalable Ad Hoc Routing in Large, Dense Wireless Networks Using Clustering and Landmarks," in Proceedings of ICC 2002, April 2002.

[15]   Y Lee, J. Chen, B. Zhou, M. Gerla, & Antonio Caruso. "'Direction' forwarding for highly mobile, large scale ad hoc networks" (full version), Technical Report TR050026, CSD, UCLA, 05.

EXTENDING THE COVERAGE OF A 4G TELECOM NETWORK USING HYBRID AD-HOC NETWORKS: A CASE STUDY

Tânia Calçada[1], and Manuel Ricardo[1,2]

[1]*INESC Porto* *
http://www.inescporto.pt
Porto, Portugal
tcalcada@inescporto.pt

[2]*Fac. Eng. Univ. Porto*
Porto, Portugal
mricardo@inescporto.pt

Abstract   Ad-hoc networks that are connected with the infrastructure Internet are named hybrid ad-hoc networks. In 4G communications scenarios, hybrid ad-hoc networks seem to be valuable since they may increase the coverage of wireless networks with minor costs. Using them, terminals out of range of an access point or a base station, or not having adequate network interfaces, may reach the operator's infrastructure via other terminals. This paper presents a hybrid ad-hoc network solution and a testbed implementation.

Keywords: Hybrid Ad-hoc Networks, 4G, Gateway Discovery Protocols

1.   Introduction

AD-HOC networks can be used to enable infrastructureless and spontaneous communications between nodes. In an ad-hoc network each terminal behaves as a router, forwarding traffic (IP packets, in this case) to other terminals. In

*The work described in this paper is based on results of IST FP6 Integrated Project DAIDALOS (http://www.ist-daidalos.org/). DAIDALOS receives research funding from the European Community's Sixth Framework Programme. Apart from this, the European Commission has no responsibility for the content of this paper. This paper may contain forward-looking statements relating to advanced information and communication technologies. Neither the DAIDALOS project consortium nor the European Community does accept any responsibility or liability for any use made of the information provided in this paper. We acknowledge the financial support of FCT (Fundação para a Ciência e Tecnologia) / POSI (Portuguese Science and Technology Foundation).

hybrid ad-hoc networks [Ruffino et al., 2005] the ad-hoc nodes can also communicate with an infrastructure network either directly or via other nodes, in a multi-hop topology.

The operator of a 4th Generation communications network will deploy IP access networks which offer connectivity to wired and wireless nodes. These nodes are miniaturized computers supporting multiple network interfaces (e.g. GPRS, UMTS, 802.11, Ethernet and DVB), and having communications capabilities analogous to a computer interconnected to the Internet. By using the hybrid network concept, the 4G networks can extend their coverage to shadow areas where it would be expensive or unfeasible to have radio coverage provided by base stations.

This paper presents a solution for deploying an hybrid ad-hoc network based in IPv6. A real prototype is described, that uses a reactive ad-hoc routing protocol and a proactive gateway discovery protocol. Combined, they optimize the interconnection from the operator's perspective.

The Section 2 of this paper describes the goals, requirements, and assumptions of this work. Section 3 presents the state-of-the-art in ad-hoc gateway discovery protocols. Section 4 proposes a solution. Section 5 gives the details about the prototype implementation. Section 6 addresses the issues open in the solution and required to be solved. The Section 7 concludes this paper.

2.   Goals, Requirements and Assumptions

The main goal of this work is to provide mobile terminals located in shadow areas, or having inadequate radio interfaces, with access to an operator infrastructured network, assuming that IPv6 is used. More than providing efficient communications within ad-hoc networks, this work aims at providing an efficient interconnection between an ad-hoc mobile node and the operator infrastructure.

The main requirements are (1) low signalling overhead, (2) resilience, and (3) support of operator driven policies. Ad-hoc networks demand routing protocols and interworking mechanisms having low signalling overheads, for good efficiency. Multiple gateways to the infrastructured network shall be supported, in order to eliminate single points of failure, balance traffic, and provide multipath connections. The infrastructured network shall have full control of communications, in order to enable security, QoS, and charging policies.

The scenario envisaged is the extension of the operator's network coverage to nodes only reachable via the ad-hoc network, and it is shown in Figure 1. Traffic flows are expected mainly between ad-hoc and infrastructure connected nodes. A few tens of nodes are expected in a single ad-hoc network.

The ad-hoc point of attachment to the infrastructured network is the gateway. The gateway forwards packets between ad-hoc and infrastructure nodes, and can be a mobile node or a fixed access router. Many functions are expected to be deployed in the gateway, such as QoS mapping, node authentication, charging, and security. In an operator driven scenario, the gateway shall preferably be a fixed access router, which is owned, managed, and trusted by the network operator.

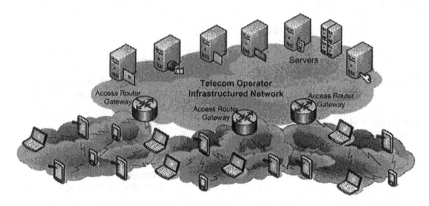

Figure 1.   Ad-hoc as an extension of the operator's infrastructure network. Three hybrid ad-hoc networks provide access to mobile nodes.

3.   Ad-Hoc Gateway Discovery Protocols

A gateway discovery protocol provides the node with Internet connectivity, that is, it enables the node to discover the address of the gateway, defines the mechanism to forward a packet towards the gateway, and may also auto-configure a globally routable address.

A gateway discovery protocol may be proactive or reactive. In the proactive mode, the gateway spreads periodically information through the ad-hoc network; this is useful if a node communicates frequently with the infrastructured network. In the reactive mode, a node requests the gateway information and the network prefix when it needs to communicate with the infrastructured network; this is useful when ad-hoc nodes communicate between them and, occasionally, access the Internet. The operation mode of the gateway discovery protocol may be selected considering the traffic scenarios, just like a routing protocol; however, these choices shall be independent.

A study of some gateway discovery protocols exists in the literature [Ghassemian et al., 2004]. However we will focus on gateway discovery protocols currently available at IETF as internet drafts [Jelger et al., 2005], [Wakikawa et al., 2003], [Cha et al., 2004], and [Cha et al., 2003]. Two of them deserve special attention: GwInfo [Jelger et al., 2005], and Global6 [Wakikawa et al.,

2003]. These methods are described in next sub-sections and are compared in Table 1. The methods presented in [Cha et al., 2004] and [Cha et al., 2003] are excluded since they are dedicated to AODV [Perkins et al., 2003]. Although AODV was the routing protocol selected for our test-bed, we require that the gateway discovery protocol works with other routing protocols.

Table 1. Evaluation of gateway discovery protocols

	GwInfo	*Global6*
Operation Mode	Proactive	Proactive, with proactive routing Reactive, with reactive routing
Routing Protocol Compatibility	Any Tests made with OLSR	Any Tests and examples with AODV
Signaling	GwInfo messages	Extended AODV routing protocol messages Extended NDP messages
Multiple Gateway Support	Possible, but node uses one GW at time Mentioned multihoming Selection algorithms specified	Possible with restrictions Selection algorithms not specified
Packet Forwarding Towards the Gateway	Prefix continuity Next hop forwarding Default route on proactive routing	Default route via the gateway Routing extension header

GwInfo

Similarly to IPv6, the GwInfo [Jelger et al., 2005] protocol forces the gateway to announce periodically a network prefix. The method supports multiple gateways, which announce different global network prefixes. An ad-hoc node may listen announces from multiple gateways. In order to select one of them, some algorithms are proposed based on metrics such as distance to the gateway, or stability (keep the network prefix as long as possible). The method is independent of the underlying routing protocol, and it can be used with proactive and reactive routing protocols.

Each gateway broadcasts periodically an advertisement message whose destination is a link local multicast address, reaching 1 hop distant nodes. This message carries the gateway address, the network prefix length, and the distance to the gateway. When a node receives this message, it may decide to use the prefix announced. In this case, the node configures a global address, using the network prefix information received and its 64-bit interface ID; then, the node updates its hop count, and multicasts the message again to its one hop neighbours.

The node that delivered the prefix information is named upstream neighbour. Even in the presence of multiple network prefixes, the prefix selection policy and the propagation method lead to the concept of "prefix continuity". The prefix continuity property ensures that all nodes on the path to the gateway have the same network prefix and, together, they form a tree towards the gateway.

When used with proactive routing protocols (e.g. OLSR [Clausen and Jacquet, 2003]), each node creates a default route which uses its upstream neighbour as the next hop; the prefix continuity property avoids the use of an IPv6 routing header, if the link to the upstream neighbour is bi-directional. When used with reactive routing protocols (e.g. AODV [Perkins et al., 2003]), the periodic announcement message is not used to add a default route, since a default route is said to be incompatible with the reactive routing paradigm; in alternative, the route to the gateway can be obtained using the route lookup method of the routing protocol. GwInfo has been tested with OLSR.

Global6

The Global6 [Wakikawa et al., 2003] protocol provides two solutions, proactive and reactive, which shall be combined with proactive and reactive routing protocols, respectively. The proactive solution disseminates periodically gateway advertisements to all nodes in the ad-hoc network; the reactive solution uses solicitation and advertisement messages, which are exchanged between a node and the gateway. The Neighbour Discovery Protocol or the routing protocol messages are extended in order to support the solicitation and advertisement information.

After accepting an advertisement from a gateway, the node configures a routable IP address using the network prefix announced and its 64-bit interface ID; then, the node creates a default route using the gateway as the next hop, and a host route to the gateway using the routing protocol. The packets for the infrastructure network are, thus, forwarded to the gateway and may carry out a routing header containing the gateway address and the address of the infrastructure destination node. If allowed by the routing protocol, hop-by-hop forwarding can also be used but, in this case, there is no guarantee that the correct gateway is used. If Mobile IPv6 is used, the node can use the address acquired as its care-of-address. Global6 is said to be independent of the routing protocol, but the implementations known are integrated only with AODV.

4.   Proposed Solution

In order to carry out our experience we used an ad-hoc routing protocol, a gateway discovery protocol, and an interface between them.

Several routing protocols have been proposed for mobile ad-hoc networks during the last years. AODV [Perkins et al., 2003] was the routing protocol selected for our experience, since it fits well in the scenario envisioned: small ad-hoc networks, some node mobility, and most of the flows destined to infrastructure nodes. AODV has reduced control traffic when compared with pro-active protocols, but increases the latency when new routes are required. This increase is mostly caused by the discovery and update of the routes which are created and maintained when needed.

The gateway discovery protocol selected was the GwInfo protocol. Prefix continuity is a relevant characteristic of this solution since it enables the creation of topologically coherent networks. From the operator management perspective, an organized network is preferable; that is, users take advantage of the ad-hoc facilities, but the operator still has an organized network. Another benefit of prefix continuity is that it enables hop-by-hop default routing, and does not demand an additional routing header mentioning the gateway. The proactive nature of the GwInfo protocol, even when combined with reactive routing protocols, is also an advantage from the operator's perspective. Using it, the operator announces itself and its gateway, and may force the node to authenticate, even before this node needs to communicate. As consequences, the operator becomes aware of the node's location, and the other ad-hoc nodes may start using the recently authenticated node to forward their packets. The GwInfo method can interact with any routing protocol, which is an advantage when comparing with the other methods. Although Global6 also supports every routing protocol, its operation mode follows the proactive or reactive nature of the routing protocol.

The GwInfo protocol running on an operator access router (the gateway) sends periodically the advertisement message through the ad-hoc network; when receiving this information, a node may configure a default route. AODV is a reactive routing protocol, so it does not maintain an extensive routing table to all the nodes in the ad-hoc network, and it should not have a default route. In order to AODV interoperate with the GwInfo protocol, it must suffer some modifications. A possibility would be not to use the default route and to forward internet packets directly to the gateway relying on a path accumulation paradigm [Perkins et al., 2004] on the route discovery. Another solution is to change the forwarding table lookup process. When a node has a packet to send or forward, it first checks if the destination address is outside the ad-hoc network. If the destination address has the same network prefix of the source node, then AODV finds a route as it usually does. Otherwise, the node forwards the packet through the default route, which uses the node's upstream neighbour as next hop. The solution is not optimal for routing between ad-hoc nodes associated to different gateways and using different network prefixes, since the packets must visit the two gateways; however, this is not a big problem since the communications towards the gateway are expected to be the most frequent. This method is simple, and it has low overheads when compared with the first possibility.

5. Implementation And Validation

A prototype was implemented in order to validate the solution advocated in last section. This prototype, shown in Figure 2, consists of a gateway (GW), 3 ad-hoc nodes (MN1, MN2, and MN3), and a computer in the infrastructure network (Server). The nodes are laptops and the gateway is a desktop, all running Mandrake 10.0 Linux, and equipped with wireless LAN cards (Cisco Aironet 350 series) configured in ad-hoc mode. The nodes and the gateway run AODV, based on the UU-AODV [1]; changes were made to this implementation, in order to support IPv6 addressing and to run on kernel version 2.6. The nodes and the gateway also run the GwInfo protocol implementation [2]. In order to let the GwInfo and the AODV modules interoperate, the modification in the forwarding table lookup process described above was implemented in the AODV code. The information about the selected network prefix is passed from the GwInfo module to the AODV module using UNIX sockets.

The tests using these equipments were made indoors, all computers in the same room, with all the WLAN cards configured with the same ESSID. For that reason, the powers transmitted enabled every computer to reach all the others. In order to overcome this situation, and simulate an ad-hoc environment, MAC filtering was implemented using the ip6tables tool of the Linux distribution.

The initial configuration of the network is presented on the top of Figure 2 and the messages exchanged by the GwInfo modules are shown just below. The GWINFO message is propagated hop-by-hop, and each node receiving the message (1) configures a global address (MN1 - 20::A, MN2 - 20::B, and MN3 - 20::C), (2) configures a default route using the network information received, and (3) informs the AODV module about the ad-hoc network prefix. The AODV HELLO messages are exchanged between neighbours who are used to create host routes to adjacent neighbours in each node forwarding table; in order to simplify the figure, the HELLO messages are not represented. After these steps, the forwarding tables of the nodes have the information shown in

---

[1] AODV-UU v0.8 implementation from Uppsala University by E. Nordstrom and H. Lundgren
[2] GWINFO implementation from Université Louis Pasteur - LSIIT by A. Frey

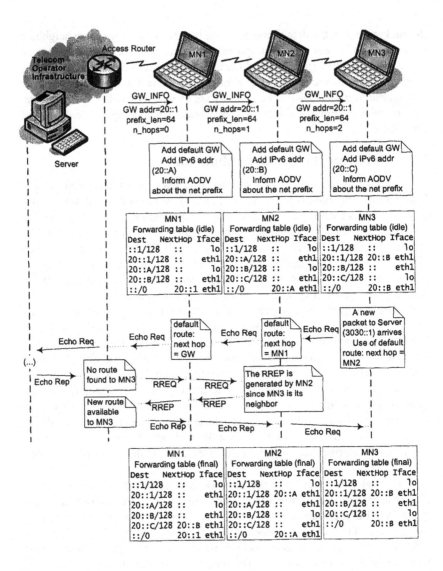

Figure 2.   Prototype of the Ad-hoc Integration Scenario and messages exchanged. The tested scenario is shown on top. Initial messages and actions, and the resulting forwarding tables of the mobile nodes are shown in the middle of the figure. On the bottom we present the forwarding tables when data packets are sent between an ad-hoc node and a server located in the infrastructure network.

the center of Figure 2. Entries to link local and multicast addresses are hidden, since they are irrelevant for this discussion; the route for 20::/64 is also hidden since it is never used.

The AODV implementation intercepts every outbound packet and compares its destination network prefix with the one delivered by the GwInfo module. If its destination address belongs to the ad-hoc network, in this case 20::/64, the packet is retained until a host route is found; the other packets are released immediately, i.e. queued in the Linux IPQueue, and follow the default route.

In order to show the network behavior and the interoperation between GwInfo and AODV, a simple experience is described; having all the nodes configured as shown in Figure 2, MN3 will ping the Server in the infrastructure network. To ping, consists in sending a set of ICMP Echo Request packets and receiving ICMP Echo reply packets. The bottom of Figure 2 describes this communication. The source of the first packet is MN3; since the network prefix of the destination address is different from 20::/64, the default route is used to forward the packet in each ad-hoc node in the path towards the gateway. When the ICMP Echo Reply message, sent by Server to MN3, arrives to the gateway and there is no host route to it, the conventional AODV route lookup is started: RREQ messages are propagated hop-by-hop and the MN2, which already has a route to MN3, sends a RREP back to the gateway. In this process, MN1 also learns the route to MN3. Then, the ICMP Echo Reply message is sent hop-by-hop to MN3.

6. Future Work

Many issues related to this topic need to be further investigated, which include: 1) a multiple gateway solution, capable of integrating the GwInfo protocol and multi-homing; 2) handover between gateways, keeping context information such as charging, authentication, and QoS; 3) improve the routing between ad-hoc networks holding different prefixes; 4) support the node automatic "handover" between infrastructure and ad-hoc modes; 5) secure the GwInfo protocol; 6) support multiple L2 technologies; 7) port the solution for PDAs and mobile phones.

7. Conclusions

In this paper we proposed a solution for integrating ad-hoc with IPv6 infrastructure networks. For that purpose, we carefully characterized the state of the art in gateway discovery protocols. Based on previously identified requirements, we proposed a solution which consists in integrating GwInfo with AODV, and in introducing modifications on the forwarding table look up mechanism: for a host route not in the forwarding table, AODV is used only when the packet destination address belongs to the ad-hoc network prefix; otherwise, a route via the nodet's upstream neighbour is used. In order to demonstrate the value of this solution, we implemented a prototype network and carried out meaningful experiments.

Acknowledgments

The authors wish to thank Eng. Filipe Abrantes for his valuable help on the implementation work, and Dr. Norbert Vicari for porting the AODV implementation to IPv6.

References

Cha, Hyun-Wook, Park, Jung-Soo, and Kim, Hyoung-Jun (2003). Extended support for global connectivity for ipv6 mobile ad hoc networks. Internet-draft, IETF.

Cha, Hyun-Wook, Park, Jung-Soo, and Kim, Hyoung-Jun (2004). Support of internet connectivity for aodv. Internet-draft, IETF.

Clausen, T. and Jacquet, P. (2003). Optimized link state routing protocol (olsr). RFC 3626, IETF.

Ghassemian, Mona, Hofmann, Philipp, Prehofer, Christian, Friderikos, Vasilis, and Aghvami, Hamid (2004). Performance analysis of internet gateway discovery protocols in ad hoc networks. In *WCNC 2004*.

Jelger, C., Noel, T., and Frey, A. (2005). Gateway and address autoconfiguration for ipv6 adhoc networks. Internet-draft, IETF.

Perkins, C., Belding-Royer, E., and Das, S. (2003). Ad hoc on-demand distance vector (aodv) routing. RFC 3561, IETF.

Perkins, Charles E., Belding-Royer, Elizabeth M., and Chakeres, Ian D. (2004). Ad hoc on-demand distance vector (aodv) routing. Internet-Draft draft-perkins-manet-aodvbis, IETF.

Ruffino, S., Stupar, P., Clausen, T., and Singh, S. (2005). Connectivity scenarios for manet. Internet-Draft draft-ruffino-manet-autoconf-scenarios-00.txt, IETF.

Wakikawa, Ryuji, Malinen, Jari T., Perkins, Charles E., Nilsson, Anders, and Tuominen, Antti J. (2003). Global connectivity for ipv6 mobile ad hoc networks. Internet-draft, IETF.

INTEGRATION OF MOBILE-IPV6 AND OLSR FOR INTER-MONET COMMUNICATIONS

Ines b. Hamida[1], Hakim Badis[1,2], Lila Boukhatem[1] and Khaldoun Alagha[1,2]

[1] *LRI Laboratory, University of Paris XI*
Orsay, France

[2] *INRIA Laboratory*
Rocquencourt, France
{badis, benhamida, boukhatem, alagha}-@lri.fr

Abstract

Trends in fourth generation (4G) wireless networks are clearly identified by the *full-IP* concept where all traffic (data, control, voice and video services, etc.) will be transported in IP packets. MObile NETwork (MONET) is a group of mobile nodes moving together as a unit. Such groups are common characteristics of the vehicular environments, for example train and buses (which are attractive because of the high concentration of passengers on these vehicles). This paper investigates an ad hoc networking for Inter-MONET communications and interworking between MONETs and the global Internet. We propose a hierarchical architecture: (1) integrating Mobile IPv6 and OLSR, a routing protocol for ad hoc networks, to manage universal mobility; (2) connecting this ad hoc network to Internet. The heterogeneous communication is established with the help of specific access routers, which serve as gateways. We describe the network scenario, its basic protocol architecture and we discuss the different practical approaches for routing. A flat and hierarchical ad hoc routing comparison is studied and performance differentials are analyzed through simulation results using varying network load and mobility.

1. Introduction

With the advances in wireless communication and mobile computing technologies, wireless multihop networking (ad hoc networking) is expected to play an important role in mobile communications beyond fourth generation systems. Because of its independence on pre-existing network infrastructure and its distributed organization, ad hoc networking enables the spontaneous establishment of communication between network-enabled electronic devices (e.g., mobile phones, personal digital assistants). Especially in applications where information must be distributed quickly and is only relevant in the area around the sender, ad hoc communications have major advantages compared to *conventional* wireless systems, such as GSM and UMTS. For example, cars involved in an accident can send warning messages back over a defined number of other vehicles, thus avoiding a motorway pileup [1]. In this vehicular scenario, we can also imagine transmission of information about bad traffic or street conditions (e.g., icy roads, obstacles), or wireless communication of closed user groups (e.g., emergency teams). A mobile ad-hoc network (MANET) [2] is a collection of nodes, which are able to connect on a wireless medium forming an arbitrary and dynamic network with *wireless links*. Implicit in this definition of a network is the fact that links, due to node mobility and other factors, may appear and disappear at any time. This in a MANET implies that the topology may be dynamic and that routing of traffic through a multi-hop path is necessary if all nodes are to be able to communicate.

A MObile NETwork (MONET) [3] is an entire network, moving as a unit, which changes its point of attachment to the Internet and thus its reachability in the topology. A MONET may be composed by one or more IP-subnets and is connected to the global Internet via one or more Mobile Routers (MR). Cases of mobile networks include networks attached to people (Personal Area Network or PAN, i.e., a network composed by all Internet appliances carried by people, like a PDA, a mobile phone, a digital camera, a laptop, etc.) and sensor networks deployed in aircrafts, boats, busses, cars, trains, etc.

This paper addresses the ad hoc networking for Inter-MONETs and interworking between MONETs and Inernet using ad hoc routing, where we restrict our view to IPv6 [4]. The wireless multihop access network is entirely based on IP, uses the optimized Link State Routing protocol (OLSR) [5] and meets the requirements of future *full-IP* wireless networks, such as providing high-rate video, voice and data services.

In the flat routing, the routing information may be maintained regularly (called proactive or table-driven routing) or computed when needed (called reactive or on-demand routing). In the hierarchical routing, the mobile nodes (MN) are clustered into several groups. The routing information is maintained separately within a group and among groups. A typical route can be found in the group-level granularity first and then in the node-level granularity. Extensive simulations are carried out to study performance comparison of flat and hierarchical ad hoc routing for Inter-MONET.

The remainder of this paper is organized as follows: in Section 2, we give an overview of the MONET terminology. We present in Section 3 our proposed architecture for mobility management. Different routing and addressing mechanisms are discussed and compared in Section 4. Performance results are presented in section 5. Finally, Section 6 concludes this paper and defines topics for further research.

2.   Mobile Network (MONET)

MONET is a network that changes its Internet access point. It is formed of mobile nodes called MNNs (Mobile Network Nodes) and one or more MRs (Mobile Routers). All these nodes move together as a single unit. The MR takes in charge the handover procedure. It has one or more interfaces and maintains the Internet connectivity for the entire mobile network. It gets access to the Internet through an AR (Access Router) which is an external router. A mobile network is said to be nested when another mobile network is getting attached to it. It is said multihomed when there are more then one active interface connected to the global Internet. The reader can refer to [6] for more details in terminology.

3.   Proposed architecture for mobility management

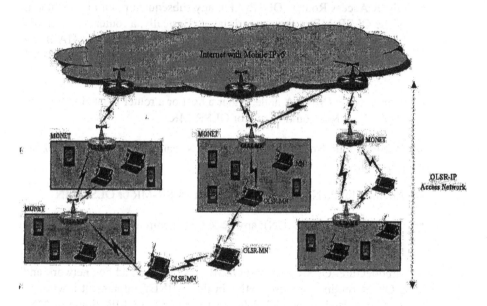

Figure 1.   Hierarchical mobility management

The proposed architecture is depicted in Figure 1. An OLSR-IP access network constitutes an IP subnetwork and its interconnected to the Internet via an OLSR Access Router (OLSR-AR). The motion of a Mobile Router (MR) inside an OLSR-IP access network is managed by the OLSR protocol and the Mobile Node (MN) inside the MONET by a wireless LAN. Mobility between different OLSR-IP access networks or IP subnetworks is managed by Mobile-IPv6.

An OLSR-IP access network consists of a random topology of ad hoc moving networks. In our MONET, an OLSR Mobile Router (OLSR-MR) provides connectivity between MONETs and OLSR-ARs. We can find more then one OLSR-MR per MONET.

The architecture is composed of several functional entities:

☞ Home Agent (HA): a Router in the MN's home network.

☞ OLSR Mobile Router (OLSR-MR): a router which changes its point of attachment to the Internet. The OLSR-MR has one or more egress interface(s) and one or more ingress interface(s) and acts as the gateway between the mobile network and the rest of the Internet. The OLSR-MR implements the OLSR protocol.

☞ OLSR Access Router (OLSR-AR): any subsequent point of attachment of the OLSR-MR at the network layer. Basically, a router on the home link or the foreign link. It can also implement the role of a HA if the OLSR-IP access network is the home network. Furthermore, OLSR-AR implements the OLSR protocol.

☞ Mobile Node (MN): A node, either a host or a router located within the MONET. A MN could be any of OLSR-MR.

☞ OLSR Mobile Node (OLSR-MN): a MN that can implement the OLSR protocol.

☞ Ad hoc Mobile Node (ad hoc MNs): an OLSR-MR or OLSR-MN.

☞ Correspondent Node (CN): any node that is communicating with one or more MN.

In our architecture, OLSR-ARs and OLSR-MNs form an ad hoc network and use the OLSR routing protocol. MNs in the MONET implement a wireless LAN, and connected to the global Internet via its OLSR-MR. Some of MNs which are the OLSR-MNs implement the OLSR protocol and have a routing table. An OLSR-MR can exchange information directly with its OLSR-MRs neighbors. If an ad hoc MN has no OLSR-AR and OLSR-MR as neighbor, it can connect to the Internet by an OLSR-MN. Any OLSR-MN that belongs to the MONET, connects to its OLSR-MR using the OLSR protocol.

4.   Routing and addressing in OLSR-IP access network

This section describes and compares different approaches for flat and hierarchical routing in our heterogeneous scenario.

4.1 Flat Routing

Let us first consider the case in which a flat routing protocol is used in our architecture (Figure 3). Such protocol regards the ad hoc network as a number of nodes without subnet partitioning. The communication in this environment can be categorized into two scenarios: (1) routing between an Internet host and a MN and (2) routing between two MNs with the same OLSR-AR or with different OLSR-ARs.

With the OLSR protocol, an ad hoc MN (OLSR-MR or OLSR-MN) senders should have an entry for the destination in its routing table, which is either a route in ad hoc network or a link to the default OLSR-AR if the destination is not reachable through the ad hoc network.

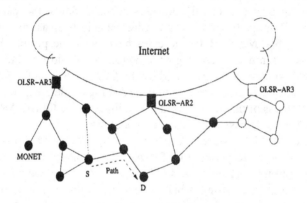

Figure 2. Flat routing in the OLSR-IP access network

Communication btw. An ad hoc MN and Internet host. After obtaining a route to the destination, an ad hoc MN can tunnel IPv6 packets through the ad hoc network to the OLSR-AR, which then forwards them to the Internet host. There are two methods to realize this tunneling. One method is that the ad hoc MN encapsulates each IPv6 packet (i.e., they add an ad hoc header with the OLSR-AR as destination). Another method is possible, the sending ad hoc MN uses the IPv6 extension header. The routing extension of this header contains the final destination address, i.e., the address of the Internet host, and the destination field of the IPv6 header contains the final destination the OLSR-AR address. Only an ad hoc MN with an IP address mentioned in the destination field of the IPv6 header of an IPv6 packet can examine the routing header of this packet [4]. The home destination option of Mobile IPv6 is used to inform the correspondent IP host about the home address of the ad hoc MN. The OLSR-AR decapsulates the incoming packets from the ad hoc MN, or it reads the routing header and puts the address of the IP host into the destination field of the IPv6 header. The resulting packet is then routed through the Internet to the IP host.

We now consider traffic from the CN to the ad hoc MN. If the CN knows the care-of address of the ad hoc MN, it puts ad hoc MN's care-of address in the IPv6 destination address field and the ad hoc MN's home address in the routing header of the routing IP packet. If the CN has no binding information about the ad hoc MN, it sends a usual IPv6 packet the ad hoc MN's home address. The home agent intercepts this packet and must tunnel it to the ad hoc MN's current care-of address using IPv6 encapsulation. In the remaining routing process, we can distinguish two design options:

- All ad hoc MNs of a single subnet have been assigned the same care-of address from the OLSR-AR, e.g., by stateful autocongiguration. The OLSR-AR possesses two IP addresses: a home address the identifies the OLSR-AR uniquely and a second address that is given as care-of address to the ad hoc MNs. Both addresses have the same prefix. With this address assignment, incoming IP packets that are addressed to an MN's care-of address can be processed by the OLSR-AR, i.e., the OLSR-AR can decapsulate packets or examine the routing header, respectively. The home address of the MNs is used in routing, i.e., the OLSR-AR uses the MN's home address as the destination address.
- Each ad hoc MN has been assigned a different care-of address with the prefix of the corresponding OLSR-AR using stateful or stateless auto-configuration (this is in our case). This address or the home address can be used in ad hoc routing, where the location information of the care-of address is not used. The content of packets from the ad hoc MN to an IP host (outgoing traffic) is the same as in the previous case. In case of in-coming traffic, the OLSR-AR does not decapsulate packets or examines routing headers that are addressed to the care-of address of ad hoc MNs.

Communication btw. Ad hoc MNs.   In order to send an IPv6 packet to another ad hoc MN in the ad hoc network, the ad hoc MN originates an IPv6 packet with the address the destination ad hoc MN in the IPv6 header. No IPv6 routing header is required in this case.

4.2   Hierarchical Routing with Care-of address

Using hierarchical routing, the ad hoc network is logically separated into subnets (i.e., cluster) (Figure 4). When an ad hoc MN receives a packet, it checks the destination address. If itself is the destination, it processes the packet for further operation. If the ad hoc MN is not the destination and the prefix of the source is different than its own prefix, the ad hoc MN ignores this packet. Inter-subnet information exchange is only possible via the OLSR-AR. In this case, a hierarchical address structure is also needed for routing in the ad hoc network, and therefore an ad hoc MN's care-of address is the right choice for addressing in the ad hoc routing protocol, since it contains the prefix of the OLSR-AR that a node is registered with. It is required that each ad hoc MN obtains a unique care-of address.

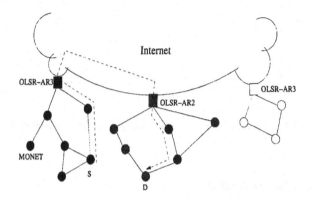

Figure 3.   Hierarchical routing in the OLSR-IP access network

If an ad hoc MN wants to send data packet to an Internet host, it knows from the prefix of the destination address that his host does not belong to its own subnet. Thus, it sends the data packets to the OLSR-AR using the OLSR protocol. Once the OLSR-AR receives the data packets, it forwards them to the Internet host.

Communication btw. Ad hoc MNs in same subnet.   if an ad hoc MN wants to communicate with another ad hoc MN that has attached to the same OLSR-AR, the ending ad hoc MN learns from the prefix of the destination's care-of address, that the destination is located in the same IP subnet (from the routing table). If the sender knows only the home address of the destination, packets will be routed to the home agent of the destination.

Communication btw. Ad hoc MNs in different subnets.   The sender learns from the IP prefix, that the destination is located in a different IP subnet. Thus, the packets are routed toward its serving OLSR-AR, and the source OLSR-AR routes the packets to the destination OLSR-AR via the fixed IP network. The destination OLSR-AR forwards the packets to the destination using the OLSR protocol.

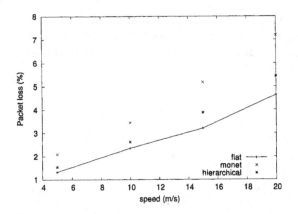

Figure 4.   Loss data packets versus mobility with 200ms as interarrival

5.   Simulation results

Figure 4 shows the results of our simulation in which the data packets sent and lost plotted against the increasing speed. The OLSR-MR's speed is increased from $5m/second$ ($18Km/hr$) up to $20m/second$ ($72Km/hr$).

In this simulation, 5 OLSR-MRs move in the same direction using our mobility model. All the 5 OLSR-MRs are packet-generating sources using $200ms$ as interarrival and. Each OLSR-MR source selects randomly one of the remaining OLSR-MR as a destination. The OLSR-AR range is a uniform value between $1000m$ and $2000m$, the OLSR-MR area range is $200m$. Each OLSR-MR node selects its speed and direction which remains valid for next $60seconds$. We can see that when the mobility (or speed) increases, the number of packet loss increases. This can be explained by the fact that when a node moves, it goes out of the neighborhood (OLSR-AR in MONET or OLSR-MR in MANET) of a node which may be sending it the data packets. There are about 2.1% of packets lost for monet classical routing at a mobility of $5meters/second$ (1.5% for hierarchical routing and 1.3% for flat routing). At a mobility of $20meters/second$, 7.2% of packets are lost for monet classical routing (5.4% for hierarchical routing and 4.6% for flat routing). The data packets are lost during the handover and Access router discovery latency. Flat routing has the highest packets delivered because during the OLSR-MR handover process, packets to this OLSR-MR are forwarded by one of its OLSR-MR neighbor. In Flat and Hierarchical routing mechanisms, the data packets are lost because the next-hop node is unreachable. A node keeps an entry about its neighbor in its neighbor table for about 6 seconds. If a neighbor moves which is the next-hop node in a route, the node continues to forward it the data packets considering it as a neighbor. Also, the next-hop is unreachable if there are interferences.

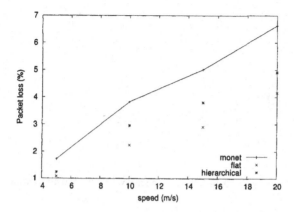

Figure 5. Loss data packets versus mobility with 400ms as interarrival

In Figure 5, we show the packet loss versus the increasing speed. We modify only the packet arrival rate using $400ms$ as interarrival parameter. The loss packet has the same behavior as that of Figure 4. However, it is clear that the packet loss in figure 5 is less than that the figure 4 (packet arrival rate used to obtain Figure 5 is less than that the figure 4).

Fig. 6 depicts end-to-end delay for both flat and hierarchical routing. Flat routing has an average delay about 130 ms. However, hierarchical routing has 300 ms. This can be explained by the fact that in flat network, the hop count number between any two ad hoc MNs is less than in hierarchical network. A low variation can be detected with increasing interarrival and speed due to the high number of ad hoc MNs.

6.   Conclusions

In this paper, we considered the Internet access of mobile devices in a wireless ad hoc network via specific access routers. We have described problems and our solution approach for access router discovery and routing. A new architecture is proposed to manage the MONET mobility using OLSR protocol. An OLSR-IP access network consists of a random topology of ad hoc moving networks. OLSR-ARs and OLSR-MNs form an ad hoc network and use the OLSR routing protocol. Simulations are carried out using an efficient simulation model to study the performance of our proposed architecture. We have shown that flat routing achieves less data packet loss and end-to-end average delay.

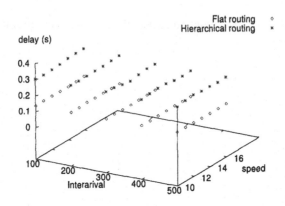

Figure 6.   Delay versus mobility and interarrival for flat and hierarchical routing

Topics for further research include the investigation of proper methods for access router selection. Furthermore, *location updating* and *multihop handover* schemes must be designed and evaluated. Also, we will propose a smooth handover with reduced packet losses.

References

[1] AW. Kellerer, C. Bettstetter, C. Schwingenschlogl, P. Sties, K.E. Steinberg and H.J. Vogel. "(Auto)Mobile communication in a heterogeneous & converged world," IEEE Personal Comm., 2001.

[2] http://www.ietf.org/html.charters/manet-charter.html.

[3] V. Devarapalli, R. Wakikawa, A. Petrescu and P. Thubert. "Network Mobility (NEMO) Basic Support Protocol," RFC 3963, 2005.

[4] S. Deering and R. Hinden. "IPv6 Specification," RFC 2460, 1998.

[5] T. Clausen and P. Jacquet. "Optimized Link State Routing Protocol," RFC 3626, 2003.

[6] T. Ernst and H. Y. Lach. "Network Mobility Support Terminology," Internet Draft, 2002.

ANALYSIS OF THE MULTI-POINT RELAY SELECTION IN OLSR AND IMPLICATIONS

Anthony Busson[1], Nathalie Mitton[2], Éric Fleury[2]

[1] *IEF - CNRS UMR 8622 - Orsay F-91405, anthony.busson@ief.u-psud.fr*
[2] *CITI/INSA Lyon - INRIA - Villeurbanne F-69621, firstname.lastname@insa-lyon.fr*

Abstract   OLSR is a promising routing protocol for multi-hop wireless networks, recently standardized by the IETF. It intensively uses the concept of MPR to minimize the routing messages and limit the harmful effects of the broadcasting in such networks. In this article, we are interested in the performances of the Multi-Point Relay selection. We analyze the mean number of selected MPR per node and their spatial distribution with a theoretical approach and simulations. Then, we discuss the implications of these results on the efficiency of a broadcasting and on the reliability of OLSR when links between nodes may fail.
keywords: ad hoc, OLSR, MPR, performances, Palm.

1.   Introduction

With the emergence of wireless technologies such as 802.11 or bluetooth, new challenges arise such as connecting wireless nodes without any infrastructure. If nodes are not in each other's radio range, packets need to be relayed by intermediate nodes which thus require forwarding capabilities and a routing protocol to find the available path to any destination. Nodes are mobile and may vanish or appear due to the wireless nature of the physical layer. The topology is thus in constant evolution. However, routing advertisements are expensive in resources since a node spends energy while transmitting as well as receiving and each message sent by a node is systematically received by all node in its transmission range. Therefore, not only the number of broadcast advertisements must be limited, but also the number of nodes which propagate them through the network. One of the recent proactive standardized protocols is OLSR (Optimized Link State Routing Algorithm) [1, 2]. Proactive routing protocols deeply rely on network broadcasting features and aim to reduce the impact of message flooding and reach scalability. In OLSR, only a subset of preselected nodes called MPR (Multi-Point Relays) are used to perform topological advertisements and to broadcast control messages. Thus, the number of emitter nodes is reduced, overhead and useless receptions of messages on nodes are minimized and the well known storm problem [3] avoided.
In this article, we are interested in the performances of the MPR selection. We

analyze the mean number of selected MPR by a single node and their spatial distribution, using a theoretical approach and simulations. We then show that the selecting algorithm is efficient for certain quantities (as *e.g.* the number of redundant packets received by a node) and that the different proposed variants always lead to very close performances (as at least 75% of the selected MPR are the same nodes whatever the selection algorithm). We also discuss the implication of the different analytical results on the reliability of the protocol.

The remaining of the paper is as follows. In Section 2, we briefly detail the OLSR protocol and the MPR selection algorithm. In Section 3, we give results about probabilities and mean quantities relative to the MPR selection algorithm. We then discuss about the implication of these results on the performances of OLSR in Section 5. Numerical results and simulations are presented in Section 4. We lastly conclude and discuss of future works in Section 6.

2.   OLSR

OLSR is a proactive routing protocol for ad-hoc networks, *i.e.*, it permanently maintains a network topology view on each node in order to provide a route as soon as needed. It uses the concept of Multi-Point Relays (MPR) to minimize the control traffic and to provide shortest routes (in number of hops) for all destination in the network. Each node chooses a subset of nodes in its neighborhood as its MPR (A MPR set is thus relative to each node) and keeps the list of its neighbors which have selected itself as a MPR. The shortest path to all possible destination is then computed from these lists, a path between two nodes being a sequence of MPR. When receiving a broadcast message M from a node u, a node v forwards it iff it is the first time v receives M and if node v is MPR of node u. This allows to reduce the number of transmitter nodes. The algorithm which allows a node u to select its MPR within its neighborhood consists in choosing nodes in such a way that the whole 2-neighborhood of u is covered by its MPR. In this way, MPR are selected in order to reach the 2-neighborhood of u in two hops from u, the k-neighborhood of u being reached within k hops. Paths are thus the shortest expected ones.

MPR selection: As the optimal MPR selection is NP-complet [7], we give here the one currently used: the Simple Greedy MPR Heuristic.

For a node u, let $N(u)$ be the neighborhood of u *e.g* the set of nodes in u's range and which share a bidirectional link with u: $v \in N(u) \Leftrightarrow u \in N(v)$. $N_2(u)$ is the 2-neighborhood of u, *e.g*, the set of nodes which are neighbors of at least one node of $N(u)$ but which do not belong to $N(u)$: $N_2(u) = \{v \text{ s.t. } \exists w \in N(u) \,|\, v \in N(w) \backslash \{u\} \cup N(u)\}$. A message sent by node u and relayed by a node $v \in N(u)$ reaches a node $w \in N_2(u) \cap N(v)$ in 2 hops.

For a node $v \in N(u)$, let $d_u^+(v)$ be the number of nodes of $N_2(u)$ which are in $N(v)$: $d_u^+(v) = |N_2(u) \cap N(v)|$. This quantity is the number of nodes of $N_2(u)$ that node u can reach in 2 hops via node v. For a node $v \in N_2(u)$, let $d_u^-(v)$ be the number of nodes of $N(u)$ which are in $N(v)$: $d_u^-(v) = |N(u) \cap N(v)|$. This quantity is the number of nodes in $N(u)$ which allow to connect nodes u and v in 2 hops. If $d_u^-(v) = 1$, there is only one node w in $N(u) \cap N(v)$ which allows to connect v and u in 2 hops. We say that v is an *isolated node* of node u. Note that "isolated nodes" are also relative to a node.

This algorithm is run at every node and selects the MPR in two steps. A node u selects in $N(u)$, a set of nodes which integrally covers $N_2(u)$. We define as $MPR(u)$ this set of MPR selected by u. $MPR(u)$ is such that: $u \cup N_2(u) \subset \bigcup_{v \in MPR(u)} N(v)$. We call $MPR_1(u) \subset MPR(u)$ the nodes that u elects at the first step. u selects as $MPR_1(u)$ the nodes which cover its isolated nodes. $MPR_1(u)$ are thus the only way to reach isolated nodes of u in 2 hops from u. Thus the first step is mandatory to totally cover $N_2(u)$ with MPR(u). At the second step, u considers the nodes in $N_2(u)$ not already covered by the $MPR_1(u)$. It chooses as MPR the node of $N(u)$ allowing to cover the maximal number of uncovered nodes of $N_2(u)$, and so on till getting $N_2(u)$ all covered. To better understand this algorithm, let's run it on the green node u on Figure 1. The isolated points of node u appear in red and $MPR_1(u)$ in blue. Node t is an isolated node as only node h allows to connect t and u in 2 hops. Node h is thus elected at the first step: $h \in MPR_1(u)$, as well as all red hatched nodes. Nodes $k, j, t, s, r, q, o, m, l$ in $N_2(u)$ are covered by them. Then, node u goes to step 2. It considers nodes of $N_2(u)$ not already covered (nodes p and n) and nodes in N_1 not selected as MPR_1 (nodes b, f, e and d). It thus only keeps the view of the topology illustrated by Figure 1(b). It first selects the node of $N(u)$ which has the highest degree on Graph 1(b): node e (e covers 2 nodes, n and p, f and d only cover one node, resp. p and n). From here, all nodes of $N_2(u)$ are covered by the selected MPR, the algorithm stops. We have: $MPR(u) = \{c, e, i, h, g\}$. Then, it is easy to see that nodes of $N(u)$ which cover "isolated nodes" must be included into the set of MPR if we want to integrally cover the $N_2(u)$, whatever the selection process. Thus, we can not skip or "compress" the first step of the algorithm in the MPR selection. Moreover, this step must be run first in order to minimize the number of MPR. Therefore, only the second step of the algorithm can be improved in order to find the minimum number of MPR.

Related works: Most of the literature about the performances of OLSR deals with the efficiency of the OLSR routing protocol itself or the different techniques using MPR ([4–7]). The goal is to minimize the number of transmitters and thus the number of selected MPR per node. Therefore, alternative algorithms to the classical MPR selection algorithm as [11, 10] aim to optimize the overlap between MPR or the global bandwidth. But, all results for the proposed algorithms are quite similar, particularly for the mean number of MPR per node. Therefore, in order to understand this phenomenon, we wished to analyze this selection more in details as only few papers have studied the different algorithm performances of the MPR selection. Only [11] gives an analysis of the MPR selection on the line. Other analytical results in different graphs are also given in [5]. Other interesting results are presented in [10].

3.   Analysis

We are interested in the properties of the MPR of a typical node. Therefore, we do not consider the whole network but only a "typical point" located at the origin of the plane and its 1 and 2-neighborhood. Our model is similar to the classical unit random graph used to model ad-hoc networks. This is a general model as we do not make any assumption about the wireless technology used.

Let $B(x, R)$ denote a ball of radius R centered in x. Let be a Poisson point process on $B(0, 2R)$ of intensity $\lambda > 0$. The intensity λ of such a process represents the mean number of points of the process by surface unit. We add a point 0 at the origin for which we study the MPR selection algorithm (Palm distribution). We assume that there is a bidirectional link between two nodes iff $d(u, v) \leq R$ where $d(u, v)$ is the Euclidean distance between u and v and $R \in \mathbb{R}^{+*}$ a constant. The neighborhood of 0 is thus constituted of the points of the Poisson process which are in $B(0, R)$. We still use N (resp. N_2) to design the 1-neighborhood (resp. the 2-neighborhood) of the point 0.

General results: Let $A(r)$ be the area of the intersection of two balls of radius R where the distance between the centers of the balls is r:

$$A(r) = 2R^2 \arccos\left(\tfrac{r}{2R}\right) - r\sqrt{R^2 - \tfrac{r^2}{4}} \text{ and } A_1(u, r, R) \text{ the area of the union}$$

of 2 discs of radius R and u where the centers of the 2 balls are distant from r:

$$A_1(u, r, R) = rR\sqrt{1 - \left(\tfrac{R^2 - u^2 + r^2}{2Rr}\right)^2} - R^2 \arccos \tfrac{u^2 - R^2 - r^2}{2Rr} - u^2 \arccos \tfrac{R^2 - u^2 - r^2}{2ur}$$

The next proposition gives several general results as the mean value of the quantities d_0^+ and d_0^- as well as the mean size of the 1 and 2-neighborhood of a node when considering a Poisson point process distribution.

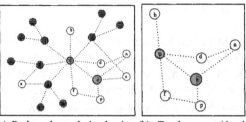

(a) Real topology - Isolated points   (b) Topology   considered
of u appear in horizontal red, by node u at the second
$MPR_1(u)$ in vertical blue.   step

Figure 1.   Illustration of the MPR selection algorithm.

Proposition 1 *Let u be a point uniformly distributed in $B(0, R)$. u is thus such that $u \in N$.*
The mean number of node u's neighbors lying in $B(0, 2R)/B(0, R)$ is given by: $\mathbb{E}\left[d_0^+(u)\right] = \frac{\lambda}{\pi R^2} \int_0^{2\pi} \int_0^R (\pi R^2 - A(r)) r dr d\theta = \lambda R^2 \frac{3\sqrt{3}}{4}$.
The idea is to count the number of the process points lying in the intersection of $B(u, R)$ and $B(0, 2R)/B(0, R)$.

Let v be a point uniformly distributed in $B(0, 2R)\backslash B(0, R)$. The mean number of node v's neighbors lying in $B(0, R)$ is given by:
$\mathbb{E}\left[d_0^-(v)\right] = \lambda \frac{2}{3R^2} \int_R^{2R} A(r) r dr = \lambda R^2 \frac{\sqrt{3}}{4}$.
The idea here is to count the number of process points in the intersection of $B(v, R)$ and $B(0, R)$. Node v may lie in $B(0, 2R)\backslash B(0, R)$ without belonging to N_2 if $N(v) \cap N = \emptyset$. So, to obtain the quantity above for nodes in N_2 we have to condition it by the probability that $v \in N_2$.
We obtain: $\mathbb{E}\left[d_0^-(v)|v \in N_2\right] = \frac{\mathbb{E}\left[d_0^-(v)\right]}{\mathbb{P}(d_0^-(v)>0)}$,
with $\mathbb{P}\left(d_0^-(v) > 0\right) = 1 - \frac{2}{3R^2} \int_R^{2R} exp\{-\lambda A(r)\} r dr$.
This last equation gives the probability that a node in $B(0, 2R)/B(0, R)$ has at least one neighbor in $B(0, R)$ which makes it a 2-neighbor of node 0.

The mean number of nodes in N is given by: $\mathbb{E}\left[\|N\|\right] = \lambda \pi R^2$.
The mean number of nodes in N_2 is given by:
$\mathbb{E}\left[\|N_2\|\right] = 3\lambda \pi R^2 \mathbb{P}\left(d_0^-(v) > 0\right) = 3\lambda \pi R^2 \left(1 - \frac{2}{3R^2} \int_R^{2R} exp\{-\lambda A(r)\} r dr\right)$.

All these quantities can be computed in the same way. We use the following properties of a Poisson point process: conditioned by the number of points in $B(0, R)$ (resp. in $B(0, 2R)\backslash B(0, R)$), the points are independently and uniformly distributed in $B(0, R)$ (resp. in $B(0, 2R)\backslash B(0, R)$) and are independent of the points of $B(0, 2R)\backslash B(0, R)$ (resp. $B(0, R)$).

Analysis of the first step of the MPR selection: In this section, we compute several quantities relative to the first step of the algorithm. In the next proposition, we give the mean number of points $v \in N_2$ such that $d_0^-(v) = 1$. These points are the isolated points of 0. The points of N, neighbors of these isolated points, necessarily belong to MPR_1 as they are the only way to reach them from node 0 in 2 hops. However, this quantity does not give the size of MPR_1, since several isolated points can be reached by the same MPR_1 point. For instance, on Figure 1(a), we have four MPR_1 nodes but seven "isolated points". MPR_1 i covers two isolated points: j and k.

Proposition 2 *Let v be uniformly distributed in $B(0, 2R)\backslash B(0, R)$ and D the set of points v such that $d_0^-(v) = 1$:*
$\mathbb{P}\left(d_0^-(v) = 1\right) = \frac{2}{3R^2} \int_R^{2R} \lambda A(r) exp\{-\lambda A(r)\} r dr$

As in Proposition 1, we only consider nodes v such that $v \in N_2$:
$$\mathbb{P}\left(d_0^-(v) = 1 | v \in N_2\right) = \frac{\mathbb{P}\left(d_0^-(v)=1\right)}{\mathbb{P}\left(d_0^-(v)>0\right)}.$$
The mean number of "isolated points" is then deduced and given by:
$$\mathbb{E}\left[\|D\|\right] = 2\pi\lambda^2 \int_R^{2R} A(r) exp\{-\lambda A(r)\} r \, dr.$$

Proposition 3 gives lower and upper bounds on the number of MPR_1.

Proposition 3 *Let u be a point uniformly distributed in $B(0, R)$:*
$$\mathbb{P}\left(u \in MPR_1\right) \geq \frac{2}{R^2}\mathbb{P}\left(d_0^+(u) > 0\right)$$
$$\times \int_0^R \int_R^{R+r} f(x, r, R) \exp\left\{-\lambda\left(2\pi R^2 - A_1(R, x, R)\right)\right\} r \, dx \, dr$$
with $f(x, r, R)$ being the probabilistic distribution function:
$$f(x, r, R) = -\frac{\lambda\left[\frac{\partial}{\partial x}A_1(x,r,R)-2\pi x\right]}{1-\exp\left\{-\lambda(A_1(R,r,R)-\pi R^2)\right\}} \exp\left\{-\lambda\left(A_1(x, r, R) - \pi x^2\right)\right\}$$
The next formula gives the mean number of MPR_1. It is the direct consequence of the formula above:
$$\mathbb{E}\left[\|MPR_1\|\right] \geq 2\lambda\pi\mathbb{P}\left(d_0^+(u) > 0\right)$$
$$\times \int_0^R \int_R^{R+r} f(x, r, R) \exp\left\{-\lambda\left(2\pi R^2 - A_1(R, x, R)\right)\right\} r \, dx \, dr$$
Moreover, since there is at least one isolated point by point of MPR_1, the mean number of isolated points offers an upper bound: $\mathbb{E}\left[\|MPR_1\|\right] \leq \mathbb{E}\left[\|D\|\right]$.

Proof 1 *To obtain a bound on the probability that a point in N belongs to MPR_1, we use a sufficient condition. Because of page restriction, we do not give here the proof but it can be found in [9].*

We are now interested in the spatial distribution of the MPR_1 points. For a node u such that $d(0, u) = r$, $r \leq R$, Proposition 4 gives lower and upper bounds on the probability that u belongs to MPR_1.

Proposition 4 *Let u be a point at distance r ($r \leq R$) from the origin. We fix the two points 0 and u and we distribute the Poisson point process in $B(0, 2R)$ independently of these two points.*
$$\mathbb{P}\left(u \in MPR_1\right) \geq \left(1 - \exp\left\{-\lambda(\pi R^2 - A(r))\right\}\right)$$
$$\times \int_R^{R+r} f(v, r, R) \exp\left\{-\lambda(2\pi R^2 - A_1(R, v, R))\right\} dv$$
$$\mathbb{P}\left(u \in MPR_1\right) \leq 1 - \left(1 - \exp\left\{-\lambda\frac{A(R+r)}{2}\right\}\right)^2$$

Proof 2 *The lower bound is obtained in the same way as the bound in Proposition 3 but given $d(0, u)$, $u \in N$. Because of page restriction, we do not give detail the proof here but it can be found in [9].*

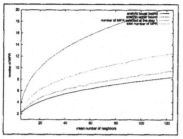 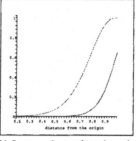

(a) Mean number of MPR and MPR_1 obtained by simulation when $\lambda\pi$ varies and comparison with analytical bounds.

(b) Lower and upper bounds on the probability of belonging to MPR_1 *w.r.t.* the distance from the origin.

Figure 2. Simulation results.

4. Numerical results and simulations

The nodes are deployed using a Poisson process in $B(0,2)$ for $R = 1$ and $\lambda > 0$. We add a point at 0 and study the number of MPR it selects at each step of the MPR selection. Figure 2(a) shows the mean number of MPR and MPR_1 obtained by simulation. We observe that approximately 75% of the MPR actually are MPR_1, which confirms that the MPR_1 almost cover the whole 2-neighborood. Figure 2(a) also show the analytic bounds. As explained before, the lower bound is very close to the mean size of the set MPR_1.

Figure 3 plots samples for different values of $\lambda\pi$ ($\lambda\pi$ being the number of a node's neighbors). The point 0 for which we compute the MPR is the black point in the middle. Points in the central circle are the points of N, the larger ones being the MPR_1. Points outside the circle are the points of N_2, the blue ones being the points of N_2 covered by the MPR_1. We note that in all cases, almost all nodes of N_2 are is covered by the MPR_1. Only one more MPR might suffice to cover the rest of N_2. We have shown in the previous section that there is an appreciable number of isolated points giving rise to a certain number of MPR_1. These MPR_1 seem to be distributed very close to the boundary of $B(0,R)$ and regularly scattered on it (which confirms the results of the Proposition 4). Therefore, they cover a very large part of N_2. The lower and upper bounds given in Proposition 4 allow us to show that the MPR_1 are very close to the boundary. Figure 2(b) show these bounds when the distance between 0 and its neighbors varies from 0.2 to 0.999 and with $\lambda = 15$. These curves incontestably show that MPR_1 points are distributed closely to the boundary of $B(0,1)$. We point out that these results depend on λ: as λ increases, the distance between MPR_1 points and 0 increases too.

5. Consequences

About the MPR distribution: When a message is sent by node u, only $MPR(u)$ forward the message. Neighbors commun to u and $MPR(u)$ thus receive several copies of the same message and spend energy uselessly. Yet, as shown in Section 4, most of $MPR_1(u)$ (and thus most of $MPR(u)$) are distributed very closely to the boundaries of the radio range of u. That means

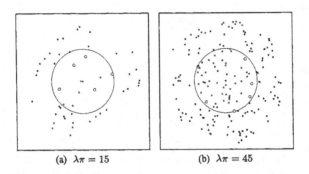

(a) $\lambda\pi = 15$ (b) $\lambda\pi = 45$

Figure 3.   MPR selection with $\lambda\pi = 15$ and $\lambda\pi = 45$.

that the intersection between u and its of each MPR radio areas is minimized
and so the number of common neighbors and so the energy uselessly spent.

The easiest way to broadcast a message over a network is the blind flooding,
where each node re-emits the message upon first reception of it. To illustrate
the number of receptions saved by the MPR, we computed by simulation the
number of receptions per node of a broadcast message. The nodes are randomly deployed using a Poisson process in a 1×1 square with various levels
of intensity λ (and thus various numbers of nodes) for $R = 0.1$. x and y
are connected if and only if $d(x,y) \leq R$. Figure 4(a) compares the results
obtained by both metrics. For the blind flooding, the number of receptions per
node corresponds to the mean number of neighbors (as every node forwards
the message once). With OLSR, approximately 40% of the nodes participate
to the diffusion. It is drastically less than the blind flooding and it is a priori
sufficiently high to be robust.

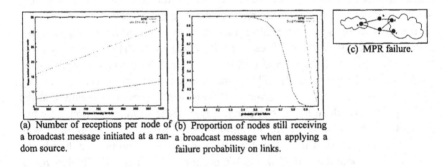

(c) MPR failure.

(a) Number of receptions per node of (b) Proportion of nodes still receiving
a broadcast message initiated at a ran- a broadcast message when applying a
dom source.   failure probability on links.

Figure 4.   Some consequences with $\lambda = 1000$.

About the MPR_1: The number of MPR elected per node aims to be as low
as possible. The Greedy heuristic of MPR selection presented here is the original one. As we mentioned in Section 1, some works have been lead in order to
enhance this algorithm and elect less MPR per node. But, only the second step

of the Greedy algorithm may be improved as the first one is mandatory to cover the whole 2-neighborhood of a node and can not be reduced. And, as the first step leads to the election of more than 75% of the MPR, the improvements can only concern less than 25% of the MPR and thus can not be significant, which explains that all works lead to similar results and minor improvements. Unfortunately, this feature also underlines a robustness problem. Indeed, if 75% of node u's MPR cover at least one isolated, if some $MPR(u)$ fail, there is a great probability that at least one node v in $N_2(u)$ does not receive messages from u. Of course, v may receive it from another path but, this path would not be optimal anymore. Because of it, parts of the network can be isolted during the broadcasting task as illustrated by Figure 4(c). Clouds represent parts of the network. As node e is an isolated point for node a, a has to elect node c as one of its MPR but does not elect node b as node d is already covered by c. Let's suppose that the link between a and c fails and a diffusion is performed before a re-computes its MPR. The network is still connected, nevertheless, as node b is not a MPR of node a, it does not forward the message. A whole part of the network is isolated. In order to measure this robustness problem, we simulate a broadcasting task, applying a failure probability over links. We measure the proportion of nodes still receiving the broadcast message. Figure 4(b) shows the results. As in the blind flooding, every node retransmits the message, if some nodes do not receive it, that means that the network is disconnected. We can see that this happens when 85% or more of links are down. However, every node does not receive the message with the MPR heuristic when only 45% of links are down whereas the network is still connected. This failure model may seem not very realist as links can fail because of congestion and, as the blind flooding induces more messages than the MPR protocol, more links fail. Nevertheless, we use the results of the blind flooding in this situation to give an information on the network connectivity. However, failures of a MPR may also be due to the node mobility. Indeed, if a MPR moves, it may leave the radio scope of the node for which it is a MPR or does not cover the same set of nodes in the 2-neighborhood anymore.

6. Conclusion

In this article, we have computed several quantities relative to the MPR selection algorithm in OLSR. We have shown that approximately 75% of the MPR are chosen during the first step of the algorithm. Since this step always is necessary for the MPR set to cover the whole 2-neighborhood, variants of the algorithm used in OLSR, trying to minimize the number of selected MPR, lead to similar performances. We have also highlighted the fact that these MPR are distributed close to the radio range boundaries, limiting the overlap between MPR. This feature also underlines a robustness problem. This robustness problem is intented to be analyzed with other robustness models. A deeper study about the influences of isolated points on the reliability of OLSR will be lead in future works. These results have been presented for a particular model using Poisson point process. Other models, more realistic, which take into account the properties of the radio layer could be considered in future works. Results obtained here could be compared to simulations considering CDMA network or 802.11 network.

References

[1] Optimized Link State Routing Protocol T. Clausen, P. Jacquet, A. Laouiti, P. Muhlethaler, A. Qayyum et L. Viennot, IEEE INMIC Pakistan 2001.

[2] Optimized Link State Routing Protocol (OLSR), Clausen, T. and P. Jacquet, Eds., RFC 3626, October 2003.

[3] The broadcast storm problem in a mobile ad hoc network. S.-Y. Ni, Y.-C. Tseng, Y.-S. Chen, and J.-P. Sheu. In Proc. of the 5th annual ACM/IEEE Int. Conference on Mobile computing and networking, pages 151–162. ACM Press, 1999.

[4] Simulation Results of the OLSR Routing Protocol for Wireless Network A. Laouiti, P. Muhlethaler, A. Najid, E. Plakoo, Med-Hoc-Net, Sardegna, Italy 2002.

[5] Performance of multipoint relaying in ad hoc mobile routing protocols P. Jacquet, A. Laouiti, P. Minet, L. Viennot, Networking 2002, Pise(Italy)2002.

[6] The Optimized Link State Routing Protocol, Evaluation through Experiments and Simulation T.H. Clausen, G. Hansen, L. Christensen and G. Behrmann, IEEE Symposium on "Wireless Personal Mobile Communications", September 2001.

[7] Performance Analysis of OLSR Multipoint Relay Flooding in Two Ad Hoc Wireless Network Models P.Jacquet, A. Laouiti, P. Minet and L. Viennot, Research Report-4260, INRIA, September 2001, RSRCP journal special issue on Mobility and Internet.

[8] Analysis of mobile Ad hoc Protocols in Random Graph Models. P. Jacquet and A. Laouiti, Research Report RR-3835, INRIA, December 1999.

[9] An analysis of the Multi-Point Relays selection in OLSR. A. Busson and N. Mitton and E. Fleury, Research Report RR-5468, INRIA, January 2005.

[10] Performance Evaluation of Approximation Algorithms for Multipoint Relay Selection Bernard Mans and Nirisha Shrestha, Med-Hoc-Net'04, Bodrum, Turkey, June 27-30, 2004.

[11] Flooding techniques in mobile Ad-Hoc networks. E. Baccelli and P. Jacquet. Research Report RR-5002, INRIA, 2003.

[12] Connectivity in ad-hoc and hybrid networks. O. Dousse, P. Thiran, and M. Hasler. In Proc. IEEE Infocom, New York, NY, USA, June 2002.

[13] Stochastic geometry and its applications. D. Stoyan, W.S. Kendall and J. Mecke, Ed John Wiley and Sons.

SELECTION METRICS FOR COOPERATIVE MULTIHOP RELAYING *

Jonghyun Kim and Stephan Bohacek
Department of Electrical and Computer Engineering
University of Delaware
Newark, DE 19716
kim,bohacek@eecis.udel.edu

Keywords: Cooperative relaying, MANETs, routing

Abstract   Cooperative relaying enables nodes to actively cooperate to deliver packets to their destination. The bestselect protocol (BSP) implements a
type of cooperative relaying that generalizes single path routing with
sets of nodes (relay-sets) replacing the concept of a single node relay.
Thus, while in traditional single path routing, packets hop from node
to node, in BSP, packets hop from relay-set to relay-set. Through the
exchange of channel gain information between relay-sets, the best node
within a relay-set is selected to transmit the data packet on behalf of the
entire relay-set. The node selected depends on the metric used. Any
metric that can be posed in a dynamic programming framework can
be used. In this paper, performance gains from a number of selection
metrics are investigated. Specific selection metrics include maximizing
the minimum channel gain along the path, minimizing end-to-end delay,
minimizing the total power, and minimizing the total energy. It will be
shown that BSP can achieve significant gains in all of these metrics.

1   Introduction

In traditional multihop wireless data networks, route search and packet
forwarding are separated; first a route is found, and then packets are forwarded along the route. In the case that multipath routing is employed,
the situation is similar, but a set of paths are found, and then, packets

*This work was prepared through collaborative participation in the Collaborative Technology
Alliance for Communications and Networks sponsored by the U.S. Army Research Laboratory
under Cooperative Agreement DAAD19- 01-2-0011. The U.S. Government is authorized to
reproduce and distribute reprints for Government purposes notwithstanding any copyright
notation thereon.

are forwarded along each route either probabilistically, or the routes are used as precomputed backups [Marina and Das, 2003]. In any case, in traditional routing, nodes act alone to forward the packet to its next hop. In cooperative relaying, a group of nodes act together to forward a packet. While several variants of cooperative relaying are possible, one approach is to generalize the single node that forwards the packet to a set of nodes that cooperate (see [Zhao and Valenti, 2005] for an alternative approach). Such a set of nodes is called a relay-set. Thus, while traditional networking forwards packets from node to node, this form of cooperative relaying forwards packets from relay-set to relay-set. Within the relay-set paradigm, there are also many possible approaches. For example, in some cases, a number of nodes transmit the same or different parts of the packet. In such cases, the total transmission power used to transmit the data packet between two relay-sets is distributed among a number of node [Sendonaris et al., 2003a]. However, in [Luo et al., 2004], it was shown that in the case of two-hop paths, if the channels are known, then the optimal approach is to allocate all power to the best node pair. Such an approach is known as best-select relaying.

Best-select protocol (BSP) is a multihop extension of best-select relaying. Hence, BSP makes extensive use of channel measurements and attempts to select the best path. A distinguishing feature of BSP is that it is highly dynamic and finds paths on a per packet basis. The path that a packet follows depends on instantaneous and smoothed channel gain measurements. As a result of the highly reactive nature of BSP, one might expect that BSP would be able to find paths that provide substantially better performance over a static path. This paper examines if this hypothesis is true.

The performance improvement attained depends on the metric used to select paths. This paper considers the performance improvements that result from maximizing the minimum channel gain along the path, minimizing end-to-end delay, minimizing the total power, and minimizing the total energy. It will be shown that BSP can achieve significant gains in all of these metrics.

This investigation examines these performance gains in two different scenarios. Specifically, we consider an idealized version of BSP when the nodes are in an urban area, and a QualNet [Scalable Network Technologies, 2005] implementation of BSP when nodes are in an urban area. The urban area simulations utilize channel gains from performing ray-tracing on a map of an urban area [Sridhara et al., 2005]. Thus, these channel gains are similar to those that would be found in an urban deployment. In each scenario, two different node densities are examined, sparse and dense.

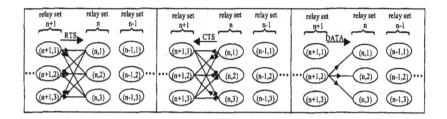

Figure 1. Best-Select Protocol

The paper proceeds as follows. In the next section a brief overview of BSP is provided. In Section 3, the methodology for evaluating the performance gains is discussed. In Section 4 the different selection metrics are evaluated. Finally, Section 5 provides a summary of the results and concluding remarks.

2 An Overview of Best-Select Protocol (BSP)

BSP groups nodes into relay-sets. The relay-set that is n hops from the destination is referred to as the n-th relay-set. The i-th node within the n-th relay-set is denoted by (n, i). The nodes within the n-th relay-set cooperate with the nodes within the $(n-1)$-th relay-set to determine which node in the n-th relay-set should transmit the data packet. Specifically, the nodes within the n-th relay-set transmit a RTS packet to the nodes in the $(n-1)$-th relay-set. These transmissions occur simultaneously using CDMA with each node using a different code. Each node in the $(n-1)$-th relay-set receives all the RTSs and records the channel gains over each channel. We denote the channel gain from node (n, i) to node $(n-1, j)$ as $R_{(n,i),(n-1,j)}$. Assuming that the channel is idle, all the nodes in the $(n-1)$-th relay-set transmit a CTS simultaneously using CDMA. These CTS packets contain the just measured channel gains along with other channel gain information. Each node in the n-th relay-set receives these CTSs along with the embedded channel gain information. Since all nodes have received the same information, they are able to make the same decision as to which node is best suited to transmit. This node then transmits the data packet using the entire bandwidth. Figure 1 illustrates the approach.

The decision as to which node is best suited to transmit does not only depend the channel gains $R_{(n,i),(n-1,j)}$, but also on the downstream channel gains, $R_{(n-1,j),(n-2,k)}$, $R_{(n-2,k),(n-3,l)}$, etc. This amount of channel gain information cannot be economically included into the CTS packets. Instead, the downstream channel information is encapsulated into a scalar, which we denote as J. Specifically, the relevant downstream channel information from node (n, i) is denoted $J_{(n,i)}$ and depends on the selection metric. In this paper we explore several different objectives, and hence J will take many different meanings. However, in all cases, J will encapsulate the downstream channel information.

3   Methodology

In order to model multihop mobile network in a more realistic urban area, a realistic propagation and mobility tool is used. This tool is described in [Sridhara et al., 2005]. Here, the Paddington area of London is considered.

Two different approaches and two different scenarios are used to evaluate the selection metrics. We refer to the approaches as urban idealized BSP and urban implemented BSP.

Idealized simulation of BSP is performed with Matlab. Once the channel gains from propagation tool are known, the selection metrics can be investigated. A source and destination are selected at random, and a least-hop path between these nodes is found. If there exists multiple least-hop paths, one is selected, and if there are no paths, a new source and destination are selected. The nodes within the least-hop path make up the initial relay-sets. If a node is able to communicate with a node in the $(n + 1)$-th relay-set and a node in the $(n − 1)$-th relay-set, then the node joins the n-th relay-set. The best path (in terms of the metric under consideration) among all paths that are made up of nodes within the relay-sets is found. The value of the metric for the best path and the value for the initial, randomly selected path are recorded. Next, time is increased by one second. As a result, the nodes may move and new channel gains result. If the nodes which had composed the least-hop path are still connected, then the process is repeated. The metrics are repeatedly evaluated until the least-hop path breaks or the simulation ends (300 seconds). Since this approach is able to always correctly build the relay-sets and always uses the correct value of the selection metric, we call this an *idealized BSP*.

Packet simulation of BSP is performed with QualNet [Scalable Network Technologies, 2005]. To evaluate the selection metrics, the same source-destination pairs, mobility, and channel gains used by the urban idealized BSP are used. The implementation of BSP is much like the idealized BSP in the sense that first a least-hop path is found. This path is then enhanced. Specifically, every time a an RTS-CTS exchanges occurs as described in the previous section, if a node can hear some node in the $(n + 1)$-th relay-set and a node in the $(n − 1)$-th relay-set, then the node joins the n-th relay-set. The value of the metric is determines in the same way as it is in the idealized BSP case. The main difference between the idealized BSP and the implement BSP is that the relay-sets grow more slowly.

4 Selection Metrics

Like routing metrics, cooperative relaying allows the selection of links according to different metrics. However, the highly dynamic nature of cooperative relaying allows new metrics to be explored. To see this, consider the channel gain. While it is possible to use the channel gain for selecting a path that will be used statically (or until it breaks), it has been shown that channel gain is only a marginal predictor of the quality of the path [Bohacek et al., 2005]. The reason for this is that the channel gain may rapidly vary and is difficult to predict, especially on the time-scales relevant for routing.

On the other hand, BSP is able to quickly adjust the way in which packets are delivered. Specifically, the exact path a packet takes is determined only as the packet is being sent through the network. Thus, BSP is able to react quickly to changes in the channel gains. The question addressed by this paper is which metrics can be used and what is the impact of using best-select with these metrics.

4.1 Maximizing the Minimum Channel Gain Along the Path

The received signal strength is the product of the transmission power and the channel gain. Thus for a fixed transmission power and noise, the SNR is a linear function of the channel gain. Thus, a high channel gain allows for a low transmission error, lower transmission power, and/or higher data rate. Here, the selection metric finds the path that has the largest minimum channel gain. That is, for each hop along the path, the channel gain is evaluated. The quality of the path is taken to be the smallest channel gain along the path. The link with the smallest channel gain can be thought of as the bottleneck of the path. Hence, we seek to select the path with the best bottleneck.

Define $J_{(n,i)}$ to be the minimum channel gain over the best path from node (n,i) to the destination. Then the following holds

$$J_{(n,i)} = \max_j \left(\min \left(R_{(n,i),(n-1,j)}, J_{(n-1,j)} \right) \right) \tag{1}$$

where the maximization is over all nodes in the $(n-1)$-th relay-set.

In order to evaluate this metric in the idealized case, we can simply examine $J_{(N,1)}$, where there are N hops between the source and destination. However, in the implementation of BSP, we evaluate the selection metric for each packet delivered by taking the minimum value of $\max_j \left(\min \left(R_{(n,i_n^*),(n-1,j)}, J_{(n-1,j)} \right) \right)$, where node (n, i_n^*) is selected to transmit the node. More specifically, suppose that the nodes that are selected to transmit the packet are $(N, 1)$, $\left(N - 1, i^*_{N-1}\right)$, $\left(N - 2, i^*_{N-2}\right)$,... Then the value of the metric is

$$\min_n \max_j \left(\min \left(R_{(n,i^*_n),(n-1,j)}, J_{(n-1,j)}\right)\right).$$

Note that in this case, the value of the metric depends of which nodes are able to decode the packet and hence the minimum gain experienced may be different from $J_{(N,1)}$. To see this how this can occur, suppose that node (n, i) is selected to transmit the data packet and $j^o = \arg\max_j \left(\min \left(R_{(n,i^*_n),(n-1,j)}, J_{(n-1,j)}\right)\right)$. This means that the best next hop is $(n - 1, j^o)$. However, there may be some other node j^+ such that $J_{(n-1,j^+)} > J_{(n-1,j^o)}$, but $\min \left(R_{(n,i^*_n),(n-1,j^o)}, J_{(n-1,j^o)}\right) > \min \left(R_{(n,i^*_n),(n-1,j^+)}, J_{(n-1,j^+)}\right)$. Thus, node $(n - 1, j^+)$ is not the best next hop. However, if node $(n - 1, j^+)$ is able to decode the packet, then, since $J_{(n-1,j^+)} > J_{(n-1,j^o)}$, node $(n - 1, j^+)$ is better suited to transmit than node $(n - 1, j^*)$. On the other hand, since $R_{(n,i^*_n),(n-1,j^o)} > R_{(n,i^*_n),(n-1,j^+)}$, node $(n - 1, j^+)$ is less likely to decode the packet than node $(n - 1, j^o)$ (this why node $(n - 1, j^o)$ is the best next hop). But in the cases that node $(n - 1, j^+)$ is able to correctly decode the packet, then its ability to deliver the packet to the designation should be utilized, which is what BSP does. The ability to use relays that, while not the most reliable, can sometimes act is good relays is called *opportunistic relaying* and is a distinctive feature of BSP that is not shared with traditional routing protocols. However, the metric discussed here does not reflect the possibility of opportunistic relaying, and hence the value of the metric for the implemented BSP might be larger than for the idealized case. Figure 2 shows that this difference is especially noticeable for small relay-set size. Below, some metrics consider the possibly of opportunistic relaying and some do not.

The performance of this selection metric is shown in the left-hand plot in Figure 2. In general, BSP is able to provide significantly higher minimum channel gain than the least-hop routing. For example, two orders of magnitude improvement is not uncommon for the idealized and implemented urban cases.

4.2   Minimizing the End-to-End Delay

Here we focus on the expected value of the end-to-end delay, i.e., the sum of each transmission delay (we do not consider queuing or processing delay).

It is assumed that if a packet is lost due to transmission error, the end-to-end delay is T, where T is a large number. The motivation for

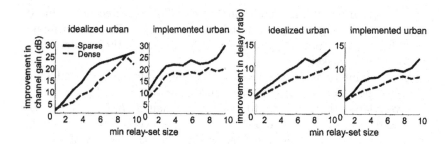

Figure 2. Left : Min Channel Gain. The average ratio of the minimum channel gain along the path with BSP to the minimum channel gain along the path with least-hop routing. Right : Delay. The average ratio of the end-to-end delay of least-hop routing to the end-to-end delay with BSP.

this is that if a packet is lost, then the transport layer will be forced to retransmit, resulting in a large delay. T is further discussed later.

Here $J_{(n,i)}$ is defined as the expected sum of the transmission delays from node (n,i) to the destination. Furthermore, let $J_{(n,i)}(B)$ be the expected delay from node (n,i) to the destination if node (n,i) transmits at bit-rate B. Let $f(V)$ be the probability of transmission error when the channel gain is V, and let $J_{(n,i)}$ be the probability of successfully delivering the packet to the destination from node (n,i). Furthermore, let $\mathcal{I}$ be an ordering of the nodes in the $(n-1)$-th relay-set such that $J_{(n-1,\mathcal{I}(1))} \geq J_{(n-1,\mathcal{I}(1))} \geq \cdots$. Then,

$$J_{(n,i)}(B) = \frac{\text{packet size}}{B}\{f\left(R_{(n,i),(n-1,\mathcal{I}(1))}X,B\right)$$
$$+ \left(1 - f\left(R_{(n,i),(n-1,\mathcal{I}(1))}X,B\right)\right) f(R_{(n,i),(n-1,\mathcal{I}(2))}X,B) + \cdots\}$$
$$+ \{f\left(R_{(n,i),(n-1,\mathcal{I}(1))}X,B\right) J_{\mathcal{I}(1)} + \left(1 - f\left(R_{(n,i),(n-1,\mathcal{I}(1))}X,B\right)\right) \times J_{\mathcal{I}(2)}$$
$$+ \cdots\}$$
$$+ T\{(1 - f\left(R_{(n,i),(n-1,\mathcal{I}(1))}X,B\right) \times \left(1 - f\left(R_{(n,i),(n-1,\mathcal{I}(2))}X,B\right)\right) \cdots\}$$

To see this, note that if the transmission is successful, then the delay from node (n,i) to the next relay-set is $\frac{\text{packet size}}{B}$. The probability of experiencing this delay is given in the first and second lines. Furthermore, if transmission is successful, it experiences an expected additional delay of $J_{(n-1,j)}$. However, the node in the next relay-set that transmits depends on which node receives the packet and its relative values of J. Specifically, if node $(n-1, I(1))$ decodes the packet, a delay of $J_{(n-1,I(1))}$ will be experienced. If the packet does not reach node $(n-1, I(1))$, but does reach $(n-1, I(2))$, then a delay of $J_{(n-1,I(2))}$ is expected. The expected delay is given in the third and fourth lines. The expected delay due to retransmission is given in the last line. Once $J_{(n,i)}(B)$ is determined, we define $J_{(n,i)} = \min_B J_{(n,i)}(B)$. And, the node with the smallest $J_{(n,i)}$ transmits the packet.

In the simulations shown, $T = 100$. However, different values of T are possible and can result in some difference in performance. Specifically, if T is very large, then, in order to make $J_{(n,i)}$ small, $f\left(R_{(n,i),(n-1,\mathcal{I}(1))}, B\right)$ will need to be very close to one. Hence, a conservative bit-rate will be selected. On the other hand, if T is smaller, then the penalty of a transmission error is not so great and the bit-rate can be increased. Thus, T acts much like a constraint on the transmission error probability. While the problem can also be framed so that the transmission error probability is fixed, in some settings, T may be a more intuitive parameter than the transmission error probability.

The right-hand plot in Figure 2 shows the performance under this selection metric. It is assumed that the least-hop approach used a fixed bit-rate. In the idealized and implemented urban cases, the delay is reduced by a factor of between 3 and 14. Note that the plot shows a small difference between the idealized urban and implemented urban cases. This contrasts the previous metrics where the implemented case gave better performance than the idealized case. The reason for this is that this selection metric does account for the possibly of opportunistic relaying.

4.3   Minimizing the Total Transmission Power Subject to per Link Channel Gain Constraint

Here we define $J_{(n,i)}$ to be the total power required to deliver a packet from node (n,i) to the destination while meeting per link channel gain constraint. Then

$$J_{(n,i)} = \min_{(n-1,j)} \frac{CH^*}{R_{(n,i),(n-1,j)}} + J_{(n-1,j)} \qquad (3)$$

where CH^* is the per link received power constraint. Note that the actual received signal power is $R_{(n,i),(n-1,j)} \times X$, where X is the transmission power. Thus, if the transmitted power is $X = \frac{CH^*}{R_{(n,i),(n-1,j)}}$, then the received power constraint will be met.

In the idealized cases, the total transmission power is the value of J at the source. In the implementation, each transmission power is summed. As in Section 4.1, (3) does not account for the possibly of opportunistic relaying and so the implementation shows better performance than the idealized case.

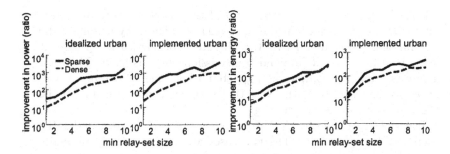

Figure 3. Left : Min power. The average ratio of the total end-to-end transmission power of least-hop routing to the total end-to-end transmission power with BSP. Right : Min energy. The average ratio of the total end-to-end transmission energy of least-hop routing to the total end-to-end transmission energy with BSP.

The left-hand plot in Figure 3 compares the performance of the BSP to least-hop in the different scenarios. Here we see that BSP yields dramatic performance improves over least-hop routing.

4.4   Minimum Total Energy

Let $J_{(n,i)}$ be the expected energy required to delivery the packet to the destination from node (n,i). Furthermore, let $J_{(n,i)}(B,X)$ be the expected total energy required to deliver the packet from node (n,i) to the destination if node (n,i) transmits at bit-rate B and with transmission power X. Then

$$J_{(n,i)}(B,X) = X\frac{\text{packet size}}{B}\{f\left(R_{(n,i),(n-1,\mathcal{I}(1))}X,B\right)$$
$$+ \left(1 - f\left(R_{(n,i),(n-1,\mathcal{I}(1))}X,B\right)\right)f(R_{(n,i),(n-1,\mathcal{I}(2))}X,B) + \cdots\}$$
$$+ \{f\left(R_{(n,i),(n-1,\mathcal{I}(1))}X,B\right)J_{\mathcal{I}(1)} + \left(1 - f\left(R_{(n,i),(n-1,\mathcal{I}(1))}X,B\right)\right) \times J_{\mathcal{I}(2)}$$
$$+ \cdots\}$$
$$+ M\{\left(1 - f\left(R_{(n,i),(n-1,\mathcal{I}(1))}X,B\right)\right) \times \left(1 - f\left(R_{(n,i),(n-1,\mathcal{I}(2))}X,B\right)\right)\cdots\}$$

where M is a parameter that represents the energy required to retransmit the packet due to transport layer retransmission. As in the minimum end-to-end delay metric examined in Section 4.2, M is set to a large value and can be used to control the probability of transmission error. The minimum energy selection metric can also be posed as a minimum energy with a constraint on the transmission error probability. Once $J_{(n,i)}(B,X)$ is known, then $J_{(n,i)}$ is found via $J_{(n,i)} = \min_{B,X} J_{(n,i)}(B,X)$.

In the idealized cases, the value of J at the source is the total energy, but for the implementation, the total energy is found by summing the transmission power divided by the bit-rate. For the least-hop case, it is assumed that the bit-rate and transmission power is fixed. The total energy is found by computing $J_{(n,i)}$ but where the relay-sets are collapsed to the least-hop path. Note that this metric does account for the possibly of opportunistic relaying.

The right-hand plot in Figure 3 shows the performance under the minimum energy metric. The two cases are able to achieve dramatic reduction in energy, often well over an order of magnitude.

5   Conclusion

This paper examined several node selection metrics for the best-select protocol (BSP), considering urban idealized and implemented BSP. It is found that BSP can be used to increase performance in a number of ways. While the exact improvement depends on the environment and on the metric, improvements of a factor of 5 to as high as 1000 is not uncommon.

Disclaimer

The views and conclusions contained in this document are those of the authors and should not be interpreted as representing the official policies, either expressed or implied, of the Army Research Laboratory or the U. S. Government.

References

Bohacek, S., Hespanha, J., Lee, J., Lim, C., and Obraczka, K. (2002). Enhancing security via stochastic routing. In *Proc. Of the 11th IEEE Int. Conf. On Comput. Communications and Networks.*

Bohacek, S., Ilic, A., and Sridhara, V. (2005). On the predictability of link lifetimes in urban MANETs. In *3rd Intl. Symposium on Modeling and Optimization in Mobile, Ad Hoc, and Wireless Networks.*

Luo, J., Blum, R. S., Greenstein, L. J., Cimini, L. J., and Haimovich, A. M. (2004). New approaches for cooperative use of multiple antennas in ad hoc wireless networks. In *Proceedings of the IEEE Vehicular Technology Conference (VTC '04-Fall).*

Marina, M. K. and Das, S. R. (2003). Ad hoc on-demand multipath distance vector routing. Technical report, SUNY - Stony Brook.

Scalable Network Technologies (2005). The QualNet simulator http://www.qualnet.com/.

Sendonaris, A., Erkip, E., and Aazhang, B. (2003a). User cooperation diversity - Part I: System description. *IEEE Transactions on Communications*, 51:1927–1938.

Sridhara, V., Kim, J., and Bohacek, S. (2005). Models and methodologies for simulating mobile ad- hoc networks. In *MobiWac.*

Zhao, B. and Valenti, M. C. (2005). Practical relay networks: A generalization of hybrid-ARQ. *IEEE Journal on Selected Areas in Communications*, 23:7–18.

SERVICE DIFFERENTIATION MECHANISM VIA COOPERATIVE MEDIUM ACCESS CONTROL PROTOCOL*

Fatma Orsun, Hakan Topakkaya, Muharrem A. Tunc and Coskun Cetinkaya
Department of Electrical and Computer Engineering
Wichita State University
{fxorsun,hxtopakkaya,matunc,coskun.cetinkaya}@wichita.edu

Abstract   Providing differentiated Quality of Service (QoS) levels is an important challenge for wireless ad hoc networks and wireless LANs when applications have diverse performance requirements. The IEEE 802.11e MAC protocol can provide a Dynamic MAC by assigning different AIFSs, contention window expansion factors (PFs), and (CW_{min}, CW_{max}) pairs for different classes and can provide a Static MAC by adjusting the durations of AIFSs based on priority levels [Aad01]. In this paper, we propose a novel and efficient service differentiation mechanism via the C-MAC. In our protocol, each node will change its backoff counter based on both its own packet's priority level and the priority level of the transmitted packet. The simulation results indicate that the Static MAC provides a service differentiation at the expense of significant goodput degradation when the amount of high priority class traffic is low. On the other hand, the Dynamic MAC fails to prevent low priority classes accessing the channel resulting in significant high priority class goodput degradation when the network load is high. However, our mechanism always provides an efficient service differentiation mechanism and high goodput with a small goodput degradation.

Keywords: Service Differentiation, MAC protocol

1.   Introduction

Supporting differentiated Quality of Service (QoS) levels is an important challenge for wireless ad hoc networks and wireless LANs when applications have diverse performance requirements such as high goodput, low delay and delay jitter. The Medium Access Control (MAC) protocols must provide an effective mechanism to support the desired QoS levels while achieving high goodput and sharing limited spectrum resources fairly among the users.

*This material is based upon work supported by the National Science Foundation under Grant No. EPS-0236913 and matching support from the State of Kansas through Kansas Technology Enterprize Corporation.

The most popular wireless LAN, the IEEE 802.11 standard [802.11], has two different configurations: infrastructure and ad hoc modes. In the infrastructure mode, the IEEE 802.11 MAC can support the desired QoS levels via the Point Coordination Function (PCF). However, several researchers show that the PCF can result in poor performance under various scenarios [Kuo97; San97]. In the ad hoc mode, a number of different MAC protocols have been proposed to provide service differentiation via a distributed reservation-based scheme or a contention-based scheme. The reservation-based scheme is explored to achieve service differentiation in [Lin99; Muir98; Sheu01]. Since these schemes require high power, memory, information exchanging, and computation complexity, they may not be suitable for some applications and environments where users have scarce resources. Further, when resources are reserved, but unused, they will be wasted, which will lead to low network utilization. In [Kon01], a packet's priority is piggybacked into the RTS/CTS/DATA/ACK frames, and each node maintains a scheduling table to provide dynamic priority. This scheme also requires high power, memory, information exchanging, and computation complexity. [Sob99; Yang02] provide service differentiation via "Black Burst" and "busy tone" which require jamming the channel before sending any data packets. However, these mechanisms can lead to significant goodput degradation under heavy network loads. It is also hard to implement these mechanisms using the IEEE 802.11 standard since they require significant changes. The IEEE 802.11e MAC protocol can provide a dynamic priority mechanism (Dynamic MAC) by assigning different Arbitration Inter Frame Spaces (AIFSs), contention window expansion factors (PFs), and (CW_{min}, CW_{max}) pairs for different classes [802.11e; Man02; Bar01; Zhu04; Ver01; Deng98; Rom03] and can provide a static priority mechanism (Static MAC) by adjusting the durations of AIFSs based on priority levels [Aad01].

In this paper, we propose a novel and efficient service differentiation mechanism via the Cooperative MAC protocol (C-MAC) [Cet04; CetTR], which is referred to as the SD-MAC. Our key technique is that each node will change its backoff counter based on both its own packet's priority level and the priority level of the transmitted packet. Specifically, a node will increase its backoff counter linearly with a higher priority (than its own) packet transmission and decrease it exponentially with a lower priority (than its own) packet transmission. We performed extensive sets of simulations in which we compared our mechanism with both the Static MAC and the Dynamic MAC in terms of the network goodput, the high priority class goodput, the packet loss rate, and admissible regions. The simulation results indicate that the Static MAC provides a service differentiation at the expense of significant goodput degradation when the amount of high priority class traffic is low. For example, when there is no high priority class traffic in the network, the Static MAC only achieves 27% goodput in the best case while the Dynamic MAC and the SD-MAC provide high goodput, up to 71%. On the other hand, the Dynamic MAC fails to prevent low priority classes accessing the channel when the network load is high. As a result, the high priority class traffic encounters a significant goodput degradation, specifically up to 25% less than the Static MAC and the SD-MAC, when the amount of low priority class traffic increases. Finally, we investigated the admissible regions, and the results show that the Dynamic MAC can not support any real time traffic when the non-real-time traffic is 70% or more of the channel data rate. On the other hand, the Static MAC encounters significant performance degradation when multiple real time traffic classes exist in the network. For example the Static MAC can support 2 voice and 12 VBR sources together while the SD-MAC supports 2 voice and 29 VBR or 12 VBR and 120 voice together. As a conclusion, the Static MAC is not an efficient mechanism to differentiate services with multiple real time classes, and the Dynamic MAC is not an efficient mechanism to protect real time traffic from greedy sources while the SD-MAC performs quite well under both scenarios. Hence, the SD-MAC is a good candidate for service differentiation.

The remainder of this paper is organized as follows. We propose a service differentiation mechanism, the SD-MAC, in Section 2, and describe the Static MAC and the Dynamic MAC in Section 3. Next, in Section 4, we present the comparison results of three mechanisms. Finally, we conclude in Section 5.

2. Service Differentiation Mechanism

In this section, we first briefly review the underlying MAC ptotocol, Cooperative MAC (C-MAC) [Cet04; CetTR]. Then, we describe the proposed service differentiation mechanism.

Review of the Cooperative-MAC Protocol

Unlike the IEEE 802.11 MAC protocol, in our protocol, we use a constant window size to reduce the amount of idle slots, and we resolve collisions among the collided nodes first by assigning these nodes a shorter DIFS than the other nodes, i.e. the other nodes have to wait for the channel to be idle for a longer duration of DIFS. The operation of the C-MAC protocol is as follows:

As in CSMA/CA, any active node senses the channel to send a packet. If it finds the channel to be idle for a duration of DIFS ($110\mu sec$), which is $50\mu sec$ in the IEEE 802.11 standard, the transmission will proceed. If the channel is determined to be busy, the node defers its transmission until the channel is idle for a duration of DIFS. Then, it generates a random backoff counter chosen uniformly from the range $[0, CW - 1]$, where CW is the contention window size. The backoff counter is decremented as long as the channel remains idle. If it becomes busy, the counter is frozen until the channel is again sensed to be idle for a duration of DIFS.

When the backoff counter reaches 0, the node transmits an RTS message if the four-way hand-shake mechanism is used. The receiving node responses with a CTS after a time period of SIF ($10\mu sec$). Any other nodes which hear RTS/CTS packets defer their transmissions and update their NAV. The sender node responses to the CTS with an actual data packet and waits for an ACK packet. If a node has a successful transmission, it chooses a new backoff counter uniformly from the range $[CW, 2 \cdot CW - 1]$ in order to let the deferred nodes capture the channel. This will lead to short-term fairness. If the sender node does not hear a CTS/ACK, it assumes that a collision has occurred and proceeds according to the procedure described below.

If a node encounters a collision, it generates a new backoff counter chosen uniformly from the range $[0, 3]$ and starts decrementing the counter if it finds the channel to be idle for a duration of Priority Inter-Frame Space (PIFS, $30\mu sec$) rather than a duration of DIFS. The DIFS ($110\mu sec$) corresponds to the sum of PIFS and $4 \cdot SlotTime$ ($20\mu sec$), since collided nodes choose their backoff counters from the range [0,3]. Therefore, the collided nodes have a higher priority than the other nodes in terms of packet transmission. If a collided node senses another collision in the channel before its counter reaches 0, it sets its counter to 0 and waits for the channel to be idle for a duration of DIFS to transmit. As a result, it has a higher priority than the nodes which are not involved in a collision. Any node that does not receive an RTS/CTS correctly is able to sense that the medium is busy since the interference power received is sufficiently higher than the noise floor. Therefore, it assumes that a collision occurred, and it sets its NAV to the Extended Interframe Space (EIFS) [802.11; Kwon03]. After a successful transmission, the node chooses a new backoff counter uniformly from the range $[CW, 2 \cdot CW - 1]$ and needs to detect a DIFS amount of idle time to reduce its backoff counter. (Please see our technical report for more details [CetTR]).

Service Differentiation Mechanism

In this section, we describe our service differentiation mechanism, SD-MAC, via the cooperative MAC protocol (C-MAC) presented above for wireless ad hoc networks and wireless LANs. Our key technique is that each node will change its backoff counter based on both its own packet's priority level and the level of the transmitted packet. Specifically, a node will increase its backoff counter linearly with a higher priority (than its own) packet transmission and decrease it exponentially with a lower priority (than its own) packet transmission. From now on, we assume that each node uses static priority among its packets to schedule the next packet transmission.

The SD-MAC first assigns different $PIFSs$ and $DIFSs$ values for different classes to provide service differentiation. We set the $PIFS^i = PIFS^{i-1} + st$ and $DIFS^i = DIFS^{i-1} + st$ in order to provide high network goodput under a low amount of high priority class traffic. Second, the SD-MAC chooses a backoff counter from the range $[0, 3]$ after a collision as in the C-MAC. However, a node with a priority level i packet to transmit will always choose its backoff counter from the range $[CW^i, 2 \cdot CW^i - 1]$ where $CW^{i+1} \geq 2 \cdot CW^i$. Therefore, the high priority classes will capture the channel initially. However, after some time period, low priority classes will decrement their backoff counter and start competing with high priority classes. As a result, the high priority classes would encounter significant goodput degradation similar to what occurs in the Dynamic MAC (Please see Figures 1).

In order to prevent this phenomenon, the SD-MAC requires the low priority classes to increase their backoff counters by one (1) when they hear a higher priority (than its own) packet transmission. However, we should limit the increment such that low priority classes should quickly capture the channel after a burst of high priority traffic in order to increase the network goodput. Therefore, the node will not increase its backoff counter more than $2 \cdot CW^i$. This method increases the chance of a high priority class packet capturing the channel while it assures that the backoff counter of low priority class does not exceed the maximum possible value, and it is very efficient under a heavy load of high priority classes. In addition, low priority classes still can capture the channel especially when a low amount of high priority traffic is present. However, to increase high priority class goodput, the high priority classes should capture the channel quickly if they hear any low priority class transmissions. To achieve this goal, upon hearing a lower priority (than its own) packet transmission, a node waits for the channel to be idle for $PIFS^i$ amount of time, instead of $DIFS^i$. Then, it reduces its backoff counter to half (exponential decrease) for each detected idle slot. This procedure enables high priority classes to capture the channel in a very short amount of time. If a collision is sensed during this procedure, the exponential decrement will be stopped and the regular linear decrement will be activated, i.e. the node will wait for the channel to be idle for a duration of $DIFS^i$ amount and decrement its backoff counter by one (1) for every detected idle slot.

The simulation results show that the SD-MAC still provides short-term fairness (2-3 packets per user) within the classes since it is based on the C-MAC protocol, and the proposed mechanism generates cohesive group movement although each user acts independently. (We omit the figures because of space limitation). However, the SD-MAC requires an additional look up into the packet header in order to identify the priority level of the transmitted packet. In simulations, we set the $PIFS^1 = 30\mu sec$, $DIFS^1 = 110\mu sec$, $PIFS^2 = 50\mu sec$, and $DIFS^2 = 130\mu sec$. We use sets of $(CW^1, CW^2) = \{(4, 8), (8, 16), (16, 32), (32, 64)\}$. We also set CW^1 to a fix number and vary the CW^2 up to 128. We found that the $CW^2 > 2 \cdot CW^1$ results in either the same as $CW^2 = 2 \cdot CW^1$ or a negligible performance improvement.

3. Reviews of the Static MAC and the Dynamic MAC Protocols

The Static MAC Protocol

The Static MAC protocol, introduced in [Aad01], employs the IEEE 802.11 DCF as an underlying access method. It uses different AIFS values, where AIFS corresponds to the DIFS in the regular IEEE 802.11 MAC, for different priority levels. The AIFS of the level $(i + 1)$ is set to the sum of the AIFS of level i and the time duration of the maximum contention window size of level i $[(CW_{max}^i + 1) * st]$ where st is the slot time. For example, in the case of two priority classes, let $AIFS^1$ be equal to $30\mu sec$, CW_{max}^1 equal to 63, and st equal to $20\mu sec$. Then, $AIFS^2 = AIFS^1 + (CW_{max}^1 + 1) * st$ which is equal to $1.31 msec$. In our simulations, we set $AIFS^1 = 30\mu sec$, $CW_{min}^1 = 15$, $CW_{min}^2 = 31$, and $CW_{max}^2 = 1023$. We vary the CW_{max}^1 from 63 to 511, then we use the above equation to calculate $AIFS^2$.

The Dynamic MAC Protocol

The IEEE 802.11e [802.11e] is the de facto standard for Quality of Service provisioning. The IEEE 802.11e uses a dynamic priority mechanism by assigning different AIFS values, contention window expansion factors (PFs), and (CW_{min}, CW_{max}) pairs for different classes to provide priority among them. The IEEE 802.11e, which is referred to as the Dynamic MAC, employs DCF as an underlying access method.

The first component is the required idle time to access the channel, i.e., AIFS. In this mechanism, the highest priority class has the shortest AIFS while the lowest class has the longest. $AIFS^i$ is calculated as: $AIFS^i = AIFS^{i-1} + st$. The second component is the backoff procedure. The basic IEEE 802.11 access mechanism always uses an exponential factor of 2. On the other hand, the Dynamic MAC provides different exponential increase factors (PFs) which increase with decreasing priority levels. Further, each class has different values of CW_{min} and CW_{max}. As a result of these settings, a high priority class waits a smaller duration to reduce its backoff counter, chooses its backoff counter from the smaller value range, and increases its CW value slower than a lower priority class. However, if high priority class has a higher density than low priority classes, it may encounter a high collision rate. Therefore, it may have a higher CW value and loss its priority. In simulations, we set $AIFS = \{30\mu sec, 50\mu sec\}$, $PF = \{2, 4\}$, $CW_{min} = \{15, 31\}$, and $CW_{max}^2 = 1023$, and we vary CW_{max}^1 from 63 to 511.

4. Comparison of the Service Differentiation Mechanisms

In this section, we describe the simulation model, then we compare the SD-MAC with the Static MAC and Dynamic MAC in terms of network goodput, Class 1 goodput, and admissible regions.

Simulation Model

We use the ns-2 simulator NS-2 with the DSSS specification and 11 Mbps Data Rate. We have three traffic models which are used in [Sheu01]. The *Voice Traffic* generates a 64Kbps constant bit rate in the *on* state and no traffic in the *off* state. We also model both the *on* and *off* states as exponential distributions with the mean duration of 1 and 1.35 seconds respectively. Additionally, the maximum delay bound for voice traffic is set to 25msec. The *VBR Traffic* generates 120Kbps minimum rate, 240Kbps average rate, and 420Kbps maximum rate. The maximum delay bound for video traffic is set to 75msec. The *Data Load* for a single source is modelled as a constant bit rate traffic with a rate of 1% of the channel data rate.

We use two performance metrics to evaluate service differentiation mechanisms: the Goodput and the Packet Loss Rate (PLR). The *Goodput* is defined as the amount of the applications' data transferred over the wireless link and normalized by the channel data rate. If a packet can not be delivered within the delay bound, it is dropped. The *Packet Loss Rate (PLR)* is defined as the ratio of dropped packets due to a delay bound violation over the total number of packets generated by real-time traffic. We use two scenarios: (1) voice traffic as Class 1 (high priority class) traffic and (2) VBR tarffic as Class 1. Data load is set to Class 2 (low priority class) traffic under both scenarios and is varied from 0 to 1.5 via adding more sources. Also, the number of voice traffic sources is varied from 0 to 300 and VBR traffic from 0 to 40.

Performance Comparison

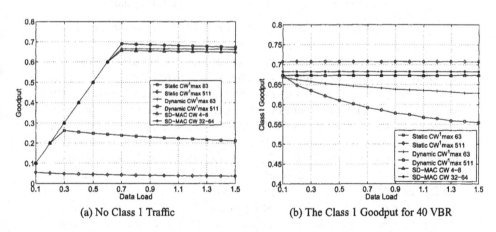

(a) No Class 1 Traffic   (b) The Class 1 Goodput for 40 VBR

Figure 1.   The Goodput Comparison

First, we investigate the case in which no Class 1 traffic is present. As shown in the Figure 1 (a), the SD-MAC and the Dynamic MAC provide high network goodput (up to 67% and 70% respectively) while the Static MAC encounters significant goodput degradation (27% maximum). Therefore, the Static MAC may not be a good mechanism for service differentiation. Next, we consider a heavy real-time traffic load case. We depicted the Class 1 goodput for 40 VBR sources in Figures 1 (b). When the Class 1 goodput is considered, the Static MAC and the SD-MAC provide steady goodput, i.e. they are able to protect the Class 1 traffic from Class 2 traffic efficiently. However, the Dynamic MAC fails to prevent low priority classes accessing the channel. As a result, the Dynamic MAC provides up to 22% and 25% less Class 1 goodput for voice and VBR traffics respectively when compared with the SD-MAC. As a conclusion, the Dynamic MAC may not be a good mechanism for service differentiation.

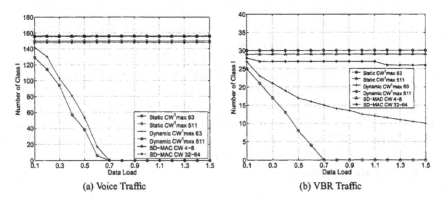

(a) Voice Traffic   (b) VBR Traffic

Figure 2.   The Admissible Region for Voice and VBR Traffic under Data Load

Next, we investigate the admissible regions, the number of users to be admitted to the network with a delay guarantee when the real-time traffic requires a maximum of (10^{-3}) packet loss rate. The first scenario sets real-time traffic as Class 1 traffic and data load as Class 2 traffic. We depicted the admissible regions for the voice traffic and VBR traffic in Figures 2 (a) and (b) respectively. The Static MAC yields the largest admissible region and supports up to 5% more real-time traffic than the SD-MAC. However, for the CW pair is (16,32) or lower values, the difference is reduced to 1%. On the other hand, the Dynamic MAC yields the smallest admissible region. For example, even in the presence of a 10% data load, the Dynamic MAC supports up to 21% less real-time traffic. Further, it can not support any real-time traffic if the data load is 70% or more of the channel data rate in the most cases.

In the second scenario, we choose voice traffic as Class 1 traffic and VBR traffic as Class 2 traffic. We depicted the admissible region in Figure 3. The SD-MAC with CW=(4,8) yields the largest admissible region, and the Dynamic MAC performs very close to the SD-MAC while the Static MAC pro-

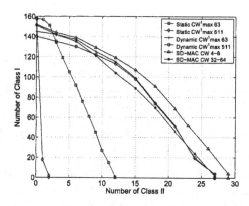

Figure 3. The Admissible Region for Voice Traffic vs. VBR Traffic

vides significantly a smaller admissible region. For example, the Static MAC can support 2 voice and 12 VBR sources together while the SD-MAC can support 2 voice and 29 VBR sources or 12 VBR and 120 voice sources. As a conclusion, the Static MAC is not an efficient mechanism to differentiate among multiple real-time traffic classes, and the Dynamic MAC fails to protect the real-time traffic from greedy sources. However, the SD-MAC performs quite well under the both scenarios. Therefore, the SD-MAC is a good candidate for service differentiation.

5. Conclusions

The goal of this work is to design a distributed medium access protocol to provide service differentiation without sacrificing the goodput, delay, and fairness when applications have diverse performance requirements. Towards this end, we propose a novel and efficient differentiated service mechanism via the C-MAC for wireless ad hoc networks and wireless LANs. Our key technique is that each node will change its backoff counter based on both its own packet's priority level and the priority level of the transmitted packet.

We compared our mechanism with both the Static MAC and the Dynamic MAC via simulations. The simulation results indicate that the Static MAC provides a service differentiation at the expense of significant goodput degradation when the amount of high priority class traffic is low. On the other hand, the Dynamic MAC fails to prevent low priority classes accessing the channel when the network load is high. Further, the Static MAC is not an efficient mechanism to differentiate among multiple real-time traffic classes, and the Dynamic MAC is not an efficient mechanism to protect real time traffic from greedy sources. However, our mechanism always provides an efficient service differentiation mechanism and high goodput with a small goodput degradation.

References

IEEE 802.11e. Medium Access Control (MAC) and Physical Layer (PHY) Specifications: MAC Enhancements for Quality of Service (QoS). May 2002.

I. Aad and C. Castelluccia. Differentiation mechanisms for IEEE 802.11. In *Proceedings of IEEE INFOCOM 2001*, Anchorage, Alaska, Apr. 2001.

C. Cetinkaya and F. Orsun. Cooperative Medium Access Control for Dense Wireless Networks-Technical Report. http://www.engr.wichita.edu/esawan/TC-Cetinkaya-CMAC.pdf.

J. Sanchez, R. Martinez, and M.W. Marcellin. A Survey of MAC Protocols Proposed for Wireless ATM. *IEEE Networks*, vol. 11, no. 6, pp. 52-62, Nov. 1997.

W.K. Kuo, C.Y. Chan, and K.C. Chen. Time bounded Services and Mobility Management in IEEE 802.11 Wireless LANs. In *Proceedings of IEEE Personal Wireless Comm.*, 1997.

C. Cetinkaya and F. Orsun. Cooperative Medium Access Control for Dense Wireless Networks. In *Proceedings of Med-HOC 2004*, Bodrum, Turkey, June 2004.

Y. Kwon, Y. Fang, and H. Latchman. A Novel MAC Protocol with Fast Collision Resolution for Wireless LANs. In *Proceedings of IEEE INFOCOM 2003*, San Francisco, CA, Apr. 2003.

VINT group. UCB/LBNL/VINT Network Simulator-ns (Version 2). http://mash.cs.berkeley.edu/ns.

IEEE. IEEE Standard 802.11: Wireless LAN Medium Access Control (MAC) and Physical Layer (PHY) Specifications. 1997

V. Kanodia, C. Li, A. Sabharwal, B. Sadeghi, and E. Knightly. Distributed Multi-hop Scheduling and Medium Access with Delay and Throughput Constraints. In *Proceedings of ACM MOBICOM '01*, Rome, Italy, July 2001.

S. Mangold et al. The IEEE 802.11e MAC for Quality of Service in Wireless LANs. In *Proceedings of European Wireless*, Feb. 2002.

X. Yang and N. H. Vaidya. Priority scheduling in wireless ad hoc networks. In *Proceedings of ACM MobiHoc '02*, Lausanne, Switzerland, July 2002.

J. L. Sobrinho and A. S. Krishnakumar. Quality-of-Service in Ad Hoc Carrier Sense Multiple Access Wireless Networks. *IEEE Journal on Selected Areas in Communications*, vol. 17, Aug. 1999.

M. Barry, A. T. Campbell, and A. Veres. Distributed Control Algorithms for Service Differentiation in Wireless Packet Networks. In *Proceedings of IEEE INFOCOM 2001*, Anchorage, Alaska, Apr. 2001.

H. Zhu, G. Cao, A. Yener, and A. D. Mathias. EDCF-DM: A Novel Enhanced Distributed Coordination Function for Wireless Ad Hoc Networks. In *Proceedings of IEEE ICCC'04*, Paris, France, June 2003.

A. Veres et al. EDCF-DM: Supporting service differentiation in wireless access packet networks using distributed control. *JSAC*, vol. 19, no. 10, Oct. 2001.

S. T. Sheu and T. F. Sheu. DBASE: A Distributed Bandwidth Allocation/Sharing/Extension Protocol for Multimedia over IEEE 802.11 Ad Hoc Wireless LAN. In *Proceedings of IEEE INFOCOM 2001*, Anchorage, Alaska, Apr. 2001.

L. Romdhani, Q. Ni, and T. Turletti. Adaptive EDCF: Enhanced Service Differentiation for IEEE 802.11 Wireless Ad Hoc Networks. In *Proceedings of IEEE WCNC'03*, 2003.

J. Deng and R. S. Chang. A priority Scheme for IEEE 802.11 DCF Access Method. *IEICE Transactions in Communications*, vol. 82-B, no. 1, Jan. 1999.

A. Muir and J. J. Garcia-Luna-Aceves. An Efficient Packet Sensing MAC Protocol for Wireless Networks. *ACM Journal on Mobile Networks and Applications*, vol. 3, no. 2, Aug. 1998.

C. R. Lin and M. Gerla. Real-time support in multihop wireless networks. *Wireless Networks*, vol. 5, 1999.